Hossein Bidgoli
California State University, Bakersfield

Information
Systems
Literacy

WordPerfect for Windows 5.2

Macmillan College Publishing Company
New York

Maxwell Macmillan Canada
Toronto

Maxwell Macmillan International
New York   Oxford   Singapore   Sydney

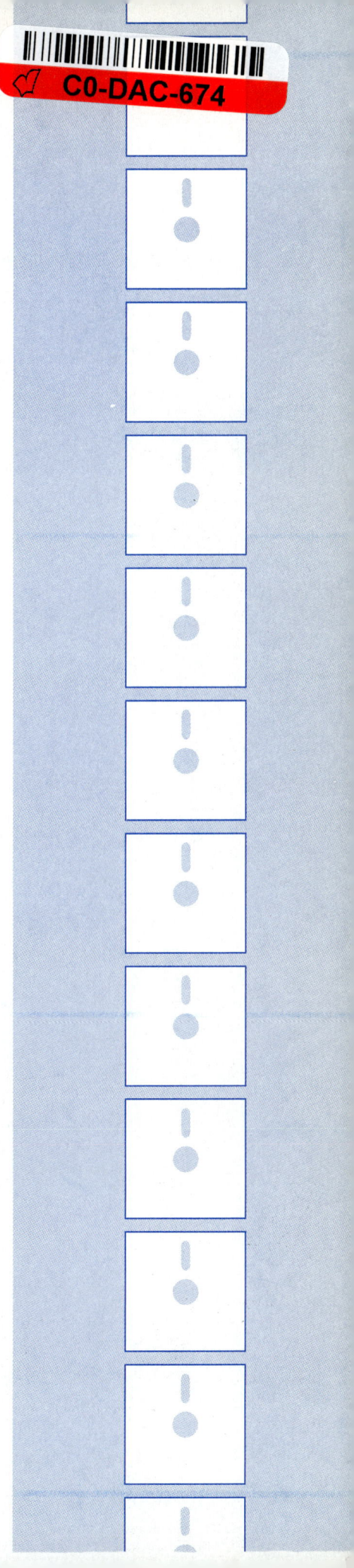

Cover art/photo: Copyright © Douglas E. Walker/Masterfile.
Cover photo insets: Courtesy of International Business Machines Corp.

Editor: Charles E. Stewart, Jr.
Production Editor: Rex Davidson
Photo Editor: Chris Migdol
Art Coordinator: Peter A. Robison
Cover Designer: Russ Maselli
Production Manager: Patricia A. Tonneman
Electronic Text Management: Marilyn Wilson Phelps, Matthew Williams, Jane Lopez, Karen L. Bretz

This book was set in ITC New Baskerville and Swiss 721 Condensed by Macmillan College Publishing Company and was printed and bound by Von Hoffman Press, Inc. The cover was printed by Von Hoffman Press, Inc.

The Publisher offers discounts on this book when ordered in bulk quantities. For more information, write to: Special Sales Department, Macmillan College Publishing Company, 445 Hutchinson Avenue, Columbus, OH 43235, or call 1-800-228-7854

Macmillan College Publishing Company
866 Third Avenue
New York, New York 10022

Macmillan College Publishing Company is part of the
Maxwell Communication Group of Companies.

Maxwell Macmillan Canada, Inc.
1200 Eglinton Avenue East, Suite 200
Don Mills, Ontario M3C 3N1

Library of Congress Cataloging-in-Publication Data
Bidgoli, Hossein.
    Information systems literacy. WordPerfect for Windows 5.2 /
Hossein Bidgoli.
        p.   cm.
    Includes index.
    ISBN 0-02-309591-1
    1. WordPerfect for Windows (Computer file). 2. Word processing.
I. Title. II. Title: WordPerfect for Windows 5.2.
    Z52.5.W655B53   1994
    652.5'536—dc20   93-44283
                                                                     CIP

Printing: 1 2 3 4 5 6 7 8 9   Year: 4 5 6 7 8

To so many fine memories of my brother, Mohsen,
for his uncompromising belief in the power of education.

Dr. Hossein Bidgoli is professor of management information systems at California State University, Bakersfield. He holds a Ph.D. degree in systems science from Portland State University with a specialization in design and implementation of MIS. His master's degree is in MIS from Colorado State University. Dr. Bidgoli's background includes experience as a systems analyst, information systems consultant, financial analyst, and he was the Director of the Microcomputer Center at Portland State University, where the first PC Lab in the United States was started.

Dr. Bidgoli, a two-time winner of the MPPP (Meritorious Performance and Professional Promise) award for outstanding performance in teaching, research, and university/community service, is the author of forty-two texts and numerous professional papers and articles presented and published throughout the United States on the topics of computers and MIS. Dr. Bidgoli has also designed and implemented over twenty executive seminars on all aspects of information systems and decision support systems.

Preface

Information Systems Literacy: WordPerfect for Windows 5.2 is a component of a modular series of textbooks developed for use in introductory computing course work. This WordPerfect for Windows text is written for first courses in word processing or for use in conjunction with texts in any course where a word processing tutorial is required.

Chapter 1 takes a comprehensive look at microcomputer hardware and software and their applications. This chapter provides a thorough discussion of the types of application software used today and provides the foundation for the hands-on section of the text.

Chapter 2 provides a quick review of MS-DOS and PC-DOS. This presentation will assist students in using their PC and WordPerfect for Windows more effectively.

Chapter 3 is an overview of Windows 3.1. The chapter will prepare the student for a better understanding of Windows principles and WordPerfect for Windows.

The software tutorials in this book (chapters 4 through 11) are designed to give the student comprehensive training and reference, all organized into manageably sized chapters. This approach gives the instructor a choice as to which and how many topics to cover, and it gives the student a valuable reference to use long after the class is completed. Advanced topics not covered in many texts are included here, as a growing number of students are coming into introductory computing courses with some software literacy; this book allows students to go further in their studies.

The software chapters are pedagogically designed with the student in mind. Consider the following features:

- Introductory sections explain, in basic terms, what the software is, why it was developed, and how it is used. Too many books "jump right in" without giving the student a sense of context.
- Illustrations of computer screens appear frequently to augment written instruction.
- Each chapter ends with 20 to 30 review questions, 5 to 8 hands-on experience assignments, and 10 multiple choice and 10 true/false questions.
- Each chapter includes a complete summary of key terms and key computer commands.
- When appropriate, chapters include a unique section titled "Misconceptions and Solutions." Common errors, improper operating procedures, and ways to avoid or solve them are highlighted.

In any hands-on computer lab, an accurate text makes managing the lab far easier. The best way to make a text accurate is to use it. During the two years I

spent developing this text, I received corrections and suggestions that make this book one that is easy to use and reliable.

Appendix A fives answers to selected end-of-chapter review questions.

Appendix B explains, in brief, how information can be shared among Windows applications.

Ancillary materials are available to instructions. The *Instructor's Manual* includes a test bank, transparency masters, and data disk that enables students to access the programs and exercises included in the text. The manual also has lecture outlines, answers to review questions/exercises, and guidelines for projects. A computerized test bank is also available.

ACKNOWLEDGMENTS

Several colleagues reviewed different versions of this manuscript and made constructive suggestions. Without their help the manuscript could not have been refined. The help and comments of the following reviewers are greatly appreciated: Kirk Arnett, Mississippi State University; Tom Berliner, University of Texas, Dallas; Glen Boswell, San Antonio College; Gary Brent, Scottsdale Community College; Chris Carter, Indiana Vocational Technical College; Michael Davis, Texas Technical University; Steve Deam, Milwaukee Area Technical College; Beth Defoor, Eastern New Mexico University, Clovis; Richard Ernst, Sullivan Junior College; Barbara Felty, Harrisburg Area Community College; Pat Fenton, West Valley College; Phyllis Helms, Randolph Community College; Mehdi Khosrowpour, Pennsylvania State University, Harrisburg; Candice Marble, Wentworth Military Academy; Ramon Mata-Toledo, James Madison University; John Miller, Williamsport Area Community College; Charles McDonald, East Texas State University; Sylvia Meyer, Community College of Vermont; J. D. Oliver, Prairie View A&M University; Greg Pierce, Penn State University; Eugene Rathswohl, University of San Diego; Mary-Ann Robbert, Bentley College; Herbert Rubhun, University of Houston, Downtown; R. D. Shelton, Loyola College; Sandra Stalker, North Shore Community College; Maureen Thommes, Bemidji State University; G. W. Willis, Baylor University; and Judy Yeager, Western Michigan University.

Many different groups assisted me in completing this project. I am grateful to over four thousand students who attended my executive seminars and various classes in information systems and software productivity tools. They helped me fine-tune the manuscript during its various stages. My friend Bahram Ahanin helped me to improve many concepts of hardware/software and put them in a non-technical and easy-to-understand format. My colleague and friend Dr. Reza Azarmsa provided support and encouragement. I am grateful for all of his encouragement. My colleague Andrew Prestage assisted me in numerous troublespots by running and debugging many of the screens presented in the book.

I am indebted to Jacki Lawson, Denise Candia, Julie Gunn, and Vivian Cochneuer, who typed and retyped various versions of this manuscript. Their thoroughness and patience made it easier to complete this project. They deserve special recognition for all this work.

A team of professionals from Macmillan College Publishing Company assisted me in this venture, including Charles Stewart, senior editor; Rex Davidson, production editor; and Jane Lopez and Pete Robison, art coordinators.

Finally, I want to thank my family for their support and encouragement throughout my life. My two sisters, Azam and Akram, deserve my special thanks and recognition. My wife, Nooshin, has been very supportive and patient. My little baby, Morvareed, has been very patient throughout this work. I extend my deepest love and appreciation to both.

WordPerfect for Windows 5.2

Contents

Contents

11
Table Handling, Working with Multiple Documents, and Changing Fonts   227

Appendix A
Answers to Selected Review Questions   251

Appendix B
Sharing Information Among Windows Applications   255

The World of Microcomputers

1

1–1   INTRODUCTION

In this chapter we discuss microcomputer fundamentals. Hardware and software for micros are described. Different classes of application software are introduced. Guidelines for successful selection and maintenance of micros are highlighted. A brief explanation of the advantages of micros compared with mainframes is presented. The chapter also includes a hands-on session with a microcomputer. The chapter concludes by defining these important concepts: computer files; types of data, values, and formulas; and priority of arithmetic operations. The information in this chapter should help you to be a more effective microcomputer user.

1–2   WHAT IS A MICROCOMPUTER?

The terms **personal computer** (PC), **micro**, or **microcomputer** refer to the smallest type of computer when measured by such attributes as memory, cost, size, speed, and sophistication. Although small, these computers are so powerful that sometimes the difference between PCs and larger computers is blurred. The reason for such confusion is the ever-increasing power and capability of PCs.

Since the beginning of the microcomputer era in roughly 1975, the capability of these computers has improved beyond imagination. Still, some experts believe this is only the beginning—there is a lot more to be done by micros.

A microcomputer consists of input, output, and memory devices. Figure 1–1 illustrates a typical microcomputer system. The **input device** is usually a keyboard. A PC keyboard is similar to a typewriter but with some additional keys. Figure 1–2 displays an IBM enhanced keyboard and a standard keyboard. In the future, voice input devices may be part of the system. Other input devices include a mouse, touch technology, light pen, graphics tablet, optical character reader (OCR), magnetic ink character recognition (MICR), camera, sensor, and bar code readers.

The common output devices for microcomputers are a cathode-ray tube (CRT) monitor, sometimes called video display terminal (VDT), and the printer. The

Figure 1–1
Typical microcomputer system (courtesy of Radio Shack, a division of Tandy Corp.).

1 Function keys	4 Shift key	7 Print Screen (PrtSc) key
2 Escape keys	5 Alt key	8 Number Lock (Num Lock) key
3 Control (Ctrl) keys	6 Shift key	9 Scroll Lock (Break) key

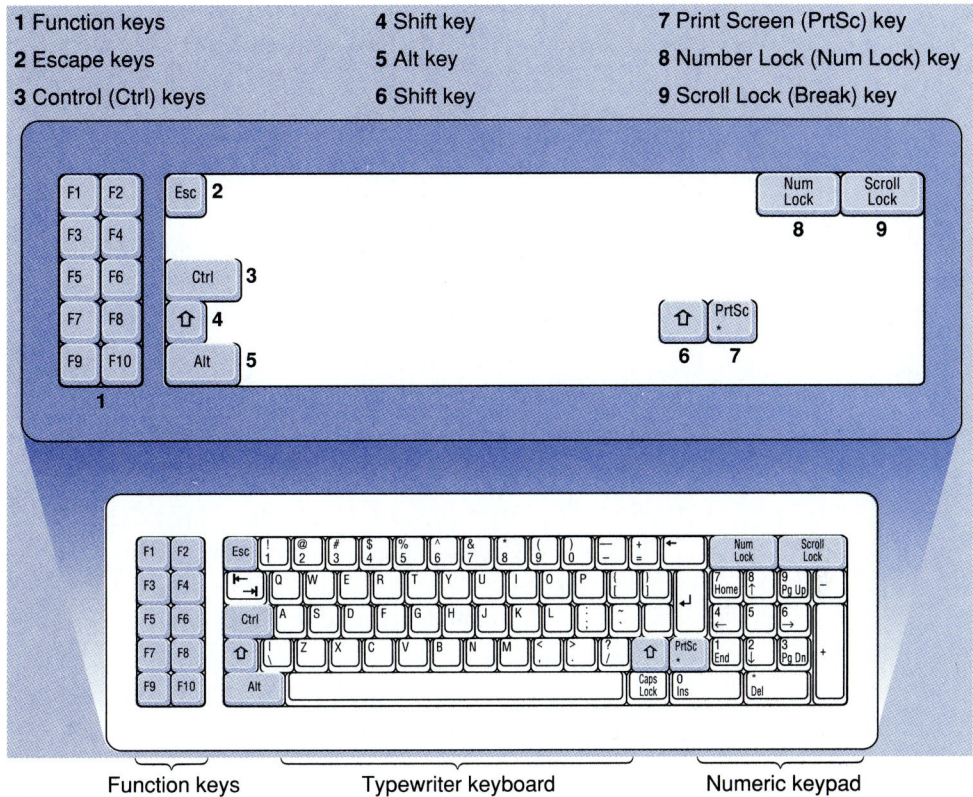

Function keys   Typewriter keyboard   Numeric keypad

A.

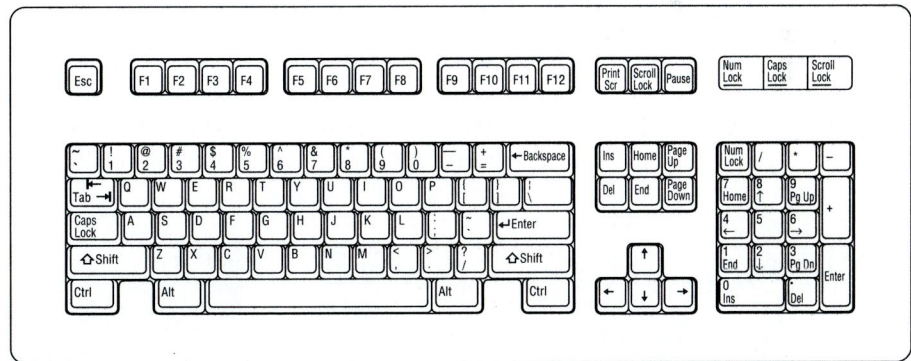

B.

Figure 1–2
A. IBM standard keyboard. B. IBM enhanced keyboard (courtesy of International Business Machines Corp.).

output generated on the monitor is called soft copy and printed output is referred to as hard copy. Other output devices include cameras, floppy disks, and plotters.

Two types of monitors display output. Some microcomputers utilize a monochrome-type screen. As the name indicates, this type of screen generates one color, such as green, although some screens are amber (orange). Either type of monochrome monitor can generate graphic output if accompanied by a graphics card or graphics adapter. The other type of monitor is called a color monitor (sometimes referred to as an **RGB** monitor—red-green-blue monitor). It shows data in a color format.

The sharpness of images on the display monitor is referred to as resolution. The intersection of a row and a column is called a pixel. The higher the number of these pixels, the higher the resolution. Color monitors come in various levels of resolution such as CGA, EGA, VGA, super VGA, and XGA:

- A color graphics adapter (CGA) displays 320-by-200 (pixels) resolution in 4 colors
- An enhanced graphics adapter (EGA) displays 640-by-350 resolution in 16 colors. More advanced versions of EGA display 640-by-480 resolution in 16 colors and 320-by-200 resolution in 256 colors.
- A video graphics array (VGA) displays 640-by-480 resolution in 16 colors and 320-by-200 resolution in 256 colors. Super VGA and XGA monitors display more than 640-by-480 resolution in many different colors. The exact resolution depends on the specific type of the monitor.

The processing part of a microcomputer, that is its **central processing unit** (CPU) or microprocessor, includes three components:

1. **Main memory** stores data, information, and instructions.
2. **Arithmetic logic unit** (ALU) performs arithmetic and logical operations. Arithmetic operations include addition, subtraction, division, and multiplication. Logical operations include any types of comparisons, such as sorting (putting data into a particular order) or searching (choosing a particular data item).
3. **Control unit** serves as the commander of the system. It tells the microcomputer what to do and how to do it.

Figure 1–3 illustrates two different microprocessor chips, or microchips, which contain the electronic components necessary for processing.

Microcomputers are getting smaller but more powerful. Among the various types are portable (laptop) micros and notebook micros (see Figure 1–4).

A.

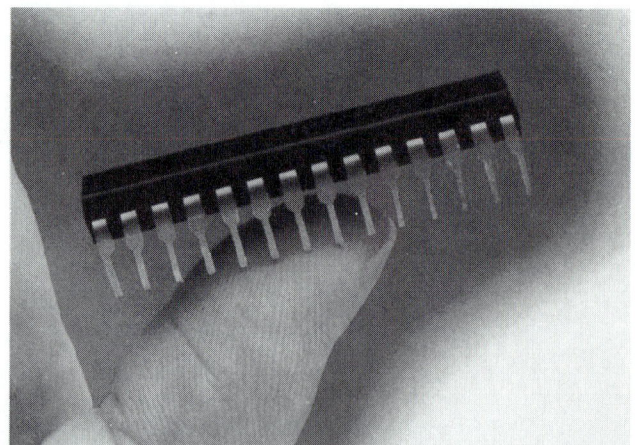

B.

Figure 1–3
A. Motorola MC 68020 microprocessor in its protective ceramic package (courtesy of Motorola, Inc.).
B. AT&T Bell Labs microprocessor (courtesy of Radio Shack, a division of Tandy Corp.).

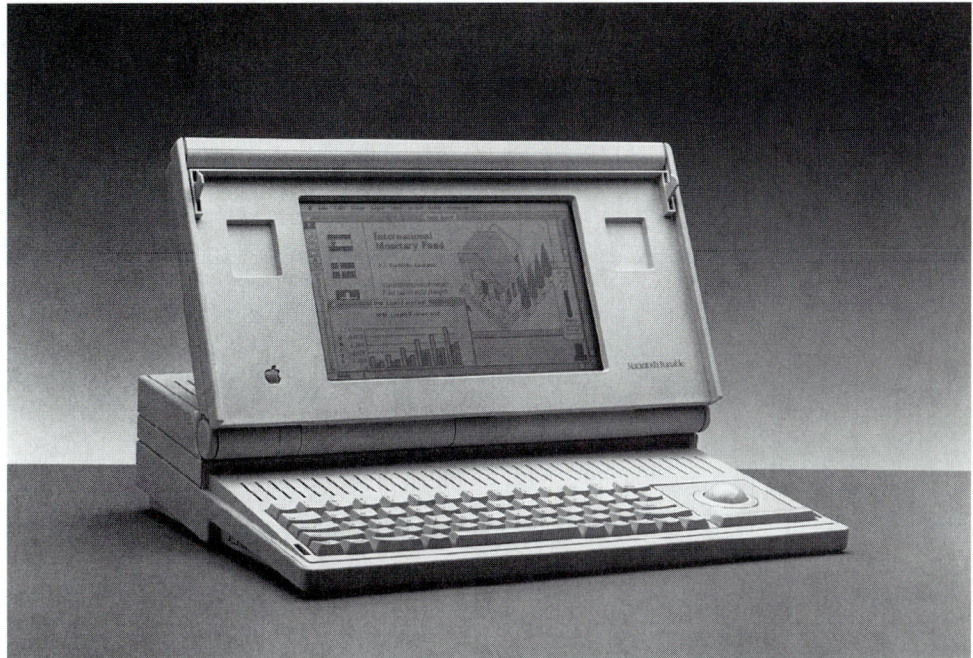

A.

B.

Figure 1–4
A. The all-in-one design of the Apple Macintosh Portable integrates the CPU, Active Matrix Liquid Crystal Display, keyboard, pointing device, battery and disk storage into a single easy-to-carry package. B. With the Macintosh PowerBook computer, customers can take advantage of notebook convenience and Macintosh power anywhere, whether at home, school or on the road for business (courtesy of Apple Computer, Inc.).

1–3   THE KEYBOARD

As you can see in Figure 1–2B, an enhanced keyboard is divided into three sections. On the top are 12 function keys. In a standard keyboard, there are only 10 function keys. Some keyboards have the function keys on the left (Figure 1–2A). With most application software, these keys perform special functions, or they can be programmed to perform a particular task. For example, Lotus 1-2-3, Quattro Pro, dBASE, and WordPerfect effectively use 12 keys (F1 through F12) for performing different tasks.

The middle part of the keyboard is similar to a typical typewriter. However, notice some special keys that a typewriter does not have (e.g., the Alt key).

The right section has a numeric key pad similar to that of an adding machine. It is used to facilitate numeric data entry (when the Num Lock key is pressed down) or for cursor movement.

The purpose of function keys and some of the special keys varies in different application programs. For example, F1 in WordPerfect 5.1 cancels a selection or performs "undelete" operations. In Lotus 1-2-3, Quattro Pro, or dBASE, it accesses the online help command.

1–4   IMPORTANT AUXILIARY DEVICES

Besides the obvious input/output devices, some additional devices are required for effective utilization of a microcomputer. Disk drives and adapter cards are two of the most important devices.

1–4–1   Disk Drives

Disk drives enable the microcomputer system to retrieve data from a disk into main memory and to store data from main memory to a disk. Disk drives come in various capacities. Your system may have one or more floppy disk drives. It may also have a hard disk drive. As you will see later, **hard disks** are capable of storing masses of information. The capacity of a hard disk is many times greater than that of a **floppy disk** (also called a diskette or just a floppy). A floppy disk can hold from 360 kilobytes (K) to 1.44 megabytes (MB) of data. Some new floppies are capable of storing 2.88 MB. The capacity of a hard disk varies from 5 to 600 MB or more.

The capacity of a storage device is measured in terms of bits or bytes of data stored on that device. Table 1–1 summarizes the memory equivalents.

1–4–2   Adapter Cards

Adapter cards are installed in expansion slots (channels) inside the computer (see Figure 1–5). These cards are used to attach a particular option to the system unit. Table 1–2 summarizes typical adapter cards.

Table 1–1
Memory Equivalents

0 or 1 is equal to one bit
8 bits is equal to one byte
1,024 (2^{10}) bytes is equal to one kilobyte
1,048,576 (2^{20}) bytes is equal to one megabyte
1,073,741,824 (2^{30}) bytes is equal to one gigabyte
10,995,627,776 (2^{40}) bytes is equal to one terabyte

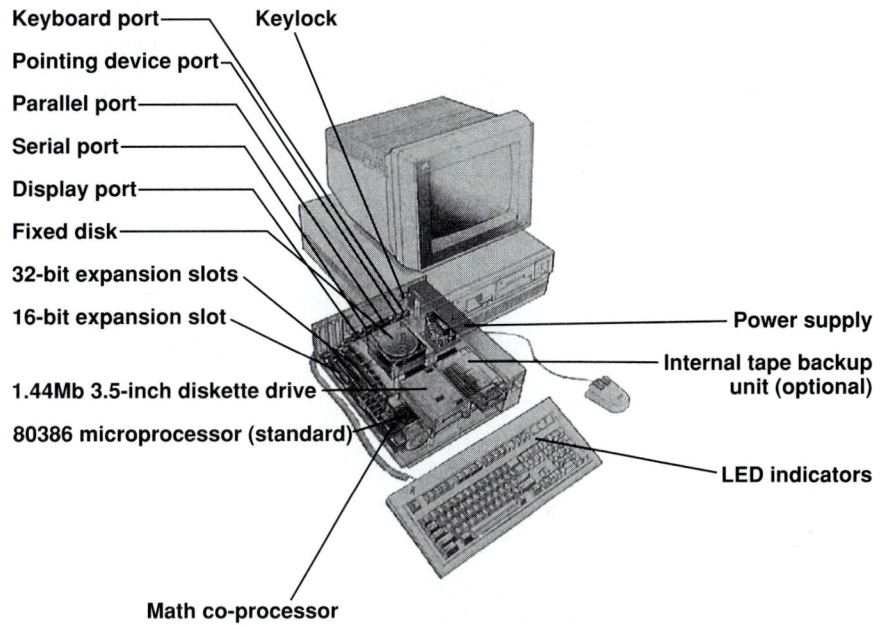

A.

Keyboard port
Pointing device port
Parallel port
Serial port
Display port
Fixed disk
32-bit expansion slots
16-bit expansion slot
1.44Mb 3.5-inch diskette drive
80386 microprocessor (standard)
Keylock
Power supply
Internal tape backup unit (optional)
LED indicators
Math co-processor

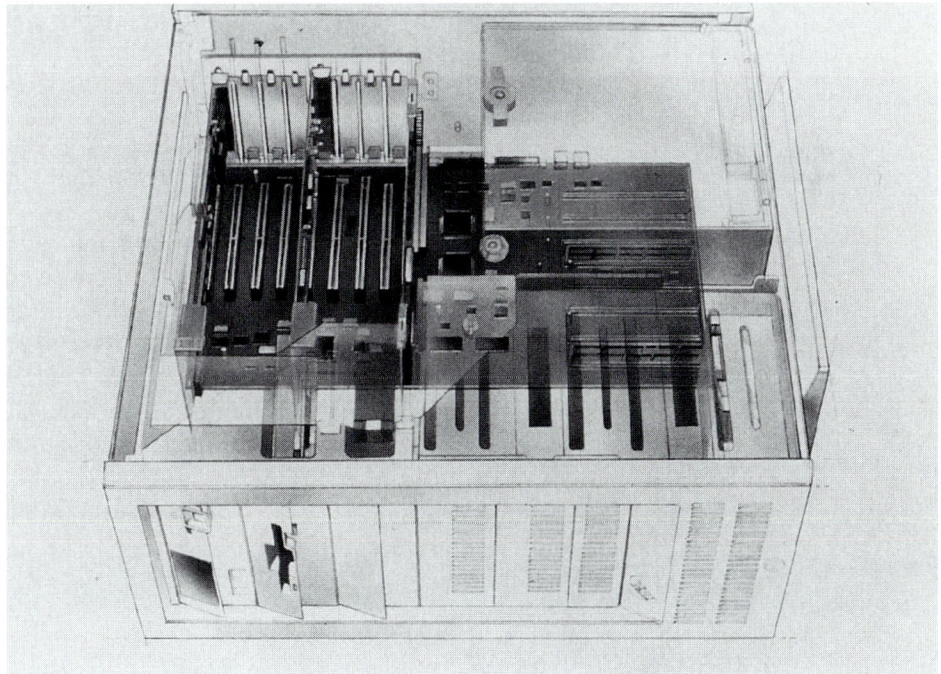

B.

Figure 1–5
Inside your PC. A. Port and expansion slots in a microcomputer (courtesy of International Business Machines Corp.). B. Inside a microcomputer. This model is IBM's PS/2 95XP 486 (courtesy of International Business Machines Corp.).

Table 1–2
Commonly Used Adapter Cards

- Disk drive card for connecting disk drives to the system unit
- Display card for connecting the CRT to the system unit
- Memory card for connecting additional RAM to existing memory
- Clock card for connecting a clock to the system unit
- Modem card for connecting the PC to the outside world
- Printer interface card for connecting a printer to the system unit

The original IBM PC has five expansion slots; the IBM XT and AT have eight slots. Adapter cards usually have outlet ports that are accessed at the back of the system unit. It is important to know that the newer PCs do not require as many adapter cards. Ports, which are either parallel or serial, connect devices to the system unit. You must connect a serial device to a serial port and a parallel device to a parallel port. Serial devices transfer one bit of data at a time; parallel devices transfer a series of bits of data at a time.

1–5   TYPES OF PRIMARY MEMORY

Computers store data in two kinds of memory: main, or primary memory, and auxiliary, or secondary memory. **Primary memory** is the heart of the microcomputer; it is usually referred to as **random-access memory** (RAM). This is a volatile memory. Data stored in RAM will be lost in the event of a power failure. To avoid this type of loss, always save your work on a permanent memory medium (i.e., secondary memory), such as a diskette.

Three other types of memory also can be referred to as main memory, but the user cannot have direct control over them:

1. **Read-only memory** (ROM): A prefabricated ROM chip is supplied by vendors. This memory stores some general-purpose instructions or programs. For example, some commands of the Disk Operating System (DOS) and some versions of the BASIC language are stored on ROM chips. DOS is the operating system for IBM microcomputers and compatible systems.

2. **Programmable read-only memory**: By using a special device, the user can program this memory. However, once programmed, the user cannot erase this type of memory.

3. **Erasable programmable read-only memory**: This type of read-only memory can be programmed by the user and, as the name indicates, erased and programmed again.

1–6   CONVENTIONAL, EXPANDED, AND EXTENDED MEMORIES

With the introduction of 386- and 486-based computers and the Pentium (the new high-powered microprocessor introduced by Intel), two new types of main memory have entered the market and have made the memory discussion even more confusing. The next few paragraphs briefly describe these two new memories and differentiate them from conventional memory.

Conventional memory, or RAM, is the first 640 K of the memory of your computer. The majority of XT-type machines come with 1 MB of memory; however, DOS can only directly reach the first 640 K of this memory. The other 384 K (1024 K–640 K) is used (as shown in Figure 1–6) by ROM BIOS (Basic Input Output System), adapter ROM, video memory, and the EMS (Expanded Memory Specification) window.

Expanded memory is located outside of the conventional memory and works based on a technique called bank switching. Lotus, Intel, and Microsoft (LIM) corporations devised the LIM Expanded Memory Specification (EMS) for expanded memory. This is like a memory storage area on an EMS-compatible expansion card inside your computer. To utilize expanded memory on your computer, you need both an EMS-compatible memory expansion card and a device driver known as Expanded Memory Manager (EMM). The EMM helps the microprocessor find a page(s) of data that your software is looking for and puts the data into a 64-K page frame as four 16-K pages. DOS can then locate the data, and your software program can use it. Expanded memory is useful for designing large spreadsheets.

Extended memory is also outside of conventional memory, but it functions basically as additional RAM and is accessible to your computer directly. No bank switching occurs with extended memory. This means that after DOS addresses the first 640 K of conventional memory, it then automatically accesses the next chunk of the memory, which is the extended memory (see Figure 1–6). A 286-based PC can access up to 16 MB of RAM, and 386- and 486-based PCs can access up to 4,096 MB of RAM.

Which memory should you get, expanded or extended? Well, the software in use dictates the type of memory. Earlier software requested expanded memory. Today's graphical environments, such as Windows, prefer extended memory. In fact, your additional memory can be configured either way using special software.

Figure 1–6
Conventional, extended, and expanded memories.

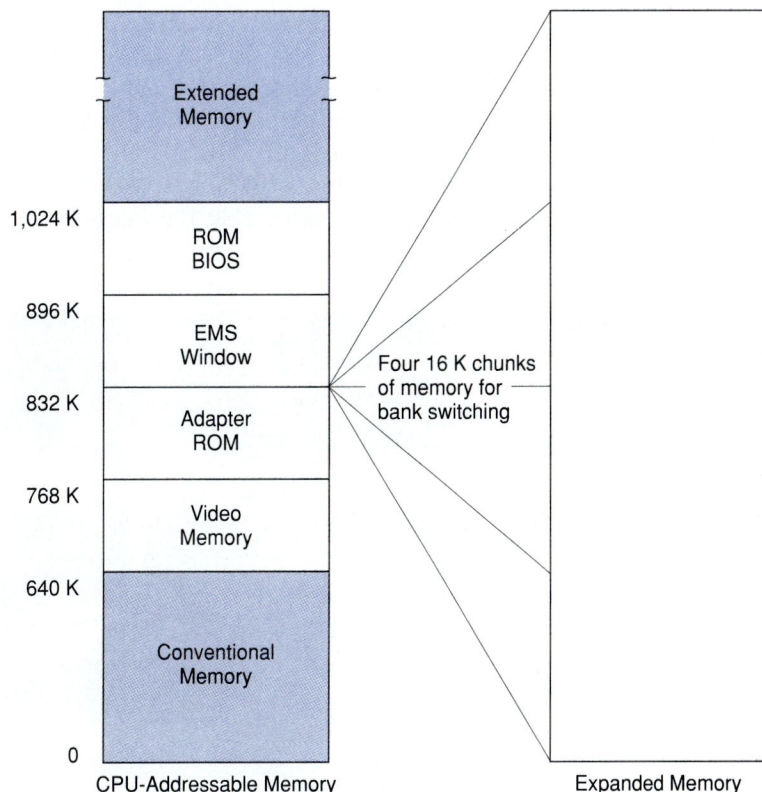

1–7   TYPES OF SECONDARY MEMORY

Since the main memory of a microcomputer is limited, expensive, and volatile, **secondary memory** storage devices are needed for mass data storage. Secondary storage is nonvolatile. Secondary storage devices are broadly classified into magnetic and optical. Let us briefly consider each group.

1–7–1   Magnetic Storage Devices

Magnetic storage devices include the diskette, mini floppy, hard disk, and Bernoulli box. The capacity of a diskette or a hard disk depends on its technical features.

There are three types of standard diskettes: 3½ inches, 5¼ inches, and 8 inches. The most recent floppy disk is a 2-inch floppy. Diskettes can be single density, double density, or high density. Density refers to the amount of information that can be stored on a disk. Diskettes can also be single sided or double sided. A 5¼-inch, single-sided, single-density floppy can hold roughly 125 K; a 5¼-inch, single-sided, double-density floppy can hold roughly 250 K; a 5¼-inch, double-sided, double-density floppy can hold roughly 360 K; a high-density (sometimes called quad-density) diskette can hold up to 1.2 MB. A 3½-inch, low-density floppy disk can store 720 K of data and a 3½-inch, high-density floppy can store 1.44 MB of data.

A hard disk (also called fixed disk or Winchester disk) can be 14, 8, 5¼ or less than 4 inches in diameter. The capacity of this device varies from 5 MB to 1 gigabyte.

A **Bernoulli box** is a removable medium. After finishing your computer work, you can pull this device out and store it in a safe location, which is not possible with a hard disk. A Bernoulli box uses high-capacity floppy disks to store 10 MB of data or more. Generally speaking, it is less prone to damage than a hard disk. This is true because the drive head of a Bernoulli box does not move as a hard disk head moves, often resulting in head crashes. In a Bernoulli box, the floppy disk moves toward the stationary read/write head through air currents. Figure 1–7 displays a Bernoulli box.

At the present time, the most commonly used secondary storage device is a 3½-inch floppy disk. However, at the beginning of the PC era, 5¼-inch floppy

Figure 1–7
A Bernoulli box.

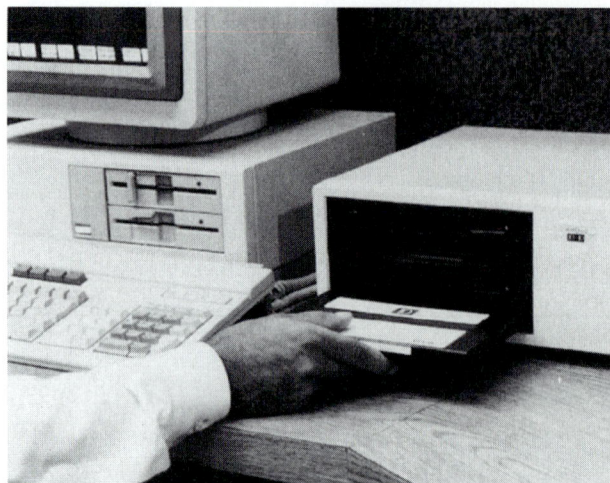

Figure 1–8
A 5¼-inch floppy disk.

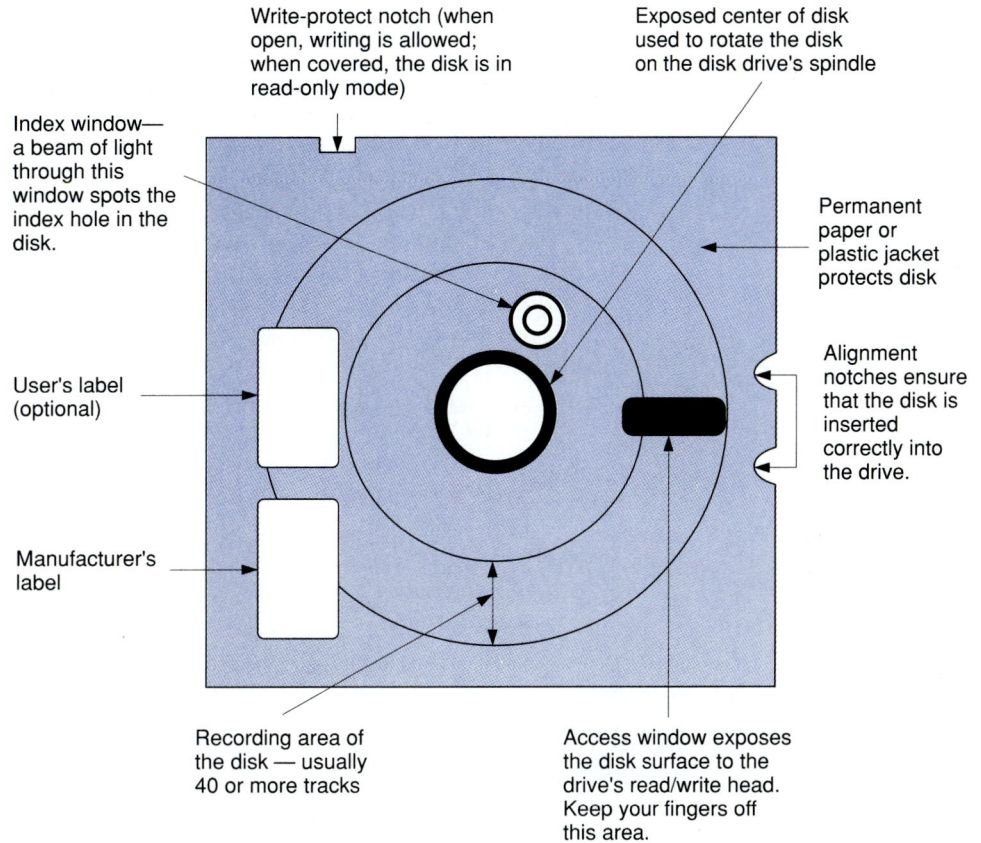

Write-protect notch (when open, writing is allowed; when covered, the disk is in read-only mode)

Exposed center of disk used to rotate the disk on the disk drive's spindle

Index window— a beam of light through this window spots the index hole in the disk.

Permanent paper or plastic jacket protects disk

User's label (optional)

Alignment notches ensure that the disk is inserted correctly into the drive.

Manufacturer's label

Recording area of the disk — usually 40 or more tracks

Access window exposes the disk surface to the drive's read/write head. Keep your fingers off this area.

disks were the most commonly used secondary storage devices. A floppy disk is made of plastic material coated with magnetic material. A 5¼-inch disk is enclosed in a permanent vinyl jacket to protect the disk. After using a floppy disk, you should put it back in its paper cover to protect it from dirt and dust. Do not touch exposed portions of the disk or data loss may result. Figure 1–8 highlights important areas of a 5¼-inch diskette. Figure 1–9 displays a 3½-inch diskette. The 3½-inch diskettes are more durable and easier to handle than the 5¼-inch disks. They also store more information.

Figure 1–9
A 3½-inch floppy disk.

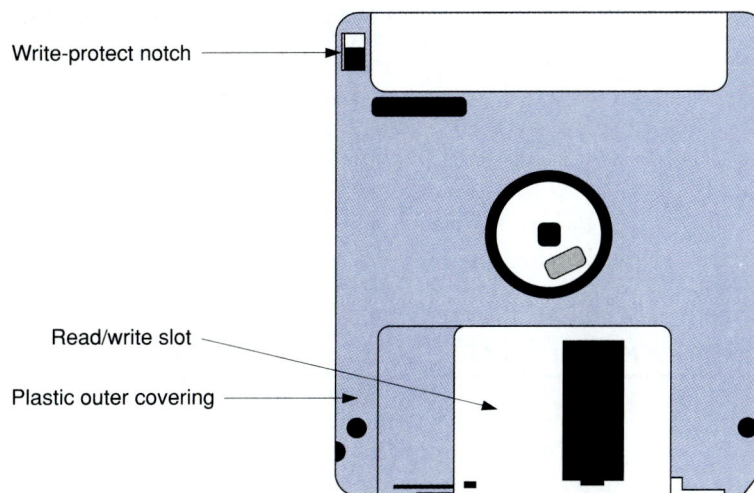

Write-protect notch

Read/write slot

Plastic outer covering

1–7–2   ## Optical Storage Technologies

Three types of optical storage have attracted much attention in recent years: CD-ROM, WORM, and erasable optical disk. The major advantages of optical technology devices are durability and massive storage capacity. The major drawback of optical technology is its slow speed; however, vendors are working rapidly to improve the technology. Let us briefly look at each type.

CD-ROM (compact disk, read-only memory), as the name indicates, is a permanent medium. In CD ROM, information is recorded by disk-mastering machines. A CD-ROM, which is similar to an audio compact disk, can be duplicated and distributed throughout an organization. Its major application is for large, permanent databases, for example, public domain databases such as libraries, real estate information, and corporate financial information.

A **WORM** (write once, read many) disk is also a permanent medium. Information can be recorded once and cannot be altered. A major drawback compared with CD-ROM is that you cannot duplicate a WORM disk. Its major application is for storing information that must be kept permanently, for example, information related to annual reports, nuclear power plants, airports, and railroads.

An **erasable optical disk** meets the needs of high-volume storage and updating. Information can be recorded and erased repeatedly.

Figure 1–10 illustrates each of the three types of optical storage.

1–8   MEMORY CAPACITY AND PROCESSOR SPEED

Microcomputer RAM capacity used to start at 512 or 640 K. Now PCs with capacities of 4 to 16 MB are becoming more common, and in the future, micros will approach minicomputer capacity.

For present and future planning, you should be able to calculate the memory requirements for your computing needs. For example, if you have a PC with 640 K of RAM, all of that memory may not be accessible to you. A large portion of that memory may be needed by software you use to carry out applications. As an example, Lotus Release 2.01 needs almost 200 K of RAM. So in your 640-K PC, you are left with only 440 K of memory to use (640 − 200 = 440).

Another consideration regarding memory is speed. The speed of the processor is measured in megahertz (MHz) and usually varies from 4 to 66. Vendors are rapidly extending this technology also. Soon, speeds of 100 MHz or more will be available. The higher the processor speed, the faster the computer.

Another factor that has direct impact on speed is the word size of the processor. Word size indicates the number of characters that can be processed simultaneously. Word size varies from 8 to 32 bits for microcomputers. The bigger the word size, the faster the computer.

The speed of your microcomputer may have a direct impact on your business operation. With a faster computer, you can process more information in a shorter period of time. However, always consider the additional cost incurred by buying a more powerful PC and the marginal benefit to be gained.

1–9   GENERAL CAPABILITIES OF MICROCOMPUTER SOFTWARE

A microcomputer can perform a variety of tasks by using either commercial software or software developed in-house. In-house developed software is usually more expensive than commercial software. However, software developed in-house

A.

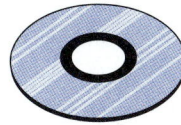

CD ROM

B.

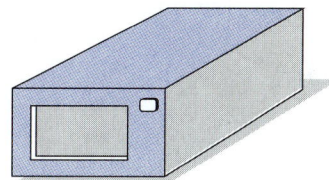

WORM disk

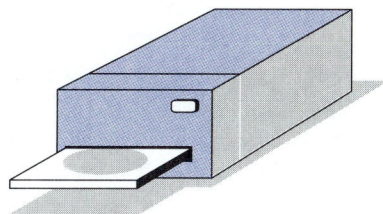

Erasable optical disk

C.

Figure 1–10

Optical storage devices for microcomputers. A. Close-up of CD-ROM (courtesy of Radio Shack, a division of Tandy Corp.). B. Disks and disk drive B (courtesy of NEC). C. Erasable optical disk.

is more customized and should better fit users' needs. Several thousands of software packages are available for PCs. For any task that can apply to several users, there is a software package on the market. The following are typical commercial packages and applications available for microcomputers.

1–9–1   Word Processing Software

A microcomputer that functions as a word processor is similar to a typewriter with a memory. With such a facility, you can generate documents, make deletions and insertions, and cut and paste. **Word processing software** is becoming more sophisticated. Some of the programs now provide limited graphics and data management features. Word processing programs allow users to save hundreds of hours by not typing the same document repeatedly. For example, organizations do not need to retype the letter that is sent to many of their customers. They need only change the names and addresses in the letters. Numerous word processing programs fill the marketplace. Some of the popular ones are WordPerfect (WordPerfect Corp.), Word (Microsoft Corporation), AmiPro (Lotus Development Corporation), and Wordstar (MicroPro International Corporation).

1–9–2   Grammar Checker Software

The ever-increasing speed and memory of microcomputers are promoting a new type of software. Most word processors now include spelling checkers, which are able to correct most of the typos in a document. The next challenge is the creation of documents that include correct verbs, subjects, adjectives, and a smooth style. Also, the creation of simple, easy-to-read, and simple sentences is of prime importance. **Grammar checker software** promotes good writing techniques.

     Grammar checkers perform text analyses through linguistic analysis, parsing, and rule matching. Parsing means simply breaking long sentences into shorter ones. More sophisticated software includes more sophisticated parsers. Grammar checkers play an especially important role when multiple authors are involved in a project. In such cases, grammar checkers help create uniformity of tone, level, style, and usage. Grammar checkers are not 100 percent perfect yet, but they have come a long way. Among the more popular grammar checkers are Grammatik Windows and Grammatik IV (Reference Software International), PowerEdit (Artificial Linguistics, Inc.), and Correct Grammar for DOS (Writing Tools Group, Inc.).

1–9–3   Spreadsheet Software

A spreadsheet is a table of rows and columns. **Spreadsheet software** can be broadly classified into two types. One type is a dedicated spreadsheet; this means the program performs only spreadsheet functions. The other type of spreadsheet package can perform more than one type of function. Lotus 1-2-3, for example, is capable of performing spreadsheet functions as well as database and graphics functions. Other popular spreadsheet packages include Symphony (Lotus), Excel (Microsoft), SuperCalc (Computer Associates International, Inc.), and Quattro Pro (Borland International).

     The number of jobs that can be performed by a spreadsheet program is unlimited. Generally speaking, any application suitable for analysis by row and column is a candidate for a typical spreadsheet. For example, say you decide to use a spreadsheet to prepare a budget. As soon as you have completed your budget, you can perform some impressive what-if analysis. This means you can manipulate variables on the spreadsheet. For example, reduce your income by 2 percent and direct the spreadsheet to calculate the effect of this change on other items in the spreadsheet.

1-9-4   Database Software

Database software is designed to perform database operations such as file creation, deletion, modification, search, sort, merge, and join (combining two files based on a common key). A file is a collection of a series of records. A record is a collection of a series of fields. A field is a collection of a series of characters. For example, the names, GPAs, and majors of all the students in our computer class constitute a student file. The name, GPA, and major of each student make up the record of each student. The name, GPA, or major is a field.

Popular database programs include dBASE III PLUS and IV (Borland), PC-File III (Buttonware, Inc.), Q&A (Symantec), Paradox (Borland), Omnis Quartz (Blyth Software), FoxBase and Fox Pro (Microsoft), and R-BASE (Microrim Corporation).

Think of a database as a table of rows and columns. The rows correspond to the occurrence of a record. The columns correspond to the fields within the record. Two common applications of database software are sorting and searching records. In sort operations, the user enters a series of records in any order, then asks the database program to sort the records in ascending or descending order based on the data in the fields. Search operations are even more interesting. You can search for data items that meet certain criteria, for example, all the MIS students who have GPAs greater than 3.60 and are younger than 20 years of age. Some databases (such as Q&A) allow you to search for key words within a text file.

1-9-5   Graphics Software

Graphics software has been designed to present data in graphic format. Data can be converted into a line graph to show a trend, to a pie chart to highlight the components of a data item, and to other types of graphs for various analyses. Masses of data can be converted to a graph and, in a glance, the reader can discover the general pattern of the data. Graphs can easily highlight patterns and the correlation of data items. They also make data presentation a more manageable job. Graphics can be done with integrated packages such as Lotus 1-2-3 or Quattro Pro or with dedicated graphics packages. Five popular graphics packages are Aldus Persuasion (Aldus Corporation), Hollywood Graphics (IBM Corporation), Harvard Graphics (Software Publishing Corporation), Freelance (Lotus), and Power Point (Microsoft Corporation).

1-9-6   Communications Software

Through a modem and **communications software**, your microcomputer can easily connect you to a wealth of information available in public and private databases. For example, several executives in different states or countries can work expeditiously on the same report by using communications software. The report is sent back and forth on computer to each location until it is completed. Communications software and a modem also make remote data entry an easy task. A modem converts computer signals (digital signals) to signals transferable on a telephone line (analog signals). Some software packages, such as Symphony by Lotus, include a communications program within the package itself. However, there are many communications software products on the market, among them Crosstalk

(Microstuf, Inc.), On-Line (Micro-Systems Software, Inc.), Pfs: Access (Software Publishing Corp.), and Smartcom II (Hayes Microcomputer Products, Inc.).

1–9–7   Desktop Publishing Software

Desktop publishing software allows you to produce professional-quality documents (with or without graphics) using relatively inexpensive hardware and software. All you need is a PC, a desktop publishing software package, and a laser or letter-quality printer. Desktop publishing has evolved as a result of three major factors: inexpensive PCs, inexpensive laser printers, and sophisticated and easy-to-use software.

With desktop publishing software, you can produce high-quality screen output and then transfer it to a printer—what you see is what you get (WYSIWYG). Today, newsletters, brochures, training manuals, transparencies, posters, and books are produced by means of desktop publishing.

Several desktop publishing software packages are available on the market. Pagemaker (Aldus) and Ventura Publisher (Xerox Corporation) are two popular ones. See Figure 1–11 for some of the output of desktop publishing software.

1–9–8   Financial Planning Software

Financial planning software works with large amounts of data and performs diverse financial analyses. These analyses include present value, future value, rate of return, cash flow analyses, depreciation analyses, and budgeting analyses. There are several packages for financial planning on the market. Among them are DTFPS (Desk Top Financial Solutions, Inc.), Excel (Microsoft), Finar (Finar Research Systems, Ltd.), Javelin (Javelin Software Corporation), Micro-DSS/Finance (Addison-Wesley Publishing Co.), Lotus 1-2-3 (Lotus), Quattro Pro (Borland), IFPS (Comshare), and Micro Plan (Chase Laboratories, Inc.).

Using these packages, you can plan and analyze your financial situation. For example, you can determine how much your $2,000 IRA will be worth at 5 percent interest in 30 years. Or, you can discount all future cash flows into today's dollars. You will know how much you have to deposit in the bank to have $90,000 in 10 years for your child's education.

1–9–9   Accounting Software

In addition to spreadsheet software which has widespread applications in the accounting field, there are dedicated **accounting software** packages that are able to perform many accounting tasks. The tasks performed by such software include general ledgers, account receivables, account payables, payrolls, balance sheets, and income statements. Depending on the price, these software packages vary in sophistication. Some of the popular accounting software packages are Business Works PC (Manzanita Software Systems), 4-in-1 Basic Accounting (Real World Corporation), Peachtree (Peachtree Software, Inc.), and DacEasy Accounting (Dac Software, Inc.).

1–9–10   Project Management Software

A project consists of a series of related activities. Building a house, designing an order entry system, or writing a thesis are examples of projects. The goal of **project management software** is to help decision makers keep time and budget under control by resolving scheduling problems. Project management software helps managers to plan and set achievable goals. Project management software highlights the bottlenecks and the relationships among different activities. This

A.

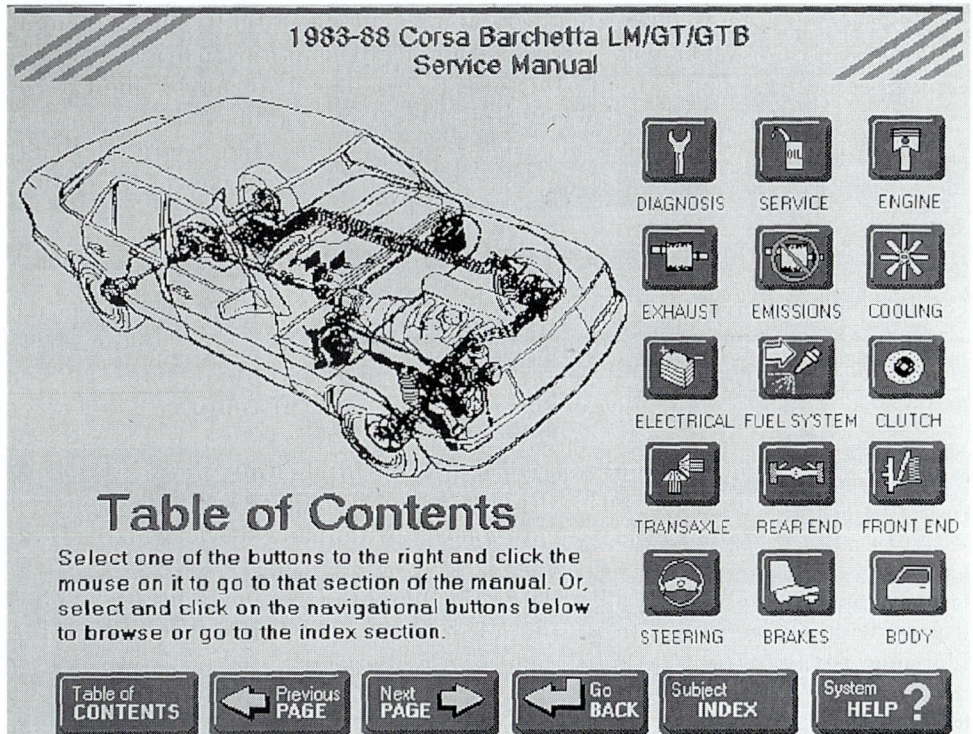

B.

Figure 1–11

Desktop publishing output. A. Desktop publishing combines text, graphics, and illustrations (courtesy of Aldus). B. With desktop publishing, business professionals can prepare high-quality documents on their own (courtesy of Ashton-Tate Corp.).

software allows the user to study the cost, time, and resource impacts of any change in the schedule. Several project management software packages are on the market: Harvard Total Project Manager (Software Publishing), Micro Planner 6 (Micro Planning International), Microsoft Project (Microsoft), Superproject Expert (Computer Associates) and Time Line (Symantec).

1–9–11   Computer-Aided Design (CAD) Software

Computer-aided design (CAD) software involves drafting and design. CAD software has replaced the traditional tools of drafting and design such as the T-square, triangle, and paper and pencil. It is used extensively in the architectural and engineering industries. CAD software no longer belongs only to large corporations. Because of the 386- and 486-based PCs and significant price reduction, small companies and individuals can afford this software. These new PCs have larger memory and are significantly faster than earlier PCs. With their enhanced power and sophistication, they are able to take advantage of most of the features offered by CAD programs. The home use of CAD software includes diverse architectural and engineering applications. There are several CAD programs on the market: AutoCAD (Autodesk), Cadkey (Cadkey), and VersaCAD (VersaCAD). See Figure 1–12 for some output from a CAD system.

A.

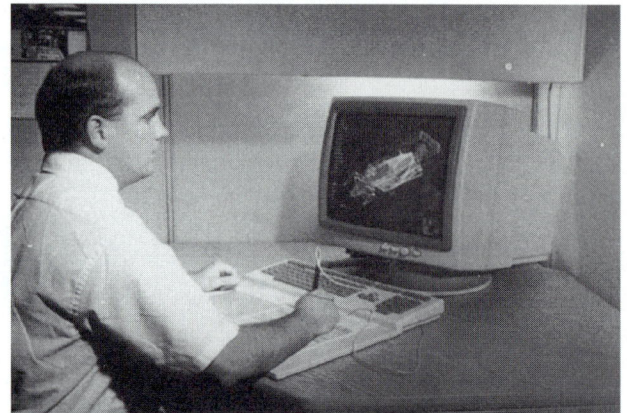

B.

Figure 1–12
A. CAD System for detailed architectural design (Larry Hamill/Macmillan). B. CAD system for design of a multicomponent product (courtesy of International Business Machines Corp.). C. CAD-supported design of aircraft landing gear (courtesy of International Business Machines Corp.).

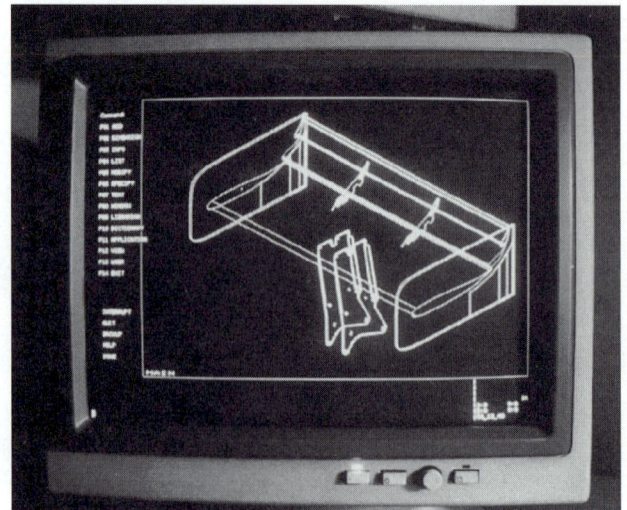

C.

1–9–12   ## Other Popular Software for Microcomputers

In addition to the 11 types of software just described, there are some others commonly used with microcomputers. Let us briefly consider them.

Utility software. These programs or utilities provide various DOS operations. Their goal is to simplify DOS operations for PC users. Depending on the sophistication of the program, various tasks are offered such as hard disk management, recovering a damaged disk or file, menu design, condensing a hard disk, and so forth.

Terminate & Stay Resident (TSR) Software. These programs are loaded when you start your PC and they stay in the background while other software applications are being used. TSR programs offer various features including screen printing, calendar, memo pad, and online calculator.

Investment Analysis Software. In addition to spreadsheet software, several other types of software are designed for investment analysis. By means of these programs, the user can track stocks, bonds, and other investment portfolios. Some of the programs are able to download financial data from public databases or stock exchanges. Others allow users to input their own financial data; then the programs perform financial analysis.

Tax Preparation software. This software assists a PC user in preparing taxes in a fairly straightforward manner. Some of the software packages enable the user to electronically download prepared tax forms to an IRS office.

Games software. Games probably form the oldest group of software for microcomputers, and they cover a broad range of activities. Although games are losing their popularity, they are still played by many PC users.

1–10   GUIDELINES FOR SUCCESSFUL SELECTION OF A MICROCOMPUTER

Because of the many microcomputers on the market, making a selection is a difficult task. The general guidelines provided here regarding the purchase and maintenance of a microcomputer may help you to choose a suitable computer and maintain it more easily.

After you define your needs, think about software. Remember, if there is software on the market, there must be hardware to run it; but the reverse is not necessarily true. After defining the software and hardware you need and want, consider the technical support provided by vendors and reputation of vendors.

Important factors regarding selection and maintenance of a microcomputer are summarized next.

Software Selection

Good software should

- be easy to use
- be able to handle the business volume
- have good documentation
- have training available

- have updates available (free of charge or for a minimum charge)
- have local support
- come from a reputable vendor
- have a low cost

Hardware Selection (Processor and Keyboard)

Good hardware should

- have a comfortable keyboard
- have function keys
- have a general operating system (e.g., OS/2, MS-DOS, PC-DOS, Windows, or UNIX)
- have 16-bit or bigger processor (word) size
- have a high speed
- be expandable (memory and peripheral)
- have enough channel capacity or expansion slots (for attachment of peripherals)
- have a low cost

Hardware Selection (CRT)

A good monitor should

- have a separate CRT (not a built-in one)
- be easy to read (high resolution, super VGA or higher)
- have a standard number of characters per row and column

Hardware Selection (Disk Drive and Hard Disk)

A good disk drive should

- have a built-in, not separate, disk drive
- have adequate storage capacity (to load and run popular software)
- have a hard disk option

Hardware Selection (Printer)

A good printer should

- have a standard printer interface (without additional devices)
- produce high-quality output
- have high speed
- have a reasonable amount of noise suppression
- let you change tape, ribbons, or toner cartridge easily
- have a low cost

Vendor Selection

A good vendor should

- have a good reputation
- have a knowledgeable staff

- have training available for hardware and software
- have a hot line available
- support newsletters and user groups
- provide a "loaner" in case of breakdown
- provide updates (e.g., trade-in options)

Maintenance Contract Selection

A good contract should

- have a warranty period
- state a flexible time for repair
- limit downtime and inconvenience by providing flexible repair visits and timely repair of the computer
- have reasonable terms for contract renewal
- allow relocation and/or reassignment of the present contract
- observe confidentiality issues

1–11   TAKING CARE OF YOUR MICROCOMPUTER

To maintain the health of your microcomputer, consider the following factors:

- Protect your microcomputer against dirt, dust, and smoke.
- Make backup copies for security reasons and keep backups in different locations.
- Avoid any kind of liquid spills.
- Maintain steady power. Use surge protectors for power fluctuations and use lightning arresters in mountainous areas.
- Protect the system from static by using humidifiers or antistatic spray devices.
- Do not start your computer with a disk that you are not familiar with (avoid computer virus—the deadly program that erases and/or corrupts all your data).
- Do not download information to your computer from unknown bulletin boards. Downloading means importing information from other computers by using a modem and telephone line.
- Acquire insurance for your computer equipment.

1–12   ADVANTAGES OF MICROCOMPUTERS COMPARED WITH MAINFRAMES

Generally speaking, a microcomputer offers several advantages over a mainframe computer. Because of their extended memory and increased speed, microcomputers can perform many of the tasks performed by a mainframe but on a smaller scale. The advantages of microcomputers in comparison with mainframes follow:

- They are easier to use.
- They are less threatening to those who are not computer experts (e.g., they are smaller).
- They give the user more control.

- They are relatively inexpensive.
- They can be portable.

1–13   YOU AND YOUR PC: A HANDS-ON SESSION

If you place the DOS diskette or "boot disk" (disk that can be used to start the computer) in drive A, when you turn the computer on, your microcomputer will ask for the date. Remember, the majority of IBM or IBM-compatible systems come with a DOS disk. Either type the date in the desired format or press the Enter key to bypass the date. The computer then asks you for the time. Either type the time in the desired format or press the Enter key to bypass the time. Now you are at the A> prompt. This means your default drive is A.

If your computer has a hard disk, this start-up procedure is slightly different. You will get the system started from the hard disk and your prompt will be C> instead of A>. See Figure 1–13.

In any case, from this mode (the DOS mode), you can go to any application software.

For example, if the software (e.g., Lotus 1-2-3) is installed in the hard disk, use the DOS CD command to change to the directory that stores the software; then type *123* and press Enter. From the DOS mode, you can access any application software.

When you are at the C> prompt, you are in RAM. This area is called a working or temporary area. Any work you do in this area will disappear if you turn the computer off. To make your work permanent, you have to transfer it to a **permanent area**. The permanent area usually is either floppy disk or hard disk. Your work stays in the permanent area until you erase it.

While you are at the C> prompt, you can send any information to RAM by using the keyboard. This information can become permanent by saving it into a permanent medium. All application programs include a command for saving your work.

Beginning computer users are always worried about making mistakes! What happens if you make a mistake? Don't panic. Your mistake can be corrected easily. Some application programs have an UNDO command. If you realize you have made a mistake, you can recover from it by using the UNDO feature. All application programs include a feature for correcting mistakes. In the worst case, you can retype the correct statement over your previous material. Remember, any address (or cell) in the computer memory can hold only one value at a time. As soon as you type and enter a new value, the old one disappears.

1–14   WHAT IS A COMPUTER FILE?

A **computer file** is basically an electronic document. One way to create a document is to type and enter it using the keyboard. As soon as you save the document, you have generated a computer file.

To differentiate one file from another, you must save each file under a unique name—a file name. A file name is any combination of up to eight valid characters. Valid characters include letters of the alphabet (upper case or lower-

Figure 1–13
Getting the system started.

```
C>
```

case), digits 0 through 9, the underscore, and some special characters. If you provide a name longer than eight characters, some application programs give you an error message; others truncate the name and accept only the first eight characters.

In addition to a file name, a file is usually saved with a file extension. A file extension is similar to a file name but uses up to three characters. Some application programs automatically provide a file extension when you save the file. In other application programs, providing a file extension is the user's responsibility.

Several characters have special meanings in different application software. The asterisk (*) can represent any number of characters up to eight. The question mark (?) can represent any single character. These two characters are called wildcard characters. These **wildcards** can significantly improve your efficiency while you work with application programs. For example, all your Lotus 1-2-3 graphic files are identified by *.PIC. The * represents any file name and the PIC indicates that your file is a Lotus 1-2-3 graphic file. For example, if you want to copy all your Lotus 1-2-3 graphic files from the disk in drive A to the disk in drive B, type this DOS command at the A> prompt: *COPY *.PIC B:* (follow by pressing the Enter key). If you did not have this wildcard feature, you would have to repeat the COPY command as many times as the number of the graphic files. The file BRANCH?.* represents BRANCH1, BRANCH2, and so on. For example, in DOS if you type *DIR *.WK?* (and press Enter), your Lotus 1-2-3 files from version 1 and 1A (WKS) files, version 2 (WK1) files, version 3 (WK3) files, and student version (WKE) files will be displayed. The asterisk as the file extension indicates that the file can have any extension. Your entire disk can be identified by *.*. Using the COPY command, for example, at the A> prompt, to copy the entire disk in drive A to drive B, type *Copy *.* B:* (and press Enter).

1–15   TYPES OF DATA

Any application program or computer language accepts different types of data. The most commonly used data types are numeric and nonnumeric.

Numeric data include any combination of digits 0 through 9 and decimal points. Numeric data can be integer or real. Integer data include only whole numbers without any decimal points, for example, 656 or 986. Real data include digits and decimal points, for example, 696.25 or 729.793. Real data is sometimes called floating point data. Floating point means that the decimal point can move from right to left, for example, 222.2, 22.22, 2.222. Another type of real data is the fixed point, meaning that the decimal point is always fixed.

Nonnumeric data, or alphanumeric data, is sometimes called labels or strings. Any types of valid characters can be nonnumeric data, for example, Jackson or 123 Broadway Street. You cannot perform any arithmetic operations with nonnumeric data.

1–16   TYPES OF VALUES

Computers usually handle two types of values: variables and constants. **Variables** are valid computer addresses (locations) that hold different values at different times. For example, in A=65, A is the variable and 65 is the **constant.** B = "Brown": B is the variable and Brown is the constant. A variable holds a given value at any given time. As soon as you enter a new value into this variable, the old value disappears. The constant is always fixed. See Figure 1–14.

Figure 1–14
Example of a variable and a constant.

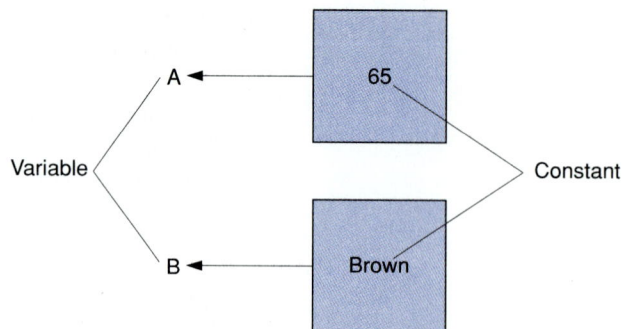

1–17 TYPES OF FORMULAS

Two types of formulas or functions are handled by computers: user-defined and built-in.

User-defined formulas or functions are a combination of computer addresses designed to perform a certain task. For example, the area of a triangle can be presented as A = B*H/2 (meaning base multiplied by height divided by 2). In this case, A is a formula or a function. When you enter different values for B and H, and a different value for A, the area of the triangle, will be calculated.

Built-in formulas or functions are already available within the application program or the computer language. As soon as the user provides values for a given variable or variables, the application program or the computer language dynamically calculates these formulas. For example, SQRT(X) is a function that calculates the square root of a variable, X. The X and any other information needed by these functions are called arguments. As soon as you provide a value for X, the square root is calculated; for example, SQRT(25) is equal to 5. The function FV(payment,interest rate,term) calculates the future value of a series of equal payments with a given interest rate over a period of time (term). This function can help you determine, for example, the future value of an IRA in which you plan to invest $2,000 for 30 years at a 10 percent interest rate.

1–18 PRIORITY OF ARITHMETIC OPERATIONS

When application programs perform arithmetic operations, they follow a series of rules. The rules for priority of arithmetic operations are as follows:

1. Expressions inside parentheses have the highest priority.
2. Exponentiation (raising to power) has the next highest priority.
3. Multiplication and division have the third highest priority.
4. Addition and subtraction have the fourth highest priority.
5. When there are two or more operations with the same priority, operations proceed from left to right.

The following examples should make the rules clear. First, an application program uses * (asterisk) for multiplication, ^ (caret) for exponentiation (raising the power), and / (slash) for division. If A=5, B=10, C=2, calculate the following:

$$A+B/C \quad = \quad 10$$
$$(A+B)/C \quad = \quad 7.5$$

$$\begin{array}{lll} A*B/C & = & 25 \\ (A*B)/C & = & 25 \\ A^\wedge C/2 & = & 12.50 \end{array}$$

SUMMARY

This chapter focused on microcomputers in general. Input, output, and primary and secondary memory devices for microcomputers were described. The general capabilities of microcomputers were introduced. The chapter presented a series of guidelines for successful selection and maintenance of a microcomputer. It also listed the advantages of micros over mainframes. A hands-on session included the basics for getting started as a computer user. The chapter concluded with a definition of computer files, types of data, types of values, types of formulas, and priority of arithmetic operations.

REVIEW QUESTIONS

*These questions are answered in Appendix A.

1. What is a microcomputer? What are some of the capabilities of a micro?
*2. What are some typical input devices for a micro?
3. What are some typical output devices for a micro?
4. Explain the difference between a primary memory device and a secondary memory device.
5. What is RAM? ROM? PROM? EPROM?
*6. What are the most commonly used secondary storage devices for a micro?
7. What is extended memory? What is expanded memory?
8. Describe optical technologies. What are their advantages and disadvantages?
9. How do you measure the memory capacity of a micro?
10. Besides memory, what other attributes are important when you buy a micro?
11. What is the difference between a floppy disk and a hard disk?
12. Give the speed range for a typical microcomputer.
*13. What is the memory size of a typical micro?
14. What is a good software?
15. What is a good hardware?
16. What is a good maintenance contract? Who are the good vendors?
*17. How should you care for your micro?
18. List some application programs for a micro.
19. What are some of the advantages of a micro compared with a mainframe?
20. What is permanent memory in a PC? What is temporary memory?
21. How do you send information from RAM to a floppy or hard disk?
*22. How do you correct your mistakes?
23. Define a computer file.
24. What is a wildcard character?
25. Describe different types of data.
26. What is a variable? What is a constant?
*27. What is the priority of arithmetic operations?
28. List the symbols used for arithmetic operations.
29. Turn on a PC. What do you see? Turn it off. Insert the DOS disk in drive A and turn the computer back on. What do you see this time?

30. Enter the correct date and time in your computer. What happens if you make a mistake?

31. Type *DIR* and press the Enter key. What is displayed at this time?

32. What types of PCs do you have on your campus? Describe different input/output devices used by the PCs in your school's micro lab. Do you have a Bernoulli box in the lab? What are some of the advantages of Bernoulli box over a hard disk?

33. What are the most commonly used disks on your campus—3½ or 5¼? Compare and contrast these two types of storage devices.

34. Consult computer magazines to find out which computers use optical disks.

35. Which of the types of software packages introduced in this chapter are available on your campus? What are the applications of each?

36. If you want to buy a PC for personal use, how should you start shopping? What attributes makes a PC attractive?

KEY TERMS

Accounting software

Arithmetic logic unit (ALU)

Bernoulli box

Built-in formulas or functions

Central processing unit (CPU)

CD-ROM

Communications software

Computer-aided design (CAD) software

Computer file

Constants

Control unit

Conventional memory

Database software

Desktop publishing software

EPROM

Erasable optical disk

Expanded memory

Extended memory

Financial planning software

Floppy disk

Grammar checker software

Graphics software

Hard disk

Input device

Main memory

Micro

Microcomputer

Nonnumeric data

Numeric data

Output device

Permanent area

Personal computer (PC)

Primary memory

Priority of arithmetic operations

Project management software

PROM

Random-access memory (RAM)

RGB monitor

Read-only memory (ROM)

Secondary memory

Spreadsheet software

User-defined formulas or functions

Variables

Wildcard

Word processing software

WORM disk

ARE YOU READY TO MOVE ON?

Multiple Choice

1. Choose the correct ranking of monitor display resolutions from lowest to highest.
   a. VGA, CGA, XGA
   b. EGA, VGA, CGA
   c. EGA, CGA, VGA
   d. CGA, EGA, XGA
   e. XGA, CGA, EGA

2. Which of the following is *not* a typical adapter card?
   a. printer interface card
   b. clock card

   c. disk drive card

   d. display card

   e. punch card

3. Of the following types of main memory, which can the user control directly?

   a. ROM

   b. REM

   c. RAM

   d. PROM

   e. all of the above

4. What is now the most commonly used secondary storage device?

   a. 5¼ inch floppy disk and a hard disk

   b. 3½ inch floppy disk and a hard disk

   c. Bernoulli box and a hard disk

   d. hard disk with no floppy disk

   e. none of the above

5. What is the major advantage of optical storage technology?

   a. storage capacity

   b. cost

   c. durability

   d. both A and C

   e. all of the above

6. When we refer to memory and storage capacity sizes, we use kilobytes (as in 360 K). 1 K equals approximately

   a. 1 byte

   b. 1,000 bytes

   c. 1,000,000 bytes

   d. 1,048,576 bytes

   e. none of the above

7. Word size directly affects

   a. the speed of the computer

   b. the ability of the user to understand what is being said

   c. the maximum amount of data that can be displayed on the CRT

   d. the choice of which type of disk drive to use

   e. the meaning of the function keys on the keyboard

8. Which of the following are disadvantages of mainframes when compared with micro-computers?

   a. They are more difficult to use.

   b. They are more threatening to users who are not computer experts.

   c. The user has less control.

   d. They are relatively more expensive.

   e. All of the above are disadvantages.

9. After booting the computer with the DOS disk (loading DOS and entering the date and time), you are at

   a. the Lotus Access menu

   b. the DOS prompt (A> or C>)

   c. the parallel/serial interface

   d. the BASIC prompt

   e. none of the above

10. An example of alphanumeric data would be

   a. 123

   b. 123.25

   c. LOTUS-123

   d. A=(123-2)/4

   e. none of the above

True/False

1. The terms *personal computer*, PC, and *microcomputer* refer to different types of computers.
2. A typical microcomputer consists of input, output, and memory devices.
3. Monochrome CRTs cannot generate graphic output.
4. The purpose of function keys and special keys on a computer keyboard does not vary in different application programs.
5. The capacity of a hard disk is greater than the capacity of a floppy disk.
6. A WORM disk can be recorded and erased repeatedly when high-volume storage and updating are essential.
7. Typical microcomputer software packages and applications include spreadsheet, database, graphics, communications, and word processing.
8. The first step in selecting a microcomputer is to define your needs; then think about software.
9. The commands DIR *.* and DIR ????????.??? produce the same results.
10. Expressions inside parentheses have the lowest priority when it comes to performing arithmetic operations.

ANSWERS

Multiple Choice		True/False	
1.	d	1.	F
2.	e	2.	T
3.	c	3.	F
4.	b	4.	F
5.	d	5.	T
6.	b	6.	F
7.	a	7.	T
8.	e	8.	T
9.	b	9.	T
10.	c	10.	F

A Quick Trip with MS-DOS and PC-DOS

2

2–1   INTRODUCTION

This chapter describes the basics of the Disk Operating System (DOS). The differences between internal and external DOS commands are explained as are the features of system date and time. After file specifications in the DOS environment are reviewed, the DIR command for generating a directory listing is discussed. Next, important keys in the DOS environment and the FORMAT command for creating a usable data disk are highlighted. Other DOS basics covered are the different versions of MS-DOS and PC-DOS, batch and AUTOEXEC files, the process of creating a directory, and commands for directories. Both DOS 5.0 and 6.0 are presented in general. A most useful feature of the chapter is a table summarizing important DOS commands.

2–2   TURNING ON YOUR PC

When you access a personal computer in a computer lab or any other location, the computer is either off or on. This text assumes that your computer has a hard disk and that the Disk Operating System (DOS) files are stored in drive C in the hard disk. DOS disks come with the computer when it is purchased.

Turn the computer on. This procedure is called a **cold boot**. Boot means getting the computer started. If the computer is already turned on, press the Ctrl, Alt, and Del keys simultaneously. This procedure is called **warm boot**. The warm boot is faster than the cold boot, because the computer does not check its memory in a warm boot as it does in a cold boot.

If your computer does not have a hard disk and you want to start it from a floppy disk, insert the boot disk in drive A and turn the computer on. When the computer is booted from the floppy disk, it asks you to enter the current date. Type the date in the format requested (mm-dd-yy). After typing the current date, press the Enter key. Your PC now asks for the current time. Type the current time in the format requested (hh:mm:ss). (Note that DOS operates on a 24-hour clock, 2:30 p.m. is 14:30, 9:15 p.m. is 21:15, etc.) After typing the time, press the Enter key. Now you should see the A> prompt. This means the necessary portions of DOS have been loaded into primary memory (RAM) and drive A is the default drive. Default drive means that from this point on this is the drive the computer accesses for executing commands. For example, if you decide to save a file, your file will be saved onto the disk in this drive. If you ask for a directory listing, the directory of the disk in this drive will be highlighted. At this point, you should be able to access any internal or external DOS commands.

If your DOS is installed on the hard disk (which is usually the C drive), your default drive will be the C drive. In a computer with hard disk, the date and time are maintained internally, so you do not need to enter them at boot-up time.

If you boot-up from the floppy disk and do not want to enter the date and time, you can bypass the prompts by pressing the Enter key twice. When the prompts are bypassed, the PC uses the default date and time when saving files. It is a good practice to enter both the correct date and time when you start the PC, so all your programs and data files are saved with this current information. The correct date and time can help you to determine the most or least recent versions of your files listed in the directory. A **directory** is the listing of all your files.

If you forget to enter the current date and time at the boot-up time, or if the date and time of your system are not correct, you can enter this information at any given time by using the DATE and TIME commands. At the DOS prompt, type *DATE* and press the Enter key. The computer will ask you to enter the current date in the format mm-dd-yy. Type the date and press the Enter key. Now type *TIME* and press the Enter key. The computer will ask you to enter the current time in the format hh:mm:ss. After typing the current time, press the Enter key. At this point the computer registers this information in its memory, where it will remain and be updated automatically until you turn the PC off. Computers with a hard disk have a battery-operated clock on their motherboard. The motherboard is where the computer's primary electronic circuitry resides. The date and time are maintained automatically, and user intervention is not required except for correcting the date or time.

Internal commands (sometimes called memory resident commands) are those commands that are loaded into the computer's memory at boot-up time. As soon as you see a DOS prompt such as A> or B> or C>, you can execute any internal command. Internal commands can be used without the DOS disk in any disk drive. CLS (clear screen) is an example of a DOS internal command. If at the DOS prompt you type *CLS* and press the Enter key, the screen will be erased.

External commands (sometimes called non-memory resident commands) are those commands that can only be executed by having the DOS disk in one of the drives. These commands are sometimes called DOS utilities. They are separate programs stored on the DOS disk. For example, DISKCOPY (generates a duplicate of a disk) is an external DOS command. A listing of most of these commands appears at the end of the chapter.

2–3   DIFFERENT DOS PROMPTS

Depending on how you get your PC started, you will see different prompts. If you have a hard disk in your system and you start the system from the hard disk, your prompt may be C>. The prompt indicates the current default drive. The default drive is the disk drive that the PC will access if no other disk drive is specified. If a file is located on a disk that is not in the default drive, the default must be changed or the disk drive containing the file must be specified. Changing the default is an easy task. At the C> prompt type *A:* (remember the colon) and press the Enter key. Now the prompt is A>. You can change this back to C> by typing *C:* and pressing the Enter key. The prompt can be customized by using the PROMPT PG command followed by pressing Enter. This command is useful when you use directories (discussed later in this chapter). By using this command, you know in which drive and/or directory you are at any given time.

2–4   DOS FILE SPECIFICATIONS

DOS files basically follow the same conventions that apply to other software. This means **file names** can be up to eight characters long. File names can contain digits 0 through 9 and some special characters such as underscore (_), pound sign (#), and so forth. To be on the safe side, limit the use of special characters in file names and do not use any space in a file name.

File extensions can be up to three characters long and contain the same characters used by file names. For example, TEST.TEX is a valid file name. Important file extensions in the DOS environment include these:

- BAK (backup): This extension indicates files generated by some word processing, spreadsheet, and database management programs; the files are backup copies of the original files.
- BAT (batch): This indicates a text file generated by the user. The file includes DOS commands and statements that are executed when the name of the file is typed.
- COM (command): This extension identifies files that can be executed by typing the name of the file.
- EXE (executable): Like COM files, files with this extension can be executed by typing the file name.
- SYS (system): This extension identifies files that can be used only by DOS.

2–5   DIR COMMAND

With DOS files installed in the hard disk, you can generate a listing of your current directory by using the DIR command. Type *DIR* and press the Enter key; information similar to Figure 2–1 will be presented to you. At the top of Figure 2–1, the listing indicates the volume in drive C is MS-DOS_6. This is the internal name for this disk. The LABEL command allows you to change this name. To do this, at the C> prompt type *LABEL* and press Enter. Specify the new label (name) of up to 11 characters and press Enter. From now on the internal name of this drive will be the name that you just specified.

The DIR command provides the name of each file, the file extension, the size of the file in bytes, and the date and time that the file was created or changed. At the end of the listing, the DIR command tells you the number of the files and the amount of bytes available on this particular disk. To erase the screen, type *CLS* and press the Enter key. To generate a listing for drive A, type *DIR A:* and press Enter. A listing of drive B can be created by typing *DIR B:* followed by pressing Enter.

The DIR command can be used with wildcard characters. Wildcard characters function as placeholders for other characters in the file name or file extension. The two valid DOS wildcards are the * (asterisk) and the ? (question mark). The asterisk replaces one or more characters in the file name or extension with any valid character. For example, *.COM refers to any file name with the extension COM. The question mark replaces only one character in the file name or extension with a valid character. For example, entering DIR *.COM displays all COM files. DIR *.PIC displays all Lotus 1-2-3 graphic files. DIR *.AB? displays any file that has AB as the first two letters of its extension, while the third character can be any valid character. DIR *.WK? displays Lotus WK1, WKS, WKE, or WK3 files. WKS are Lotus 1-2-3 files before Release 2.0, WK1 are Lotus release 2.0 and 2.01, 2.2, 2.3 and 2.4 files, WKE are Lotus 1-2-3 files in the student version of the software, and WK3 are Lotus 1-2-3 files in Release 3 or higher. It also displays Quattro Pro WKQ files.

2–6   DIR WITH DIFFERENT SWITCHES

The DIR command can be used with different switches (parameters) to provide different types of listings. DIR/W provides a wide directory; this means you get a horizontal listing of your directory. In this case, only file names and extensions

Figure 2–1
Directory listing of MS-DOS 6.

```
Volume in drive C is MS_DOS_6
Volume Serial Number is 1C22-913B
Directory of C:\DOS

.               <DIR>        06-06-92   12:24p
..              <DIR>        06-06-92   12:24p
DBLSPACE BIN     51214 03-10-93    6:00a
FORMAT   COM     22717 03-10-93    6:00a
NLSFUNC  EXE      7036 03-10-93    6:00a
COUNTRY  SYS     17066 03-10-93    6:00a
KEYB     COM     14983 03-10-93    6:00a
KEYBOARD SYS     34694 03-10-93    6:00a
SETUP    EXE     71974 03-10-93    6:00a
DOSSETUP INI      3735 03-10-93    6:00a
ANSI     SYS      9065 03-10-93    6:00a
ATTRIB   EXE     11165 03-10-93    6:00a
CHKDSK   EXE     12907 03-10-93    6:00a
EDIT     COM       413 03-10-93    6:00a
EXPAND   EXE     16129 03-10-93    6:00a
EDLIN    EXE     12642 06-13-91    5:00a
MORE     COM      2546 03-10-93    6:00a
MSD      EXE    158470 03-10-93    6:00a
QBASIC   EXE    194309 03-10-93    6:00a
RESTORE  EXE     38294 03-10-93    6:00a
MIRROR   COM     18169 06-13-91    5:00a
SYS      COM      9379 03-10-93    6:00a
UNFORMAT COM     12738 03-10-93    6:00a
SMARTDRV SYS      8335 06-13-91    5:00a
OS2      TXT      6358 03-10-93    6:00a
NETWORKS TXT     20463 03-10-93    6:00a
README   TXT     44990 03-10-93    6:00a
DEBUG    EXE     15715 03-10-93    6:00a
FDISK    EXE     29333 03-10-93    6:00a
DOSSHELL VID      9462 03-10-93    6:00a
19C1DOSC BAT        16 01-23-93    3:05p
DEFAULT  SET      4207 01-02-94   10:49a
DOSSHELL GRB      4421 03-10-93    6:00a
CHOICE   COM      1754 03-10-93    6:00a
DEFRAG   EXE     75033 03-10-93    6:00a
PACKING  LST      2507 06-13-91    5:00a
DEFRAG   HLP      9227 03-10-93    6:00a
DOSSWAP  EXE     18756 03-10-93    6:00a
EGA      CPI     58870 03-10-93    6:00a
RECOVER  EXE      9146 06-13-91    5:00a
EGA      SYS      4885 03-10-93    6:00a
HIMEM    SYS     14208 03-10-93    6:00a
MEM      EXE     32150 03-10-93    6:00a
XCOPY    EXE     15820 03-10-93    6:00a
MONEY    BAS     46225 06-13-91    5:00a
MSHERC   COM      6934 06-13-91    5:00a
DELTREE  EXE     11113 03-10-93    6:00a
GORILLA  BAS     29434 06-13-91    5:00a
4201     CPI      6404 06-13-91    5:00a
4208     CPI       720 06-13-91    5:00a
5202     CPI       395 06-13-91    5:00a
MOVE     EXE     17823 03-10-93    6:00a
ASSIGN   COM      6399 06-13-91    5:00a
RAMDRIVE SYS      5873 03-10-93    6:00a
BACKUP   EXE     36092 06-13-91    5:00a
SMARTDRV EXE     42073 03-10-93    6:00a
COMP     EXE     14282 06-13-91    5:00a
```

Figure 2–1
(continued)

```
DISPLAY   SYS     15789 03-10-93    6:00a
DOSHELP   HLP      5667 03-10-93    6:00a
DOSSHELL  COM      4620 03-10-93    6:00a
DOSSHELL  EXE    236378 03-10-93    6:00a
FASTHELP  EXE     11481 03-10-93    6:00a
GRAFTABL  COM     11205 06-13-91    5:00a
FASTOPEN  EXE     12034 03-10-93    6:00a
HELP      HLP    294741 03-10-93    6:00a
HELP      COM       413 03-10-93    6:00a
NIBBLES   BAS     24103 06-13-91    5:00a
REMLINE   BAS     12314 06-13-91    5:00a
MODE      COM     23521 03-10-93    6:00a
POWER     EXE      8052 03-10-93    6:00a
EXE2BIN   EXE      8424 06-13-91    5:00a
PRINT     EXE     15640 03-10-93    6:00a
JOIN      EXE     17870 06-13-91    5:00a
LCD       CPI     10753 06-13-91    5:00a
QBASIC    HLP    130881 03-10-93    6:00a
PRINTER   SYS     18804 06-13-91    5:00a
SHARE     EXE     10912 03-10-93    6:00a
DELOLDOS  EXE     17710 03-10-93    6:00a
SETVER    EXE     12015 03-10-93    6:00a
APPEND    EXE     10774 03-10-93    6:00a
APPNOTES  TXT      8660 06-13-91    5:00a
KEYBHP    COM     15997 06-13-91    5:00a
MODEHP    COM     23232 06-13-91    5:00a
SSTOR     SYS     37260 06-13-91    5:00a
DISKCOMP  COM     10620 03-10-93    6:00a
MOUSE     SYS     32730 06-13-91    5:00a
DISKCOPY  COM     11879 03-10-93    6:00a
B         BAT        46 06-06-92    1:53p
589DOSCM  BAT        16 01-23-93    3:01p
D5C0DOSC  BAT        16 01-23-93    6:49p
2688DOSC  BAT        16 01-23-93    3:08p
370CDOSC  BAT        16 01-23-93    4:12p
D923DOSC  BAT        16 01-23-93    5:50p
BA6EDOSC  BAT        16 01-23-93    6:43p
D329DOSC  BAT        16 01-23-93    6:49p
DRIVER    SYS      5406 03-10-93    6:00a
FC        EXE     18650 03-10-93    6:00a
FIND      EXE      6770 03-10-93    6:00a
GRAPHICS  COM     19694 03-10-93    6:00a
GRAPHICS  PRO     21232 03-10-93    6:00a
LABEL     EXE      9390 03-10-93    6:00a
SMARTMON  EXE     28672 03-10-93    6:00a
SMARTMON  HLP     10727 03-10-93    6:00a
SORT      EXE      6922 03-10-93    6:00a
LOADFIX   COM      1131 03-10-93    6:00a
MWBACKUP  EXE    309696 03-10-93    6:00a
MWBACKUP  HLP    400880 03-10-93    6:00a
REPLACE   EXE     20226 03-10-93    6:00a
SUBST     EXE     18478 03-10-93    6:00a
TREE      COM      6898 03-10-93    6:00a
DOSKEY    COM      5883 03-10-93    6:00a
VFINTD    386      5295 03-10-93    6:00a
MWBACKF   DLL     14560 03-10-93    6:00a
MWBACKR   DLL    111120 03-10-93    6:00a
MOUSE     COM     56408 03-10-93    6:00a
MSBACKUP  EXE      5506 03-10-93    6:00a
MSBACKUP  OVL    133952 03-10-93    6:00a
MSBACKFB  OVL     69066 03-10-93    6:00a
```

Figure 2–1
(continued)

```
MSBACKFR OVL      72474  03-10-93      6:00a
CHKSTATE SYS      41600  03-10-93      6:00a
UNDELETE EXE      26420  03-10-93      6:00a
MWUNDEL  EXE     130496  03-10-93      6:00a
MWUNDEL  HLP      35741  03-10-93      6:00a
MWGRAFIC DLL      36944  03-10-93      6:00a
MSBACKUP HLP     314236  03-10-93      6:00a
WNTOOLS  GRP       2205  01-02-94      6:25p
MSBACKDB OVL      63098  03-10-93      6:00a
MSBACKDR OVL      66906  03-10-93      6:00a
MSBCONFG OVL      47210  03-10-93      6:00a
MSBCONFG HLP      45780  03-10-93      6:00a
DBLSPACE EXE     274388  03-10-93      6:00a
MEMMAKER INF       1652  03-10-93      6:00a
INTERLNK EXE      17197  03-10-93      6:00a
INTERSVR EXE      37314  03-10-93      6:00a
MSCDEX   EXE      25377  03-10-93      6:00a
DBLSPACE HLP      72169  03-10-93      6:00a
DBLSPACE INF       2178  03-10-93      6:00a
DBLSPACE SYS        339  03-10-93      6:00a
DBLWIN   HLP       8597  03-10-93      6:00a
DOSSHELL HLP     161323  03-10-93      6:00a
EMM386   EXE     115294  03-10-93      6:00a
MEMMAKER EXE     118660  03-10-93      6:00a
SIZER    EXE       7169  03-10-93      6:00a
MONOUMB  386       8783  03-10-93      6:00a
MSTOOLS  DLL      13424  03-10-93      6:00a
MSAV     EXE     172198  03-10-93      6:00a
MSAV     HLP      23891  03-10-93      6:00a
MSAVHELP OVL      29828  03-10-93      6:00a
MSAVIRUS LST      35520  03-10-93      6:00a
VSAFE    COM      62576  03-10-93      6:00a
MWAVDOSL DLL      44736  03-10-93      6:00a
MWAVDRVL DLL       7744  03-10-93      6:00a
AUTOEXEC UMB        703  01-01-94      5:34p
MOUSE    INI         28  01-01-94      5:34p
CONFIG   UMB        142  01-01-94      5:34p
MEMMAKER STS        851  01-01-94      5:40p
MWAVDLG  DLL      36368  03-10-93      6:00a
MSBACKUP INI         43  01-03-94      4:46p
MWAVSCAN DLL     151568  03-10-93      6:00a
MSBACKUP RST        608  04-13-92      7:07a
MSBACKUP TMP       5014  01-02-94     10:49a
MWAV     EXE     142640  03-10-93      6:00a
MWAVABSI DLL      54576  03-10-93      6:00a
MWAV     HLP      24619  03-10-93      6:00a
MWAVSOS  DLL       7888  03-10-93      6:00a
MWAVMGR  DLL      21712  03-10-93      6:00a
MWAVTSR  EXE      17328  03-10-93      6:00a
COMMAND  COM      52925  03-10-93      6:00a
MSAV     INI          0  01-01-94      3:01p
DEFAULT  BAK       4207  01-02-94      9:56a
MSBACKUP LOG     196811  01-02-94     10:54a
DEFAULT  SLT         64  01-02-94     10:49a
DEFAULT  SAV         64  01-02-94      9:56a
DOSSHELL INI      16424  01-02-94      1:02p
       176 file(s)     6563296 bytes
                     129966080 bytes free

C>
```

are listed. Figure 2–2 was generated by typing *DIR/W* at the C> prompt and pressing the Enter key. *DIR/P* gives you one screen of the file listing. At the bottom of the screen, a prompt tells you to strike a key to see another screen. Figure 2–3 was generated by typing *DIR/P* at the C> prompt and pressing the Enter key. (Notice that this is a partial listing.)

The DIR command enables you to get a listing of files in any drive by specifying the drive. For example, say the current drive is A; type *DIR B:/W* to display a wide directory of drive B. There must be at least one space between the DIR command and a drive name when you issue the command. Remember, to execute any DOS command, you must press Enter after typing the command.

```
C>DIR/W

    Volume in drive C is MS_DOS_6
    Volume Serial Number is 1C22-913B
    Directory of C:\DOS

[.]              [..]             DBLSPACE.BIN     FORMAT.COM       NLSFUNC.EXE
COUNTRY.SYS      KEYB.COM         KEYBOARD.SYS     SETUP.EXE        DOSSETUP.INI
ANSI.SYS         ATTRIB.EXE       CHKDSK.EXE       EDIT.COM         EXPAND.EXE
EDLIN.EXE        MORE.COM         MSD.EXE          QBASIC.EXE       RESTORE.EXE
MIRROR.COM       SYS.COM          UNFORMAT.COM     SMARTDRV.SYS     OS2.TXT
NETWORKS.TXT     README.TXT       DEBUG.EXE        FDISK.EXE        DOSSHELL.VID
19C1DOSC.BAT     DEFAULT.SET      DOSSHELL.GRB     CHOICE.COM       DEFRAG.EXE
PACKING.LST      DEFRAG.HLP       DOSSWAP.EXE      EGA.CPI          RECOVER.EXE
EGA.SYS          HIMEM.SYS        MEM.EXE          XCOPY.EXE        MONEY.BAS
MSHERC.COM       DELTREE.EXE      GORILLA.BAS      4201.CPI         4208.CPI
5202.CPI         MOVE.EXE         ASSIGN.COM       RAMDRIVE.SYS     BACKUP.EXE
SMARTDRV.EXE     COMP.EXE         DISPLAY.SYS      DOSHELP.HLP      DOSSHELL.COM
DOSSHELL.EXE     FASTHELP.EXE     GRAFTABL.COM     EDIT.HLP         FASTOPEN.EXE
HELP.HLP         HELP.COM         NIBBLES.BAS      REMLINE.BAS      MODE.COM
POWER.EXE        EXE2BIN.EXE      PRINT.EXE        JOIN.EXE         LCD.CPI
QBASIC.HLP       PRINTER.SYS      SHARE.EXE        DELOLDOS.EXE     SETVER.EXE
APPEND.EXE       APPNOTES.TXT     KEYBHP.COM       MODEHP.COM       SSTOR.SYS
DISKCOMP.COM     MOUSE.SYS        DISKCOPY.COM     B.BAT            589DOSCM.BAT
D5C0DOSC.BAT     2688DOSC.BAT     370CDOSC.BAT     D923DOSC.BAT     BA6EDOSC.BAT
D329DOSC.BAT     DRIVER.SYS       FC.EXE           FIND.EXE         GRAPHICS.COM
GRAPHICS.PRO     LABEL.EXE        SMARTMON.EXE     SMARTMON.HLP     SORT.EXE
LOADFIX.COM      MWBACKUP.EXE     MWBACKUP.HLP     REPLACE.EXE      SUBST.EXE
TREE.COM         DOSKEY.COM       VFINTD.386       MWBACKF.DLL      MWBACKR.DLL
MOUSE.COM        MSBACKUP.EXE     MSBACKUP.OVL     MSBACKFB.OVL     MSBACKFR.OVL
CHKSTATE.SYS     UNDELETE.EXE     MWUNDEL.EXE      MWUNDEL.HLP      MWGRAFIC.DLL
MSBACKUP.HLP     WNTOOLS.GRP      MSBACKDB.OVL     MSBACKDR.OVL     MSBCONFG.OVL
MSBCONFG.HLP     DBLSPACE.EXE     MEMMAKER.HLP     MEMMAKER.INF     INTERLNK.EXE
INTERSVR.EXE     MSCDEX.EXE       DBLSPACE.HLP     DBLSPACE.INF     DBLSPACE.SYS
DBLWIN.HLP       DOSSHELL.HLP     EMM386.EXE       MEMMAKER.EXE     SIZER.EXE
MONOUMB.386      MSTOOLS.DLL      MSAV.EXE         MSAV.HLP         MSAVHELP.OVL
MSAVIRUS.LST     VSAFE.COM        MWAVDOSL.DLL     MWAVDRVL.DLL     AUTOEXEC.UMB
MOUSE.INI        CONFIG.UMB       MEMMAKER.STS     MWAVDLG.DLL      MSBACKUP.INI
MWAVSCAN.DLL     MSBACKUP.RST     MSBACKUP.TMP     MWAV.EXE         MWAVABSI.DLL
MWAV.HLP         MWAVSOS.DLL      MWAVMGR.DLL      MWAVTSR.EXE      COMMAND.COM
MSAV.INI         DEFAULT.BAK      MSBACKUP.LOG     DEFAULT.SLT      DEFAULT.SAV
DOSSHELL.INI
        176 file(s)      6563296  bytes
                       129966080  bytes free

C>
```

Figure 2–2
Directory listing with DIR/W command.

Figure 2–3
Directory listing with DIR/P command.

```
C>DIR/P

 Volume in drive C is MS_DOS_6
 Volume Serial Number is 1C22-913B
 Directory of C:\DOS

 .             <DIR>         06-06-92   12:24p
 ..            <DIR>         06-06-92   12:24p
 DBLSPACE BIN     51214 03-10-93    6:00a
 FORMAT   COM     22717 03-10-93    6:00a
 NLSFUNC  EXE      7036 03-10-93    6:00a
 COUNTRY  SYS     17066 03-10-93    6:00a
 KEYB     COM     14983 03-10-93    6:00a
 KEYBOARD SYS     34694 03-10-93    6:00a
 SETUP    EXE     71974 03-10-93    6:00a
 DOSSETUP INI      3735 03-10-93    6:00a
 ANSI     SYS      9065 03-10-93    6:00a
 ATTRIB   EXE     11165 03-10-93    6:00a
 CHKDSK   EXE     12907 03-10-93    6:00a
 EDIT     COM       413 03-10-93    6:00a
 EXPAND   EXE     16129 03-10-93    6:00a
 EDLIN    EXE     12642 06-13-91    5:00a
 MORE     COM      2546 03-10-93    6:00a
 MSD      EXE    158470 03-10-93    6:00a
 QBASIC   EXE    194309 03-10-93    6:00a
Press any key to continue . . .

(continuing C:\DOS)
 RESTORE  EXE     38294 03-10-93    6:00a
 MIRROR   COM     18169 06-13-91    5:00a
 SYS      COM      9379 03-10-93    6:00a
 UNFORMAT COM     12738 03-10-93    6:00a
 SMARTDRV SYS      8335 06-13-91    5:00a
 OS2      TXT      6358 03-10-93    6:00a
 NETWORKS TXT     20463 03-10-93    6:00a
 README   TXT     44990 03-10-93    6:00a
 DEBUG    EXE     15715 03-10-93    6:00a
 FDISK    EXE     29333 03-10-93    6:00a
 DOSSHELL VID      9462 03-10-93    6:00a
 19C1DOSC BAT        16 01-23-93    3:05p
 DEFAULT  SET      4207 01-02-94   10:49a
 DOSSHELL GRB      4421 03-10-93    6:00a
 CHOICE   COM      1754 03-10-93    6:00a
 DEFRAG   EXE     75033 03-10-93    6:00a
 PACKING  LST      2507 06-13-91    5:00a
 DEFRAG   HLP      9227 03-10-93    6:00a
 DOSSWAP  EXE     18756 03-10-93    6:00a
 EGA      CPI     58870 03-10-93    6:00a
 RECOVER  EXE      9146 06-13-91    5:00a
 EGA      SYS      4885 03-10-93    6:00a
Press any key to continue . . .

(continuing C:\DOS)
 HIMEM    SYS     14208 03-10-93    6:00a
 MEM      EXE     32150 03-10-93    6:00a
 XCOPY    EXE     15820 03-10-93    6:00a
 MONEY    BAS     46225 06-13-91    5:00a
 MSHERC   COM      6934 06-13-91    5:00a
 DELTREE  EXE     11113 03-10-93    6:00a
 GORILLA  BAS     29434 06-13-91    5:00a
 4201     CPI      6404 06-13-91    5:00a
 4208     CPI       720 06-13-91    5:00a
 5202     CPI       395 06-13-91    5:00a
 MOVE     EXE     17823 03-10-93    6:00a
 ASSIGN   COM      6399 06-13-91    5:00a
 RAMDRIVE SYS      5873 03-10-93    6:00a
 BACKUP   EXE     36092 06-13-91    5:00a
```

Figure 2–4
IBM enhanced keyboard (courtesy of International Business Machines Corp.).

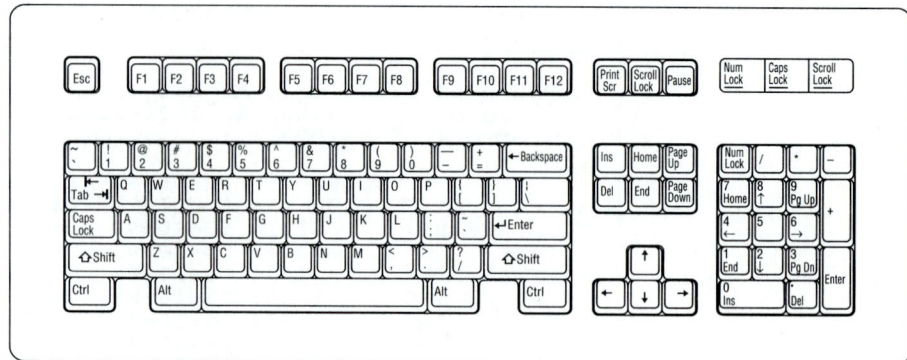

2–7   IMPORTANT KEYS IN DOS ENVIRONMENT

Examine the picture of a typical keyboard in Figure 2–4. Several of the keys perform special tasks in the DOS environment. Table 2–1 briefly explains these keys.

2–8   CREATING YOUR OWN DATA DISK: THE FORMAT COMMAND

Before using a newly purchased floppy disk on your PC, you must format the disk. To format a disk at the C> prompt insert a blank disk in drive A; type *FORMAT A:* and press the Enter key. When the process is finished, DOS asks you if you would like to format another disk. If you answer Y (for yes), you will be prompted to insert a new disk. If you answer N (for no), the C> prompt will return. Various computers use different versions of the FORMAT command. Consult your DOS manual for the specific version of the FORMAT command for your computer.

When you format a disk, the operating system checks your entire disk for defective spots. It tells you if your disk is usable or not. The FORMAT command also divides a disk into tracks and sectors and creates the *File Allocation Table* (FAT). The FAT indicates where data is saved on a disk.

When you format a disk, that disk is completely erased. Make sure the disk you are formatting is either a new disk or an old disk with files for which you have no need. Figure 2–5 shows the formatting procedure. At the C> prompt we typed *FORMAT A:*, pressed Enter, and followed the prompt.

You can format a disk in a different drive than A. For example, at the C> prompt type *FORMAT B:* and press the Enter key; the disk in drive B will be formatted.

Having a formatted disk at hand, you are ready to use it as a data disk or to copy other programs onto it.

2–9   DIFFERENT VERSIONS OF MS-DOS AND PC-DOS

PC-DOS is for IBM microcomputers and MS-DOS is for IBM compatibles. Both of these programs have gone through several revisions. The first version was 1.0 and the latest is version 6.0. Each version has added new commands and corrected some of the bugs in the earlier versions. Major enhancements occurred in version 3.0 and later versions. Versions 3.1 and later include commands for the local area network (LAN) environment. Minor revisions are indicated as .1, .2, and so on. Major revisions are indicated as 2, 3, and so forth.

Table 2–1
Special Keys on the Keyboard

Keys	Description
Backspace	Backs up and erases the character typed
Ctrl+Alt+Del	A key combination used to warm boot the system—equivalent to turning your computer off, then turning it back on (without memory check)
Ctrl+C or Ctrl+Break	Cancels a command while it is being executed (Note: Look for Break on the side of the Pause key.)
Ctrl+Print Scr or Ctrl+P	Sends a copy of each line on the screen to the printer as it is being displayed, assuming you are connected to a printer and the printer is on. This command toggles the printer on. (Toggle means the key combination remains in effect until you press Ctrl and PrtScr or P again.) When the printer is toggled on, everything displayed on the screen will be printed.
Ctrl+S or Ctrl+Num Lock	Pauses the directory listing for viewing
Esc	Erases the current command or statement
F1 (function key)	Displays one character of the previous command by each press. Useful for editing a DOS command.
F3 (function key)	Displays the entire previous command. You can perform editing or just press F3 and then the Enter key to execute the command again.
Print Scr (one key)	In enhanced keyboards, does the same job as Shift+Prtsc
Shift+Prtsc	Sends a copy of the screen to the printer. This command does not toggle the printer on.

Figure 2–5
Formatting procedure.

```
C>FORMAT A:
Insert new diskette for drive A:
and press ENTER when ready...

Checking existing disk format.
Formatting 1.2M
Format complete.

Volume label (11 characters, ENTER for none)?

   1213952 bytes total disk space
   1213952 bytes available on disk

      512 bytes in each allocation unit.
     2371 allocation units available on disk.

Volume Serial Number is 0362-1BEC

Format another (Y/N)?N


C>
```

Versions of MS-DOS and PC-DOS are upwardly compatible: all the commands in earlier versions are available in the newer versions, but not vice versa. To a typical microcomputer user, PC-DOS and MS-DOS are almost identical. To find out which version of DOS you are using, at the DOS prompt, type *VER* and press the Enter key. This command displays the current version of DOS in the default drive. Figure 2–6 illustrates this process. It shows this DOS is version 6.0. In this text, DOS version 6.0 is used. All the commands discussed in the text work with all versions of DOS unless otherwise specified.

2–10   BATCH AND AUTOEXEC FILES

Batch files are disk files designed for a specific use. A batch file can have any standard name, but the extension must always be BAT. In theory, batch files can be of any length. You can include any valid command or statement in a batch file. To enter a command, you must always press the Enter key after the specific command. To generate a batch file you can use EDLIN, the line editor available on DOS prior to version 5.0, or any word processing program. DOS 5.0 and 6.0 include an impressive full-screen editor called EDIT. For simple batch files, you can use a version of the COPY command, which allows you to copy one or a series of files. For example, if the default drive is C, to copy a file named TEST from drive C to drive A, type *COPY TEST A:* and press Enter. To generate a simple batch file using the COPY command, the process is as follows:

```
C>COPY CON MYFILE.BAT     (press Enter)
Command or statement      (press Enter)
Command or statement      (press Enter)
Command or statement      (press Enter)
```

To terminate a batch file, press Ctrl and Z together (or the F6 function key). To execute a batch file, all you need to do is to insert the disk that includes the batch file and type the name of the file at the C> prompt.

A simple batch file follows:

```
C>COPY CON HELLO.BAT      (press Enter)
DIR                       (press Enter)
CLS                       (press Enter)
BASICA                    (press Enter)
                          (press Ctrl and Z keys together or press F6)
```

If you type *HELLO* at the C> prompt, you will see a listing of a directory of drive C, the screen will clear, and BASICA will be loaded to RAM. (The assumption is that drive C includes BASICA, a programming language available in the majority of computers.)

Figure 2–6
Finding out your version of DOS.

```
C>VER

MS-DOS Version 6.00


C>
```

The only limitation with COPY CON is that you cannot edit a file that has been created. For editing, you have to redo the entire file or use EDLIN, EDIT, or use some other word processing or editor-type system.

To stop the execution of a batch file, press Ctrl and Break at the same time.

If you name your file AUTOEXEC.BAT, it will be executed automatically as soon as you start the system. As a matter of fact, DOS always looks for the **autoexec file** first. If you have such a file, all its commands and statements will be executed. This facility can be very helpful. In addition to designing a menu or customizing your system, you can help people who are unfamiliar with computers by providing a question-and-answer type environment. Batch files in general are very helpful if you have to do a series of repetitive operations.

2–11   DEFINING A DIRECTORY

When you format a disk, DOS automatically creates a directory for you. This directory usually is called the **root directory**.

As a result of advances in disk technology, more and more files can be stored on a disk. These files are stored based on the date that they were created. As the number of files increases, it becomes extremely difficult to manage them properly. It becomes a time-consuming process to locate one file among several hundred.

There is a limit to the number of files that can be stored on a floppy disk or a hard disk. The root directory on a single-sided disk can hold up to 64 files; on a double-sided disk there can be up to 112 files. The root directory of a high-density disk can hold up to 224 files, and on a hard disk, up to 512 files. To create a better mechanism for storing and maintaining files and to bypass these file limitations, you can create **subdirectories**. A subdirectory is similar to a folder that contains a listing of files that you have grouped together based on a given scheme. (Subdirectory names follow the same conventions as file names.)

Consider a file cabinet in your office. Suppose that you store all important sales documents in this file cabinet. One method of storage is to throw all the sales documents in the cabinet as they arrive. In this case, retrieving information is a very difficult task. Another method is to divide the file cabinet into three separate parts (three subdirectories) by using some type of folders. You can then divide these folders into more logical parts (lower-level subdirectories). After this segmentation, you can put each document into its proper folder. This method, which is illustrated in Figure 2–7, improves retrieval time.

The directory below the root directory is considered a subdirectory to the root directory. A directory immediately below a subdirectory is considered a subdirectory to that subdirectory. In Figure 2–7, the WEST, SOUTH, and EAST regions are subdirectories to the root directory. OREGON and CALIFORNIA are subdirectories to the WEST region. They can be broken down further into SOUTHERN and NORTHERN (California) and so on.

As another example, suppose that on your hard disk you create four subdirectories for WordPerfect, Lotus 1-2-3, dBASE, and Quattro Pro. All your word processing documents will be saved in the WordPerfect directory, all your spreadsheets will be saved in the Lotus 1-2-3 directory, and so forth. Under Lotus 1-2-3, you may want to create two subdirectories, one for graphics files and one for database files. You can continue this process for several levels based on your specific needs.

The root directory is always identified by a back slash (\). The current subdirectory is identified by a period (.) and the parent subdirectory (the directory immediately above the current directory) is identified by two periods(..).

Figure 2–7
Example of directory structure.

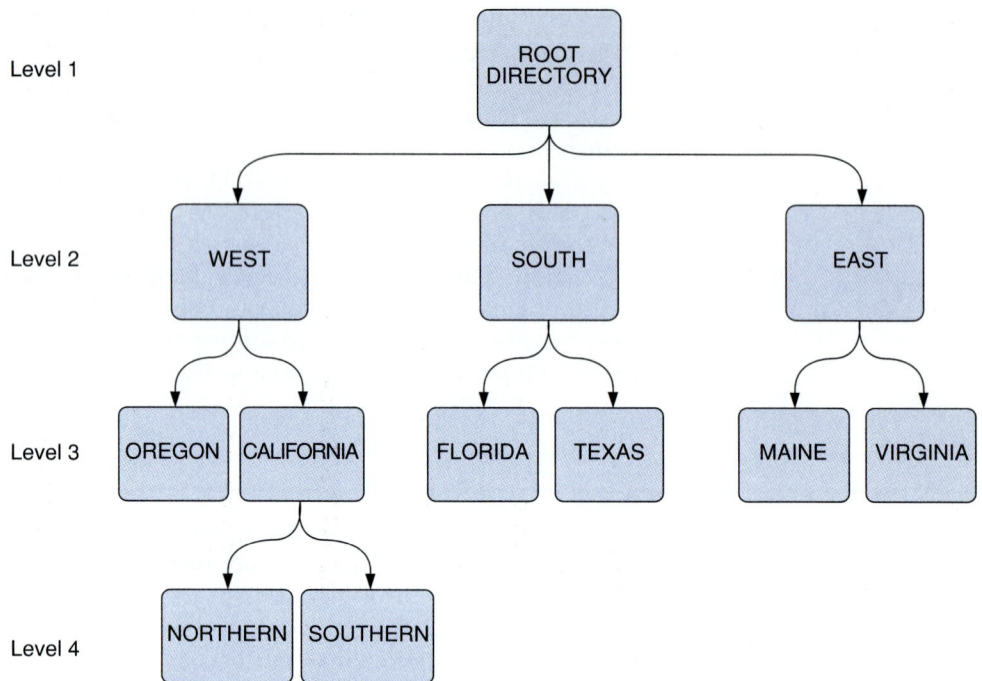

2–12   IMPORTANT COMMANDS FOR DIRECTORIES

To create a subdirectory, use the DOS command MKDIR (make directory) or MD. You must be in the directory immediately above the subdirectory you are creating. To change to a subdirectory or make a subdirectory the current directory, use the CHDIR (change directory) or CD command. The CD command uses several different parameters as shown in Table 2–2.

To remove a subdirectory, you first must erase all the files and subsequent subdirectories by using either the DEL or ERASE command. Then get in the root directory and use the RMDIR (remove directory) or RD command.

If you do not know in which directory you are working, use the PROMPT PG command. At the DOS prompt, type *PROMPT PG* and press Enter. The default prompt changes to a prompt that identifies the current directory. For example, if you are working in the OREGON directory, your new prompt will read C:\OREGON>.

To display the structure of your directory, use the TREE command. Type *TREE /F* to display each directory on your disk and the files stored within each directory.

Another powerful command that you can use with directories is the PATH command. This command establishes a search path. Suppose that the DOS disk is in drive A and you are working with a data disk in drive B. If you issue an external DOS command from drive B, you will receive an error message (because the DOS disk is in drive A). When you type *PATH A:* at the A> prompt, DOS searches the root directory on drive A for any commands that it cannot find in the current drive or directory (in this case drive B). You also can establish multiple search paths by using the PATH command and a semicolon (;). Suppose that you want to tell your computer to search for DOS commands in drive B and in a subdirectory on drive C called EXTERNAL. Type the following search path to do the job: *PATH B:\; C:\EXTERNAL.*

Table 2–2
Change Directory (CD) Command
Parameters

Parameter	Function
CD.	Displays the current directory
CD..	Moves up one directory level
CD\	Moves up to the root directory from any directory level
CD..\..	Moves up two directory levels
CD\WEST\OREGON	OREGON becomes the current directory

When you establish a search path, it remains in effect until you turn off your PC. To cancel a search path, type *PATH* and press Enter. To make a search path permanent, enter the command into your AUTOEXEC.BAT file. Then, as soon as you start your computer, the search path will be activated.

2–13   DOS 5: AN OVERVIEW

In 1991, Microsoft Corporation released a new version of MS-DOS: **DOS 5.0**. In all ways, this release is a major improvement over the earlier releases of DOS. DOS 5 is uniquely identified by the following features:

■ Memory management. DOS 5.0 allows the memory of your computer to be used more effectively. This is because DOS 5.0 loads itself to memory other than conventional memory. For example, DOS 5.0 loads drivers and TSR programs to the upper memory area, leaving you with more conventional memory.

■ A shell program providing some of the features of Windows 3.0/3.1. Using the shell program, you enter a graphical-type environment. In this environment, you can access various options through the keyboard or simply through the mouse, which simplifies your DOS work.

■ A DOS macro capability. Through a DOSKEY you can assign a series of options to a DOS command and then use this DOS command by only typing its name. This is almost like creating a mini batch file.

■ Support for higher capacity disks. DOS 5.0 basically lets you utilize as much memory as your computer can support.

■ Some command enhancement. Many new commands and new options in existing commands have been added in DOS 5.0. For example, two of the most important new commands are UNDELETE and UNFORMAT, which allow you to rescue your work erased mistakenly.

■ Capability of task swapping. Using DOS 5.0, you can exit one application program such as a word processor and enter another application program such as Quattro Pro and easily get back to the word processor without closing the Quattro Pro program.

■ A new and complete online help facility. DOS 5.0 enables you to receive online help for all DOS commands. At the DOS prompt, type *HELP* and press Enter for complete information on the help facility. Or type *HELP*, then the command name, and press Enter. This provides you with specific help on a given command. For example, type *HELP DIR* and press Enter to receive online help for the DIR command.

■ Full-screen editing feature. DOS 5.0 includes an impressive full-screen editing component that is similar to a word processor. (The EDLIN utility is still available for people who are familiar with it.)

All commands presented in this chapter work in DOS 5.0 and 6.0.. Consult Table 2–3 for summary of important DOS commands. The commands simplify DOS operations and your PC work.

Table 2–3
Important DOS Commands*

Command	Function
ATTRIB +R (Release 3 and higher)	Makes a file a read-only file, e.g., ATTRIB +R COMMAND.COM (press Enter). This makes COMMAND.COM a read-only file.
ATTRIB –R (Release 3 and higher)	Removes the read-only status, e.g., ATTRIB –R COMMAND.COM (press Enter)
CHDIR (CD)	Changes the current directory or displays the current directory path. For example, CD\ changes the current directory of a drive to its root directory
CHKDSK	Displays free space on diskette
CHKDSK B:	Displays free space on diskette in drive B
CLS	Clears the screen
COMP	Compares two files to determine if they are the same or if they are different, e.g., COMP A:TEXT.JOE B:TEXT.JAC
COPY Filename.ext B:	Copies Filename.ext to the B drive
COPY B:Filename.ext	Copies Filename.ext to the C drive
COPY *.ext B:	Copies all files with the same ext from the C drive to the B drive
COPY B:*.ext	Copies all files with the same ext from the B drive to the C drive
COPY *.* B:	Copies all files from the C drive to the B drive
COPY B:*.*	Copies all files from the B drive to the C drive
COPY Filename1.ext Filename2.ext	Copies a file from C to C with a different name
COPY B:Filename1.ext B:Filename2.ext	Copies a file from B to B with a different name
COPY Filename1.ext B:Filename2.ext	Copies a file from C to B with a different name

*To execute all of these commands, the C prompt is assumed. An A stands for A drive; B stands for B drive; ext stands for file extension (any three valid characters). Filename can be any valid file name.

Table 2–3
(continued)

Command	Function
COPY B:Filename1.ext Filename2.ext	Copies a file from B to C with a different name
COPY CON B:Filename.BAT	Creates a batch file in drive B. To terminate the file creation, press F6 then Enter.
CTRL-ALT-DEL	Resets the system (a warm boot)
DATE	Resets the system date
DEL Filename.ext	Erases Filename.ext from drive C
DEL B:Filename.ext	Erases Filename.ext from drive B
DEL B:Filename.*	Erases all Filenames with any extension from drive B
DEL B:*.ext	Erases all files with the same extension from drive B
DIR	Displays a directory of C
DIR B:	Displays a directory of B
DIR/P	Displays a complete directory of drive C with a pause before scrolling off the screen
DIR B:/P	Does the same as above for drive B
DIR/W	Displays a wide directory of drive C
DIR B:/W	Does the same as above for drive B
DIR|SORT (| This character is the broken line found on back-slash key)	Displays a sorted directory of drive C
DIR B:|SORT	Displays a sorted directory of drive B
DISKCOMP	Compares two diskettes track by track, sector for sector, to determine if their contents are identical, e.g., DISKCOMP A: B:
DISKCOPY A: B:	Copies a diskette in drive A to a diskette in drive B. The two drives must be identical.
ERASE Filename.ext	Erases Filename.ext on C
ERASE B:Filename.ext	Erases Filename.ext on B
ERASE *.ext	Erases all files with the same .ext on C
ERASE B:*.ext	Erases all files with the same .ext on B
FORMAT A:	Erases and formats a diskette in drive A
FORMAT B:	Erases and formats a diskette in drive B
FORMAT A:/V	Formats a diskette in drive A with a volume label (a name with up to 11 characters long)
FORMAT B:/V	Formats a new diskette with a volume label (a name with up to 11 characters long) in drive B

Table 2–3
(continued)

Command	Function
LABEL	Creates, changes, or deletes a volume label for a disk, e.g., type *LABEL* and press Enter; follow the prompt
MKDIR (MD)	Creates a subdirectory on C drive, e.g., MD CLIENTS
PATH	Instructs DOS to search a specified directory for a program that cannot be found in the current directory, e.g., PATH C:\
PROMPT	Customizes the DOS system prompt, e.g., PROMPT Hello
PROMPT PG	Displays the current subdirectory that you are in
RENAME Filename1.ext Filename2.ext	Renames a file on C
RENAME B:Filename1.ext B:Filename2.ext	Renames a file on B
RMDIR (RD)	Removes a subdirectory from a disk, e.g., RD C:CPA. Remember, the subdirectory must be empty
SHIFT-PrtSc or Print Scr	Prints a copy of the screen
SYS	Puts a copy of operating system files IBMDOS.COM and IBMBIO.COM on the specified diskette or hard disk, e.g., SYS B:
TIME	Resets system time
TREE	Displays the structure of the current directory
TYPE Filename.ext	Displays the content of Filename.ext
TYPE B:Filename.ext	Displays the content of Filename.ext on B
VER	Displays the DOS version number on the screen
VERIFY	Checks the data just written to a disk to be sure the data has been correctly recorded and then displays if the data has been checked, e.g., VERIFY ON sets verify status on, VERIFY OFF sets verify status off, and VERIFY shows verify status.
VOL	Displays the volume label of a disk, if the label exists

2–14   HIGHLIGHTS OF DOS 6.0

DOS 6.0, which was released in April 1993, offers features not available in the previous versions of DOS. Some of the important features of this release are listed next:

- Disk compression that can almost double the capacity of your hard disk
- Back-up facility for easy backing up of your hard disk
- Antivirus feature which eliminates known viruses. Computer viruses are a series of computer codes that can wipe out your computer hard disk.
- Memory management, more powerful than DOS 5.0, that can increase availability of your RAM by up to 100 K
- Advanced communications capabilities for accessing files and peripherals on other PCs with compatible software.
- Availability of electronic mail (E-mail) program. By means of this feature, you can send and receive mail through your computer
- File sharing utility for exchanging files with another microcomputer.
- Ease of use by improving online help
- New commands such as *MOVE* for moving files and DELTREE for deleting a directory and its contents and all its subdirectories

SUMMARY

This chapter introduced you to elementary DOS operations, beginning with differences between internal and external DOS commands. Types of DOS prompts and file name specifications in the DOS environment were described, and the DIR command with different switches was highlighted. Important keys used frequently in DOS environment were introduced. The chapter also examined the FORMAT command, which is necessary for preparing blank disks. After a brief discussion of different versions of MS-DOS and PC-DOS, DOS 5 and 6.0 were outlined briefly. The chapter featured with a table of the most commonly used DOS commands.

REVIEW QUESTIONS

*These questions are answered in Appendix A.
1. What is a cold boot?
2. What is a warm boot?
*3. Why is it important to enter the correct time and date at boot-up time (if the system does not have an internal battery)?
4. What are internal DOS commands?
5. What are external DOS commands?
6. How many different DOS prompts are there?
*7. How do you change from drive C to A and from A to C?
8. What is the default drive?
9. Describe a valid DOS file name.
10. Give three examples of file extensions.
11. How many different ways can you use the DIR command?
12. Name the two DOS wildcards.

13. Describe the functions of the F1, F3, and F6 keys.
14. Why must a new disk be formatted before it can be used?
*15. What is a batch file? What is an autoexec file?
*16. Give three examples of DOS internal and three examples of DOS external commands.
17. What is a directory?
18. Why should you use directories?
19. List some directory commands.
20. How do you get to the root directory from a three-layered subdirectory?
21. How do you remove a directory?
22. What are some of the features of DOS 5.0?
23. How can you receive online help in DOS 5.0?

HANDS-ON EXPERIENCE

1. Start your computer. At the C> prompt enter the date as *1-1-95*. Change it back to today's date.
2. Change the default drive from C to A or from A to C. Type *DIR* and press Enter. What are the contents of drive A and of drive C?
3. By using Ctrl+Alt+Del, warm boot your computer. Type *DIR* and press Enter. How many different types of file extensions do you see in the directory?
4. Type *DIR/W* and press Enter; then type *DIR/P* and press Enter. What is the difference between these two commands?
5. By using the asterisk wildcard (*), generate listings of all COM files, of all EXE files, and of all SYS files.
6. Format a new disk. Use the COPY command to copy all COM files from drive C to this formatted disk.
7. Use the VER command to determine the version of DOS that you are using.
8. Create two directories on a diskette in drive A; name them TEST1 and TEST2. Copy two COM files from drive C to TEST1. Now copy the contents of TEST1 to TEST2.
9. Remove TEST1 from your disk.

KEY TERMS

Autoexec files	DOS 5.0	Internal command
Batch files	DOS 6.0	Root directory
Cold boot	External command	Subdirectory
Directory	File allocation table (FAT)	Warm boot
Disk operating system (DOS)	File extension	
	File name	

KEY COMMANDS

See Tables 2–1 through 2–3

MISCONCEPTIONS AND SOLUTIONS

Misconception You turn on your PC and you see a message that is not familiar to you, for example:

```
NON-SYSTEM DISK
```

> **Solution** You forgot to put the DOS disk in drive A, or you inserted your disk on the wrong side, or you inserted a data disk instead of the DOS disk. Insert the DOS disk into drive A properly and reboot the system.

Misconception You are trying to format a disk in the A drive and receive this error message:

```
ATTEMPTED WRITE-PROTECT VIOLATION
```

> **Solution** The disk in drive A has the write-protection notch covered. Either remove the protection or insert another disk.

Misconception You are using the FORMAT command and receive this error message:

```
DRIVE NOT READY
```

> **Solution** Either the target drive door is not closed or there is no disk in that drive. Insert a disk in this drive, close the drive door, and press Enter.

Misconception You are using a DOS command and receive one of these error messages:

```
SYNTAX ERROR   BAD COMMAND   FILENAME ERROR
```

> **Solution** Check the spelling of the command. Most likely, you have misspelled a command.

ARE YOU READY TO MOVE ON?

Multiple Choice

1. The procedure known as warm boot means
   a. inserting the DOS disk in drive A and turning on the computer
   b. typing the name of the program to be run and pressing Enter
   c. simultaneously pressing the Ctrl, Alt, and Del keys
   d. formatting a disk
   e. none of the above
2. Which of the following prompts are you most likely to see after performing a cold boot with the DOS disk in drive A?
   a. A>
   b. B>
   c. C>
   d. OK
   e. C:/DOS>
3. If the correct date and time are not entered during the boot process or if you want to change them at any time, the commands are
   a. HOUR and DAY
   b. DAY and HOUR

   c. DATE and CLOCK
   d. DATE and TIME
   e. none of the above

4. To change the default drive from drive B to drive A, what should you type at the DOS prompt before pressing Enter?

   a. *A*
   b. *DRIVE=A*
   c. *B+A*
   d. *GO TO A:*
   e. *A:*

5. File names with these extensions can be executed by typing the name of the file. (Remember, both extensions in each pair must be correct.)

   a. COM and SYS
   b. COM and EXE
   c. EXE and SYS
   d. BAK and SYS
   e. BAK and BAT

6. The command DIR/P will yield

   a. the same as DIR
   b. a wide directory listing
   c. one screen at a time of the file listing
   d. a hard copy output to the printer
   e. nothing—it is not a valid command

7. The command to format a disk in drive B is

   a. ERASE B:
   b. DELETE *.*
   c. SYS B:
   d. FORMAT B:
   e. A or B

8. The file allocation table indicates

   a. where data are saved on a disk
   b. the maximum number of files that can be saved on disk
   c. how much disk space is available
   d. how much memory (RAM) is available
   e. none of the above

9. A typical computer response to the command VER is

   a. Disk Verified OK
   b. MS_DOS Version 5.0
   c. File Verified OK
   d. Insert new disk and strike Enter when ready
   e. A or B

10. When you format a disk,

   a. all data is erased
   b. the file allocation table is created
   c. the operating system checks for defective spots
   d. the disk is divided into sectors and tracks
   e. all of the above occur

True/False

1. If the computer is off and the system does not have a hard disk, the DOS disk must be placed in drive A to boot the computer.

2. A cold boot is faster than a warm boot because the computer does not check the memory.

3. To get back to the root directory from a subdirectory, type *CD* and press Enter.

4. External DOS commands are those loaded into the computer memory at boot-up time.

5. The DOS prompt indicates the current default drive.

6. The DIR command generates a listing of the files in the default directory.

7. DOS wildcards act as placeholders for other characters and include *, ?, @, $, %, and |.

8. DIR and DIR/W yield exactly the same information except that DIR/W places it in a wide format.

9. To move up two directory levels, type *CD..\..* and press Enter.

10. Versions of MS-DOS and PC-DOS are not upwardly compatible.

ANSWERS

Multiple Choice		True/False	
1.	c	1.	T
2.	a	2.	F
3.	d	3.	T
4.	e	4.	F
5.	b	5.	T
6.	c	6.	T
7.	d	7.	F
8.	a	8.	F
9.	b	9.	T
10.	e	10.	F

A Quick Trip Through
Microsoft Windows

3

3–1   INTRODUCTION

This chapter presents some of the unique advantages of Microsoft Windows[1] as a graphical-based environment compared with a character-based environment such as DOS. After discussing how to get in and out of Windows, the chapter looks at the procedures for using a mouse and the keyboard in the Windows environment. Next, the help and tutorial facilities of Windows are introduced. The chapter then describes different parts of a Windows screen, the role of the Program Manager, running applications in Windows, working with the Clipboard, quitting an application, and Windows groups.

3–2   WINDOWS 3.1: AN OVERVIEW

Windows 3.1 is an environment based on a graphical user interface (GUI—pronounced "gooey") that runs on top of DOS (i.e., you must have DOS to run Windows). This graphical environment has several advantages not found in the DOS character-based environment. Let us summarize some of these advantages:

1. Windows is easier to use than DOS because with Windows you do not need to memorize the strict DOS command syntax. In Windows, you can perform all DOS functions and more through a series of pull-down menus.

2. All Windows applications share the same principles. When you learn one Windows application, you can easily transfer some or all of what you have learned to other Windows applications.

3. You can work with Windows applications using a mouse, the keyboard, or shortcut keys for speed (described later in this chapter). All these options enable you to become more efficient as you work with Windows programs.

4. Windows presents a **multitasking** environment. This means that you can run more than one program at the same time. Imagine that you are typing a report using WordPerfect and decide you need a spreadsheet created in Lotus 1-2-3. If you are using Windows, you can easily switch to Lotus 1-2-3 and incorporate the desired spreadsheet into your report. You can even integrate a graph into your report. Perhaps you decide that you need a telephone number out of your online telephone directory. You can easily run your telephone directory software, retrieve the correct phone number, then exit the telephone directory software without ever exiting WordPerfect.

5. Windows applications and DOS applications can be run simultaneously. You can even run multiple DOS programs and multiple Windows programs at the same time.

6. Several files can be linked together. If you change data in one file, the same data in the other file will be changed automatically.

7. Windows allows better memory management. You are not restricted by 640 K, the traditional DOS barrier. Windows enables you to use memory well beyond 640 K. It makes your hard disk an extension of your RAM. If a program does not fit into your RAM, it simply spills over to your hard disk.

8. Windows allows you to display on the screen exactly what will appear on printed output. This is called what-you-see-is-what-you-get (WYSIWYG). By

---

[1] For a detailed discussion of Microsoft Windows, consult *Information Systems Literacy: Windows 3.1* by Hossein Bidgoli, published by Macmillan Publishing Company 1993.

Table 3–1
Unique Advantages of Windows

Ease of use

Shared principles among Windows programs

Use of mouse, keyboard, and shortcut keys

Multitasking

Ability to run Windows and DOS applications at the same time

Linkage of several files

Better memory management

True WYSIWYG

Free accessories

means of this feature, you have a pretty good idea of the output of an application before printing it.

9. Accessory programs are free of charge. Windows comes with a group of accessories that are readily available to you at no extra cost: Windows Write—a simple word processor; Windows Paintbrush—a drawing program; Windows Terminal—a communications program; Windows Print Manager—a program that allows you to work and print at the same time; and other more useful programs such as the Calculator, Calendar, Notepad, Cardfile, and Clock.

The unique advantages of Windows are listed in Table 3–1.

3–3   UNDERSTANDING WINDOWS TERMINOLOGY

Windows, just like other software, has its own terminology. Among the important terms are desktop, icon, and mouse. Let us briefly explain each.

Desktop in Windows is similar to the surface of a desk. All your Windows work takes place in the desktop. When you start Windows you start at the desktop. You can do a number of tasks from the desktop; among the most common are the following:

- Fast application switching—going from one application program to another
- Icon spacing change—moving around the existing icons, deleting the unwanted ones, and so forth
- Displaying your document
- Changing colors

An **icon** is a graphic representation of an application, a document, or an object. You can move the mouse pointer to the desired application icon and double-click the left button of the mouse to start the application or open a document.

The **mouse** will be explained in detail in section 3–5. It is the main interface between you and Windows and Windows applications. Although you can use the keyboard or the shortcut keys, using the mouse is probably the most efficient way to accomplish most Windows tasks.

3–4   GETTING IN AND OUT OF WINDOWS

The first step is to install Windows on a hard disk system. Windows will not run on a floppy system. After installing Windows, switch to the drive and directory containing your Windows files by using the DOS CD command (e.g., type *CD WIN31* and press Enter); then type *WIN* and press Enter. You will be presented with a screen similar to the one shown in Figure 3–1. Your screen might be different from what is presented here depending how Windows has been configured.

Three methods allow you to get out of Windows. The first is to move the mouse pointer (see Section 3–5) to the File option at the upper left of the screen and click the left button of the mouse. You will be presented with a screen similar to the one shown in Figure 3–2. Move the mouse pointer to the Exit Windows option and click the left button. The second method is to move the mouse pointer to the control-menu box, at the extreme upper left of the screen, and double-click the left button of the mouse. The third method is to move the mouse pointer to the control-menu box and click the left button once. You will be presented with a screen similar to the one shown in Figure 3–3. Move the mouse pointer to the Close option and click the left button.

Regardless of which of these three methods you use, you will be presented with a screen similar to the one shown in Figure 3–4. Move the mouse pointer to OK and click the left button of the mouse to leave Windows. If you click with the mouse pointer on Cancel, you have indicated that you changed your mind and wish to stay in Windows. When you exit Windows you exit either to DOS or to your starting menu, depending on how you started Windows in the first place.

You can also use the keyboard to exit Windows. To do so, press Alt+F to open the File menu. Then either press the X key or move the cursor to Exit Windows and press Enter. Press Enter again to exit Windows.

Figure 3–1
Windows starting screen.

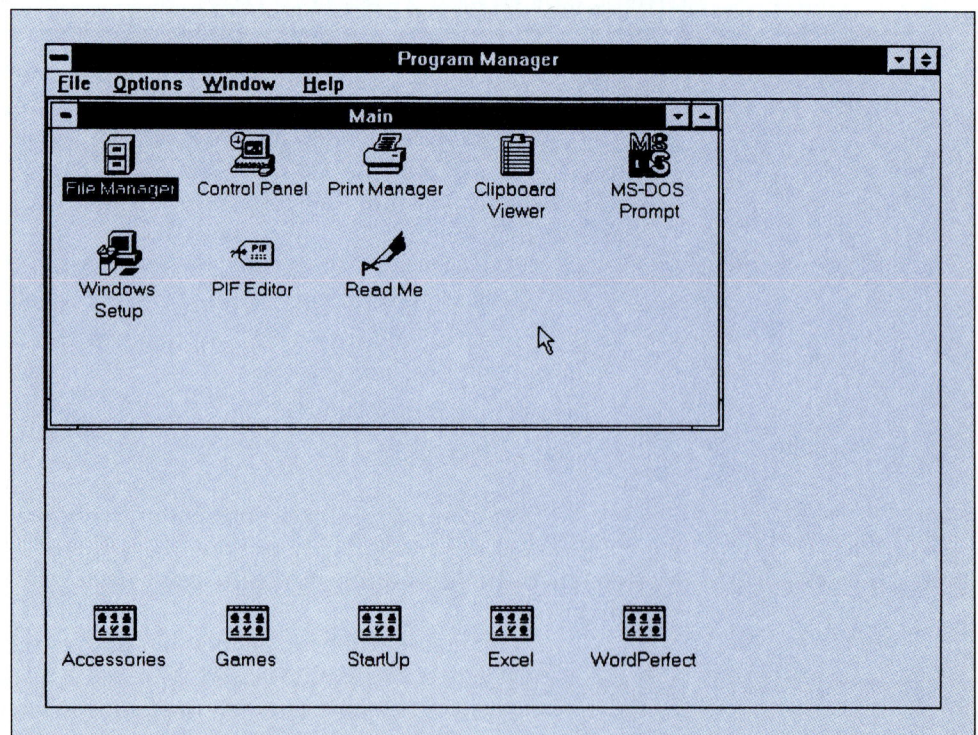

Figure 3-2
File pull-down menu.

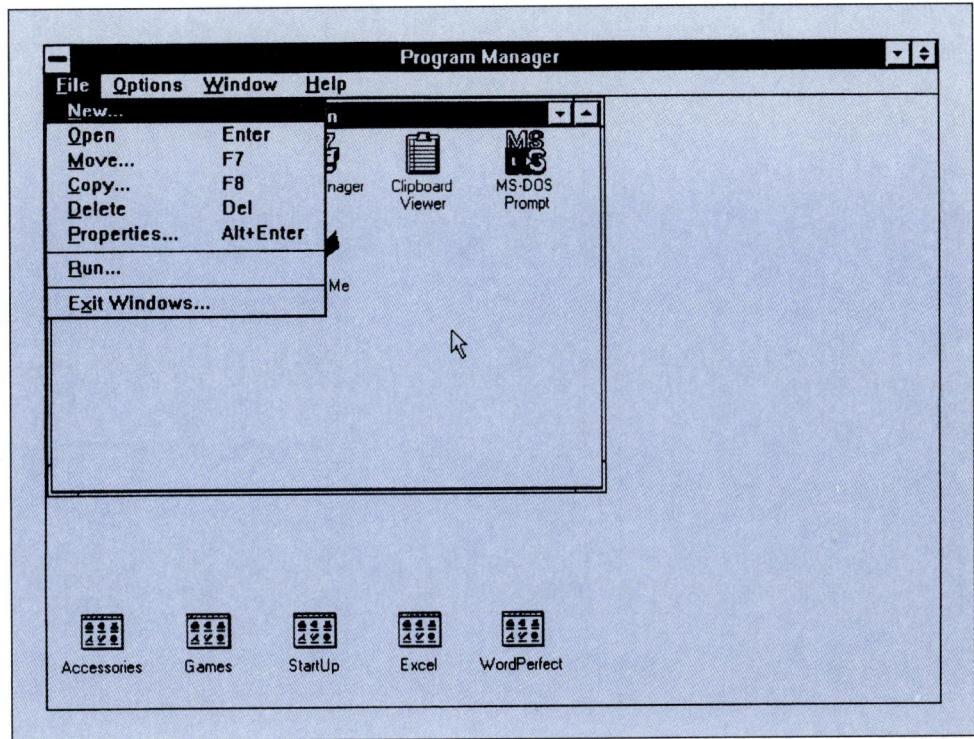

Figure 3-3
Control-menu box options.

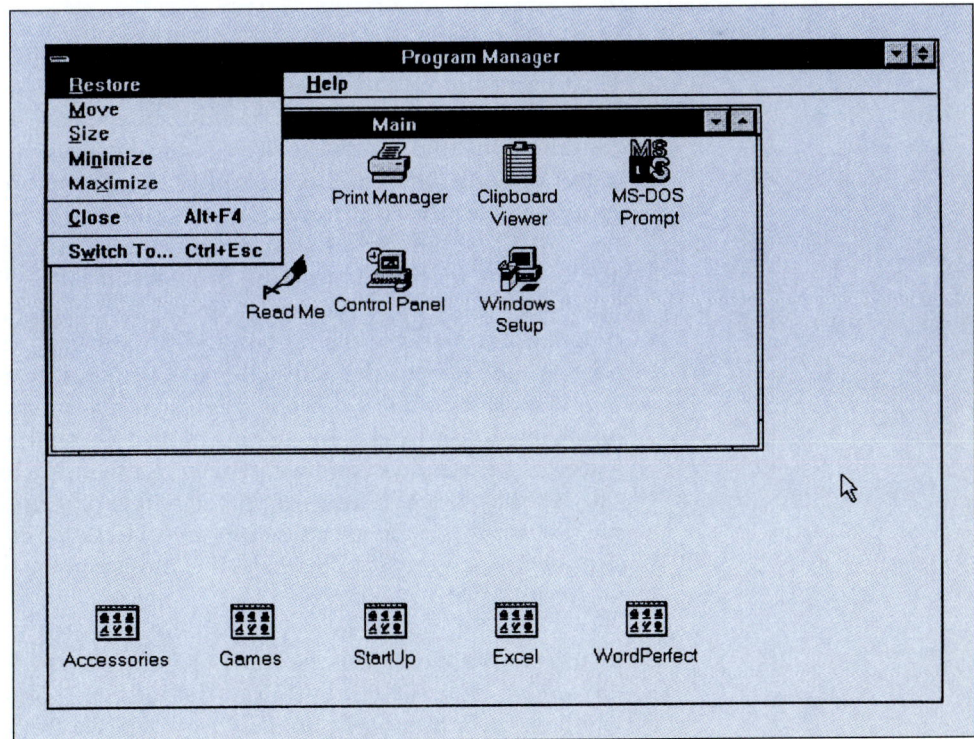

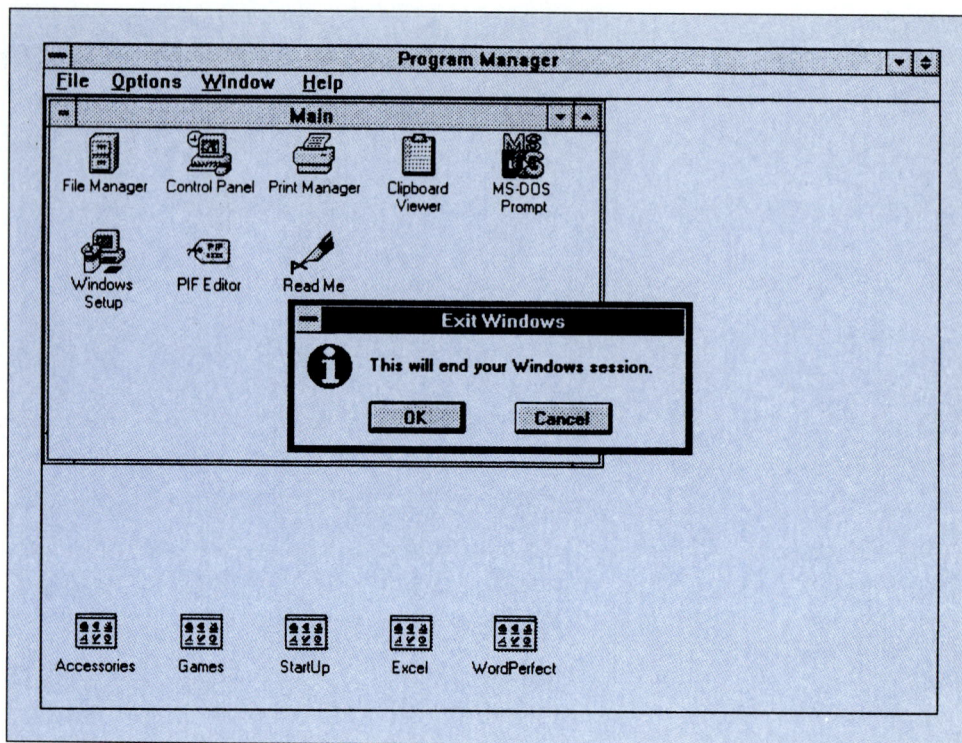

3–5   USING A MOUSE IN THE WINDOWS ENVIRONMENT

Windows offers three user interface options: keyboard, mouse, and shortcut keys. Most users agree that a mouse is preferable to a keyboard in graphical environments such as Windows because of its speed, accuracy, ease of use, and other special functions that it can provide. Using a mouse, you can easily select pull-down menu options, quickly execute application programs, move and/or resize group windows, relocate icons to new locations on the screen, and much more.

If you are right handed, hold the mouse in your right hand, and if you are left handed, hold the mouse in your left hand. Place the mouse on a flat surface (preferably on a mouse pad) and rest your hand on top of it. Place your thumb on one side of the mouse and the two fingers on the opposite end of your hand on the other side. This will leave your index finger and middle finger positioned over the mouse buttons. Lightly rest your fingers on these buttons. To see how the mouse works, move the mouse in a circular motion and look at the screen for the **mouse pointer**, which can be an arrow or some other shape. You will see that it is also moving in a circular pattern, matching the movements of the mouse. If you move the mouse to the left, the mouse pointer moves to the left side of the screen; if you move the mouse away from you, the mouse pointer moves to the top of the screen.

Now let's try selecting some menu items using the mouse. Move the mouse so that the mouse pointer is pointing to the File option at the upper left of the screen; click the left button of the mouse. If you have done this correctly, the File pull-down menu will be displayed (see Figure 3–2). Move the mouse pointer to the Window option and click the left button again to display the Window pull-down menu (Figure 3–5). Notice that positioning the mouse pointer and clicking the left button selects the desired menu item automatically. For now, move the mouse pointer back into the middle of the screen and click the left button to "deselect" any currently highlighted menu items.

Figure 3–5
Window pull-down menu.

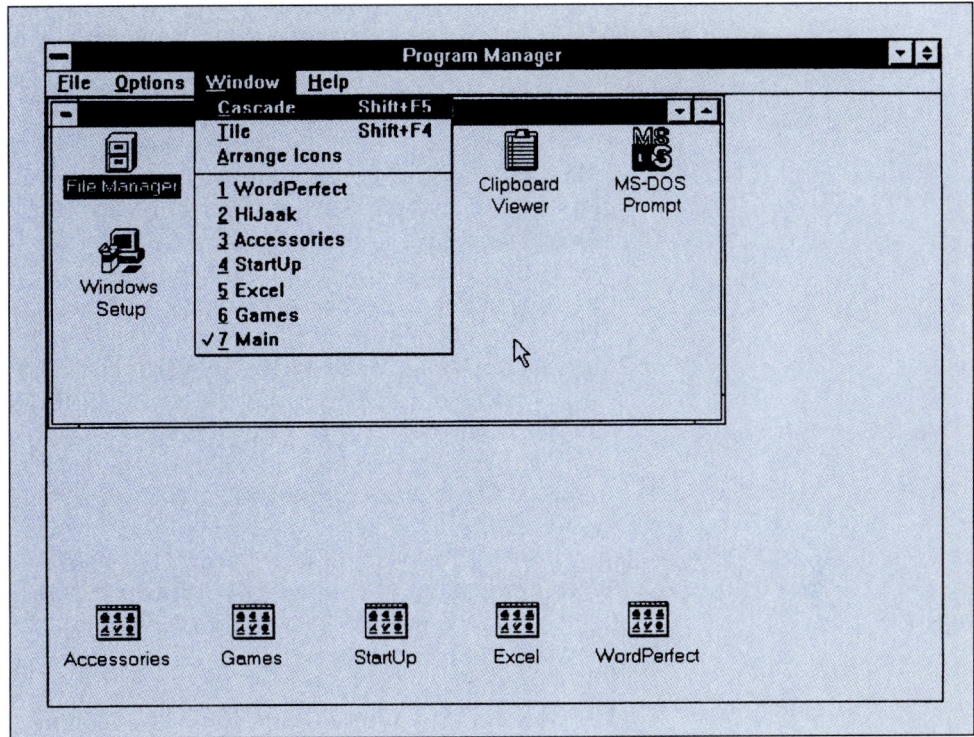

Rapid double-clicking of the left button while pointing the mouse pointer onto an icon automatically executes the application that the icon represents. To see how this works, move the mouse pointer to the accessories icon and double-click the left button. This automatically opens the Accessories window (Figure 3–6). Now you can double-click on any of the options shown to open them.

Figure 3–6
Applications in the Accessories group.

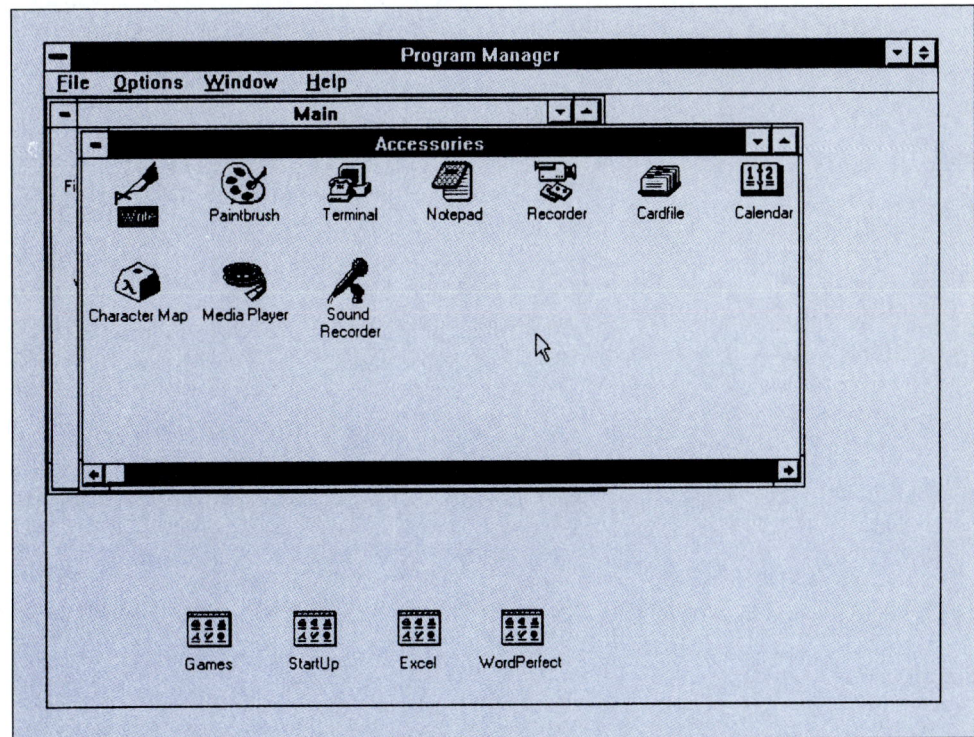

Let's try another example. Move the mouse pointer to the MS-DOS Prompt option in the Main group (see Figure 3–1) and double-click the left button. Windows responds by displaying a DOS prompt. Type the command *EXIT* (press Enter) to return to the Windows main screen.

You can move windows, group icons, application icons, and so forth to other locations on the screen using a method called **click and drag**. To try this, point the mouse pointer onto the title bar of the Main group window (where the word "Main" appears; see Figure 3–1). Click the left button; then, while holding the button down, drag the mouse pointer to a new location on the screen. You will notice that an outline form of the Main group moves with the mouse pointer. When you release the left button, your window will be relocated to the position of the mouse pointer when you released the left button.

Let's try changing the size of the Main group window. Move the mouse pointer to the right edge of the Main group window. Notice that at a certain position over the edge of the window the mouse pointer becomes a double-pointing arrow. When you see this, click and drag a small distance to the right. Again notice the outline form; when you release the mouse button, your window will conform to the size you just constructed by dragging the mouse. If you change your mind, before releasing the left button of the mouse, press the Esc key.

As a final example of moving screen items to new locations, move the mouse pointer onto the MS-DOS Prompt option inside the Main group window. Click and drag the icon to a new location inside of the window, then release the left button of the mouse. The icon will obediently follow your command to position itself in a new location. For now, drag the icon back into its original location.

3–6   USING THE KEYBOARD IN THE WINDOWS ENVIRONMENT

As mentioned, Windows and Windows programs allow use of the keyboard in addition to the mouse. Keyboards are comfortable for experienced typists, and since keyboards have been around for years, people are more familiar with them than with the mouse. If you prefer working with a keyboard, the following areas of it may be used with Windows:

- The typing keys located in the center of the keyboard. These keys are similar to the keys of a typewriter.

- The numeric and cursor movement keys located on the right side of the keyboard. Enhanced keyboards have a dedicated cursor movement pad. For standard keyboards, if you press the Num Lock key, the numeric pad serves as a 10-key machine for entering numbers. Arrow keys are used to move the cursor around.

- The function keys: F1 through F12 located across the top of the enhanced keyboard or F1 through F10 on the left side of the standard keyboard. All these keys perform different functions depending on the application program you are using.

Windows and Windows applications can also be accessed through the combination of keys called shortcut keys. The key-combination method always involves one of the following special keys—Shift, Alt, and Ctrl—combined with another key. For example, Alt+F invokes the File menu. To use a key combination, first press either the Shift, Alt, or Ctrl key and hold it down; then press another key. In this book, the mouse is emphasized as the major Windows interface.

3–7   HELP FACILITIES OF WINDOWS

As you can see in Figure 3–1, one of the options in the Program Manager is Help. The Program Manager, which is the heart of Windows, is used to start other applications and organize applications and files into groups. If you move the mouse pointer to the Help option and click the left button, you will see a screen similar to the one presented in Figure 3–7. You can move the mouse pointer to any of these options and click the left button to execute the desired option. For example, if you click left on the Contents option, you will receive a screen similar to Figure 3–8. As you can see in this figure, the Search option is available; it enables you to search for a particular topic. To exit Search, click on Cancel. You can also select the Glossary option to generate an alphabetized listing of all the topics in Windows. To receive help on commands, click on the underlined command. You can always exit any of these options by clicking the control-menu box and selecting the Close option.

If you select the Windows Tutorial option from the Help pull-down menu, you will be presented with a screen similar to Figure 3–9. The **online tutorial** provides an overview of Windows and mouse operations. If you have not used a mouse before, this tutorial is very helpful.

Figure 3–7
Starting screen of the Help option.

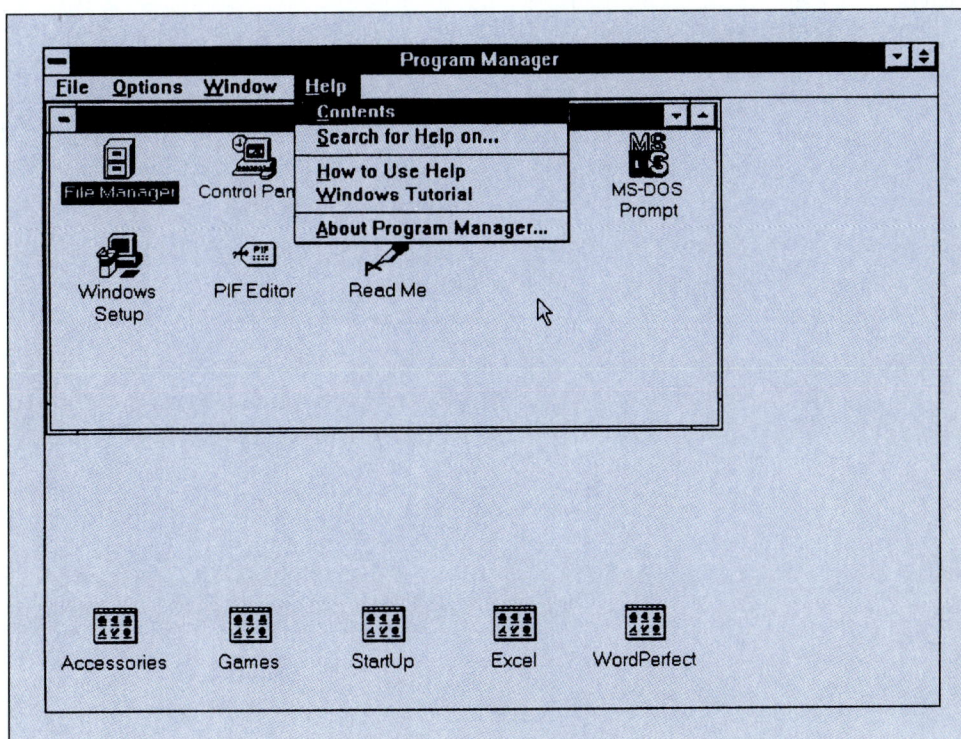

Figure 3–8
Information under the Contents option of the Help menu.

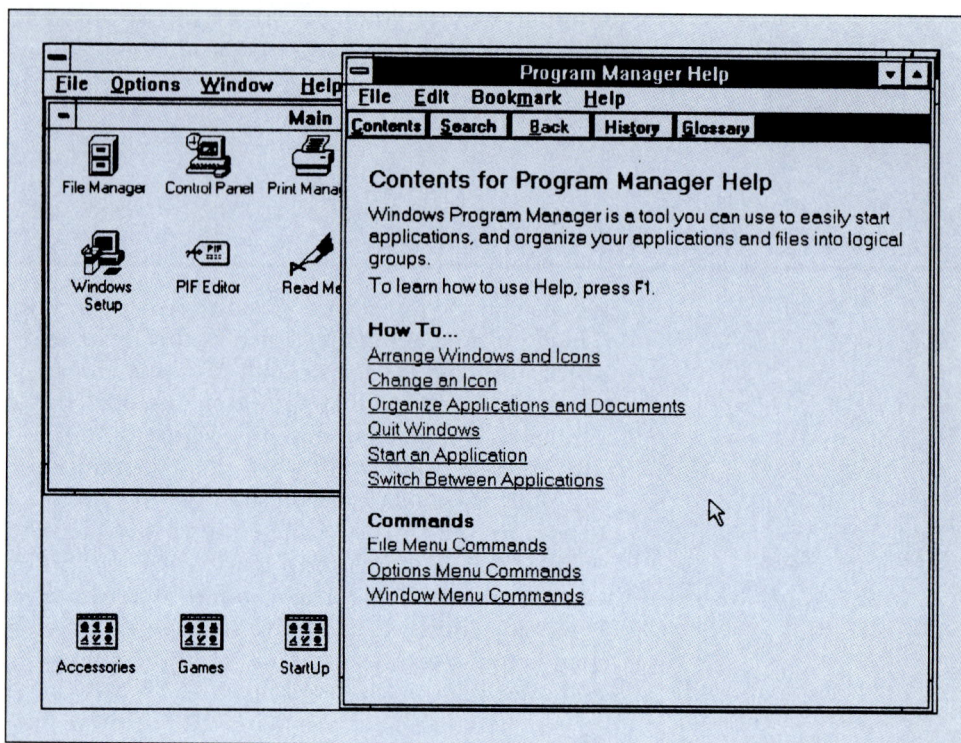

Figure 3–9
Starting screen of the Windows tutorial.

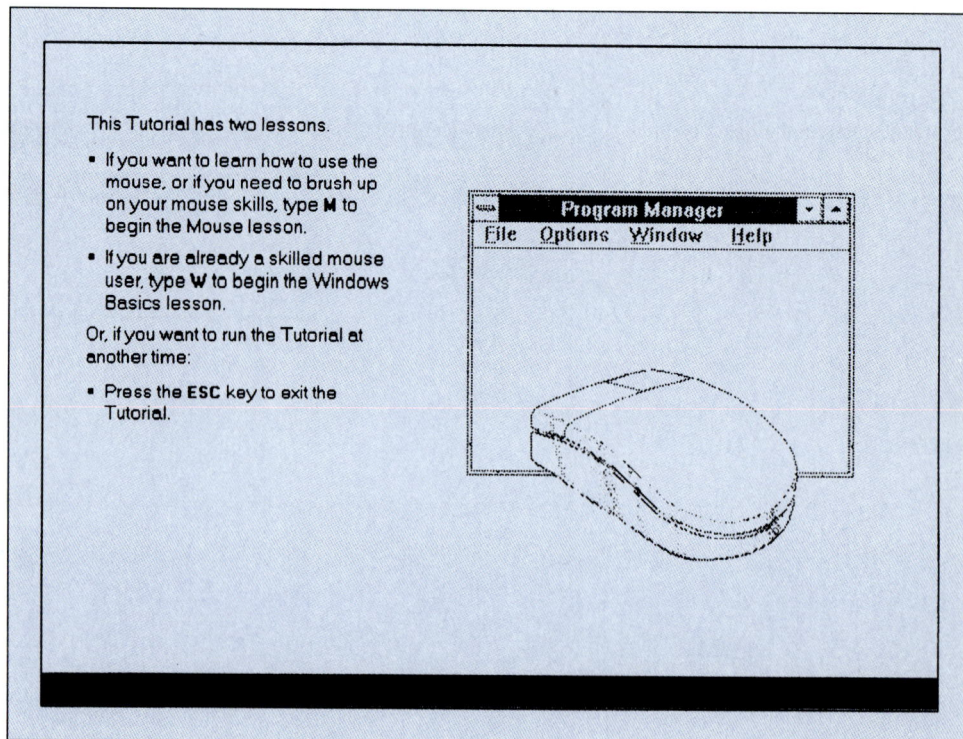

3–8   DIFFERENT PARTS OF A WINDOWS SCREEN

Most Windows screens include the elements illustrated in Figure 3–10. A **window** can be a whole screen or part of a screen. Refer to the figure as you read the following descriptions:

- The window title (in the title bar) is usually the name of the application, name of a document, or name of a file. In Figure 3–10 the title is Notepad - [Untitled] because no document has been opened yet.
- The control-menu box appears at the upper left of each window. The control-menu box is helpful if you are using the keyboard to work with Windows. By using control-menu commands, you can resize, move, maximize, minimize, close windows, and switch to applications. If you use a mouse, you can perform all of the tasks just mentioned by clicking and dragging. Probably the most common application of the control-menu box is closing a window. To do this, just double-click on the control-menu box.
- Insertion point indicates the current position of the cursor at any give time in your document. Text and graphs will be inserted at this point.
- The menu bar lists available menu options. In Figure 3–10, the menu bar includes File, Edit, Search, and Help.

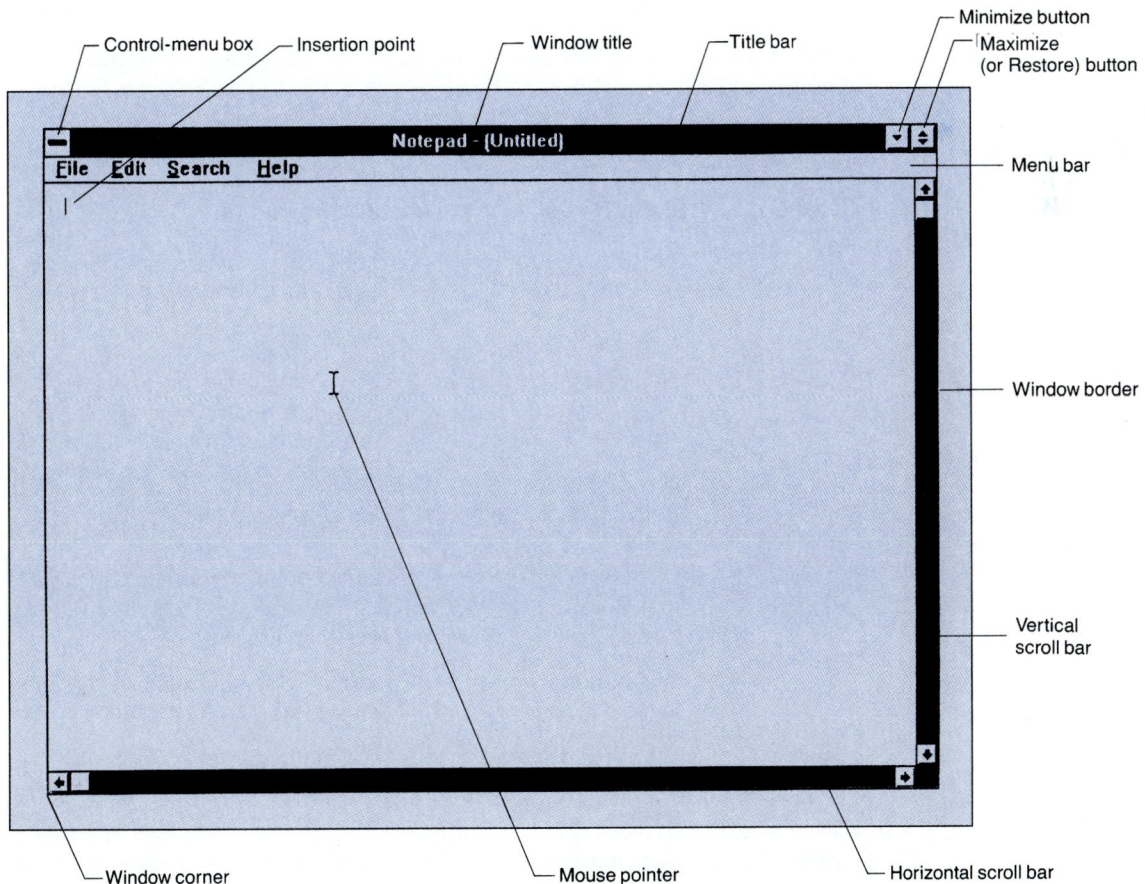

Figure 3–10
Elements of the Windows screen.

- The minimize button can reduce the window to an icon.
- The maximize button can enlarge the active application window so that it fills the entire desktop. After you enlarge a window, the maximize button is replaced by the restore button. You can click the restore button to return a window to its previous size.
- The window border is the outside edge of a window. You can lengthen or shorten the border on each side of a window.
- The vertical and horizontal scroll bars are used to view parts of a document that do not fit on the current screen.
- The mouse pointer is a small arrow that moves on the screen corresponding to the movement of the mouse on your desktop. The mouse pointer changes to a double-pointed arrow when it is moved to the edge of a window. Other common pointer shapes are summarized in Table 3–2.

Table 3–3 summarizes the control menu commands, which are accessible through the control-menu box. Some applications do not have all of these commands. For example, Figure 3–11 does not include all the commands outlined in Table 3–3.

3–9   WHAT IS THE PROGRAM MANAGER?

As soon as you start Windows you start the **Program Manager.** The Program Manager always runs during a Windows session. As you will see later in this chap-

Table 3–2
Mouse Pointer Shapes

Shape	Description	Allows you to
⇒	Arrow	select an option from the menu bar, select an icon, and move a window.
I	I–Beam	enter text.
⌛	Hourglass	do nothing while this shape is visible. Windows is performing a task. You must wait until the pointer changes shape before you can continue.
🖑	Pointing hand	jump between Help topics.
👆	Pointing finger	select one or more items in a graph.
🖐	Hand	move an item in a graph.
↕	Two-headed vertical arrow	split a worksheet window vertically and resize a row.
⟺	White (with line border) two-headed arrow	adjust the size of a window by "dragging" the side or corner of a window.
↔	Two-headed horizontal arrow (in one color)	split a worksheet window horizontally and resize a column.

Figure 3–11
Control Menu options.

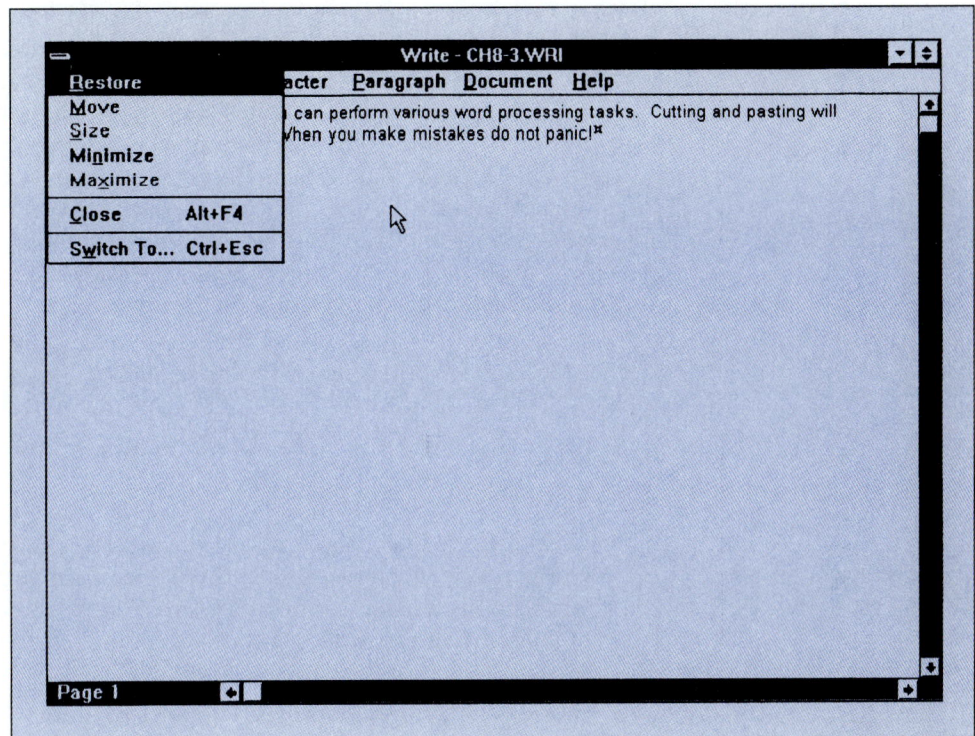

Table 3–3
Control Menu Commands

Command	Function
Restore	Restores the window to its former size after you have enlarged it (by using the Maximize command) or reduced it to an icon (by using the Minimize command)
Move	Uses the keyboard to move a window to another location
Size	Uses the keyboard to change the size of a window
Minimize	Reduces a window to an icon
Maximize	Enlarges a window to its maximum size
Close	Closes a window or a dialog box. You can also use this command to quit an application from an application window.
Switch To	Opens the Task List (discussed later in this chapter). This feature enables you to switch between running applications. It also arranges windows and icons on your desktop.
Next	Switches you between open document windows and icons. This is available for document windows only.
Edit	Displays a cascading menu with additional commands

ter, a variety of tasks can be performed through the Program Manager. When you run other applications, the Program Manager runs either in the background or as an icon on your desktop.

When you first start Windows, the Program Manager opens on your desktop with the Main group window open inside the Program Manager window. See Figure 3–12. This may appear different in your system, depending on how Windows has been configured. The Accessories group, the Games group, the StartUp group, and various applications groups are represented as group icons along the lower border of the Program Manager window. Remember, your screen might be different from what is presented in Figure 3–12.

3–9–1

Different Parts of the Program Manager Window

Refer to Figure 3–13 as you read the following descriptions of the different parts of the Program Manager window:

- **Group window** is a separate window inside the Program Manager window. As you can see in Figure 3–13, this window includes icons that start different applications. Group windows are affected by the commands from the Program Manager menu bar: File, Options, Window, and Help.

- Program-item icons are displayed inside a group window and represent applications, documents, accessories, and so forth. You can select program-item icons to start particular applications; for example, double-click on the File Manager icon to start it.

- Group icon is a minimized group window. These icons are displayed in the lower border of the Program Manager window. Figure 3–13 shows five of these icons.

Figure 3–12
Program Manager window.

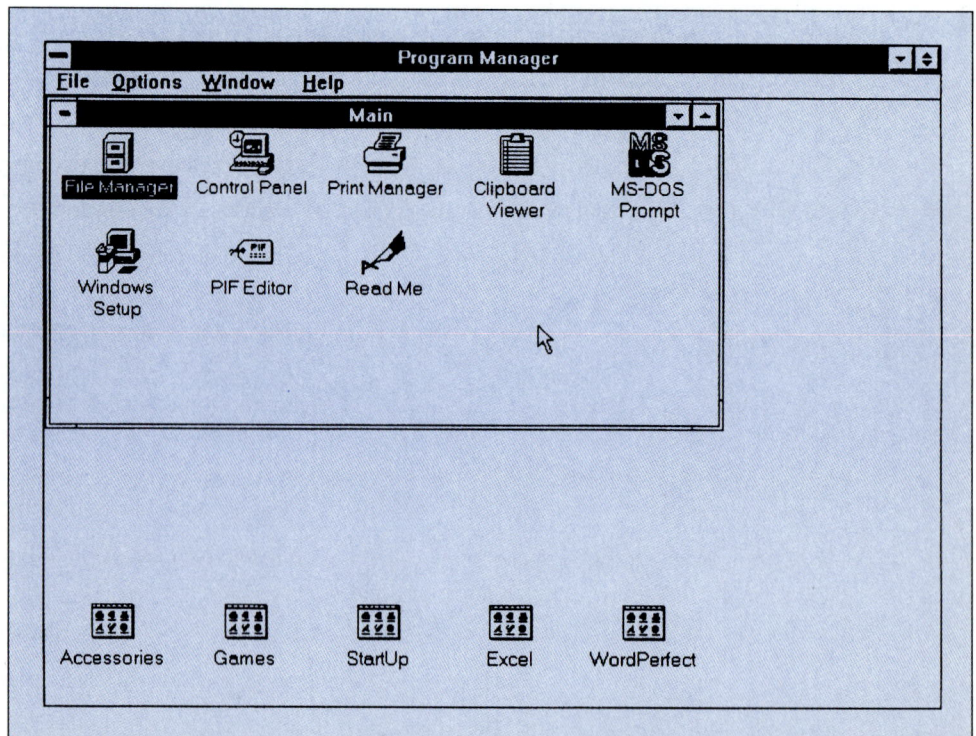

Program-item icon

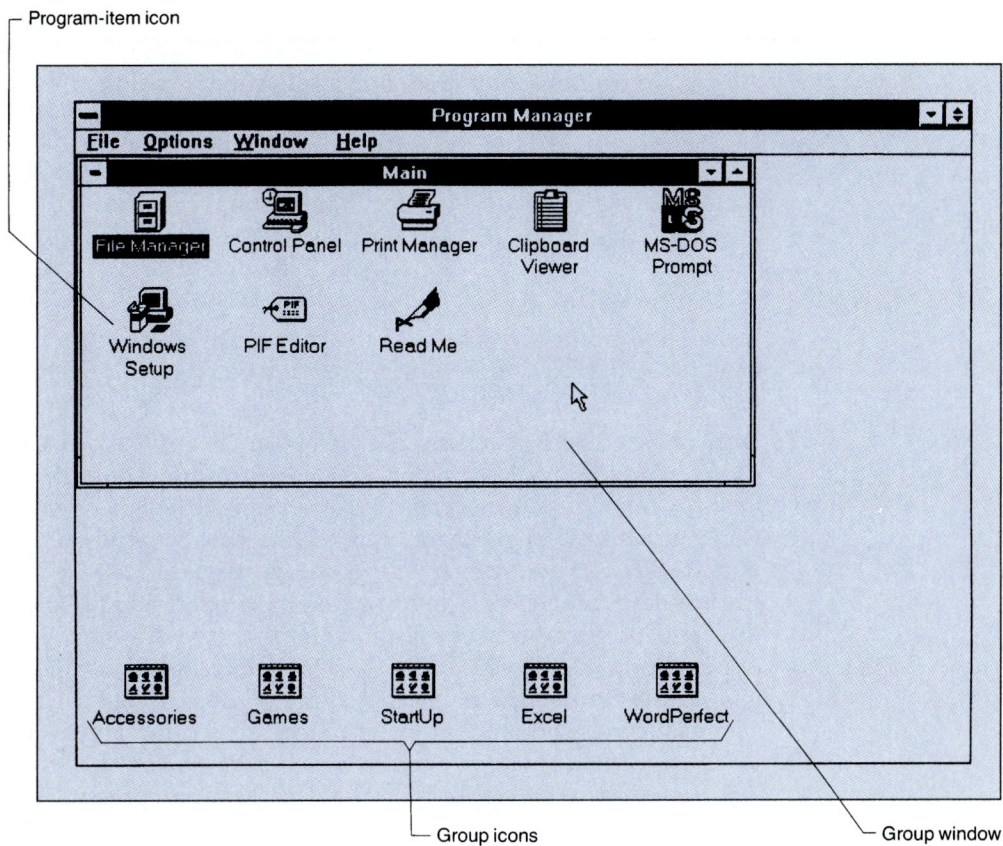

Figure 3–13
Parts of the Program Manager window.

3–9–2   Starting an Application from the Program Manager

Use the mouse and follow these steps to start an application:

1. Open the Program Manager window (if it is not already open).
2. Open the group window (if it is not already open) that includes your desired application by double-clicking on the group icon.
3. Double-click on the program-item icon for your desired application.

3–10   RUNNING TWO OR MORE APPLICATIONS AT THE SAME TIME

Windows allows you to run more than one application at one time. When you run multiple applications at the same time, the processing speed may be slower than normal. Processing speed also depends on the type of computer that you are using. To start several applications, start them in the desired sequence using the method that we just discussed.

3–11   SWITCHING BETWEEN APPLICATIONS

When you are running more than one application at a time, the window in which you are currently working is called the active window. The active window appears in the foreground. It might overlap or completely block other application windows that are also running on your system. To make another application active, you must select its window.

To switch between applications, you can choose one of the following methods:

1. If the application is visible, click the mouse anywhere in the application's window. If the application is running as an icon, click left on its icon, then click left on the Restore option.

2. Display Task List by pressing the Ctrl+Esc keys. A **Task List** is a window that shows all the applications that you have running and allows you to switch between them. Open the Task List by choosing the Switch To option from the Control menu or by pressing the Ctrl+Esc key combination. You will be presented with a screen similar to the one displayed in Figure 3–14. In the Task List window, double-click on the name of the desired application or highlight the name of the desired application and then select Switch To option from the options available in the dialog box. A **dialog box** is a window that appears temporarily to request information. Many dialog boxes include options that you must choose before Windows can execute a command.

To return to the application that you last used, press Alt+Tab.

Figure 3–14
Task List dialog box.

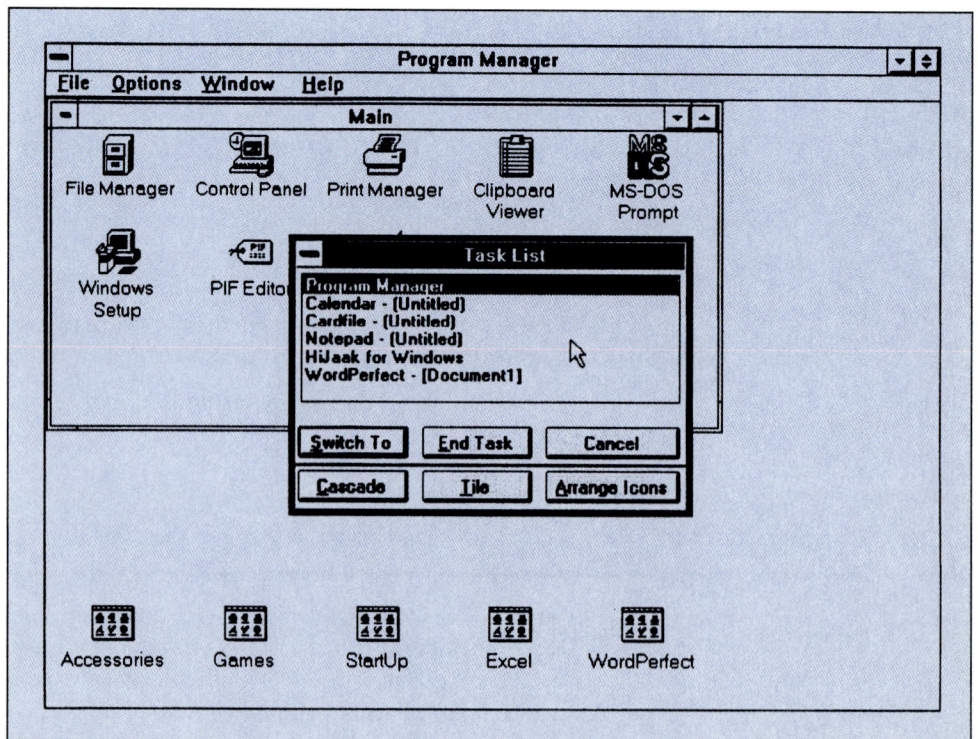

3-12   TRANSFERRING INFORMATION USING THE CLIPBOARD

The Windows **Clipboard** serves as a temporary location that stores information. The Clipboard enables you to copy or move information from one application and then copy ("paste") it in another application. The information that you copy to the Clipboard stays there until you clear the contents of the Clipboard or copy other information to it.

The Clipboard can also serve as a buffer for exchanging information among several applications.

3-12-1   Moving or Copying Information to the Clipboard

How information is moved or copied to the Clipboard depends on the type of application that you are running—a Windows application or a non-Windows application. It also depends on whether your application is running as a window or a full screen.

A Windows application allows you to easily move or copy information or an image to the Clipboard. To copy or move information to the Clipboard, follow these steps:

1. Highlight or select the text or the information that you want to move or copy. (For highlighting text, see the next section.) You can copy or move text, graphics, or both.
2. From the application's Edit menu (e.g., the Edit menu of Lotus 1-2-3), select Cut or Copy. Cut removes the selected text from its current position to the Clipboard. Copy only takes a snapshot for the Clipboard; the existing information remains intact.

You can copy the contents of an entire screen to the Clipboard by displaying the information then pressing the Print Screen key, or Shift+PrtSc or Alt+Prtsc. This process puts a snapshot (also called a bitmap) of the screen onto the Clipboard.

3-12-2   Selecting Text or Graphs

Editing commands can be performed on a block of text instead of on a single character. First you must select (highlight or block) the text. Then you can select various commands such as Cut, Copy, and so forth from the Edit menu of the application software.

To select text using the mouse, follow these steps:

1. Point to the first character of the desired text and click left.
2. Drag the insertion point to the end of the desired text.
3. Release the mouse button.

To cancel the selection, click the mouse button again anywhere in the document. Some applications such as WordPerfect for Windows allow you to select a word by double-clicking on it, a sentence by triple-clicking, an entire paragraph by quadruple-clicking, and so on.

To select a graph in the majority of Windows applications, you can click left on it.

3–12–3   ### Transferring Information from the Clipboard

To transfer the contents of the Clipboard to another application, follow these steps:

1. Start the desired application.
2. Position the insertion point at the place that you want the information from the Clipboard to appear.
3. From the Edit menu of the application (e.g., the Edit menu of Lotus 1-2-3), select Paste.

3–13   QUITTING AN APPLICATION

When you are finished working with an application, you should exit from it. Use one of the following methods to exit a Windows application:

- Select Exit from the application's File menu.
- Press Alt+F4.

To quit a non-Windows application, select the application's Exit or Quit command.

3–14   WORKING WITH GROUPS

Figure 3–15 shows **groups** containing program-item icons that represent applications, accessories, or documents. To start an application from a group, you have to select the application's icon. As you can see in Figure 3–15, Windows includes several predefined groups as follows:

1. The Main group, which is already open in Figure 3–15, contains Windows system applications:
   - File Manager—manages your files and disk drives
   - Control Panel—allows you to change the configuration of your system
   - Print Manager—allows you to install and configure printers
   - Clipboard Viewer—allows you to view, edit, and save the contents of the Clipboard
   - MS-DOS Prompt—allows you to exit to the DOS prompt
   - Windows Setup—displays the system configuration
   - PIF Editor—is a tool for editing program information files
   - Read Me—includes basic information about Windows
2. The Accessories group includes several interesting applications such as word processing, drawing, painting, communications, and so forth.
3. The Games group includes several games that you can use for learning the basics of Windows or for fun.

Figure 3–15
Example of groups.

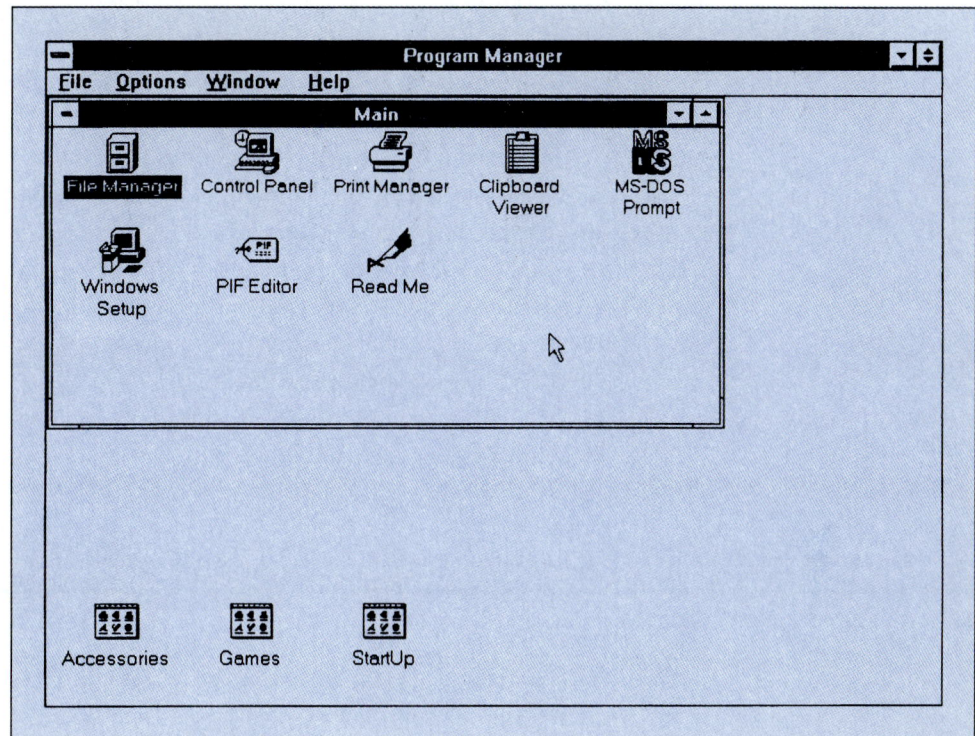

4. The StartUp group contains applications that start when you start Windows. This group is empty until you add applications to it. You can add any application to the group.

5. The Applications group contains applications found on the hard disk during setup. If you select the custom setup, and select not to have Windows set up applications from your hard disk, your Program Manager window will not contain an application group. This is the case in our example.

To start an application, you must first open its group window and select the appropriate program-item icon. To open a group window, double-click on the group icon.

SUMMARY

This chapter provided an overview of the Windows operating environment. The advantages of Windows as a graphical-based environment were highlighted. After the process of getting in and out of Windows was explained, some of the basic features of Windows were discussed: using the mouse, selecting from the Windows screen, using the Program Manager, running an application, working with the Clipboard, and working with a group.

REVIEW QUESTIONS

*These questions are answered in Appendix A.

1. What are some of the advantages of Windows?
*2. How do you start Windows?
3. What is a desktop? What is an icon?

4. How do you use the mouse in the Windows environment? How do you use the keyboard? Which one is easier to use?

5. Explain how to obtain online help in Windows.

6. How is the tutorial facility of Windows started?

7. What is the Control menu? How do you activate it?

*8. Give some of the commands in the Control menu.

9. What is the Program Manager?

10. How do you start an application from the Program Manager?

11. How can you run more than one application in Windows at the same time?

*12. How do you switch between applications?

13. Describe the Clipboard.

14. How do you transfer information from an application to the Clipboard?

15. How do you quit an application?

16. What is a group? How do you start a group?

HANDS-ON EXPERIENCE

1. Start Windows. Use the mouse to invoke the File pull-down menu; select Exit and then OK to leave Windows.

2. Start Windows again. This time exit Windows by means of the keyboard. To do this, first press Alt+F to access the File pull-down menu; then move the cursor to Exit Windows and press the Enter key twice.

3. Start Windows again. Using the mouse, select (one at a time) the File, Options, Window, and Help menus from inside the Program Manager. What is available under each option?

4. By double-clicking the left button of the mouse, open the accessories icon. What is available in this group?

5. Invoke the Windows tutorial program and spend an hour with it. What is available?

6. Use the Glossary option in the Help menu to display the first 20 items in the list.

7. Print the Contents screen by using the Print option from the File menu in the Program Manager Help window.

8. Use the mouse to enlarge the Main group window. Then return it to its previous size.

9. Double-click on the MS-DOS prompt icon. At the DOS prompt, use the DIR command to generate a listing of the current directory. Type *EXIT* and press Enter to return to Windows.

10. Press the Ctrl+Esc key combination to start the Task List. What is available in the Task List dialog box?

KEY TERMS

Click and drag	Group	Mouse pointer
Clipboard	Group Window	Online tutorial
Desktop	Icon	Program Manager
Dialog box	Multitasking	Task List
Graphical user interface (GUI)	Mouse	Window

KEY COMMANDS

Alt+F (to invoke the File menu)

Alt+Tab (to return to the previous application)

Commands for Program Manager (see Figure 3–1)

Ctrl+Esc (to invoke the Task List)

MISCONCEPTIONS AND SOLUTIONS

Misconception   Press the Alt key to activate the menu and move the cursor to an option to execute the option; this is time consuming.

> **Solution**   If a name in the menu bar has an underlined letter, you can press Alt to activate the menu bar and open the desired menu; then press the letter that is underlined. For example, to exit Windows: from the File Manager press Alt+F; then press the X key. An even faster method is to click the left button of the mouse while on the desired menu item.

Misconception   Performing search operations in the Help menu by typing the entire word in the Search for box is time consuming.

> **Solution**   The help facility matches characters you type as closely as possible with the available key words. Just type the closest word or a part of the word that comes to mind.

Misconception   Sometimes you see more than one control-menu box. This is confusing.

> **Solution**   The control-menu box at the far upper left of the screen controls the application (e.g., WordPerfect). The others control the windows inside the application window (e.g., a document in WordPerfect). The extreme upper left control-menu box is usually for the Program Manager.

Misconception   To maximize a window, you click on the maximize button, but this is time consuming.

> **Solution**   You can also maximize a window by double-clicking on its title bar. To restore an application window to its previous size, double-click on the title bar again.

ARE YOU READY TO MOVE ON?

Multiple Choice

1. The following statements about Windows are all true except for which one?
   a. It will run without DOS being in your computer.
   b. It is a graphical environment.
   c. It is a multitasking environment.
   d. It is easier to operate than DOS.
   e. All are true.

2. The following statements about Windows are all true except for which one?
   a. You can run Windows and DOS applications at the same time.
   b. You can link several files together.
   c. Windows provides better memory management than DOS.
   d. All are true.
   e. Only A and B are true.

3. Of the following items, which is not included in the accessories group of Windows 3.1?
   a. File Transfer
   b. Write
   c. Paintbrush
   d. Terminal
   e. Print Manager

4. To start Windows, first change to the drive and directory that contain your Windows files then, before pressing Enter, type
   a. *FILE*
   b. *FUN*
   c. *WIN*
   d. *TEST*
   e. *GO*

5. All the following tasks can be performed from the Windows desktop except
   a. fast application switching
   b. icon spacing changes
   c. displaying your document
   d. changing colors
   e. all are possible

6. The following are all possible applications of a mouse except
   a. invoking a menu
   b. exiting from Windows
   c. deselecting a menu
   d. all are possible
   e. only A and C are possible

7. If you are using a keyboard in the Windows environment, which of the following is *Not* true?
   a. You can use the middle part of the keyboard.
   b. You cannot use the function keys.
   c. You can use the key combinations.
   d. You can use the numeric keypad.
   e. These are all correct.

8. To activate the Task List, which key combination should you press?
   a. Alt+Tab
   b. Ctrl+Esc
   c. Ctrl+Tab
   d. Esc
   e. Alt+F10

9. To start the help facility of Windows,
   a. type *HELP* at the DOS prompt and press Enter
   b. select the Help option from any Windows application menu
   c. type *TUTOR* at the C> prompt and press Enter
   d. select Help from the File menu
   e. none of the above

10. The following are all parts of a Windows screen except
    a. window title
    b. control-menu box
    c. insertion point
    d. title bar
    e. DOS prompt

True/False

1. The minimize button is used to reduce the window to an icon.
2. The window border is the outside edge of a window.
3. The vertical and horizontal scroll bars are used to view only the first five lines of a window.
4. The mouse pointer indicates the present position of the pointer.
5. To return to your previous application, you must press Alt+Esc.
6. Windows applications do not all follow the same principles.
7. Windows presents a multitasking environment.
8. Windows cannot be used to link several files together.
9. The Accessories group is one of the predefined groups in Windows.
10. Application switching is *Not* possible from the Windows desktop.

ANSWERS

Multiple Choice		**True/False**	
1.	a	1.	T
2.	d	2.	T
3.	a	3.	F
4.	c	4.	T
5.	e	5.	F
6.	d	6.	F
7.	b	7.	T
8.	b	8.	F
9.	b	9.	T
10.	e	10.	F

WordPerfect For Windows at a Glance

4

4–1   INTRODUCTION

This chapter introduces WordPerfect for Windows—one of the most popular word processing packages on the market. A brief comparison of a typewriter and a word processor is followed by a description of the various generations of word processing machines. Next, the different capabilities of WordPerfect for Windows are explained. After outlining the general aspects of WordPerfect for Windows, the chapter introduces a complete cycle of word processing operations, including file creation, modification, saving, printing, retrieving, and exiting.

4–2   A WORD PROCESSOR AND A TYPEWRITER: A COMPARISON

A **word processor** offers many features not found in a typewriter, although it is similar to a typewriter that has a large memory. Using a word processor, you can create a document, edit it, revise it, do cutting and pasting, save it on the disk, and print it on a printer. No longer do you need correction fluid (e.g., Liquid Paper) to erase an unwanted word or scissors for cutting and pasting! The word processor helps you do everything electronically with a high degree of efficiency and effectiveness. Throughout this book you will learn many powerful features of WordPerfect for Windows as one of the most popular word processing programs on the market.

4–3   WORD PROCESSING REVOLUTION

Word processing machines have gone through a major revolution. The earliest machines were **dedicated word processors**, meaning they were only capable of performing word processing tasks. These machines were relatively expensive, and only medium-size and large organizations could afford them.

    In the past mainframe computers also performed word processing tasks. A **mainframe-based word processor** is usually difficult to use and lacks flexibility.

    The microcomputer era has brought a new meaning to word processing operations. **Microcomputer-based word processors** are relatively inexpensive and easy to use, and they perform major word processing tasks in an efficient and effective manner.

4–4   WORDPERFECT FOR WINDOWS: THE ENTIRE PACKAGE

WordPerfect for Windows is considered to be one of the best word processing programs on the market. The tasks performed by WordPerfect for Windows can be classified into five major components: word processor, speller, thesaurus, merge, and advanced features.

    The word processor component is a full-featured word processing program. A document can be created, indented, underlined, put in boldface, saved, and printed. Electronic cut and paste and variable spacing are easy with this component of the WordPerfect program.

    The speller component contains a comprehensive dictionary. You can check your spelling against this dictionary, so you should be able to create documents with no spelling errors.

The thesaurus component includes antonyms and synonyms. This feature helps you to create reports that are more meaningful. The thesaurus gives you a variety of word choices from which you can choose.

The merge component allows you to merge or combine a "boilerplate" document (i.e., standardized text) with another document that is not constant. For example, using the merge feature you can generate one letter and send it to hundreds or thousands of people. In this case, the letter document is constant (it is a boilerplate). A second document that contains all the names and addresses is not constant. The merge feature combines the letter with all of the names and addresses to generate a letter for each recipient.

The fifth feature of WordPerfect for Windows is called the advanced component. This feature enables you to perform math functions, perform search and sort, draw lines, incorporate graphics into your documents, and develop keyboard macros. We will discuss most of these features in future chapters.

WordPerfect for Windows is available for PC and PC-compatible machines. Both a floppy and a hard disk are required. A 386 or higher computer with 4 MB or more of RAM and about 7.5 MB of free hard disk space is recommended. Your computer must also have Microsoft Windows version 3.0 or higher.

4–5   GETTING WORDPERFECT FOR WINDOWS STARTED

The easiest method for starting WordPerfect for Windows is through the WordPerfect group. If you double-click on the WordPerfect icon, you will be presented with a screen similar to the one in Figure 4–1. From this screen, double-click on the WordPerfect icon. As you can see, from the WordPerfect group you can start the File Manager, Speller, Thesaurus, QuickFinder File Indexer, and WPWin Installation. The File Manager lists the files stored in a directory. It allows you to switch to

Figure 4–1
WordPerfect group.

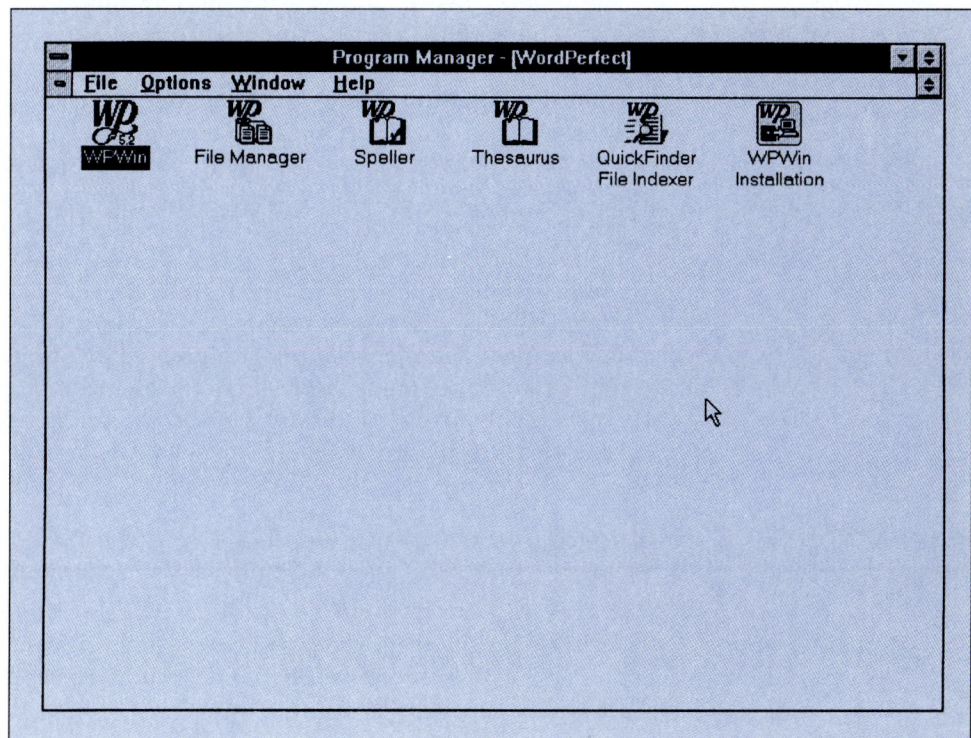

Figure 4–2
WordPerfect for Windows data
entry window.

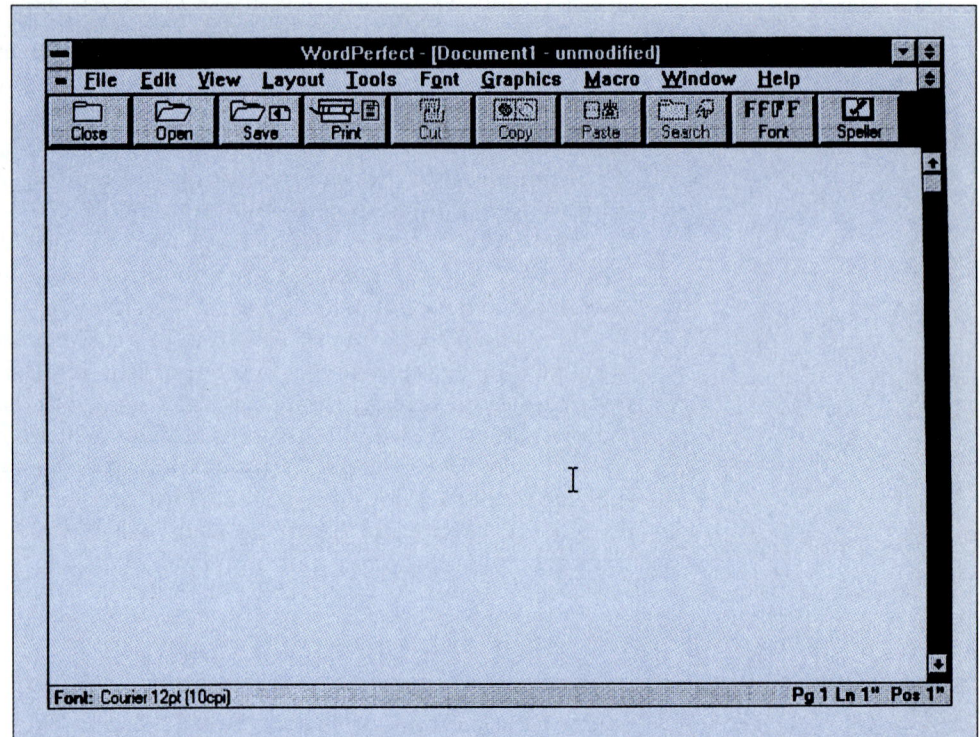

different directories and view files stored in each one. Using the File Manager you can open, delete, rename, move, print, and copy files. The speller component allows you to correct typographical mistakes. The thesaurus component enables you to find synonyms and antonyms for the words in your document. QuickFinder File Indexer helps you to create and edit indexes. WPWin Installation is used for installing WordPerfect for Windows or changing existing specifications.

You an also start WordPerfect for Windows by using the Run command from the Program Manager File menu. To do this type *C:\WPWIN\WPWIN* and press Enter.

In either case, you will be presented with a screen similar to one presented in Figure 4–2. This screen is called the *data entry window*. The line at the bottom of the screen is called the **status line**. It tells you that you are in page 1 (Pg 1), line 1 inch (Ln 1"), position 1 inch (Pos 1"). The quotation symbols indicate that the line the insertion point is on is 1 inch from the top margin and 1 inch from the left margin of the page. When you move the insertion point by entering text, the status line changes automatically to constantly reflect the position of the insertion point. The default type font is displayed in the lower left corner of the screen.

The position indicator (Pos) in the status line gives you valuable information. If it is displayed as POS, it means the Caps Lock key is enabled.

4–6   DATA ENTRY WINDOW

As you can see in Figure 4–2, the starting screen of WordPerfect for Windows includes several distinct areas. Let us briefly explain them.

At the extreme upper left corner notice the application control-menu box. Use this icon to control the size of the application window. You can also resize the window, change its location on the desktop, close the window, and perform other "housekeeping" tasks.

Immediately below the application control-menu box is the document control-menu box. Use this icon to control the size and location of the document window.

To the right of the application control-menu icon notice the title bar, which indicates WordPerfect-[Document1-unmodified]. As soon as you save a document, the name of your document will replace these words.

To the right of the title bar you can see the minimize and maximize (or restore) boxes for the application, which is WordPerfect for Windows in this case. As mentioned in the previous chapter, the minimize button can reduce the application window to an icon. Also note the document restore button. When you minimize a WordPerfect document, if the document window is not maximized (meaning it has not occupied the entire screen), it takes on the appearance of a WordPerfect for Windows icon with the title of the document beneath it. Double-clicking on the document icon will restore it to the window. The maximize icon expands the window to its maximum size.

The main menu of WordPerfect for Windows (just below the titles bar) includes the following options, all of which will be discussed in more detail in subsequent chapters.

The File menu is used to create files, open existing files, save files, and print files. Through the File menu you can also access the WordPerfect for Windows File Manager, which we will talk about in detail in Chapter 7.

The Edit menu allows you to cut, copy, paste, and append documents. It also allows you to perform search and replace operations and, most important of all, this menu allows you to "undo" your mistakes.

The View menu allows you to use the WordPerfect for Windows Ruler to control margin and tab settings, to look at reveal codes, and to work with button bars.

The Layout menu includes commands for controlling paragraphs, pages, and columns. It also enables you to include footnotes and endnotes in your documents.

The Tools menu includes the speller and thesaurus, the word count option, and spreadsheet-handling feature.

The Font menu allows you to change the appearance of your text through boldface, italics, and underlining.

By means of the Graphics menu you can control the way graphics are created and edited and control borders around graphic objects. You also can incorporate graphs into your documents.

The Macro menu enables you to record and play back a series of keyboard or mouse actions as macros to simplify your WordPerfect tasks.

The Window menu allows you to work with various windows. It also lets you organize the open windows in tile or cascade formats. In Tile mode you see open windows side by side, with no window overlapping any other window. In Cascade mode you see open windows in overlapping format; this format shows you the name of each open document.

The Help menu gives you access to the various online help screens available in WordPerfect for Windows operations.

The **button bar** for WordPerfect for Windows appears below the menu bar. Buttons represent different commands. For example, to print a document just click on the Print button. You can create your own button bars, modify the existing ones, and so forth. If you do not like them at all, you can hide them by selecting View from the menu bar, then clicking on the Button Bar.

If you have any questions about the other parts of Figure 4–2, refer to the previous chapter. Most of the menu options will be explained further in future chapters.

4–7   YOUR FIRST ELECTRONIC DOCUMENT

To get started with WordPerfect for Windows, have a formatted disk ready. In this text we are using a computer equipped with two diskette drives and a hard disk. Start WordPerfect for Windows by following the instructions explained in section 4–5. Insert a formatted disk in drive A; it will be used to save your documents. If you do not specify a drive, WordPerfect for Windows will save documents in the default directory in drive C.

Type the following two lines:

Using WordPerfect for Windows we can generate documents that can be revised later. Cut and paste become an easy task.

Figure 4–3 illustrates this document. Do *not* press the Enter key at the end of a line. WordPerfect for Windows automatically does **word wrap.** This means that as you type and the insertion point approaches the right side of the screen, if WordPerfect for Windows cannot fit the entire word on the current line it moves the entire word to the next line automatically. At the end of each line WordPerfect for Windows places a **soft return.** The soft return marks the end of the line where the word wrap occurred. If you want to cut a line short, or for any reason you want to break a line, you must press the Enter key right after the character that marks the end of the line. This is called a **hard return.** A hard return is used to mark the end of a line or a paragraph. Each hard return in a blank line inserts a blank line in the document.

Figure 4–3
Your first electronic document.

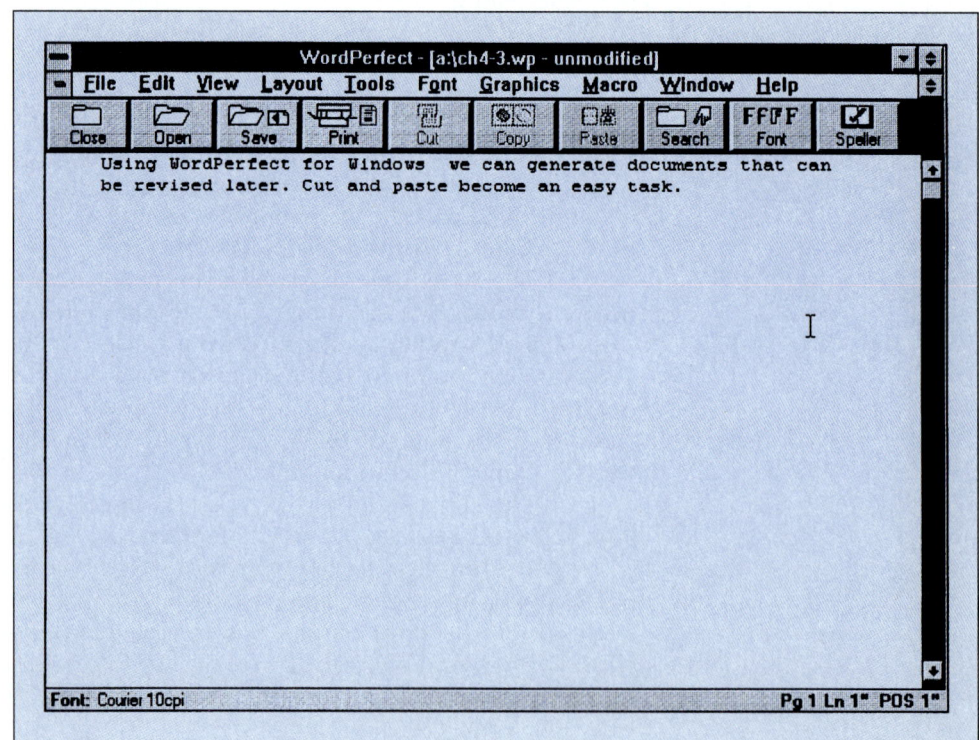

In this example we started from the first available column, at position 1". If you want to start a paragraph (indent a line), press the Tab key once. This key will move the insertion point over by $^1/_2$ inch to the 1.5" position.

At any given time you can see one screen of your document. When you type one additional line beyond one screen, the first line of the document will scroll off the top of the screen.

4–8   MOVING AROUND IN THE DOCUMENT

While you are using WordPerfect for Windows, you can move the insertion point to any location of your document. Table 4–1 provides a summary of important arrow movement keys using the keyboard, and Table 4–2 provides a summary of the important mouse actions for moving around.

Remember, when you move the insertion point from one line to another line or from one screen to another screen, WordPerfect for Windows keeps track

Table 4–1
Important Arrow Movement Keys
Using the Keyboard

Key(s) Used	Function Performed
→ (right arrow)	Moves the insertion point one position to the right
← (left arrow)	Moves the insertion point one position to the left
↑ (up arrow)	Moves the insertion point up one line
↓ (down arrow)	Moves the insertion point down one line
Ctrl + →	Moves the insertion point to the first character of the next word to the right
Ctrl + ←	Moves the insertion point to the first character of the previous word to the left
End	Moves the insertion point to the end of the line
Page Down (PgDn)	Moves the insertion point to the first line of the document on the next page
Page Up (PgUp)	Moves the insertion point to the first line of the document on the previous page

Table 4–2
Important Mouse Actions for Moving Around

To move insertion point to	Place the mouse pointer
any place in the document	on the scroll box in the vertical scroll bar (at far right of screen) and click and drag the scroll box to the desired location in the document, or move the mouse pointer to any location and click left.
one line up	on the up scroll arrow at the top of the vertical scroll bar and click once.
one line down	on the down scroll arrow at the bottom of the vertical scroll bar and click once.
up one window	above the scroll box and click once.
down one window	below the scroll box and click once.

Figure 4–4
Go To dialog box.

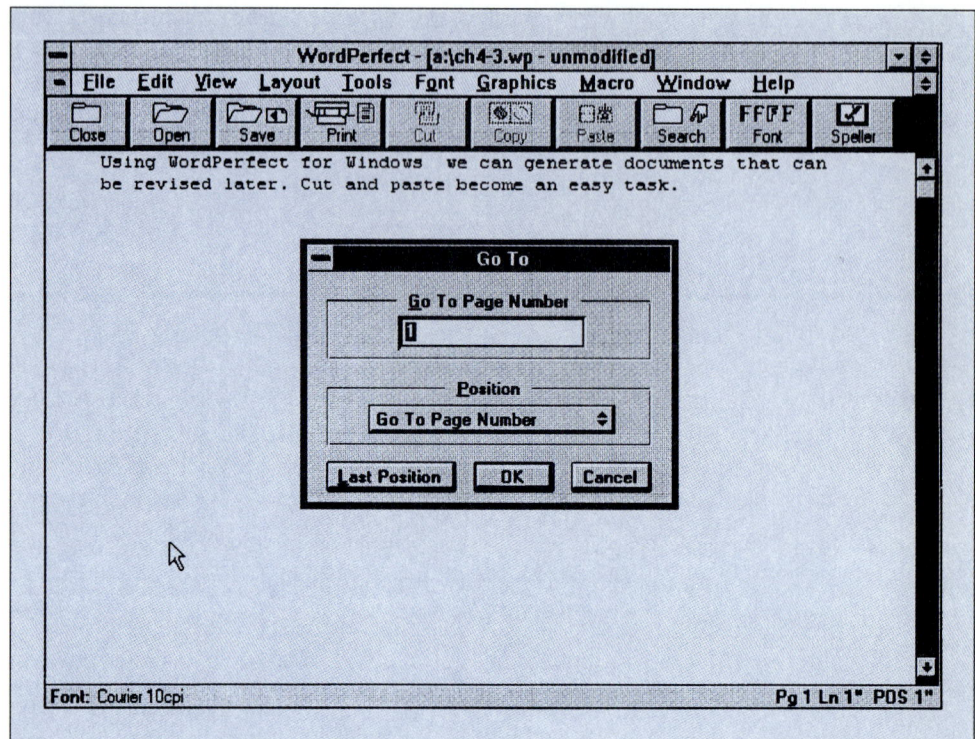

of the relative position. For example, if the insertion point is in position 30 and you move to the next screen, you will go to position 30 in the next screen. If the line in the receiving screen is shorter, the insertion point will move to the right-most character position.

You can also use the Edit menu to move around. To do this click on Edit and on Go To (Ctrl+G). You will see a dialog box similar to the one in Figure 4–4. Type in the desired page number and click on OK or press Enter. You can also click and drag the **pop-out icon** in the Position box to move to the top of the current page or bottom of current page. Click on one of these options; then click on OK. By clicking on the Last Position box, you can return to the previous location of the insertion point. This feature is especially useful after you have moved the insertion point using features such as Go To on the Page Up or Page Down keys.

4–9   CONVENTIONS USED IN THIS BOOK

Throughout this book we use the following conventions:

■ Whenever there is a shortcut key or key combination available for a command, we list it immediately after the menu option. For example, Ctrl+G can be used to invoke the Go To dialog box. These shortcut keys allow you to access an option without going through the WordPerfect for Windows menus.

■ Whenever there is a key combination, such as the Ctrl+G key combination, you must press and hold down the first key then press the second key.

■ The key and key combinations used in this book are based on the common user access (CUA) keyboard template. This template consists of a set of terminology, keystrokes, and commands designed by IBM to provide standardization among

Windows applications. The WordPerfect for Windows default is the CUA keyboard.

■ To change the CUA keyboard to other formats select the Preferences option from the File menu; then select the Keyboard option. From this menu click on the Select button and select your desired option, such as WPDOS51.WWK (WordPerfect 5.1 for DOS—the most popular version of WordPerfect before WordPerfect for Windows).

Please note: if you select a keyboard other than the CUA, the key and key combinations used throughout this text often will not agree with those shown on your screen.

4–10   CORRECTING MISTAKES

When you make mistakes, do not panic. Correcting mistakes using WordPerfect for Windows is an easy task. If you make a mistake and discover it immediately, you can use the Backspace key to correct the mistake. Each press of the Backspace key erases one character to the left of the insertion point. If you discover a mistake after the document is completely typed, you can use the arrow keys or the mouse pointer to move the insertion point to the error location and correct the mistake. Characters can also be deleted by using the Delete (Del) key. The Del key erases the character to the right of the insertion point.

To insert a series of characters in a WordPerfect for Windows document, you have two options. The first option is the **Insert mode,** which is the default for WordPerfect for Windows. This means you can move the insertion point to any location and type all the characters that were left out. As you type, the existing text will be moved to the right. As soon as you finish typing, use the down-arrow key to move the insertion point down one line; the text will be reformatted.

The second option is the **typeover mode**. This means you can type over the existing text. To activate the typeover option, press the Insert (Ins) key once. The word "Typeover" will be displayed at the lower left of the screen. To exit this mode press the Ins key again.

To see how these two options work, move the insertion point to the beginning of the word "documents" in Figure 4–3. Let us say you would like to replace "documents" with "reports." Press the Ins key to activate the Typeover mode. You will see the word "Typeover" displayed at the lower left of the screen. Now type *reports*. There will be two additional characters ("ts") that can be eliminated by using the Del key. Press the Ins key again to exit the Typeover mode. Press Del twice. The extra characters disappear and their spaces are closed up. Now let us insert "or any other word processing program" right after the word "Windows." Move the insertion point to the position just after the character "s" in Windows. Start typing, *or any other word processing program*. When you type, the existing text is moved to the right. When you are finished typing, move the insertion point down one line and the text will be reformatted. The final report is presented in Figure 4–5. To slide the existing text to the right by one position, press the space bar once.

Figure 4–5
Revised document.

```
Using WordPerfect for Windows or any other word processing program,
we can generate documents that can be revised later. Cut and paste
become an easy task.
```

4–11   SAVING YOUR DOCUMENT ON DISK

Saving a file to a disk involves selecting either Save (Shift+F3) or Save As (F3) from the File menu. If this is the first time that you are saving your document, there is no difference between the Save and Save As commands. Selecting either of these commands will present the Save As dialog box as displayed in Figure 4–6. Type a name of up to eight characters and click on the Save button. This procedure saves your document on the disk in the default drive and directory. If you want to save in a directory and/or a drive other than the default directory/drive you must specify it. For example, if you type *A:FIRST.WP*, your file will be saved under the name FIRST in the A drive. The .WP extension is optional, but the .WP will remind you that this file is a WordPerfect file. You can use any three letters as your file extension, for example, LTR for letters, MEM for memos, and so forth.

WordPerfect for Windows also provides an automatic backup feature. The user can define the interval between automatic backups. For example, backups can be performed automatically every 5 minutes, 10 minutes, and so forth. This is done through the Preferences option of the File menu. It is a good idea to use the Save option every 10 minutes or so to protect yourself against unexpected events such as a power failure. Selecting the Save option saves your document under its current name.

If a file is already saved, by selecting the Save As option you can save it again under a different name. By doing this you are creating two versions of your document. If your document is saved and you select the Save As option to save it under its present name, WordPerfect for Windows displays the Replace dialog box as presented in Figure 4–7. Selecting the Yes option will replace the old document with the new one regardless of any differences in size. By selecting the No

Figure 4–6
Save as dialog box.

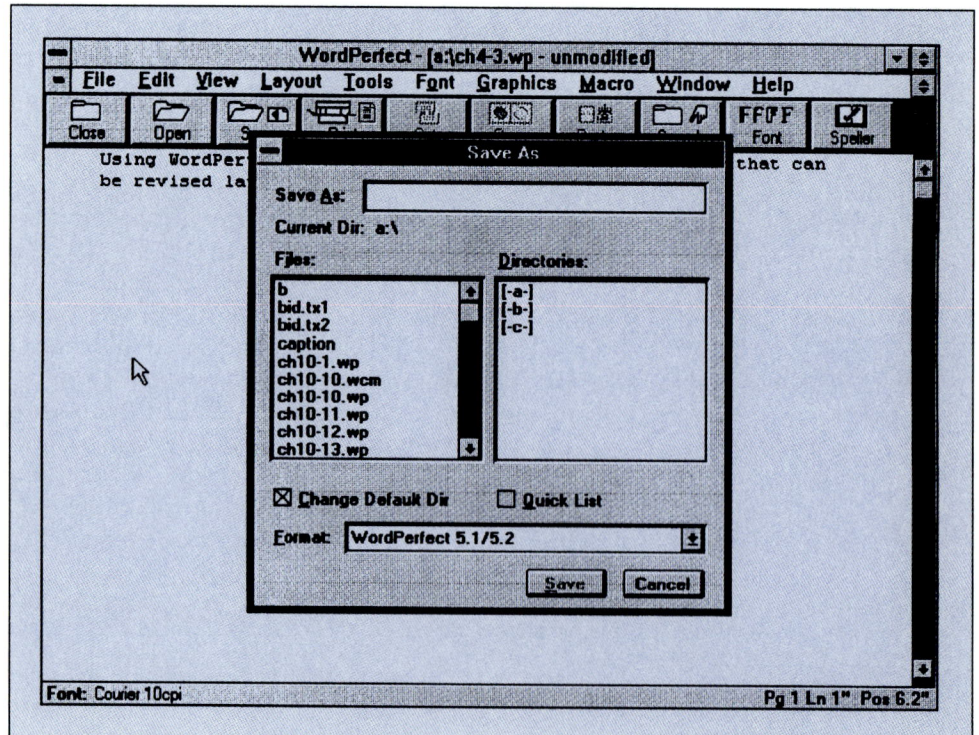

Figure 4–7
Replace dialog box.

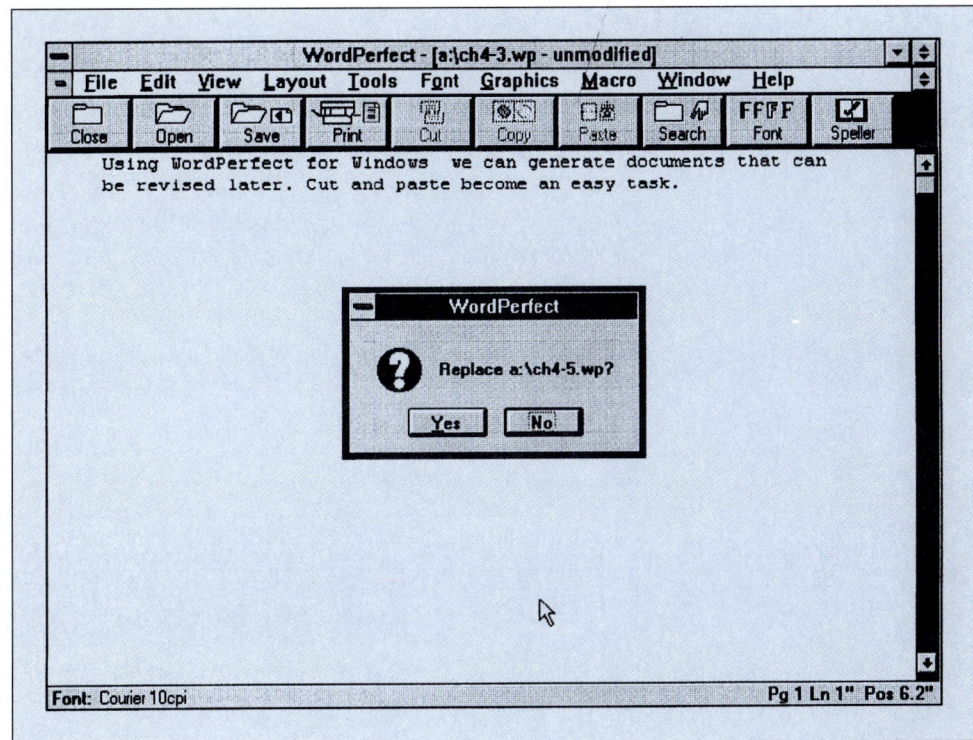

option, you are in effect changing your mind, and you will be presented with the Save As dialog box again.

As you can see in Figure 4–6, all the drives and directories in your system are displayed in the Directories box. To change to any of them just double-click on it. For example, if you double-click the drive shown as [-b-], your default drive will be changed to drive B. The root directory is identified by [..].

Also note in Figure 4–6 that all the files in the current directory are displayed in the Files box. To save your current file under one of these names, first double-click on the desired name; then click on the Save button.

Let us say you just finished writing a term paper for one of your classes. Now you want to write a letter. Save the term paper by using the Save or Save As command. Then, from the File menu select the Close (Ctrl+F4) option. You will be presented with a clear screen onto which you can start typing the letter.

4–12   PRINTING A DOCUMENT

Printing a document involves selecting the Print (F5) option from the File menu. You will be presented with a screen similar to the one in Figure 4–8. Click on Print at the lower right of the screen. Your document will be printed with the default settings of WordPerfect for Windows, which are summarized in Table 4–3.

As you can see in Figure 4–8, the Print command gives you a variety of options. For example, you can specify the number of copies by clicking on the Number of Copies box and typing the desired number. Then click on Print. Click on the Current Page option to print the current page. You can print a range of pages by clicking on the Multiple Pages button and then clicking on Print; you will see another dialog box that allows you to print any section of the document. You can also print a document on disk by clicking on Document on Disk.

Table 4–3
WordPerfect Default Options

Left margin	1 inch (9 spaces)
Right margin	1 inch (9 spaces)
Top margin	1 inch (6 lines)
Bottom margin	1 inch (6 lines)
Length of the page	54 lines
Starting character	Column 10 or 1."
Ending character	Column 74 or 7.4"
Spacing	Single

Figure 4–8
Print dialog box.

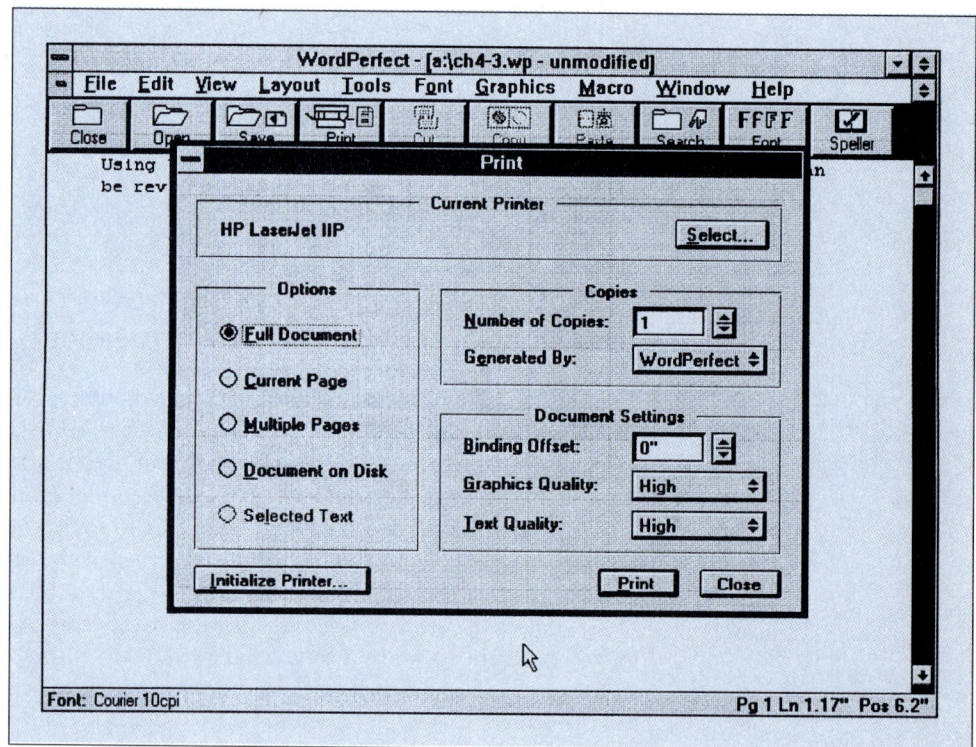

4–13   RETRIEVING AN EXISTING DOCUMENT

Retrieving a file that has already been saved involves selecting the Open (F4) option from the File menu. You will be presented with the Open dialog box as shown in Figure 4–9. In the Filename box type the desired name and click on Open. As before, you can select a different drive and/or directory by double-clicking on its name. You can also double-click Filename in the Open File dialog box in order to bring it to the screen.

One nice feature about WordPerfect for Windows is that it always remembers the last four files that you used. To see a listing of these files, click on the File option. You can open any of these four files by double-clicking on it. Figure 4–10 shows the four files that we used at the end of the File pull-down menu.

Figure 4–9
Open dialog box.

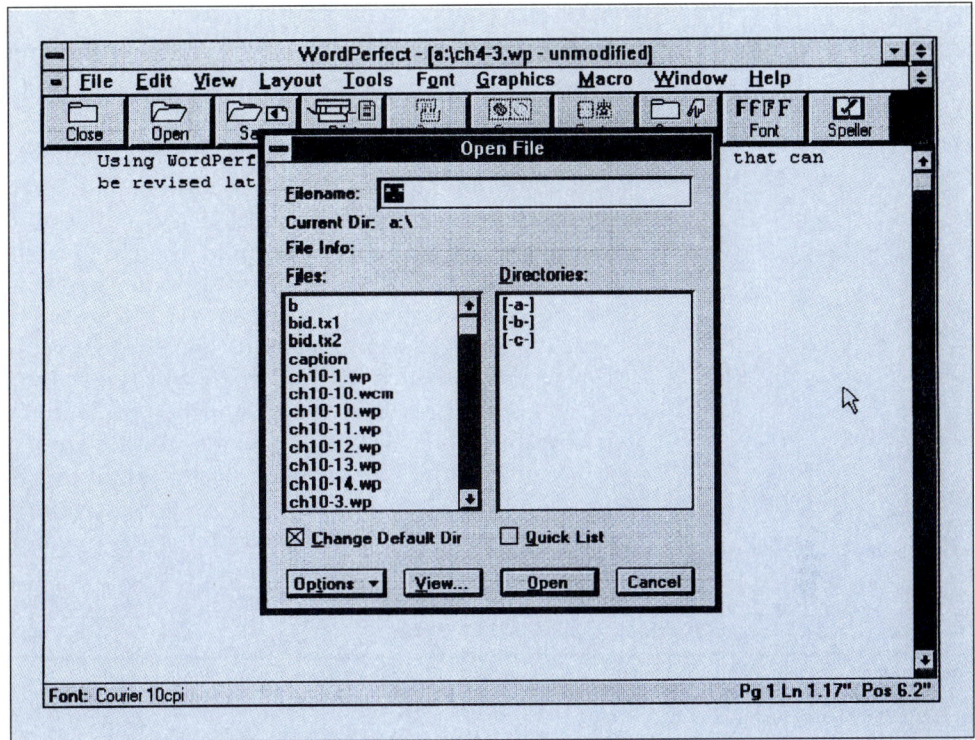

Figure 4–10
Listing of the four most recent files used.

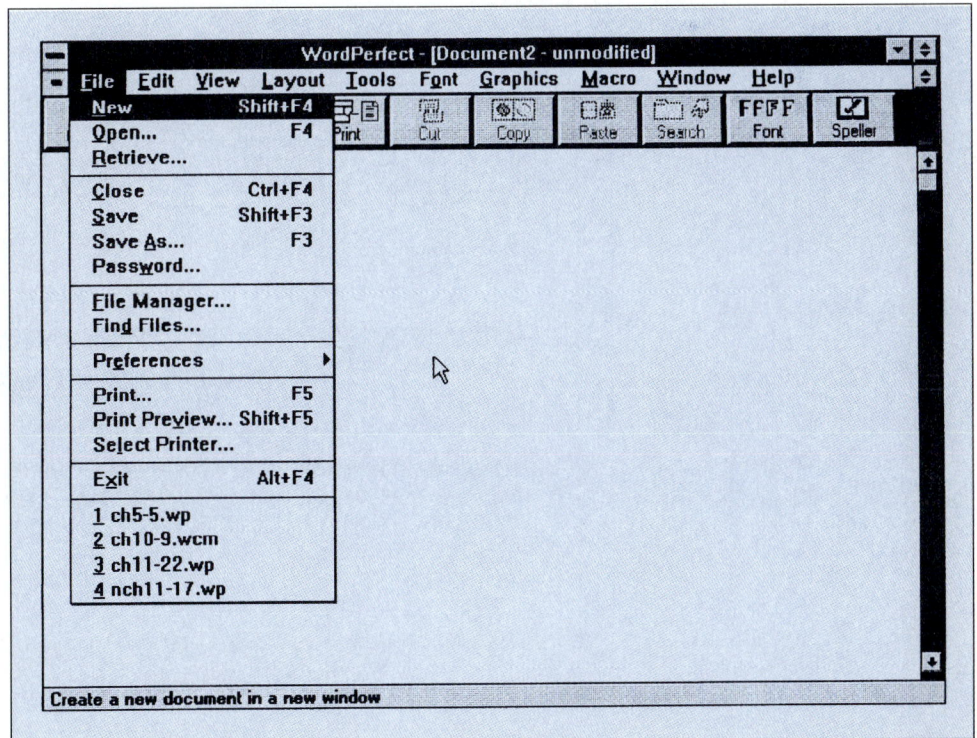

4–14   USING THE UNDO AND UNDELETE FEATURES

WordPerfect for Windows has an option that undoes the last action regardless of what the last action might have been. For example, if mistakenly you erase an entire page, select the Undo (Alt+Backspace) command from the Edit menu. Your text will be restored to its previous condition. The Undo option works with more complex tasks as well. For example, if you replace all occurrences of one word with another and you change your mind, the Undo feature easily reverses your action.

The Undelete (Alt+Shift+Backspace) feature allows you to **undelete** the last three deletions you made, so you can restore text or graphs that you mistakenly deleted. For example, let us say that first you delete one paragraph and then delete one sentence. If you decide to restore the paragraph, select the Undelete option from the Edit menu. You will be presented with a screen similar to the one in Figure 4–11. Click on Previous; the deleted paragraph will be highlighted. Click on Restore; the Restore button always restores the highlighted text. The Next button allows you to restore your deleted sentence. The Cancel button returns you to the document without restoring any deleted text.

4–15   USING THE BUTTON BAR

The basic tasks performed so far in this chapter can also be done by using the button bar near the top of the screen as follows:

■ To save your document click on the Save button. WordPerfect for Windows will display the Save As dialog box.

Figure 4–11
Undelete dialog box.

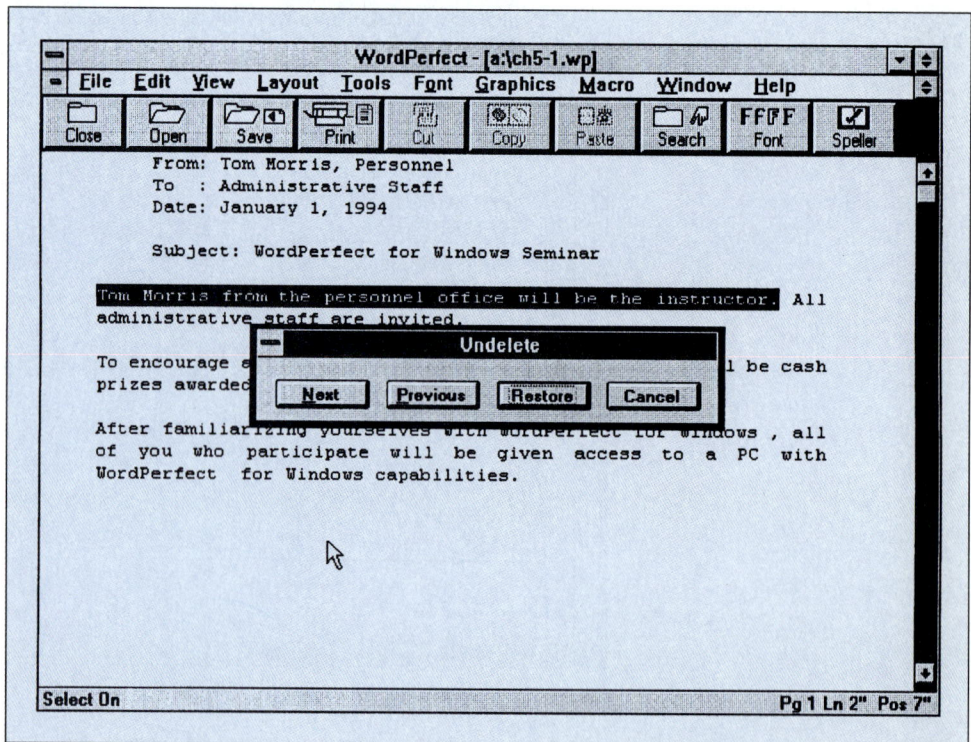

- To retrieve a saved document click on the Open button. WordPerfect for Windows will display the Open File dialog box.

- To clear the screen click on the Close button. If your file is saved, WordPerfect for Windows clears the screen. If your file is not saved, WordPerfect for Windows gives you Yes, No, and Cancel options from which you can choose.

- To print a document click on the Print button. You will be presented with a Print dialog box.

These are the buttons described in this chapter; we will discuss the button bar in detail in Chapter 7.

4–16 EXITING WORDPERFECT FOR WINDOWS

To exit WordPerfect for Windows select the Exit (Alt+F4) option from the File menu. If your file is already saved, you will return to Program Manager. If your file has not been saved yet, you will be presented with a dialog box similar to the one in Figure 4–12. If you select the Yes option, WordPerfect for Windows will present you with the Save As dialog box so you can specify a name. If you select No, your file will not be saved and you will return to the Program Manager. The Cancel option keeps you in the document.

Figure 4–12
Exit dialog box.

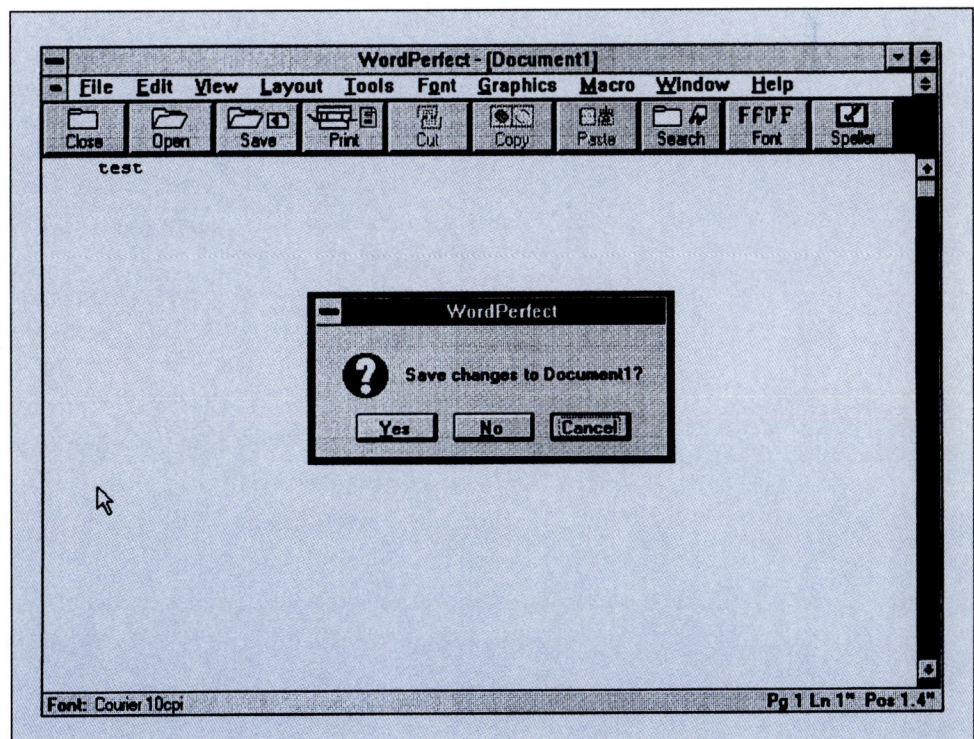

SUMMARY

This chapter provided a quick overview of WordPerfect for Windows. Different capabilities of WordPerfect for Windows were introduced. The entire word processing cycle of file creation, correction, saving, printing, retrieving, and exiting was described. In addition, the chapter explained two useful options: Undo and Undelete for restoring deleted text. The chapter also briefly described the WordPerfect for Windows button bar. In the next chapter, more advanced features of WordPerfect for Windows will be introduced.

REVIEW QUESTIONS

*These questions are answered in Appendix A.

1. What are three major advantages of a word processor compared with a typewriter?
2. How were word processing tasks performed 20 years ago?
*3. List five 5 major capabilities of WordPerfect for Windows.
4. What does the thesaurus feature do?
5. What kind of a system can run WordPerfect for Windows?
6. How do you start WordPerfect for Windows from the WordPerfect group?
7. How do you start WordPerfect from the File Manager?
*8. What is the button bar?
9. How do you indent a line?
10. How many lines can be displayed in the WordPerfect for Windows data entry window?
11. Explain soft returns and hard returns.
12. How do you move from one page to the next page?
13. How do you move from page 1 to page 24?
14. What is the shortcut key for the Go To command?
15. What are the functions of Page Down and Page Up?
*16. What is the default option for entering text when you are creating a document? What is the Typeover option?
17. How do you insert two blank lines in a document?
18. How do you delete an entire line? How do you delete an entire paragraph and an entire page?
*19. How do you save a WordPerfect for Windows document?
20. Why should you identify a drive and/or a directory when you save a file?
*21. How do you print a document?
22. Describe how to retrieve a saved file.
23. How can you undo your last action?
24. How can you undelete one of your last three deletions?
25. Explain how to exit from WordPerfect for Windows.
26. How do you clear the screen without saving?
*27. When you exit, does WordPerfect for Windows automatically save your file?
28. How many buttons are available on the button bar?
29. Describe how to save a file under two different names.

HANDS-ON EXPERIENCE

1. Start WordPerfect for Windows. How many options are available in the main menu? What is available under each menu choice? How do you select a menu option? How do you change your mind?

2. In a clear screen type the following document:

> Using WordPerfect for Windows, numerous documents can be created. The nice feature about the program is its user-friendliness. Mistakes can be easily corrected.

   Do the following:
   a. Replace the words "WordPerfect for Windows" with "a word processing program."
   b. Replace the word "mistakes" with "errors."
   c. Insert a blank line between lines 2 and 3.
   d. Save this file on your disk in drive A under EXCE1.WP.
   e. Using the default options, print this document.
   f. By using the Exit option from the File menu, exit WordPerfect for Windows.

3. Start WordPerfect for Windows again and type sections 4–2 through 4–4 of this chapter as one document. (You can also retrieve it from the disk provided; the file is named EXERCISE.WP). Do the following:
   a. Save your document under EXERCISE.WP.
   b. Print the document.
   c. Move the insertion point to the beginning of the first page.
   d. Move the insertion point to the beginning of the last page.
   e. Erase the first paragraph. By using the Undelete command, restore it.
   f. By using the Save As option, save this document under A:TEST.WP.
   g. Try all the arrow movement keys highlighted in Table 4–1.
   h. Try all the mouse actions highlighted in Table 4–2.
   i. Use the Close command to erase the screen.
   j. By using the Open button, retrieve the EXCE1.WP document.
   k. Add the following message to the end of this document:

> It is exciting to learn all these word processing features in this book. This knowledge should help you in writing reports and papers.

   l. Save this document under a new name called A:PRACTICE.WP.

4. Create a directory listing of drive C by double-clicking on the drive icon. Create a directory list of drive A.

5. Generate two printed copies of your current document. Open the EXERCISE.WP file and print only the second page.

KEY TERMS

Button bar	Microcomputer-based word processor	Status line
Data entry window		Typeover mode
Dedicated word processor	Pop-out icon	Undelete
Hard return	Printing a document	Word processor
Insert mode	Retrieving a file	Word wrap
Mainframe-based word processor	Saving a file	
	Soft return	

KEY COMMANDS

Alt+Backspace (to undo the last action)

Alt+Shift+Backspace (to invoke the Undelete dialog box)

Ctrl+F4 (to close a file and clear the screen)

Ctrl+G (to invoke the Go To dialog box)

F3 (to save a file, Save As)

F4 (to retrieve a file)

F5 (to print a file)

Insert (to activate the Typeover mode)

Shift+F3 (to save a document)

Table 4–1 (arrow movement commands)

Table 4–2 (mouse actions for moving insertion point around)

MISCONCEPTIONS AND SOLUTIONS

Misconception   After a WordPerfect for Windows session you try to terminate the session by turning the computer off.

> **Solution**   This may damage segments of your program. Always exit the program by selecting the Exit option from the File menu.

Misconception   Pressing the Backspace key to erase a character sometimes generates unpredictable results.

> **Solution**   Using Backspace in Insert Mode erases the characters to the left and closes the gap. In Typeover mode, using Backspace erases the characters to the left and inserts spaces. Before using the Backspace key, check the mode.

Misconception   Pressing the space bar to erase a character or to insert spaces creates unpredictable results.

> **Solution**   Check the mode first. In Typeover mode, the space bar erases the characters and leaves their place empty. In Insert mode the space bar inserts spaces and moves the existing text to the right.

ARE YOU READY TO MOVE ON?

Multiple Choice

1. Using a word processor, you can
   a. create text
   b. edit the document
   c. do cut and paste
   d. do all of the above
   e. do none of the above

2. Which of the following is *not* a component of WordPerfect for Windows?
   a. spreadsheet (similar to Lotus 1-2-3)
   b. full-feature word processor
   c. speller
   d. thesaurus
   e. all of the above

3. To start WordPerfect for Windows you can
   a. start it from the WordPerfect group
   b. start it from the File Manager using the Run command
   c. do both a and b
   d. start it by typing *Start* at the C> prompt
   e. do none of the above

4. The line at the bottom of the data entry window is called the
   a. comment line
   b. status line
   c. command line
   d. memo line
   e. control line

5. Which of the following commands is used to access the online help facility in Word-Perfect for Windows?
   a. File
   b. View
   c. Window
   d. Alt+F1
   e. Help

6. The F4 key can be used to
   a. stop text from printing once the Print command has been given
   b. exit from WordPerfect for Windows
   c. retrieve a file
   d. save a file
   e. do none of the above

7. Which function key is used to save a file on disk?
   a. F3
   b. Shift+F3
   c. either a or b
   d. F1
   e. Ctrl+F5

8. Under which menu can you find the Undelete option?
   a. File
   b. Edit
   c. View
   d. Layout
   e. Font

9. The shortcut for the Go To command is
   a. F1
   b. Ctrl+T
   c. F10
   d. Ctrl+G
   e. none of the above

10. Using the Print command
   a. you can print the current page
   b. you can print the entire document
   c. you can generate several copies
   d. you can print a document from disk
   e. you can do all of the above

True/False

1. The shortcut for the Undo command is Alt+Backspace.

2. WordPerfect for Windows has only one major component, the word processor, whereas other programs include other components such as speller, thesaurus, and merge.

3. WordPerfect for Windows provides two commands for saving a document.

4. The standard display for WordPerfect for Windows gives the cursor position in inches from the top margin and inches from the left margin.

5. When using WordPerfect for Windows, press the Enter key to create a soft return at the end of each line.

6. When you use the arrow keys to move around the document, WordPerfect for Windows does not keep track of the insertion point's relative position.

7. Pressing Ctrl+G will invoke the Go To dialog box.

8. When you exit WordPerfect for Windows, the program does not give you the option of saving your work.

9. Once you select the Exit option, and if your document is not saved, you cannot stay in the program; you cannot change your mind.

10. You can usually select an option from a WordPerfect for Windows menu by clicking on it.

ANSWERS

Multiple Choice		True/False	
1.	d	1.	T
2.	a	2.	F
3.	c	3.	T
4.	b	4.	T
5.	e	5.	F
6.	c	6.	F
7.	c	7.	T
8.	b	8.	F
9.	d	9.	F
10.	e	10.	T

Formatting and Emphasizing Text, Speller, and Thesaurus

5

5–1   INTRODUCTION

This chapter presents various commands for changing the appearance of your documents and emphasizing text. These commands include centering, underlining, boldfacing, case conversion, indenting, and line spacing. The chapter also explains the speller and the thesaurus—two features to help you generate documents that are more readable and that do not contain typographical errors.

5–2   FORMATTING TEXT

WordPerfect for Windows provides various commands for formatting text. This chapter introduces the most commonly used options.

5–2–1   Indenting Text Using the Tab Key

To indent a line, press the Tab key and start typing. To show this process, let us type a memo. Start WordPerfect for Windows. The status line reads:

```
Pg 1  Ln 1"  Pos 1"
```

Press the Tab key. (Pos is changed to 1.5".) Now type the following material and press the keys indicated.

From: Tom Morris, Personnel (press Enter)
(press Tab)
To: Administrative Staff (press Enter)
(press Tab)
Date: January 1, 1994 (press Enter)
(press Enter)
(press Tab)
Subject: WordPerfect for Windows Seminar (press Enter)
(press Enter)
WordPerfect for Windows is one of the most popular word processing programs on the market. The personnel office is planning to conduct a brief seminar on this package. (press Enter)
(press Enter)
Tom Morris from the personnel office will be the instructor. All administrative staff are invited. (press Enter)
(press Enter)
To encourage all of you to attend the seminar, there will be cash prizes awarded to three seminar participants. (press Enter)
(press Enter)
After familiarizing yourselves with WordPerfect for Windows, all of you who participate will be given access to a PC with WordPerfect for Windows capabilities. (press Enter)

At this point your screen should be similar to the one presented in Figure 5–1. We saved this document by using the Save As (F3) command. The name of this file is CH5-1.WP.

Figure 5–1
Sample memo.

```
From: Tom Morris, Personnel
To  : Administrative Staff
Date: January 1, 1994

Subject: WordPerfect for Windows Seminar

WordPerfect for Windows is one of the most popular word processing
programs on the market. The personnel office is planning to conduct
a brief seminar on this package.

Tom Morris from the personnel office will be the instructor. All
administrative staff are invited.

To encourage all of you to attend the seminar, there will be cash
prizes awarded to three of the participants.

After familiarizing yourselves with WordPerfect for Windows , all
of  you  who  participate  will  be  given  access  to  a  PC  with
WordPerfect  for Windows capabilities.
```

5–2–2

Indenting Text Using the Indent Option

The temporary indent command resets the left margin to the next tab stop. The default tab stops occur every 1/2 inch. A temporary indentation remains in effect until the Enter key is pressed. To access the temporary indent from the Layout menu, select Paragraph; then select Indent (F7). One situation in which you might use the temporary indent is in quoting material. The temporary indent draws attention to the quotation and clearly shows (by distinguishing it from the rest of your document) that the statement is not yours.

5–2–3

Blocking Data

A block can be any portion of your text; it can be a character, a word, a sentence, a paragraph, or even the entire document. When you **block** (or highlight or select) data, the blocked data stands out. In color monitors, the blocked data appears in a different foreground and background color than the rest of the text. When you block data, you can apply various commands to the block. For example, say you block a paragraph; by pressing the Del key you can erase the entire paragraph. Table 5–1 summarizes blocking techniques using the mouse.

You can also block data from a menu. To block a sentence, select Edit, then Select, then Sentence. Choose Edit, then Select, then Paragraph, to block a paragraph. To unblock data, click the left mouse button.

We will talk more about blocks of data in the next chapter.

Table 5–1
Blocking Techniques

To block a	Click
word	twice on the word.
sentence	three times anywhere in, or next to, the sentence.
paragraph	four times anywhere in, or next to, the paragraph.

5–2–4

Centering Text

There are many cases in which you have to **center** text. Let us say you are typing a brief report. The title of the report is Sales Report for Western Regions. To center this title, move the insertion point to the beginning of the line. From the Layout menu select Line (Shift+F9); then select Center (Shift+F7). You can also invoke the command first and then type the text. As soon as you invoke the command, the insertion point is moved to the center of the line. You can type the title with all capital letters by pressing the Caps Lock key. When you press the Caps Lock key, the Pos indicator in the status line at the bottom of the screen will be capitalized (POS). To disengage this key, press it again. The indicator at the bottom of the screen will now appear in lowercase letters (Pos).

5–2–5

Flush Right Command

By using the Layout, Line, Flush Right (Alt+F7) commands you can align text against the right-hand margin. Let's say you would like to use this feature on the following message: 1993 has been a good year for all of us. Follow these steps:

1. Block the message.
2. Select Layout, then Line, then Flush Right.

Your message will be aligned against the right margin. This feature is used mostly to position headings, footings, dates, and special messages. You can also invoke the flush right command first and then type your text.

5–2–6

Double Indent

Double indentation means indenting both left- and right-hand margins of a single paragraph. To do this, follow these steps:

1. Move the insertion point to the beginning of the paragraph.
2. Select Layout and Paragraph; then select Double Indent (Ctrl+Shift+F7).

Your paragraph is indented from both margins. When you press the Enter key, the text that you type from this point on will be displayed in the normal fashion.

5–2–7

Justifying Text Using the Menu

WordPerfect for Windows offers four different types of **justification**. You can format your documents with left, center, right, or full justification, thereby arranging text to fit your needs. To see this feature in action, start with a clear screen, and follow the steps outlined:

1. From the Layout menu select Justification.
2. From this menu select Left (Ctrl+L).
3. Type this text.

Using left justification, your text will be aligned along the left margin, and will have a flush left margin and a ragged right margin, as you can see in this example. Note that you can see the effects of left justification on the screen and on the printed output.

4. Press Enter twice to insert one blank line into the document.
5. From the Layout menu select Justification.
6. From this menu select Center (Ctrl+J).
7. Type the following text:

> Notice that when using center justification, your text will be centered between the left and right margins. Both the left and right margins will be ragged, as this example shows. Note that you can see the effect of center justification on the screen as well as the printed output.

8. Press Enter twice to insert one blank line into the document.
9. From the Layout menu select Justification.
10. From this menu select Right (Ctrl+R).
11. Type the following text:

> Notice that when you use right justification, the text appears on the right side of the screen as you type it, and is pushed to the left as more text is typed. This text is flush on the right side, and ragged on the left. Note that you can see the effect of right justification on the screen as well as on the printed output.

12. Press Enter twice to insert one blank line into the document.
13. From the Layout menu select Justification.
14. From this menu select Full (Ctrl+F).
15. Type the following text:

> Full justification means that both the right and the left sides of the text will be flush with their respective margins. Note that you can see the effect of full justification on the screen, as well as on the printed output.

16. From the File menu select the Print option.
17. Click on Print.

Take a look at the effects of the various types of justification. Each has its own distinct appearance. Your work should be similar to that in Figure 5–2.

5-2-8   Justifying Text Using the Ruler

Using the justification feature can even be easier than what we just discussed. If your text is already typed, block the text; then do the following:

1. Click on View; then click on Ruler (Alt+Shift+F3). A screen similar to Figure 5–3 will be displayed.
2. Click and hold the mouse button on the justification icon (the icon before the last) and select the Left, Right, Center, or Full option. The highlighted text will be justified accordingly.

The justification that you choose stays in effect until you select a different one. To leave the Ruler, click on View and on Ruler again.

Figure 5–2
Different types of justification.

```
Using left justification, your text will be aligned along the
left margin, and will have a flush left margin and a ragged right
margin, as you can see in this example. Note that you can see the
effects of left justification on the screen and on the printed
output.

        Notice that when using center justification, your text is
      centered between the left and right margins. Both the left and
       right margins will be ragged, as this example shows. Note that
       you can see the effect of center justification on the screen as
                   well as on the printed output.

Notice that when you use right justification, the text appears on
the right side of the screen as you type it, and is pushed to the
          left as more text is typed.  This text is flush on the right
    side, and ragged on the left.  Note that you can see the effect
       of right justification on the screen as well as on the printed
                                                            output.

Full justification means that both the right and left sides of the
text will be flush with their respective margins.  Note that you
can see the effect of full justification on the screen,as well as
on the printed output.
```

Figure 5–3
WordPerfect for Windows Ruler.

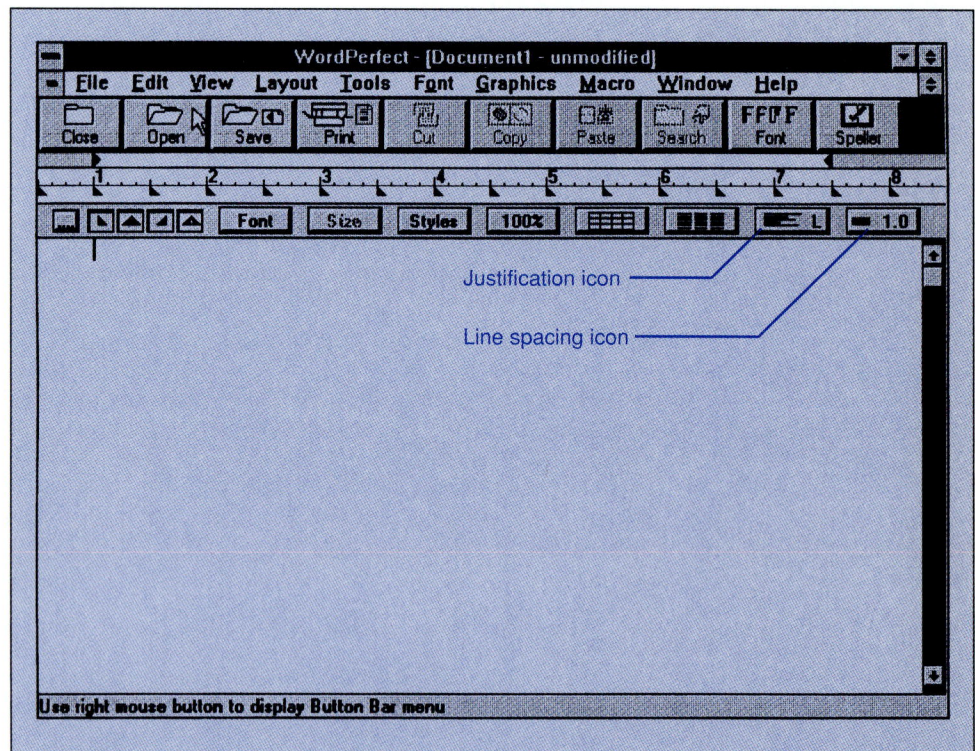

If you have not typed your text yet, select View, then Ruler; then click and hold the mouse button on the justification icon and select the desired justification format (e.g., Left, Right, Center, or Full). Type your text.

There are many other applications of the Ruler that we will talk about later in this book.

| 5–2–9 | ## Line Spacing |

By default, WordPerfect for Windows maintains your document in a single-space format, but you can change this format. One way to change the spacing format is through the Layout Line menu. Select Layout Line; then select Spacing. The line spacing dialog box will be displayed. Using the up- or down-arrow icon, select the desired format and click on OK. The spacing format will be changed from the present position of the insertion point to the end of text. You can block a section of the document then change the line spacing format for that section.

Line spacing can also be done by using the Ruler. As you can see in Figure 5–3, the last icon from the right is the line spacing icon. Click on this icon and select the desired spacing format.

| 5–2–10 | ## Revealing Codes |

When you generate a document, WordPerfect for Windows adds special formatting codes to it. Although you do not see these codes, WordPerfect for Windows keeps track of them internally. These formatting codes are essential when you are trying to change the appearance of your document.

Let us say in Figure 5–1 you would like to combine the first two paragraphs. To do so you have to eliminate certain codes. Move the insertion point to the blank line between the two paragraphs. To reveal the formatting codes select Reveal Codes (Alt+F3) from the View menu. A screen similar to the one shown in Figure 5–4 will be displayed. Notice that the screen is split horizontally into two screens. The screens are separated by a solid double-line. The insertion point is in the same position in both screens. In the lower screen soft returns are represented by [SRt] and hard returns by [HRt]. To connect the two paragraphs you

Figure 5–4
Reveal codes for Figure 5–1.

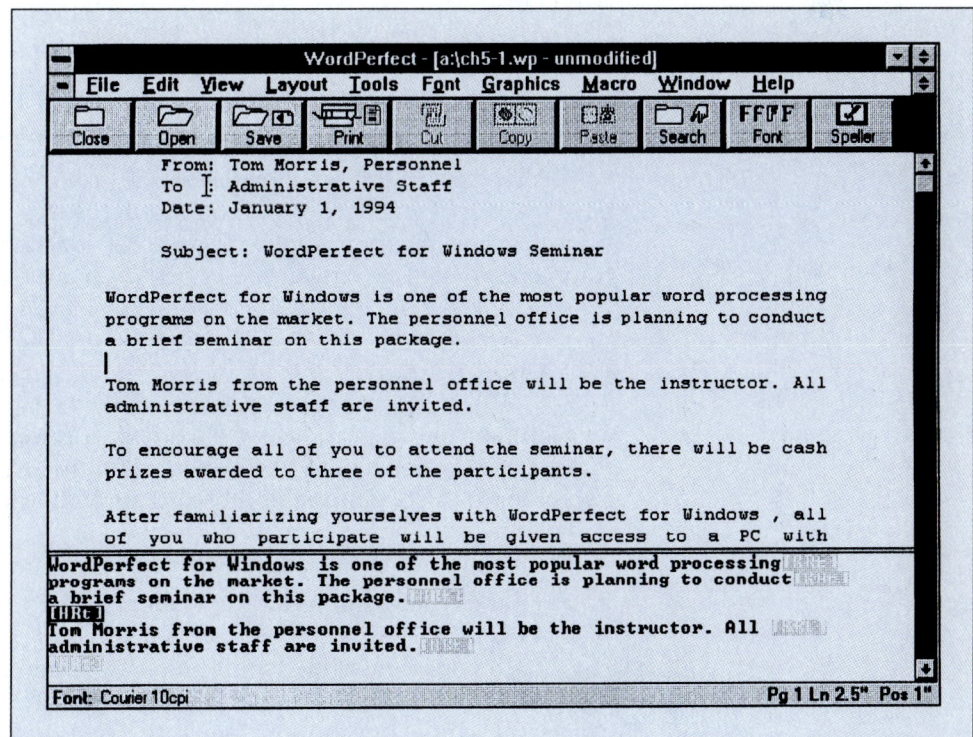

Figure 5–5
Two paragraphs are connected.

```
          From: Tom Morris, Personnel
          To  : Administrative Staff
          Date: January 1, 1994

          Subject: WordPerfect for Windows Seminar

WordPerfect for Windows is one of the most popular word processing
programs on the market. The personnel office is planning to conduct
a brief seminar on this package. Tom Morris from the personnel
office will be the instructor. All  administrative staff are
invited.

To encourage all of you to attend the seminar, there will be cash
prizes awarded to three of the participants.

After familiarizing yourselves with WordPerfect for Windows , all
of you who participate will be given access to a PC with
WordPerfect  for Windows capabilities.
```

must eliminate both of the hard returns. Move the insertion point to the first [HRt] and press the Del key to delete the HRt on the line between paragraphs. Then move the insertion point to the hard return in the first paragraph and press the Del key. The two paragraphs will be connected. To leave the Reveal Codes screen click on View then on Reveal Codes (Alt+F3) again. As you see in Figure 5–5, the first two paragraphs are connected. Now your memo includes only three paragraphs.

To split the two paragraphs again, move the insertion point to the space right after the period at the end of the first sentence and press the Enter key twice.

Other commonly used formatting codes are [Center] for centering text; [Bold On] for boldfacing text [Bold Off]; and [Und On] for underlining text [Und Off].

5–3   EMPHASIZING TEXT

WordPerfect for Windows provides several commands for emphasizing text. The next few pages introduce the commonly used commands, which are accessed from the Font menu. A **font** is a group of letters, numbers, and symbols with a common typeface. Fonts are described by name, weight, and size, for example, Courier Bold 12 pt. We will discuss fonts in Chapter 11.

5–3–1   Underlining Text

To highlight the importance of a word or a series of words, you may **underline** them. Let's say you would like to underline the word "Western." Move the insertion point to the beginning of the word and follow these steps:

1. Block the word by clicking and dragging the mouse pointer.
2. From the Font menu select the Underline (Ctrl+U) option.

To underline while typing the text, either select the Font then Underline options, or press the Ctrl+U key combination first and then type your text. To cancel the Underline option, block the text and press Ctrl+U once again or select Underline from the Font menu.

5–3–2   ## Italicizing Text

To make text **italic** select Font; then select Italic (Ctrl+I). To cancel the italic option, select the command again.

5–3–3   ## Boldfacing Text

The **boldface** feature creates words highlighted in dark print. Various printers perform boldfacing differently. Let us say you want to boldface the phrase "past three years." Do the following:

1. From the Font menu select Bold (Ctrl+B).
2. Type the phrase.

If the phrase is already typed, block the phrase and invoke the Bold command.

5–3–4   ## Combining Commands

Formatting commands can be combined. For example, you can combine the Bold and Underline commands. To do so, you must turn on both features; it does not matter which feature is turned on first. Let us say you would like to boldface and underline the phrase "new advertising campaign." Follow these steps:

1. Block the phrase.
2. Select Font; then select Underline.
3. Select Font; then select Bold.

When you select a formatting feature, it stays in effect until you disable it by selecting it again. However, if you use the blocking feature and apply a formatting feature, the formatting feature is disabled as soon as the block is no longer highlighted.

5–3–5   ## Subscript and Superscript

Sometimes scientific reports require superscript (text above the line) or subscript (text below the line).
To subscript text, select Font; then select the Subscript option. After typing the text, select the command again to disable it. To superscript text, select Font; then select the Superscript option. After typing the text, select the command again to disable it. If the text is already typed, block it first, then apply the command.

5–3–6   ## Other Text Formatting Commands

The Font menu has other text formatting commands. One of the popular ones is the Double Underline command, which can be used to further emphasize a point by drawing two lines under the text.
Redline and Strikeout commands have specific applications. Redlined text stands out from the rest of the document by appearing dimmed on the screen. Use this feature to draw attention to a specific part of a text. Strikeout is appropriate for editorial functions such as deleting a portion of text. WordPerfect

Figure 5–6
Examples of emphasized text.

```
This is an example of Bold

This is an example of Italic

This is an example of Underline

This is an example of Double Underline

This is an example of Redline

This is an example of Strikeout

This is an example of Subscript--X₁+X₂=22

This is an example of Superscript--2⁸=8
```

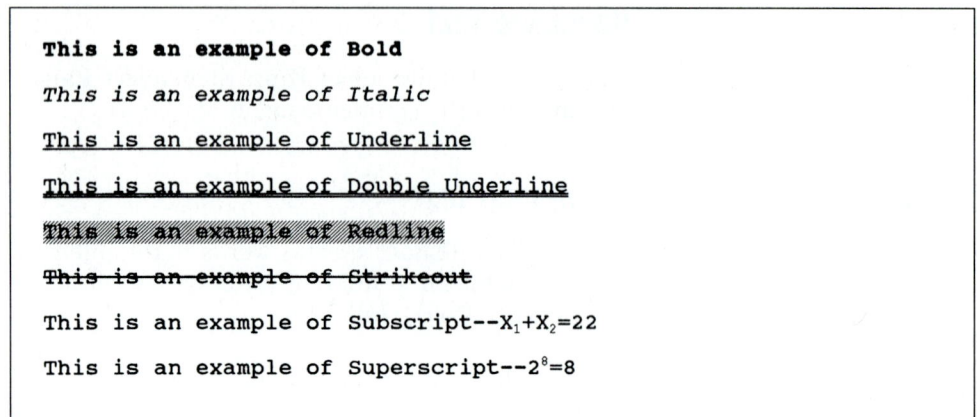

for Windows places a series of hyphens through the strikeout text. Figure 5–6 presents examples of various formatting features.

5–3–7

Case Conversion Command

To change a phrase from uppercase to lowercase or vice versa, WordPerfect for Windows provides a simple **case conversion** feature. Let us say you would like to change this message to lowercase letters: SALES REPORT FOR WESTERN REGIONS. Follow these steps:

1. Block the message.
2. From the Edit menu select the Convert Case option. The following menu will be displayed:

```
Uppercase
Lowercase
```

3. Select the Lowercase option.

At this point the message will be:

```
sales report for western regions
```

5–4   WHAT IS THE SPELLER?

The **speller** component of WordPerfect for Windows checks all the words in a document against a built-in dictionary or a supplemental dictionary that you specify. If a misspelled word is found, it is highlighted. You can change the word, leave it as it is, or add it to the dictionary.

Different word processing programs have different spellers. The level of sophistication varies with the package. Be aware, however, that a speller cannot catch all mistakes. Many times a word is spelled correctly but it is used in the wrong context. For example, "Too students dropped the computer class." The word "too" will not be highlighted by the speller, but it is a misspelled word in this context.

5–4–1   Getting the Speller Started

The document presented in Figure 5–7 contains several intentional mistakes. Let's correct these mistakes using the speller.

To start the speller, from the Tools menu select the Speller (Ctrl+F1) option. You will be presented with a screen similar to the one in Figure 5–8. Refer to options at the lower right as you read the following explanation.

The Close button at the lower right allows you to leave the speller.

The Start button instructs the speller to start checking the spellings. The contents of this button may change to Resume or Replace. Clicking the Resume

Figure 5–7
Document with misspellings.

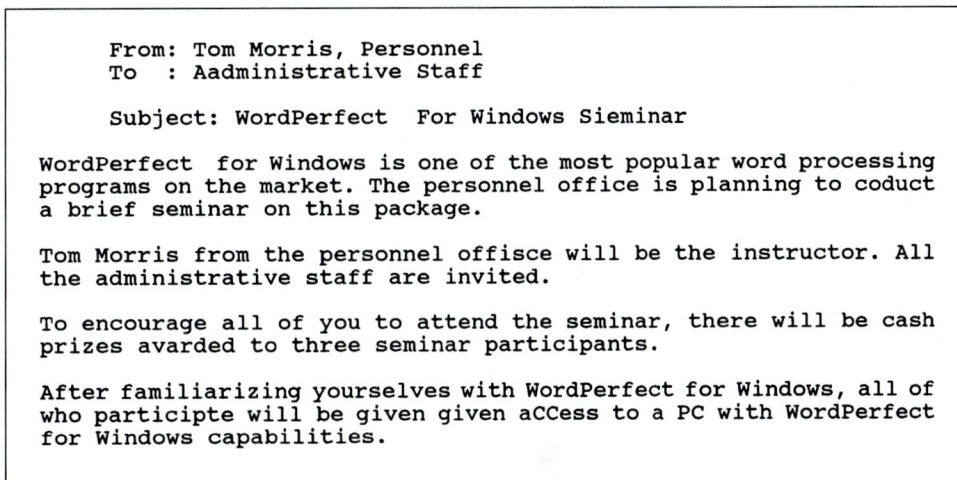

```
From: Tom Morris, Personnel
To  : Aadministrative Staff

Subject: WordPerfect  For Windows Sieminar

WordPerfect  for Windows is one of the most popular word processing
programs on the market. The personnel office is planning to coduct
a brief seminar on this package.

Tom Morris from the personnel offisce will be the instructor. All
the administrative staff are invited.

To encourage all of you to attend the seminar, there will be cash
prizes avarded to three seminar participants.

After familiarizing yourselves with WordPerfect for Windows, all of
who participte will be given given aCCess to a PC with WordPerfect
for Windows capabilities.
```

Figure 5–8
Speller starting menu.

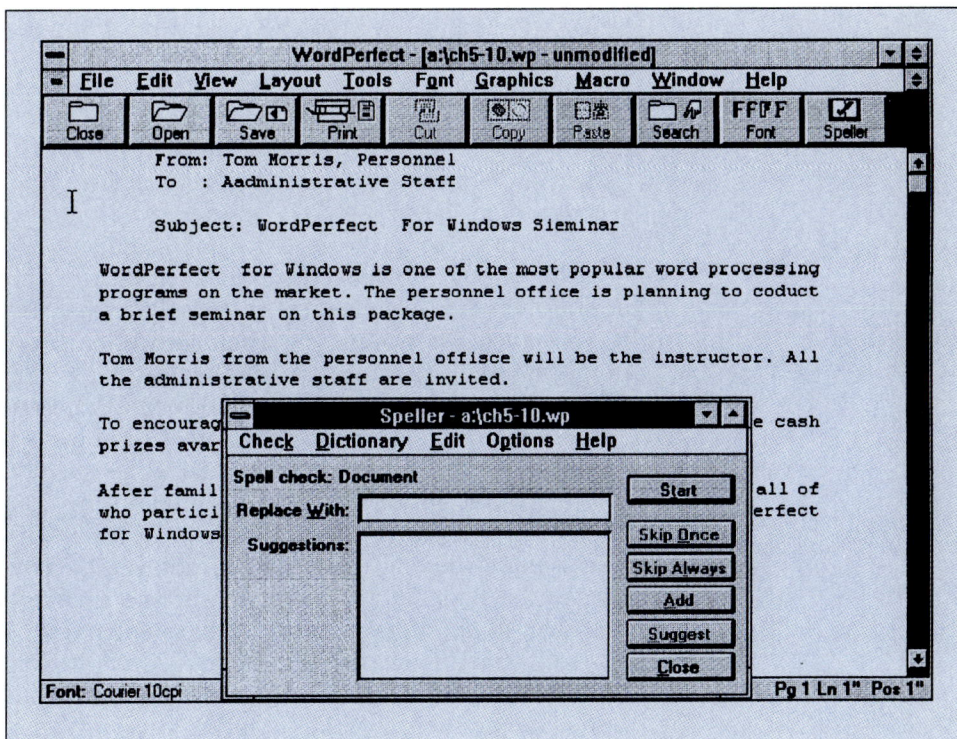

button resumes the spell checking process. The function of the Replace button is to replace the highlighted misspelled word in the document with the option that you choose from the suggestions box.

The Skip Always button instructs the speller to ignore other occurrences of this particular word throughout this document. For example, if you have used a name in a document several times, selecting Skip Always alerts the speller that this is a correct spelling, although it is not in the dictionary, and that it can be ignored.

The Skip Once button ignores the highlighted word once. If the word is encountered again, it will be highlighted.

The Add button allows you to add a particular word to the dictionary. For example, if you add your name to the dictionary, it will not be highlighted from this point on as a spelling error.

The Suggest button instructs the speller to provide alternative spelling suggestions from which you can select the correct spelling. Type a word in the Replace With box and click on the Suggest button to ask for alternative spellings.

The Check default option (in the menu bar) refers to the entire document. However, you can click on the Check option to change it to one of these options: Word, To End of Document (from the insertion point), Page, To End of Page, or Selected Text.

5–4–2   Going Through the Spell Checking Process

While the document shown in Figure 5–7 is displayed on the screen (you can load it from the disk provided), select the Speller option from the Tools menu. You will see a screen similar to the one in Figure 5–8.

Click on Start. As soon as you do this, the Start option is changed to Replace and the first mistake, which is "Aadministrative," is highlighted. The Suggestions box displays a correct spelling. To replace the mistake with this option either press Enter, or click on the Replace button, or double-click on the correct spelling in the Suggestions box.

Now the second typo, which is "Sieminar," is displayed. This time Word-Perfect for Windows gives you two options. Double-click on the correct option.

The third typo is "Coduct." Double-click on the correct spelling. The fourth typo is "offisce." Double-click on the correct spelling. The next typo is "avarded." This time the speller gives you three options. Double-click on the correct spelling. The next typo is "participte." Double-click on the correct spelling.

At this point the speller displays a dialog box similar to the one in Figure 5–9. Because it has encountered a duplicate word ("given"), you have three options: (1) You can click on Disable Checking. If you do this, WordPerfect for Windows will not prompt you when it encounters duplicate words for the remainder of the spell checking session. For the time being, do *not* select this option. (2) You can select the Continue option to continue and leave the second word. (3) You can select the Delete 2nd option to eliminate the second occurrence of the duplicate word. This is the option that we selected.

At this point you will be presented with a dialog box similar to the one in Figure 5–10. Note in the line before the last we intentionally typed "aCCess." This is not a spelling error, but it is not standard writing either. The WordPerfect for Windows speller is capable of finding such problems. To make this option available, in the Options menu of the speller enable the Irregular Capitalization option. Click on the Replace button. This will change "aCCess" to "ACCESS." Now you will see a dialog box similar to the one in Figure 5–11. Click on Yes to terminate the spell checking process.

Figure 5–9
Duplicate words dialog box.

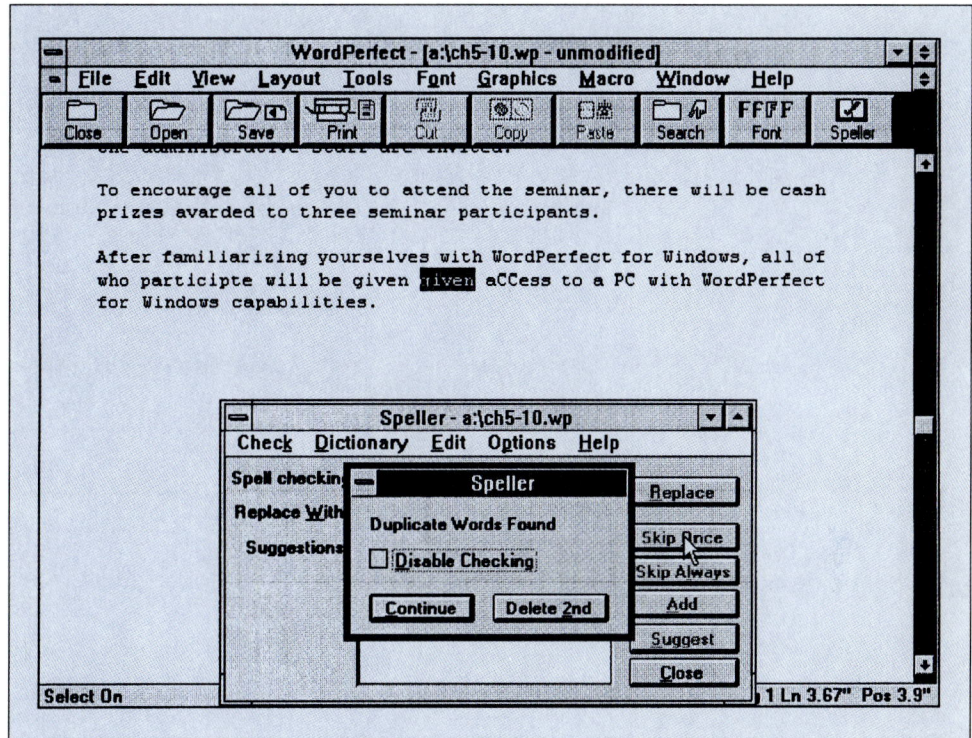

Figure 5–10
Irregular capitalization dialog box.

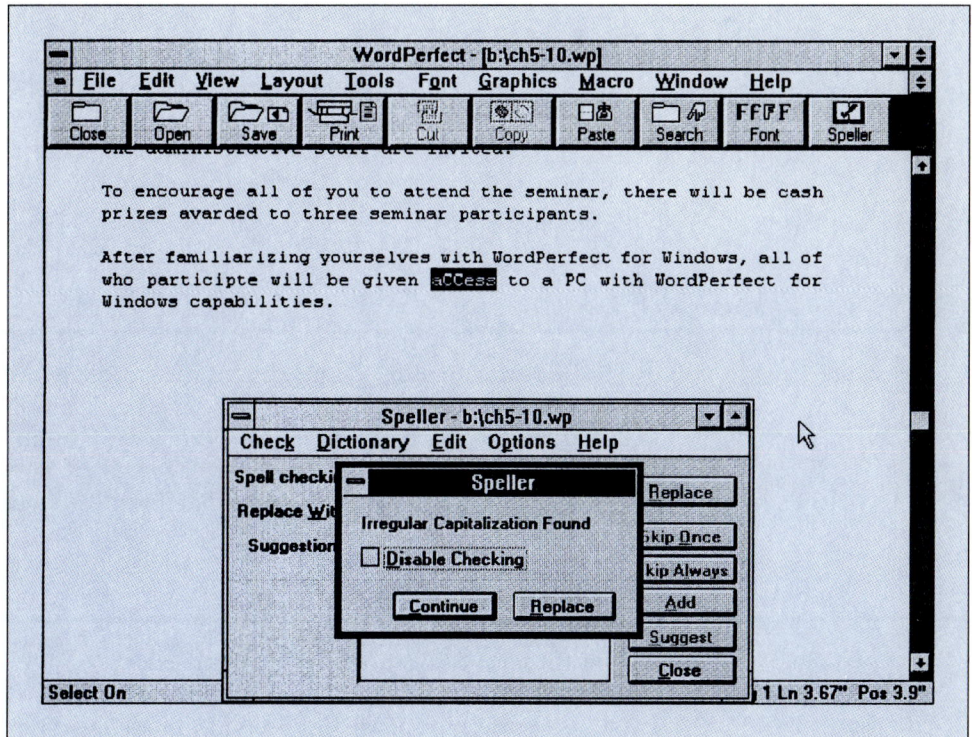

Figure 5–11
Speller completion box.

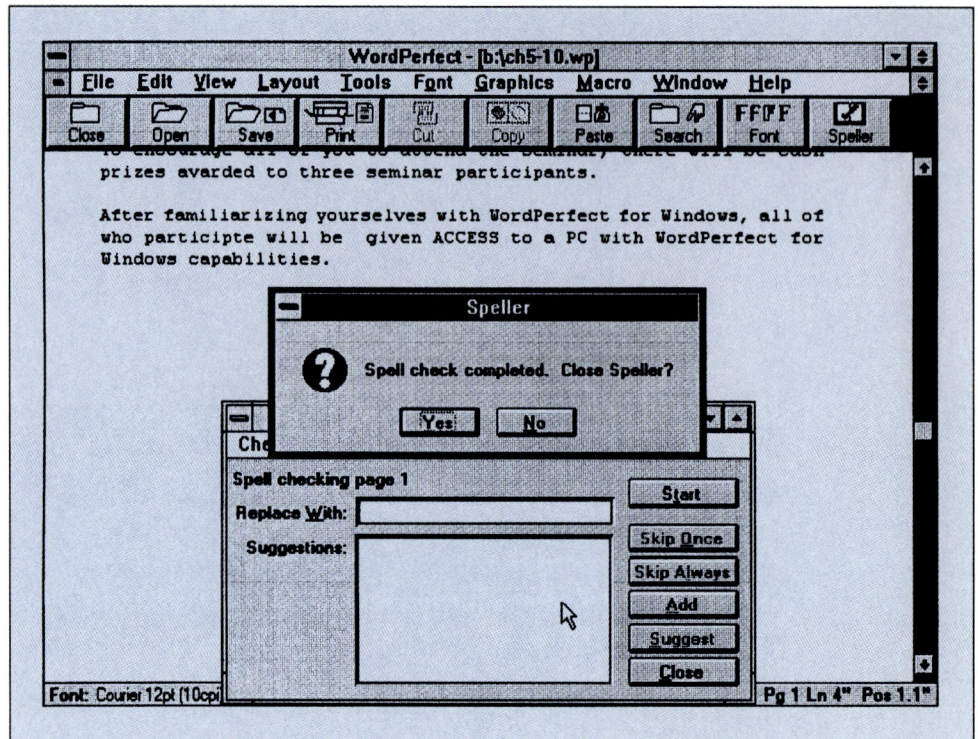

5–4–3   Creating Your Own Dictionary

If a word is not included in the WordPerfect for Windows dictionary, it will always be highlighted as a misspelled word (e.g., your name or the name of a company). To avoid this, you can add specific words to the dictionary by selecting the Add option from the Speller dialog box.

The added word(s) will be stored in a file named WP{WP}US.LEX. You can view the contents of this file and edit it just like any other file. Open the file by using the Open command. After editing, save it by using the Save command.

5–5   COUNTING WORDS

The Tools menu allows you to **count the words** in a document. Let us say you have been asked to write an abstract that can be at most 150 words. The Word Count option of WordPerfect for Windows can come to your rescue. From the Tools menu select the Word Count option. A message will display how many words you have in the document. This option told us that Figure 5–7 has 99 words.

5–6   WHAT IS THE THESAURUS?

The **thesaurus** component of WordPerfect for Windows provides a list of synonyms and antonyms for various words. This feature can help you to create documents that are more meaningful and readable. The word you look up (called the headword) is displayed in the Word box. The suggestions from the thesaurus are displayed as nouns (n), verbs (v), adjectives (a), and antonyms (ant).

To start the thesaurus component of WordPerfect for Windows, click on the Thesaurus (Alt+F1) option in the Tools menu. You will be presented with a screen similar to the one presented in Figure 5–12.

Figure 5–12
Thesaurus dialog box.

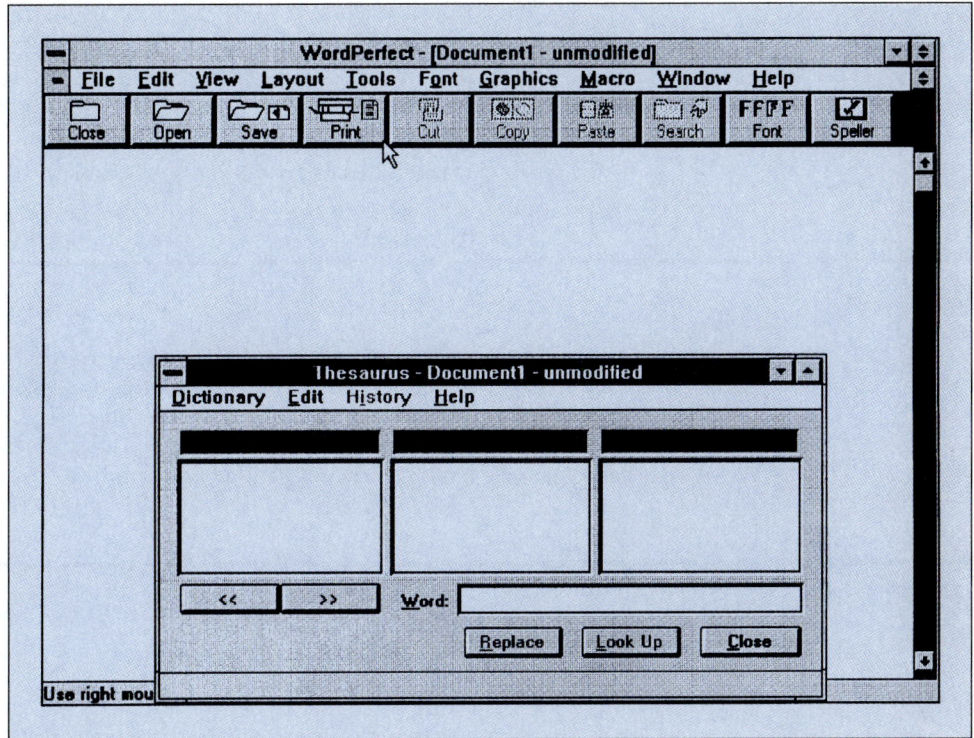

As an example, type the word "explain" in the Word box. Then click on the Look Up button. You will be presented with a screen similar to the one in Figure 5–13. Scroll through the options by using the up or down arrow to see additional choices. Click on the Replace button to replace the highlighted word by one of the options provided by the thesaurus.

Figure 5–13
Options provided by the thesaurus for the word "explain."

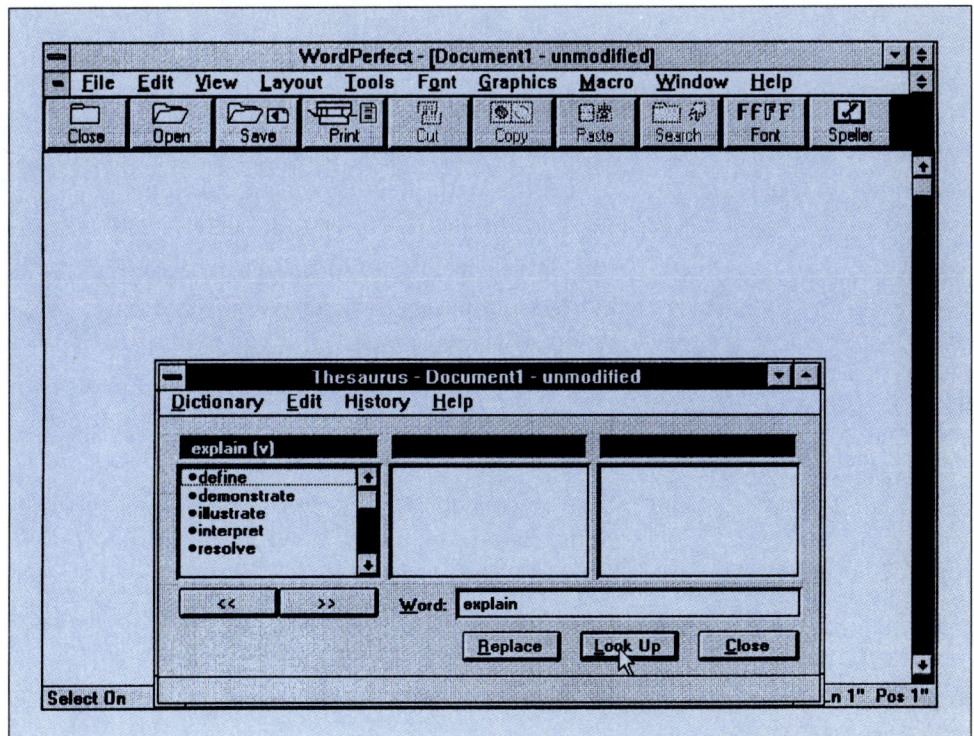

If you double-click on one of the options in the first column of the Thesaurus dialog box, additional words will be displayed for that option in the second column. And if you double-click on one of the options in the second column of the Thesaurus dialog box, additional options will be displayed on the third column.

To exit the Thesaurus dialog box, click on the Close button.

SUMMARY

This chapter introduced commands for enhancing the appearance of documents. The commands allow you to justify, center, boldface, use uppercase and lowercase letters, add subscript and superscript, and change text in other ways. The chapter also described the speller and the thesaurus. These two features of WordPerfect for Windows can assist you in creating documents that do not include typographical errors and that are more readable.

REVIEW QUESTIONS

*These questions are answered in Appendix A.

*1. How do you center a line?

2. Explain how to underline a word and a sentence.

3. Why might you boldface a word? How do you do this?

4. Can the Underline and Bold commands be combined? Is there any priority of one command over the other?

*5. How do you make text a subscript or a superscript?

6. How do you block data?

7. What is the Flush Right command? What are some applications of this command?

8. Give some applications of the Indent option. What is the difference between the Indent option and the Tab key?

9. How do you make text italic?

10. What is double indent? How do you double indent a paragraph?

*11. How can you change from lowercase to uppercase letters? Can all uppercase characters be replaced with lowercase characters?

12. How can you make text flush right?

13. How many different ways can text be justified?

14. Describe how to justify text using the Ruler.

15. How can you change text spacing?

16. Can you only change spacing of a paragraph?

17. What is the speller?

*18. How do you start the speller?

19. Can you add a word to the WordPerfect for Windows dictionary?

20. What is the thesaurus?

21. Explain the process of counting words in a document. What are some of the applications of counting words?

*22. How do you start the thesaurus?

23. How do you ask for more options on one of the choices displayed by the thesaurus?

HANDS ON EXPERIENCE

1. Start WordPerfect for Windows. Begin with a blank screen. Do the following:
   a. Center the following line:

      In 1995 our company will celebrate its 50th anniversary.

   b. Boldface 1995.
   c. Boldface and underline "its 50th."
   d. Make the following message flush right:

      It will be fun to go to Disneyland!

   e. Indent the following paragraph:

      In 50 years of their existence computers have grown beyond imagination. A $1000 computer today has as much power as a million dollar computer of 50 years ago.

   f. Double indent the above paragraph.
   g. Convert "I am happy" to uppercase letters.

2. Type the word "companeon" in a blank screen; start the speller. Find the correct spelling for this word.

3. Start the thesaurus. Generate all the synonyms for the word "glory." Choose the best replacement.

4. Retrieve the EXERCISE.WP document that you created in the last chapter. Do the following:
   a. By using the speller, determine if there are any typos in the document.
   b. Underline the first three lines of the document.
   c. Boldface the last three lines of the document.
   d. Boldface and underline the fifth line of the document.
   e. Make the last line of the document flush right.
   f. Convert the first paragraph to all uppercase letters.
   g. Count all the words in the document.

5. Using the Subscript option, enter the following equations:

   $$X_1+X_2+X_3+X_4=a$$
   $$X_1-X_2+2X_3-X_4=b$$
   $$2X_1+X_2-X_3+2X_4=c$$
   $$X_1+3X_2+5X_3-2X_4=d$$

6. Using the superscript option, enter the following equations:

   $$2^3 + 2^2 = 12$$
   $$2^5 + 2^4 = 48$$

KEY TERMS

Blocking	Counting words	Speller
Boldfacing	Font	Thesaurus
Case conversion	Italicizing	Underlining
Centering	Justification	

KEY COMMANDS

Alt+Shift+F3 (to display the Ruler)

Blocking Techniques (see Table 5–1)

Alt+F1 (to start the thesaurus)

Alt+F3 (to reveal formatting codes)

Alt+F7 (to make text flush Right)

Ctrl+B (to boldface text)

Ctrl+F (to full justify text)

Ctrl+F1 (to start the speller)

Ctrl+J (to center justify text)

Ctrl+I (to italicize text)

Ctrl+L (to left justify text)

Ctrl+R (to right justify text)

Ctrl+U (to underline text)

Ctrl+Shift+F7 (to double indent text)

F3 (Save As) (to Save a Document)

F7 (to temporarily indent text)

Shift+F7 (to Center text)

Shift+F9 (to invoke the Line menu)

MISCONCEPTIONS AND SOLUTIONS

Misconception   You apply a particular attribute, such as boldface, to a portion of your document and later decide that's not what you want.

  Solution   You can delete the unwanted attribute by using the Reveal Code options. Delete the code representing the unwanted attribute.

Misconception   You are in the spell checking process in a document and you discover that you left out a portion of text. You decide to get out of the speller, type the missing text, and restart the speller.

  Solution   Even if you are in the middle of a spell checking process, you can click anywhere inside the document and make changes or type new text. When you are finished, click the Resume button in the Speller dialog box to continue.

Misconception   After the spell checking process is complete, you notice irregular cases or numbers or duplicate words. But WordPerfect for Windows did not notify you about these problems.

  Solution   Check the Options menu in the Speller dialog box. Words with Numbers, Duplicate Words, or Irregular Capitalization must be enabled (must have a check mark). If they are not enabled, Speller will not signal the situations mentioned.

Misconception   You correspond with some individuals and companies on a regular basis. The speller always signals these names as typing errors.

  Solution   Use the Add option in the Speller dialog box to add these names to the dictionary. By doing this, you increase the efficiency of the spell checking process.

ARE YOU READY TO MOVE ON?

Multiple Choice

1. To center text, press
   a. F7
   b. Alt+F2
   c. Shift+F7
   d. F10
   e. F5

2. To underline text, press
   a. Ctrl+U
   b. F10
   c. Shift+F1
   d. Shift+F5
   e. Shift+F7

3. Flush right means
   a. text is aligned against the left margin
   b. text is aligned against the right margin
   c. text is centered on the line
   d. text is centered on the page
   e. text has passed the spell check

4. Ctrl+Shift+F7 is used to
   a. start a new paragraph, similar to the Tab key
   b. insert a hard page break
   c. indent the left margin only
   d. indent both the left and right margins
   e. underline the text

5. Under which menu can you find the Convert Case command?
   a. Font
   b. Tools
   c. Layout
   d. View
   e. Edit

6. After the speller has identified a potentially misspelled word, you have the option to
   a. replace the word with one of the choices provided
   b. skip the word, leaving it in its current form
   c. add the word to your personal dictionary
   d. edit the word yourself
   e. do all of the above

7. Which menu should you use to count the number of words in a document?
   a. File
   b. Edit
   c. Tools
   d. View
   e. Layout

8. The F7 key is used to
   a. start a new paragraph, similar to the Tab key
   b. insert a hard page break
   c. indent the left margin only
   d. indent both the left and right margins
   e. underline the text

9. To find a substitute word to make your document more meaningful and readable, you would probably choose the
   a. thesaurus
   b. speller
   c. replace feature
   d. switch feature
   e. none of the above

10. WordPerfect for Windows default tab stops are every
    a. 2 inches
    b. 1/2 inch
    c. 3 spaces

    d. 1 inch
    e. none of the above

True/False

1. The Tab key can be used to indent a line.
2. To underline text that you have already typed, you must block the text before pressing Ctrl+U.
3. You cannot boldface text you have already typed; you must delete it first and press Ctrl+B before typing the text.
4. Boldface and Underline commands cannot be combined.
5. The Flush Right command is accessed through the Layout Line menu.
6. To indent only the left margin two tab stops, press F7 twice.
7. The speller will find all spelling and grammar mistakes.
8. The thesaurus suggests only synonyms (same meaning); it does not suggest antonyms (opposite meaning).
9. When the Caps Lock key is activated, the cursor position indicator appears as POS.
10. The Subscript and Superscript options are under the Edit menu.

ANSWERS

Multiple Choice		True/False	
1.	c	1.	T
2.	a	2.	T
3.	b	3.	F
4.	d	4.	F
5.	e	5.	T
6.	e	6.	T
7.	c	7.	F
8.	c	8.	F
9.	a	9.	T
10.	b	10.	F

Search and Replace Operations, Tabs, Blocks of Data, and the Help Facility

6

6–1   INTRODUCTION

This chapter concentrates on several useful features of WordPerfect for Windows. First, the process of searching and replacing text and codes is explained. Next, the Ruler for establishing tabs and setting margins is examined. In the discussion on working with blocks of data, the following operations are reviewed: cutting, copying, deleting, saving, and printing. The chapter concludes with a description on the help facility.

6–2   SEARCHING FOR TEXT

In many instances you might be interested in locating a particular word or phrase in your document. You might also be interested in locating a formatting code such as bold, italic, and so forth. The **search** facility of WordPerfect for Windows enables you to accomplish these actions and more. Let us walk through an example.

Type or retrieve the sample document presented in Figure 6–1. Move the insertion point to the beginning of the document. To start the search facility, select Search (F2) from the Edit menu. You will be presented with the Search dialog box as shown in Figure 6–2. In the Search For box, type your desired text, for example, *Tom Morris.* Click on the Search button and WordPerfect for Windows immediately locates the *first* occurrence of the specified text, in this case Tom Morris.

By default, WordPerfect for Windows searches in a forward manner starting from the position of the insertion point. The limit of the size of the phrase that you can search for is 82 characters. To conduct a backward search, click on the Forward pop-out menu and select the Backward option. At this point the search will be conducted from the present position of the insertion point to the beginning of the document.

After WordPerfect for Windows locates the first occurrence of the text, to see the other occurrences one by one, you must select the Search Next (Shift+F2) option from the Edit menu. The Search Previous (Alt+F2) option from the Edit menu allows you to search for previous occurrences of the word or phrase from the present position of the insertion point.

As you can see in Figure 6–2, WordPerfect for Windows also allows you to search for codes. For example, you can search for bold or italic codes. To do this in Figure 6–2 click on Codes. You will be presented with a screen similar to the

Figure 6–1
Sample document.

```
              From: Tom Morris, Personnel
              To  : Administrative Staff
              Date: January 1, 1994

              Subject: WordPerfect  for Windows Seminar

WordPerfect for Windows is one of the most popular word processing
programs on the market. The personnel office is planning to conduct
a brief seminar on this package.

Tom Morris from the personnel office will be the instructor. All
administrative staff are invited.

To encourage all of you to attend the seminar, there will be cash
prizes awarded to three of the participants.

After familiarizing yourselves with WordPerfect for Windows , all
of you who  participate will be given access to a PC with
WordPerfect for Windows  capabilities.
```

one in Figure 6–3. The codes are listed in alphabetical order. You can scroll through this box until you find the desired code, then double-click on it. This code will then be displayed in the Search For box. Now click on the Search button to locate the next occurrence of this code in your document.

Figure 6–2
Search dialog box.

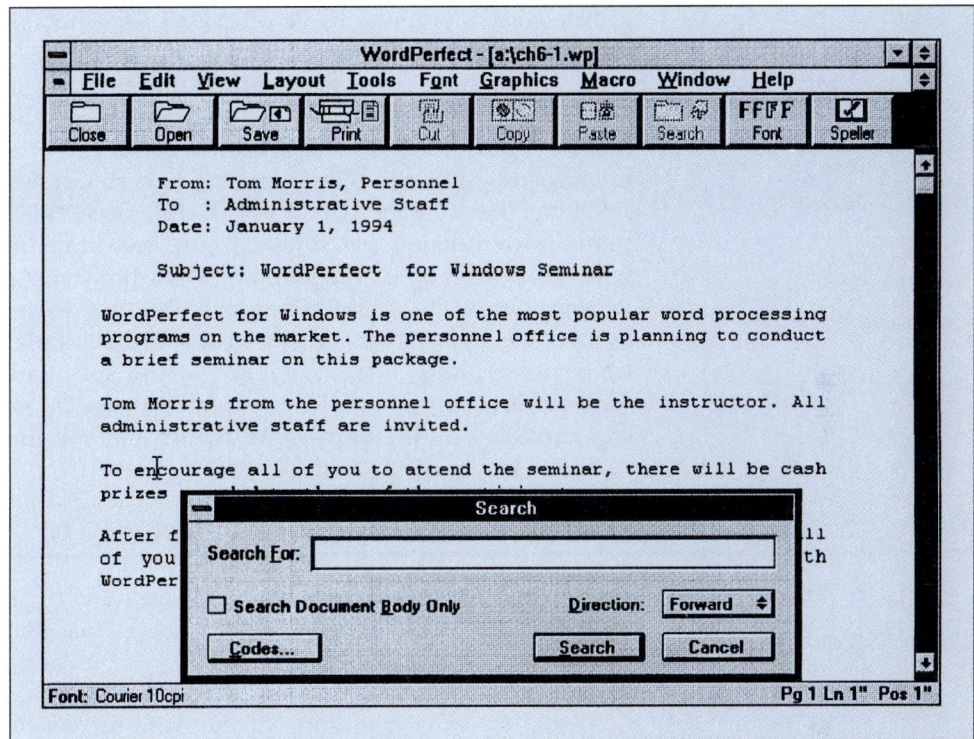

Figure 6–3
Search and Codes dialog boxes.

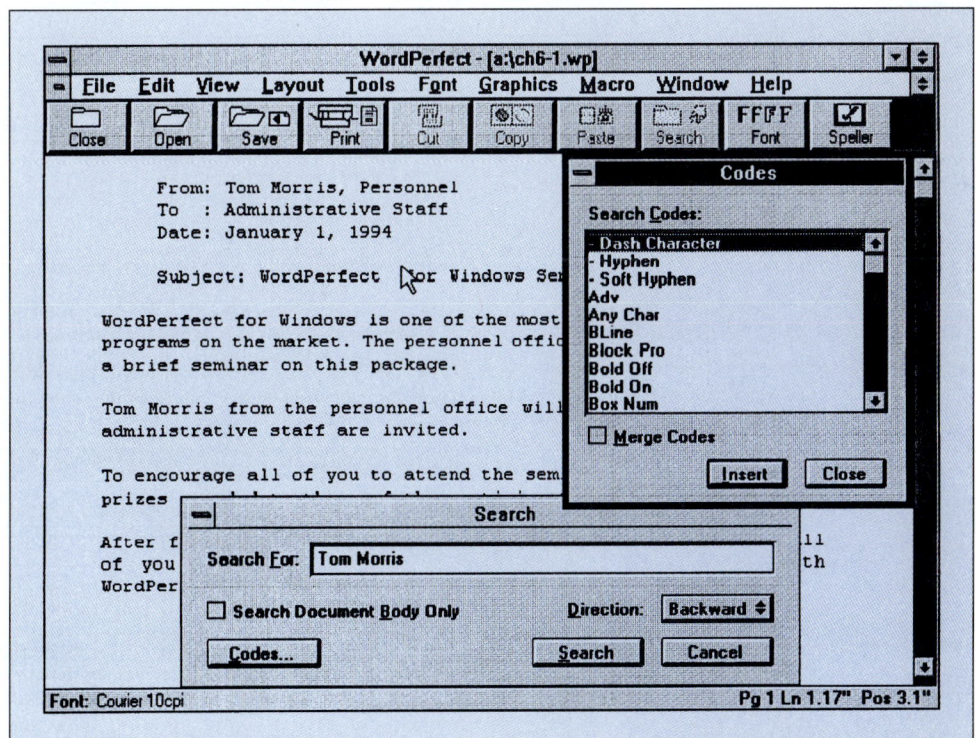

6–3   SEARCHING FOR AND REPLACING TEXT

Many times you will want to **replace** a word or a series of words with a new word or series of words. The length of the word or words does not matter as long as it is limited to 82 characters. WordPerfect for Windows can replace any word or phrase with another word or phrase. To see how this feature works, let us walk through another example.

Tom Morris was just notified that he has to go to Europe; Bob Brown has been asked to take his place. In the memo shown in Figure 6–1, we would like to replace Tom Morris with Bob Brown. Move the insertion point to the top of the memo, and enter the search and replace facility of WordPerfect for Windows by selecting the Replace (Ctrl+F2) option from the Edit menu. You will be presented with a dialog box similar to the one in Figure 6–4. In the Search For box type *Tom Morris*. In the Replace With box type *Bob Brown* and click on the Replace button. In a blink of an eye, the first occurrence of Tom Morris is highlighted. To replace that with Bob Brown, click Replace again. The Replace option finds and replaces one occurrence of the specified text at a time. To find and replace all occurrences of the search string of characters with the replace string, you must click on the Replace All button also shown in Figure 6–4.

6–4   SEARCH AND REPLACE OPERATIONS FOR CODES

Let us say that in a long document you want to replace all occurrences of the underline attribute with the bold attribute. This is how you do it:

1. Before you start the search and replace operations for codes, make sure the cursor is at the beginning of the code for which you are searching. The best

Figure 6–4
Search and Replace dialog box.

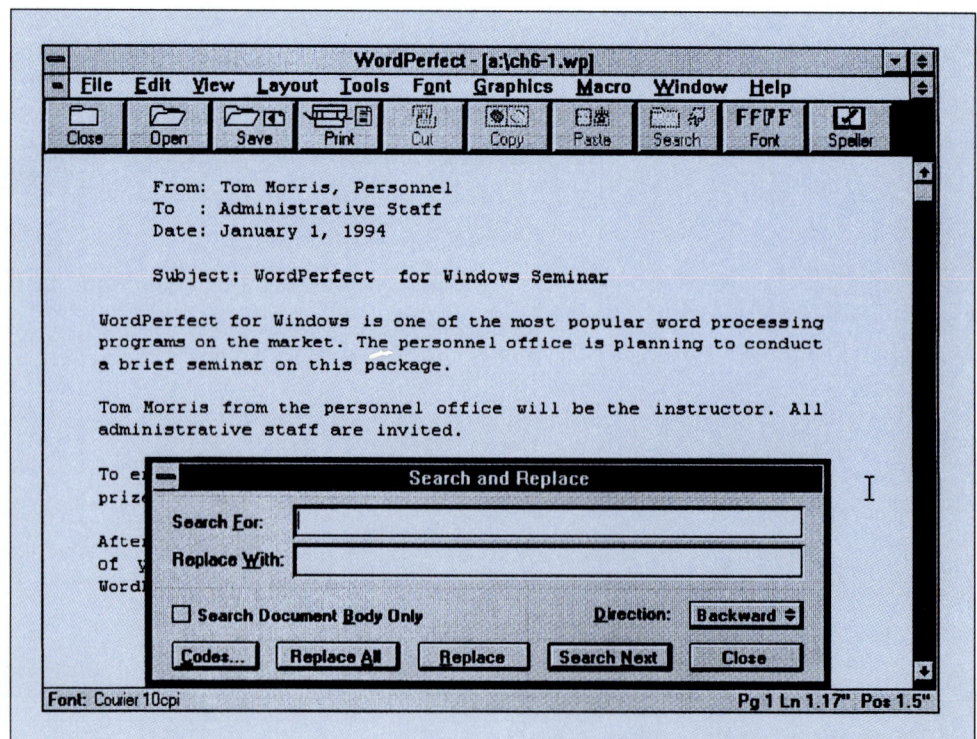

method to check this is to reveal codes by pressing the Alt+F3 key combination. Then use the arrow keys to move the cursor to the beginning of the desired code (if it is not already there). From the Edit menu select the Replace option (Ctrl+F2). You will be presented with a dialog box similar to the one presented in Figure 6–4.

2. In this dialog box click on the Codes button. You will see a screen similar to the one in Figure 6–5. In the Codes dialog box scroll through until you find the code called Und on. Double-click on it. As soon as you do this, the [Und on] code will be displayed in the Search For box.

3. Move the insertion point to the Replace With box and click on it.

4. In the Search Codes box locate the Bold On code and double-click on it; the [Bold On] code will appear in the Replace With box.

5. At this point your screen should be similar to the one in Figure 6–6. Click on the Replace All button. In a few seconds all of the underlined phrases will be changed to bold phrases.

6–5   DISPLAYING THE RULER

The **Ruler** displays margins, tab stops, and other valuable information, as you can see in Figure 6–7. It displays different information as you move through a document. A solid right triangle (▶) on the Ruler indicates a **tab** stop, which appears every half an inch. By default, the left margin is at the 1-inch position and the right margin is at the 7½-inch position. You can easily modify these positions by clicking on these icons (i.e., the right triangles) and dragging them to the desired position. When you position the mouse pointer at the desired position, release the mouse button. As soon as you click and drag the icon, a dotted line appears and moves

Figure 6–5
Search and replace operations for Codes.

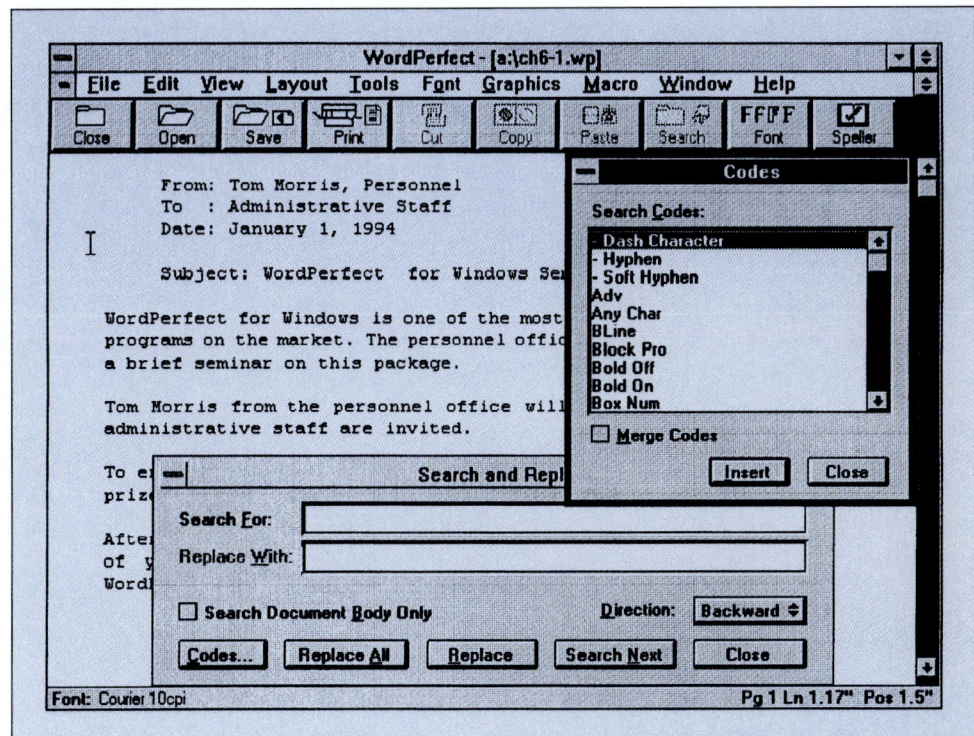

Figure 6–6
Two desired codes displayed.

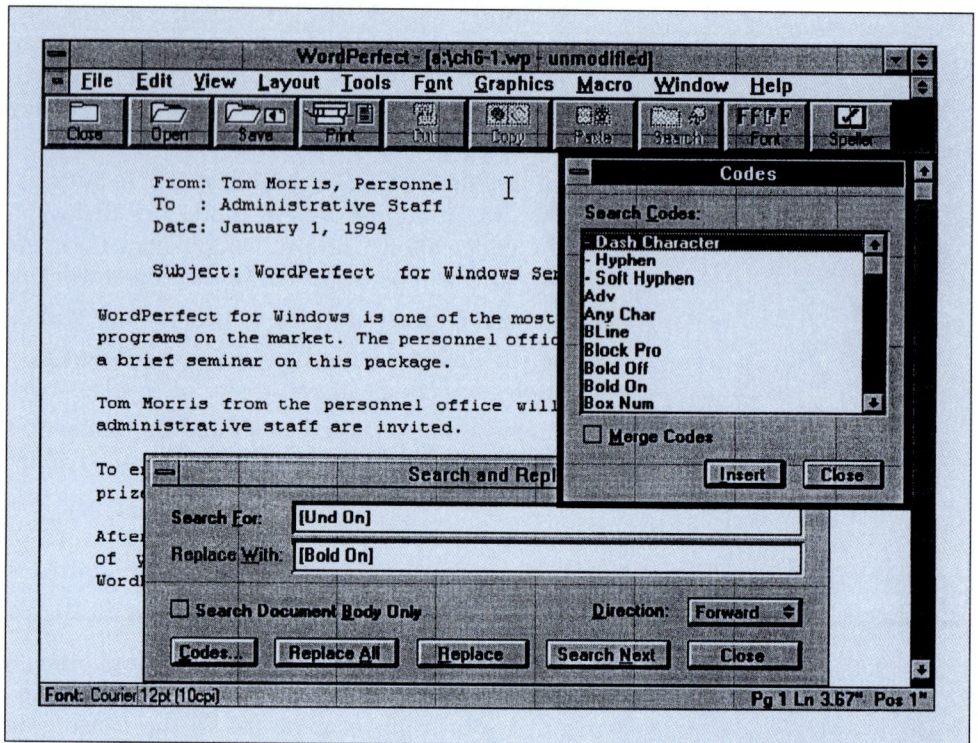

Figure 6–7
WordPerfect for Windows Ruler.

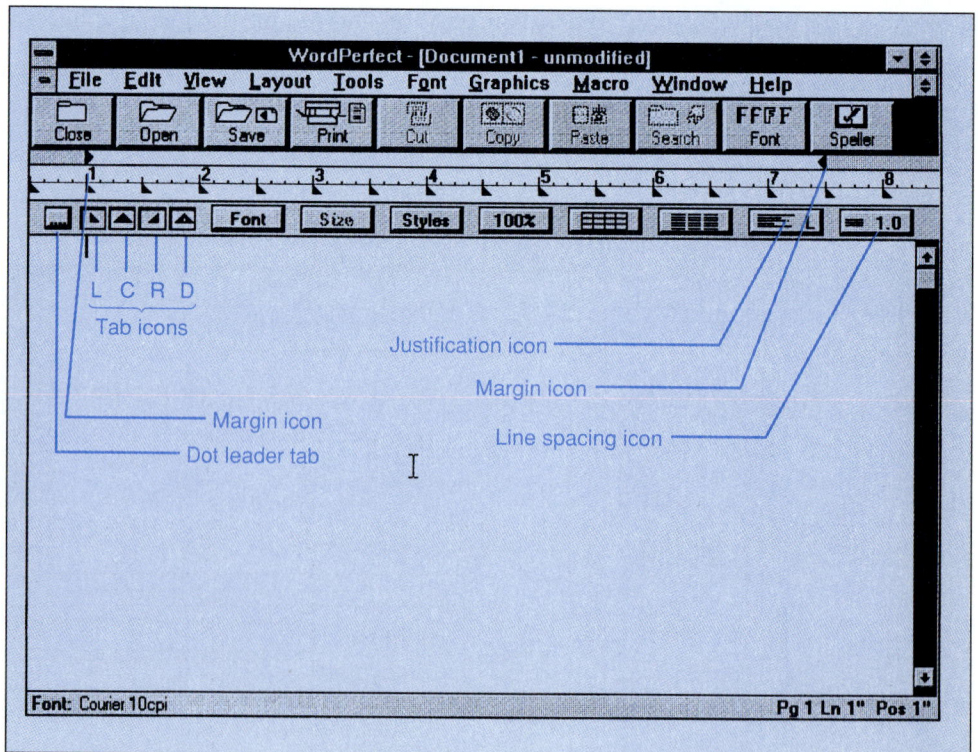

with the direction of the mouse pointer. After you release the mouse button, the insertion point appears in this new location. If you change your mind, simply click the icon again and drag the mouse pointer back to the original position and release it, or just select the Undo option from the Edit menu.

6–5–1

Different Tabs on the Ruler

Figure 6–7 shows the types of tabs on the Ruler. Let us briefly explain each type:

1. The left tab (L) aligns text to the right of the tab setting. Your typed text moves to the right one character at a time when you type.
2. The center tab (C) centers the typed text around the tab setting.
3. The right tab (R) aligns text to the left of the tab setting.
4. The decimal tab (D) aligns text around the decimal point.

   To create dot leaders (a series of periods between text and the next tab) for a tab stop, select the dot leader tab.

6–5–2

Clearing Tabs

In some cases you may not want to use the standard tabs provided by WordPerfect for Windows. For example, you want to set up columns in different positions than the default ones. You can clear all tabs or clear selected ones. To clear tabs use the mouse and the Ruler, or you can do it through the Tab dialog box. To clear one tab stop, follow these steps:

1. Position the mouse pointer on the desired tab stop.
2. Click and drag a very small distance until you see a small gray box.
3. Release the mouse button.
4. Click and drag the small gray box off the Ruler.

   To clear all the tab stops or several of them at once, click and drag the mouse pointer over all the desired tab stops; then release the mouse button. Now click on the gray box and drag it off the Ruler. If you change your mind, click on Edit; then click on Undo. This will reset tabs to their previous positions.
   To clear tab stops using the Tab dialog box follow these steps:

1. Select Line from the Layout menu.
2. Select Tab Set. You will be presented with a dialog box similar to the one in Figure 6–8.
3. Click on the Clear Tabs button.
4. Click on OK.

6–5–3

An Example of the Four Tab Types

To see how the four different tabs function, let us walk through an example. We would like to set four tabs in positions 1, 3, 4, and 7 inches to indicate left, center, right and decimal tabs, respectively. Start with a clear screen and follow these steps:

1. Click on View; then click on Ruler (Alt+Shift+F3). The Ruler will be displayed.

Figure 6–8
Tab Set dialog box.

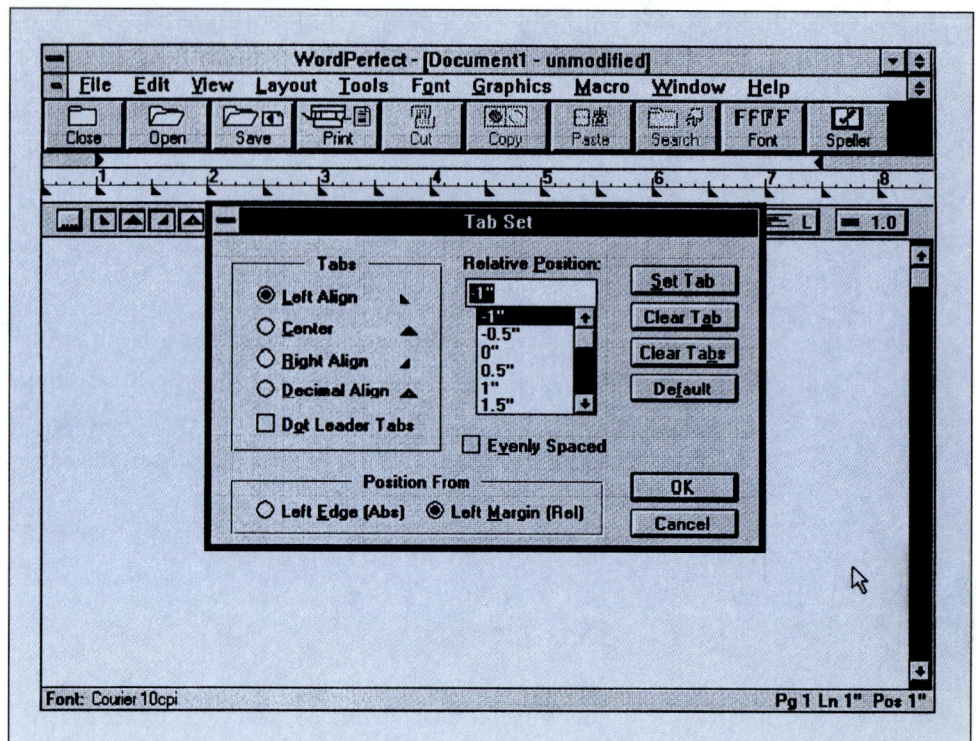

2. Using the mouse or the Tab Set dialog box, clear all the existing tabs.

3. Position the mouse pointer on the left tab icon, then click and drag it to the 1-inch position and release it.

4. Position the mouse pointer on the center tab icon, then click and drag it to the 3-inch position and release it.

5. Position the mouse pointer on the right tab icon, then click and drag it to the 5-inch position and release it.

6. Position the mouse pointer on the decimal tab icon, then click and drag it to the 7-inch position and release it.

At this point you should see four new tab stops on the Ruler with the respective icons. Now follow these instructions:

1. Type *Left Tab* and press the Tab key on the keyboard. The insertion point jumps to the 3-inch position.

2. Type *Center Tab* and press the Tab key on the keyboard. The insertion point jumps to the 5-inch position.

3. Type *Right Tab* and press the Tab key on the keyboard. The insertion point jumps to the 7-inch position.

4. Type *Decimal Tab* and press Enter.

5. Type *Jacki* and press the Tab key.

6. Type *Jacki* and press the Tab key.

7. Type *Jacki* and press the Tab key.

8. Type *11.111* and press Enter.

9. Type *WordPerfect,* press Tab, type *WordPerfect,* press Tab, type *WordPerfect,* press Tab, type *126.121,* and press Enter.

Figure 6–9
Example of four different tabs.

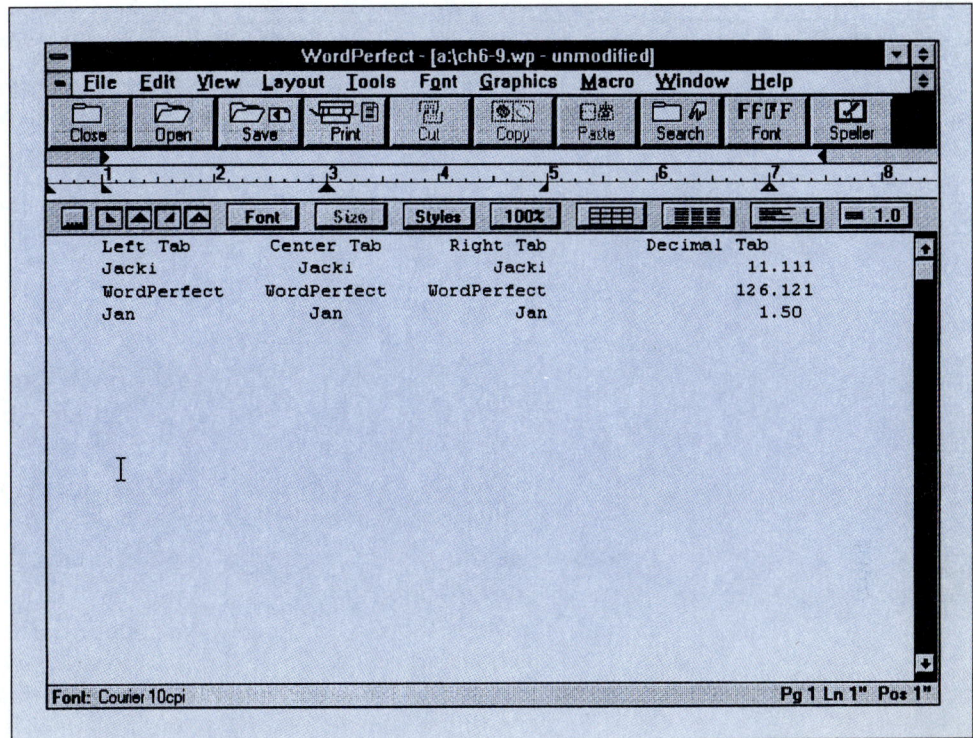

Figure 6–9
Example of four different tabs.

10. Type *Jan*, press Tab, type *Jan*, press Tab, type *Jan*, press Tab, type *1.50*. Your final work should be similar to Figure 6–9.

6–5–4   Modifying Standard Tabs: Another Example

Figure 6–10 is a portion of a report that we would like to create using WordPerfect for Windows. We would like to set up two tabs: one for region and one for total sales. Start with a clear screen and do the following:

1. Click on Layout, Line, and Center. The insertion point jumps to the middle of the screen. Type *Sales Report for Western Regions*.
2. Press Enter twice.
3. Type the next two lines as shown in Figure 6–10.
4. After typing the word "campaign" press Enter twice.

    Now you are ready to set the two tabs. Let us say the first tab is in the 2-inch position and the second tab in the 5.5-inch position. The first is a left tab and the second tab is a decimal tab. Continue with these steps:

5. Press the Tab key twice on the keyboard and type *Region*. Make sure to underline it.
6. Press the Tab key four times on the keyboard and type *Total Sales (in thousands)*. Make sure to underline it. Press the Enter key.
7. Click on View then on Ruler to display the ruler.
8. By selecting Layout, Line, Tab Set and clicking on the Clear Tabs button and clicking on OK, clear all the tab stops.

Figure 6–10
Portion of a financial report.

Sales Report for Western Regions

For the past three years western regions have demonstrated a significant increase in total sales. The major factor for this increase is due to the new advertising campaign.

Region	Total Sales (in thousands)
Los Angeles	696,272.18
Portland	11,121.65
San Diego	28,169.22
Seattle	9,171.82

Figure 6–10
Portion of a financial report.

9. Position the mouse pointer on the left tab icon. Click and drag it to 2-inch position and release it.

10. Position the mouse pointer on the decimal tab icon. Click and drag it to the 5.5-inch position and release it.

11. Press the Tab key on the keyboard; the insertion point jumps to 2-inch position. Type *Los Angeles.*

12. Press the Tab key on the keyboard; the insertion point jumps to the 5.5-inch position. Type *696,272.18.* Press Enter. Now you are ready to type the rest of the data. For example, press Tab, type *Portland,* press Tab, type *11,121.65.* Press Enter. Your final work should be similar to Figure 6–11.

6–6   INSERTING THE DATE IN A DOCUMENT

One option is to type the date as text in a document. If you do this, your date text is static; this means it will not change if you retrieve this document later. You can also enter the static date from a menu by following these steps:

1. Select Tools from the main menu; then select Date.

2. Select Text (Ctrl+F5).

The current system date will be inserted at the insertion point.

WordPerfect for Windows contains a function option that makes the date dynamic. To use this function, first move the insertion point to the desired location in your document. Then select Tools, Date, and Code (Ctrl+Shift+F5); this action enters the system date into your document. Now, whenever you retrieve your document the current system date is displayed in this position. This option can be useful because it tells you, for example, when a particular document was printed.

Figure 6–11
Report with two tabs: left and decimal.

```
                Sales Report for Western Regions

     For  the  past  three  years  western  regions  have  demonstrated  a
     significant  increase  in  total  sales.  The  major  factor  for  this
     increase  is  the  new  advertising  campaign.

               Region                    Total Sales(in thousands)
               Los Angeles                     696,272.18
               Portland                         11,121.65
               San Diego                        28,169.22
               Seattle                           9,171.82
```

Figure 6–12
Document with the system's date.

```
January 1, 1994

       From: Tom Morris, Personnel
       To  : Administrative Staff

       Subject: WordPerfect for Windows Seminar

WordPerfect for Windows is one of the most popular word processing
programs on the market. The personnel office is planning to conduct
a brief seminar on this package.

Tom Morris from the personnel office will be the instructor. All
administrative staff are invited.

To encourage all of you to attend the seminar, there will be cash
prizes awarded to three of the participants.

After familiarizing yourselves with WordPerfect for Windows, all of
you who  participate will be given access to a PC with WordPerfect
for Windows capabilities.
```

In Figure 6–12 we entered the system date at the top of the document. To do this, move the insertion point to the top of the document and press Enter twice. Click on Tools, Date, and Code. To skip a line press Enter.

6–7   WORKING WITH BLOCKS OF DATA

Most word processing programs handle documents as **blocks of data**. A block can be a character, a word, a series of words, a paragraph, a series of paragraphs, or the entire document. Using WordPerfect for Windows you can define a block first and then issue the appropriate command.

To work with a block of data, follow these steps:

1. Move the insertion point to the beginning of the data with which you wish to work.
2. Highlight the desired block by using the click and drag technique. The highlighted data always stands out. On color monitors, the highlighted data is shown by different foreground and background colors.
3. Issue the desired command.

WordPerfect for Windows handles four types of blocks: sentence, paragraph, tabular column, and rectangle. A sentence is the text from the beginning of a sentence to the first occurrence of a period or decimal point. Paragraphs are identified by hard returns. Columns are identified by tab stops, indents, hard returns, or tab aligns. Rectangles are blocks of data with rows and columns. You can issue Cut, Copy, Delete, Save, and Print commands on blocks of data.

To make this discussion clearer, in a blank screen create a document as follows:

1. Click on File and New (Shift+F4) and type *Div 1*. Press the Tab to move to the next tab stop.
2. Type *10* and press Tab.

3. Type *20* and press Tab.
4. Type *30* and press Tab.
5. Type *40* and press Tab.
6. Press Enter.
7. Type *Div 2* and press Tab.
8. Type *50* and press Tab.
9. Type *60* and press Tab.
10. Type *70* and press Tab.
11. Type *80* and press Tab.
12. Press Enter.
13. Type *Div 3* and press Tab.
14. Type *90* and press Tab.
15. Type *100* and press Tab.
16. Type *110* and press Tab.
17. Type *120* and press Tab.

Figure 6–13 illustrates this figure.

Let's say you want to move the second column of Figure 6–13 to column 6 (which does not exist yet). Do the following:

1. Move the insertion point to the beginning of the second column, that is, the 1 of the number 10.
2. By the click and drag technique, highlight the entire column. To do this, click on the 1 of 10 in the first row and drag the mouse pointer down until the 9 of 90 in the third row is highlighted. The entire third row must *not* be highlighted; only Div 3 and 9 might be highlighted. Some other areas are highlighted when you move the insertion point down. Don't worry.
3. Click on Edit to display the Edit menu.
4. From this menu choose the Select option. A new menu will be presented.
5. From this menu, select Tabular Column. Only column 2 will be highlighted.
6. Click on Edit and select Cut. At this point the second column has been cut and stored into the buffer and the table is closed up. The table now has four columns.

To move the removed column to the end of the table, move the mouse pointer to the right of number 40 and click left to move the insertion point. Click on Edit and then on Paste. This is the result:

```
Div 1   20    30    40    10
Div 2   60    70    80    50
Div 3   100   110   120   90
```

Figure 6–13

Sample document.

```
Div 1       10    20    30    40
Div 2       50    60    70    80
Div 3       90   100   110   120
```

6–7–1   Moving Text Around: Cut and Paste Operations

Cut and paste operations apply to tables as well as to regular text. WordPerfect for Windows allows you to move any portion of a document from one location to another location. Let us say in Figure 6–1 you would like to move the second paragraph to the end of the memo. Move the insertion point to the beginning of the second paragraph. By using the click and drag technique, highlight the paragraph. Click on Edit then on Cut. Move the mouse pointer to the end of the document and click left. Press Enter twice to skip a line; then click on Edit and on Paste. See Figure 6–14.

6–7–2   Deleting Blocks of Text

Let us say in Figure 6–1 you would like to delete the second paragraph. Move the insertion point to the beginning of the paragraph. Highlight the area that you intend to delete. Press the Del key. The block disappears.

If you change your mind, the undelete feature of WordPerfect for Windows allows you to restore the deleted text. To do so, select Undelete from the Edit menu. The most recently deleted paragraph will be highlighted. Click on Restore. Only the most recent deletion and the two previous deletions may be recalled in this manner. Also, the portion of the text stored in the undelete buffer can be restored to any place in the document, not just the area from which it was initially deleted. In addition, the text in the buffer can be restored in several locations as many times as needed.

6–7–3   Saving and Copying Blocks of Text

Let us say that you want to save a block of text as a file and use it later. Follow these steps:

1. Use the click and drag technique to highlight the block.
2. Select the Save or Save As command from the File menu.
3. Enter a name consisting of up to eight characters.
4. Click on Save.

Figure 6–14
Second paragraph from Figure 6–1 is moved to the end of the memo.

```
From: Tom Morris, Personnel
To  : Administrative Staff
Date: January 1, 1994

Subject: WordPerfect  for Windows Seminar

WordPerfect for Windows is one of the most popular word processing
programs on the market. The personnel office is planning to conduct
a brief seminar on this package.


To encourage all of you to attend the seminar, there will be cash
prizes awarded to three of the participants.

After familiarizing yourselves with WordPerfect for Windows , all
of you who  participate will be given access to a PC with
WordPerfect for Windows  capabilities.

Tom Morris from the personnel office will be the instructor. All
administrative staff are invited.
```

To **copy** a block of data from one place to another, highlight the data then select the Copy command from the Edit menu. Move the insertion point to the desired location then select Paste from the Edit menu.

6–7–4   Printing a Block of Text

To print a block of text, follow these steps:

1. Use the click and drag technique to highlight the block.
2. Select the Print command from the File menu. Notice that the Selected Text option in the Print dialog box is enabled. This happened because you highlighted a block and then invoked the Print command.
3. Click on Print.

Naturally, you can check the spelling of a block, change the appearance of the block, and apply any formatting commands to it.

6–8   HELP FACILITY

As you have seen all along, one of the main menu options of WordPerfect for Windows is the Help option. If you click on Help you will see a screen similar to the one in Figure 6–15. The WordPerfect for Windows **help facility** is similar to the Windows help facility explained in Chapter 3. It can be accessed in the same manner.

The Help menu shows several options. The Contents option serves as an index to the help facility. When you click on Contents, a dialog box is displayed and you can select from various topics by double-clicking on them.

Figure 6–15
Help menu.

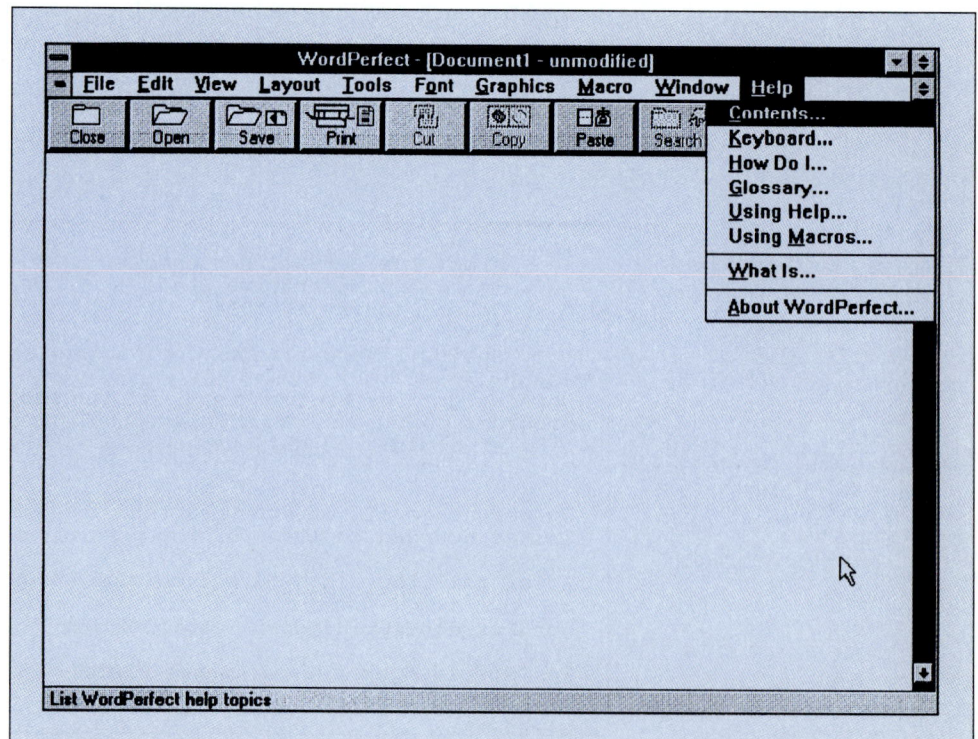

The Keyboard option includes information related to different keyboard layouts such as the CUA keyboard template. It also provides information related to all Alt, Ctrl, and Shift key combinations.

The How Do I option lists the most common tasks of WordPerfect for Windows. The Glossary option provides an alphabetical list of terms used in the help facility. To quickly move to a portion of the glossary, click one of the letters provided.

The Using Help option explains how the help facility works. The Using Macros option explains macro basics, commands, and creating dialog boxes. Macros will be discussed in Chapter 10.

The What Is option switches the mouse and keyboard into a context-sensitive mode (explained in the next section), which allows you to click on various screen regions or press keystroke combinations to get help.

The About WordPerfect option displays your license number and the program release date. A license number is the number issued by the WordPerfect Corporation to identify authorized users. (You can also edit your license number.)

6–8–1   Context-Sensitive Help

The WordPerfect for Windows context-sensitive mode offers help on whatever feature that you specify throughout your WordPerfect session. That is why it is called context sensitive. You can use context-sensitive help in two ways:

1. Whenever you need help on a particular option or menu choice press the F1 function key. Let us say that the Save As dialog box is displayed and you need help. Just press the F1 function key. A screen of help instructions will be displayed.

2. The second method for receiving context-sensitive help is by selecting the What Is option from the Help menu. This provides a cursor that looks like a question mark—called a question pointer. Now move this question pointer to the desired option and click the mouse button. A screen of help on the desired option will be displayed and you can choose from its options.

To exit a help screen either double-click on the control-menu box or select Exit from the Help File menu.

SUMMARY

The first of several features discussed in this chapter was search and replace operations. The chapter also highlighted the Ruler—a means for working with tabs. Next, blocks of data were considered: cutting, copying, deleting, saving, and printing. The chapter concluded with a review of the online help facility of WordPerfect for Windows.

REVIEW QUESTIONS

*These questions are answered in Appendix A.
1. How do you start the search process?
2. How do you tell WordPerfect for Windows to replace a word with another word?
*3. In search and replace operations, must the two words (original and replacement) be of equal length?
4. How do you search for codes?

5. What are the applications of searching for codes?

*6. How do you replace one code with another?

7. How do you display the Ruler?

8. What is the meaning of solid right triangles on the Ruler?

9. How many tab icons are in the Ruler?

10. Explain how to set margins using the Ruler.

*11. How do you set the margins back to the default using the Ruler?

12. Describe how to erase the tab stops using the mouse.

13. How do you modify standard tabs?

14. Why might you want to reset the standard tabs?

*15. How do you erase the standard tabs using the Tab Set dialog box?

16. Can you erase only one tab stop?

17. What are the applications of decimal tabs?

18. How do you insert a dynamic date into your document?

19. What is the difference between using the dynamic date function versus typing the date directly as text?

*20. What is a block of data?

21. Explain how to block a paragraph.

22. List some of the operations that can be done on blocks of data.

23. How do you move a column of a table to another column of the same table?

24. What are some applications of the Cut command?

25. How do you delete a block of data?

*26. Can you change your mind after deleting a block? How do you restore the deleted text?

27. How do you save a block? How do you print it? Can you copy a block?

28. What is context-sensitive help?

HANDS-ON EXPERIENCE

1. Use Figure 6–1 to do the following:

    a. Add this paragraph to the text:

    > After the WordPerfect for Windows seminar, the personnel office is planning to conduct a Lotus 1-2-3 for Windows seminar.

    b. Indent the first line of this paragraph.
    c. Replace "WordPerfect" with "Word."
    d. Replace all occurrences of "M" with "N".
    e. Change all occurrences of "N" back to "M".
    f. Join paragraphs 4 and 5.
    g. Split paragraph 1 into 2 paragraphs.
    h. Display the Ruler.
    i. Locate the dot leader on the Ruler.

2. Start with a clear screen and create the following table in the 3-, 5-, and 7-inch positions.

Quarter 1	Quarter 2	Quarter 3
10	40	70
20	50	80
30	60	90

Do the following:

- **a.** Copy Quarter 1 after Quarter 3.
- **b.** Cut Quarter 1 and paste it after Quarter 3.

3. In Figure 6–1, use the block feature and cut paragraph 1 and paste it at the end of the text.

4. In Figure 6–1, by using the block feature, delete paragraph 2. By using the Undo feature, restore paragraph 2.

5. In a clear screen set up tabs in these columns: 1.5, 3, 4.5, and 6 inch. Do the following:

- **a.** Column 1.5 inch: right justify.
- **b.** Column 3.0 inch: center.
- **c.** Column 4.5: left justify.
- **d.** Column 6.0 inch: align on decimal.

Enter the following data in these columns:

Portland	Johnny	Nooshin	22.91
Los Angeles	Tom	Morvareed	121.52
London	William	Tonia	1.16

How is your data presented on the screen?

6. By using the date function, insert the system date in your previous screen as a function.

7. Retrieve the EXERCISE.WP document and do the following:

- **a.** Copy the last paragraph and paste it to the beginning of the text.
- **b.** Replace all occurrences of "the" with "xxx".
- **c.** Replace all the occurrences of "xxx" with "the".
- **d.** Insert the system date at the top of the document.
- **e.** Delete the first paragraph.

KEY TERMS

Block of data	Help facility	Searching
Cut and paste	Indentation	Ruler
Copying	Replacing	Tab

KEY COMMANDS

F2 (to start the search facility)	Ctrl+F5 (to enter the system date as text)	Shift+F4 (to start a new document)
Alt+F2 (to search previous text)	Ctrl+Shift+F5 (to enter the system date as a function)	Del (to delete a character or a block)
Alt+Shift+F3 (to display the Ruler)	Shift+F2 (to search for the next occurrence of some specified text)	Tab (to move the insertion point to the next tab stop)
Ctrl+F2 (to invoke the search and replace facility)		

MISCONCEPTIONS AND SOLUTIONS

Misconception   You try to justify a line or paragraph but you do not get the correct result.

Solution   You can only justify if the line or paragraph is ended by a hard return. Press the Enter key first then try to justify the text.

Misconception   Going through the codes to find a desired one in search and replace operations is time consuming.

Solution   A quicker way is to enter the first letter of the desired code, thereby moving to that section of the listing.

ARE YOU READY TO MOVE ON?

Multiple Choice

1. Under which menu will you find the Search command?
   a. File
   b. View
   c. Edit
   d. Tools
   e. none of the above

2. The formatting code for centering text is
   a. [CNTR] (text) [cntr]
   b. [C] (text) [c]
   c. [Center] (text)
   d. [CNTR] (text) [C/A/flrt]
   e. [CENTER] (text) [uncenter]

3. On the Ruler, a tab stop is indicated by a
   a. bracket
   b. solid right triangle
   c. brace
   d. parenthesis
   e. star

4. To display the Ruler, press
   a. F4
   b. F1
   c. Alt+Shift
   d. Alt+Shift+F3
   e. none of the above

5. A block of text can be
   a. a character
   b. a word
   c. a series of words
   d. an entire document
   e. all of the above

6. To work with a block of data, move the insertion point to the beginning of the data to be altered and
   a. click and drag
   b. click
   c. double click
   d. press F3
   e. press F4

7. By means of the block feature and the Edit command, WordPerfect for Windows can
   a. move text
   b. copy text
   c. delete text
   d. do both a and c
   e. do all of the above

8. Using search and replace operations,
   a. you can search forward
   b. you can search backward
   c. you can search for codes
   d. you can do all of the above
   e. you can do only A and B

9. To receive context-sensitive help, what function key should you press?
   a. F10
   b. F9
   c. F8
   d. F1
   e. F7

10. To make the date entry dynamic so that it changes automatically, from the Date menu select
    a. Code
    b. Text
    c. Format
    d. Outline
    e. Paragraph Number

True/False

1. The only way to leave a help screen is to double-click on the control-menu box.
2. A decimal tab stop can be created that will align numbers on the decimal point.
3. You can enter the current system date automatically with the Date command.
4. When using search and replace options, there is a limit to the length of a word or words being searched or replaced.
5. WordPerfect for Windows does not allow search and replace operations using lower-case characters.
6. To invoke the Search dialog box press the F2 function key.
7. The Ruler displays only tab stops.
8. Blocks cannot be saved individually.
9. Cut and paste operations cannot be applied to tables.
10. Once you have deleted text, there is no way to undelete it.

ANSWERS

Multiple Choice		True/False	
1.	c	1.	F
2.	c	2.	T
3.	b	3.	T
4.	d	4.	T
5.	e	5.	F
6.	a	6.	T
7.	e	7.	F
8.	d	8.	F
9.	d	9.	F
10.	a	10.	F

Button Bars and the File Manager

7

7–1   INTRODUCTION

This chapter focuses on two of the most exciting features of WordPerfect for Windows: button bars and the File Manager. The first part of the chapter explains how to access button bars, modify them, and create your own button bars. The second part of the chapter explains the File Manager, which helps you to organize, view, copy, move, and find your WordPerfect and other files very effectively.

7–2   WHAT IS THE BUTTON BAR?

The **button bar**, which was introduced in Chapter 4, is one of the most useful features of WordPerfect for Windows because it simplifies commonly used word processing operations. The button bar that you see in Figure 7–1 includes 10 popular tasks of WordPerfect for Windows; the options shown are Close, Open, Save, Print, Cut, Copy, Paste, Search, Font, and Speller. As you will see later in this chapter, you can create your own button bars, move them around on the screen, hide them, and so forth.

When you click on these different buttons, a specific task is performed. For example, if you click on the Print button, the Print dialog box will appear. If you click on the Save button, the Save As dialog box will appear.

If you do not want to see the button bar on your screen, click on View; then click on the Button Bar option. A check mark next to the Button Bar option means the button bar is visible. Removing the check mark hides the button bar.

7–2–1   Moving the Button Bar Around

As you can see in Figure 7–1, by default the button bar is displayed on the top of the screen. However, this position can be changed. To change the position of the button bar, follow these steps:

Figure 7–1
Ten buttons on the button bar.

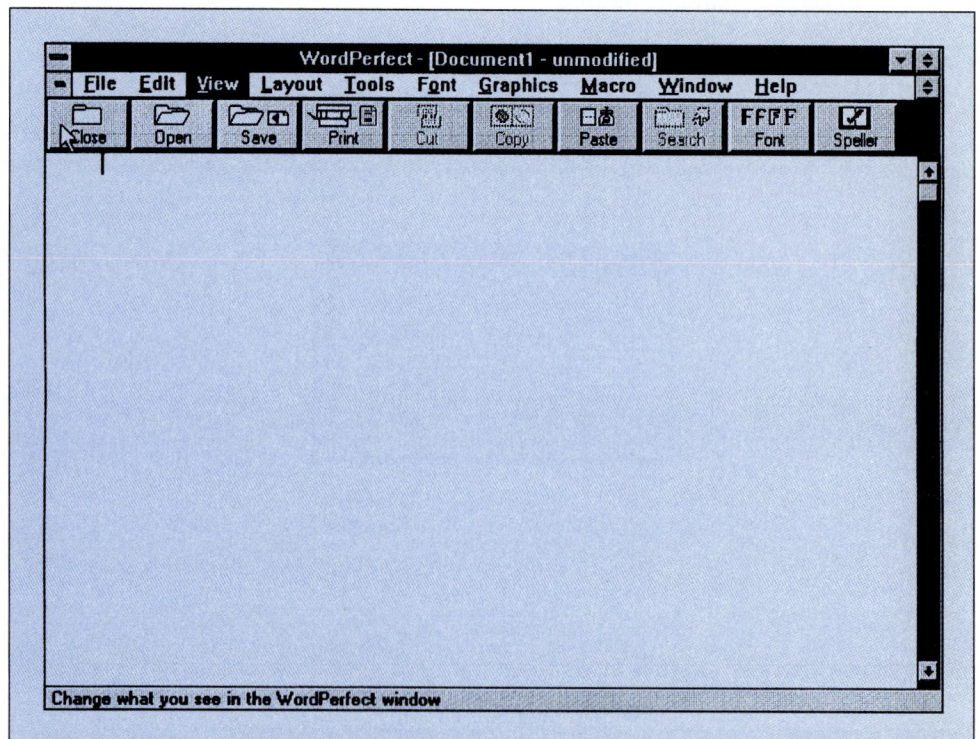

1. Select the View option; then click on Button Bar Setup. Figure 7–2 will be displayed.
2. Click on Options. You will see a screen similar to the one in Figure 7–3.

Figure 7–2
Options under the Button Bar Setup.

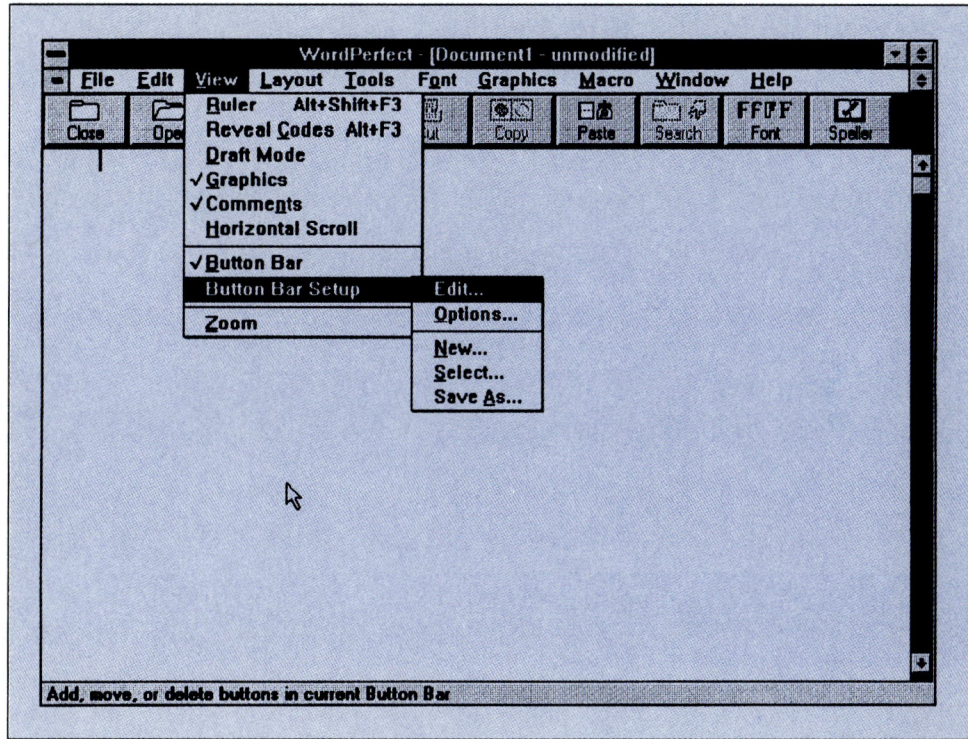

Figure 7–3
Button Bar Options dialog box.

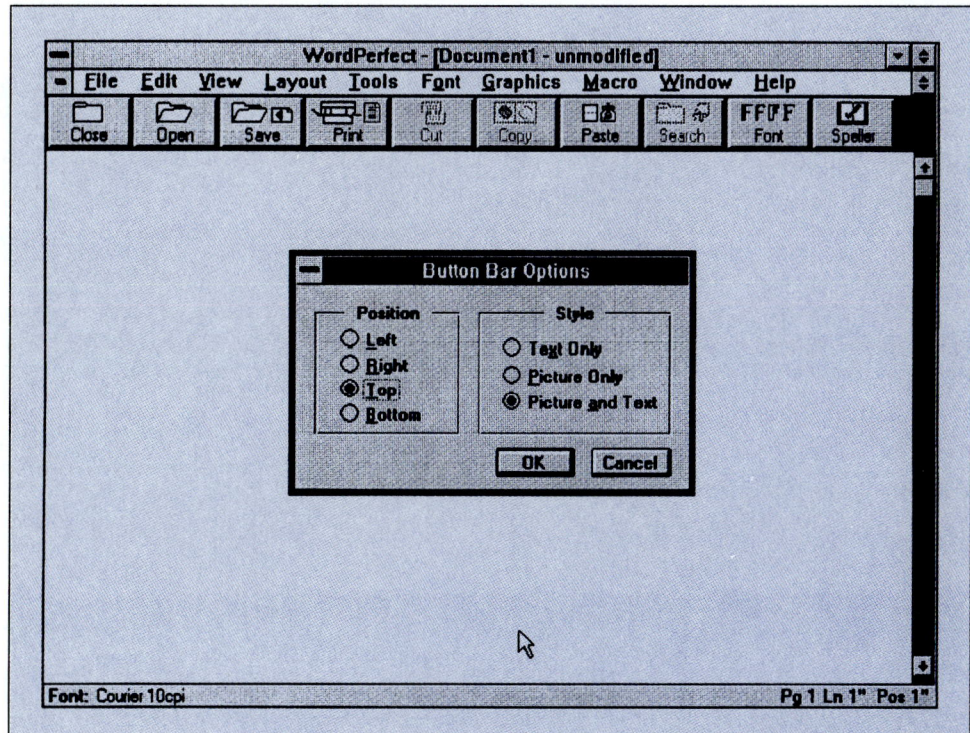

Figure 7–3 shows that you can select one of the following four positions for the button bar to be displayed: left, right, top, or bottom. The default position is top. To display the button bar on the left side of the screen, for example, click on Left; then click on OK. The button bar will be displayed on the left side of the screen.

Also, as you can see in Figure 7–3, you can choose the Text Only, Picture Only, or Picture and Text option, which is the default option. In the Text Only option you see only the text; no icon is displayed. In this mode, the buttons require less room, thereby allowing you to add more buttons. (Creating a custom button bar is discussed in the next section.) In the Picture Only option you only see the icons. In the Picture and Text option you see both the icons and the text.

7–2–2

Creating Your Own Button Bar

To simplify the tasks you perform using WordPerfect for Windows on a daily basis, you might want to create custom button bars. Each button bar can include several buttons that represent different tasks. Let us say you want to create a button bar that includes buttons for various text justification options such as left, right, center, and full. Call this button bar FORMAT. To create a button for centering text, follow these steps:

1. Select the Button Bar Setup option from the View menu. You will see a screen similar to the one in Figure 7–2.
2. From this menu select New. You will see a dialog box similar to the one in Figure 7–4. This figure provides you with instructions about button bar creation.
3. Select the Layout menu. Notice that the mouse pointer takes the shape of a hand holding a button.

Figure 7–4
Edit Button Bar dialog box.

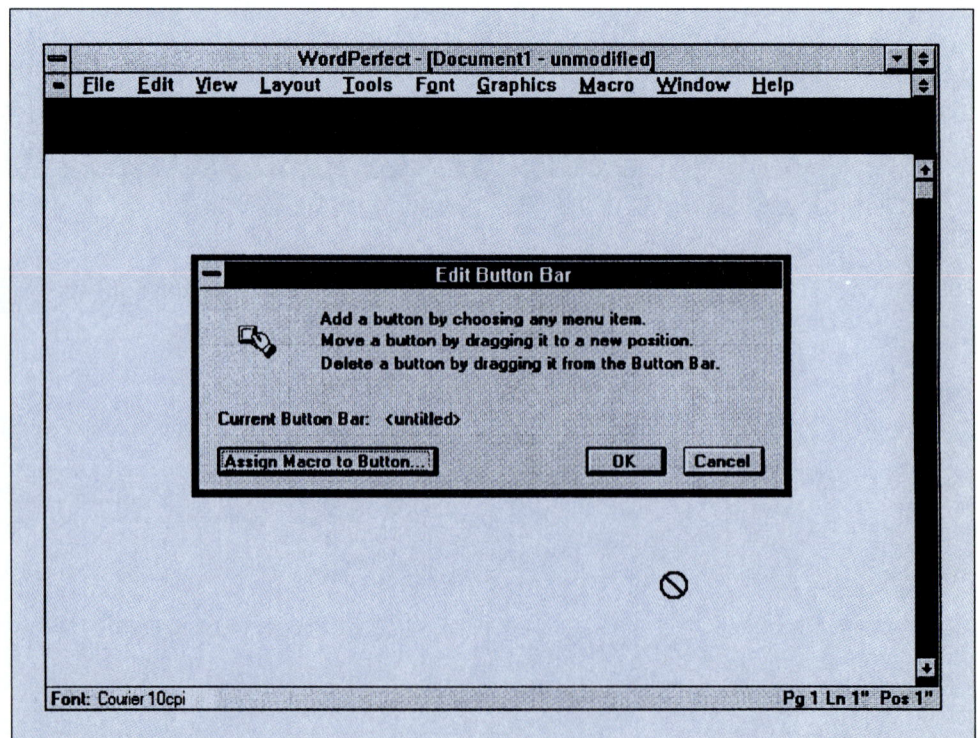

4. In the Layout menu, click on Justification; then click on Center. That is it! A center justification button appears on the button bar.

5. Click on OK.

6. The Save Button Bar dialog box appears. Type *A:FORMAT* and click on the Save button. WordPerfect for Windows saves this button bar under FORMAT (a file name) with a WWB extension—WordPerfect for Windows Button.

7–2–3   Adding a Button

Now let us add the full justification option to the button bar that we just created. Follow these steps:

1. First make sure that your button bar is displayed. If it is not, select the Button Bar Setup option from the View menu; then choose the Select option. Scroll through the names and double-click on the desired one. In our case, double-click on FORMAT.WWB.

2. From the Button Bar Setup menu select Edit. The Edit Button Bar dialog box appears.

3. Move the cursor to Layout (notice the hand holding a button); then click on Justification and click on Full. The second button is created.

4. Click on OK.

At this point your screen should be similar to Figure 7–5.

7–2–4   Changing the Order of the Buttons

You can change the order in which buttons appear on the button bar. To do this, select Edit from the Button Bar Setup menu; click and drag the button anywhere

Figure 7–5
Two buttons on the button bar.

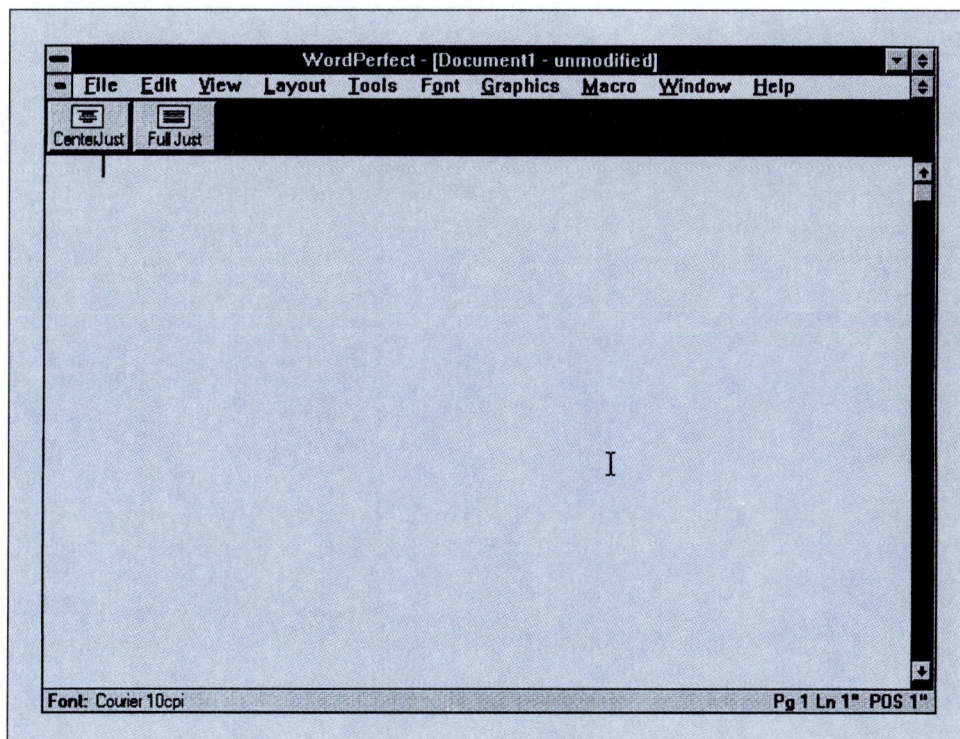

you want on the bar. When you are satisfied with the new position, release the mouse button. To finalize the process click on OK.

7–2–5

Deleting a Button

To delete a button from the bar, follow these steps:

1. Make sure the button bar is visible.
2. Select Edit from the Button Bar Setup menu.
3. Click and drag the desired button off the button bar.
4. Click on OK.

When you delete a button, it is gone for good. To have it back, you must create it again.

7–2–6

Selecting Different Button Bars

WordPerfect for Windows comes with several predefined button bars. The one that you have seen all along is saved as wp{wp}.wwb. To access a different button bar, follow these steps:

1. From the View menu select the Button Bar Setup option.
2. From this menu choose the Select option. You will be presented with a screen similar to the one in Figure 7–6.
3. Double-click on your choice. For example, if you double-click on page.wwb you will see a screen similar to the one in Figure 7–7. The page.wwb button bar includes buttons for various operations performed on a page of a document.

Figure 7–6
Select Button Bar dialog box.

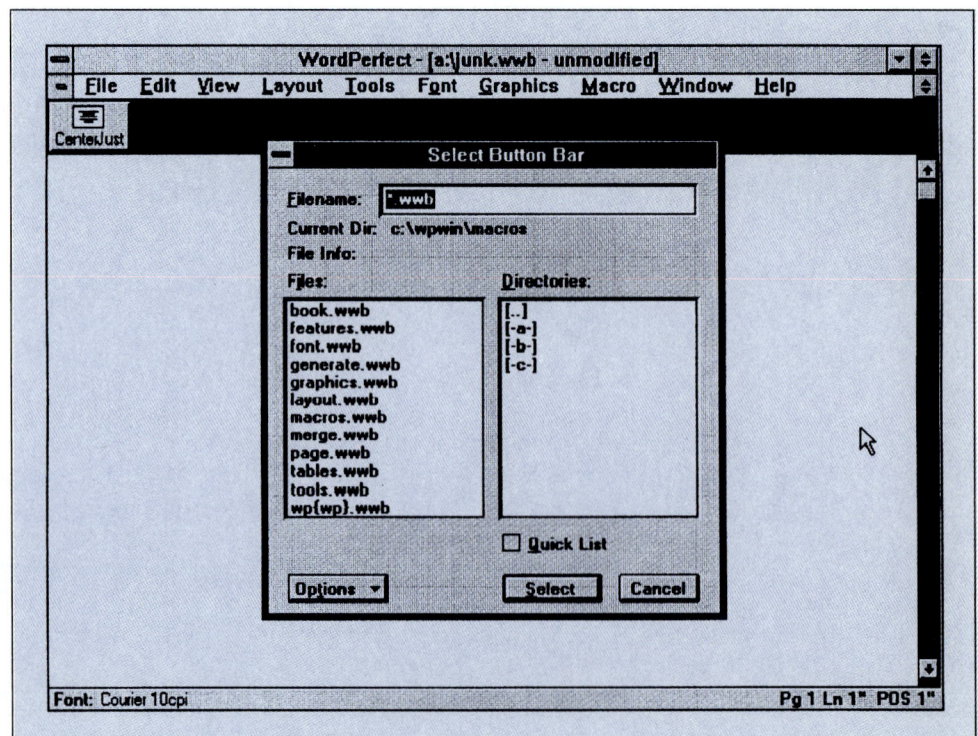

Figure 7-7
The page.wwb button bar.

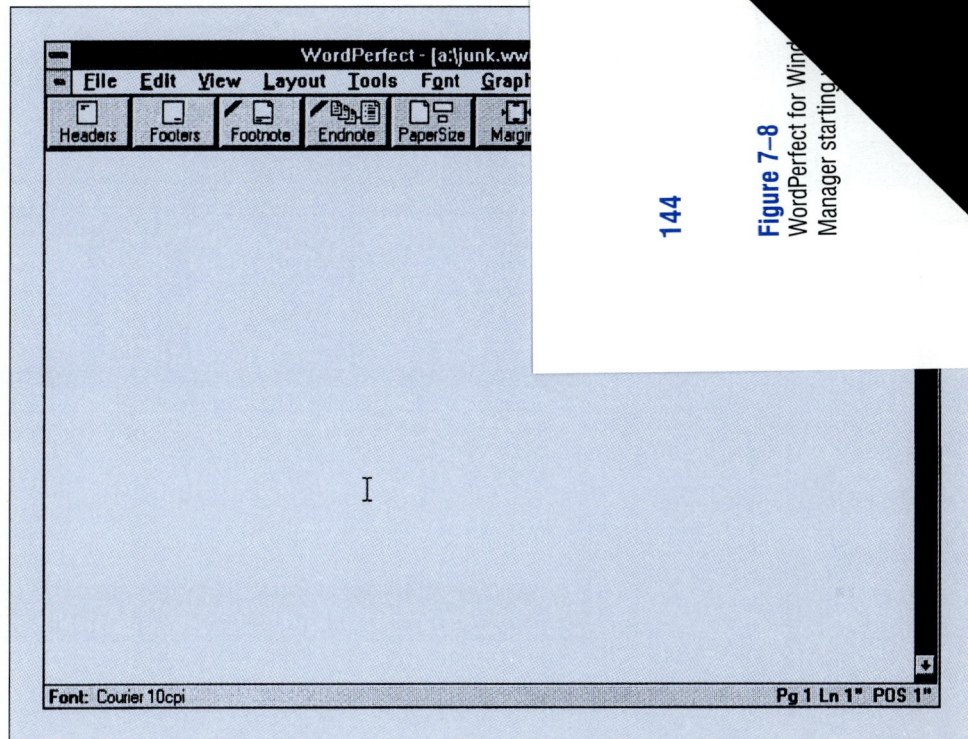

7-3 WHAT IS THE FILE MANAGER?

The **File Manger** of WordPerfect for Windows is a sophisticated program that allows you to perform various housekeeping and housecleaning tasks. The File Manager performs the basic DOS functions discussed in Chapter 2 and much more.

Using the File Manager is much easier than using DOS, because all the functions performed by the File Manager are accessed through the pull-down menus and button bars. Some of the tasks performed by the File Manager include copying files, editing files, viewing files, and search operations. The next few pages describe the major tasks performed by the File Manager.

7-3-1 Starting the File Manager

To start the File Manager, select the File Manager option from the File menu. You will be presented with a screen similar to the one in Figure 7-8. As you can see in this figure, the File Manager has its own menu, which includes the following options: File, Edit, Search, View, Info, Applications, Window, and Help.

Inside the File Manager Window notice the **Navigator window**. Similar to other windows, this window can be maximized by clicking on the maximize box and minimized by clicking on the minimize box.

The left side of the Navigator window shows the drives in your system. In our example, three drives are identified: [-a-], [-b-], and [-c-]. The current drive is identified by a small hand.

The second column indicates the contents of the current drive. The third column shows the contents of a selected directory in the second column. The fourth column could list the contents of a selected directory from the third col-

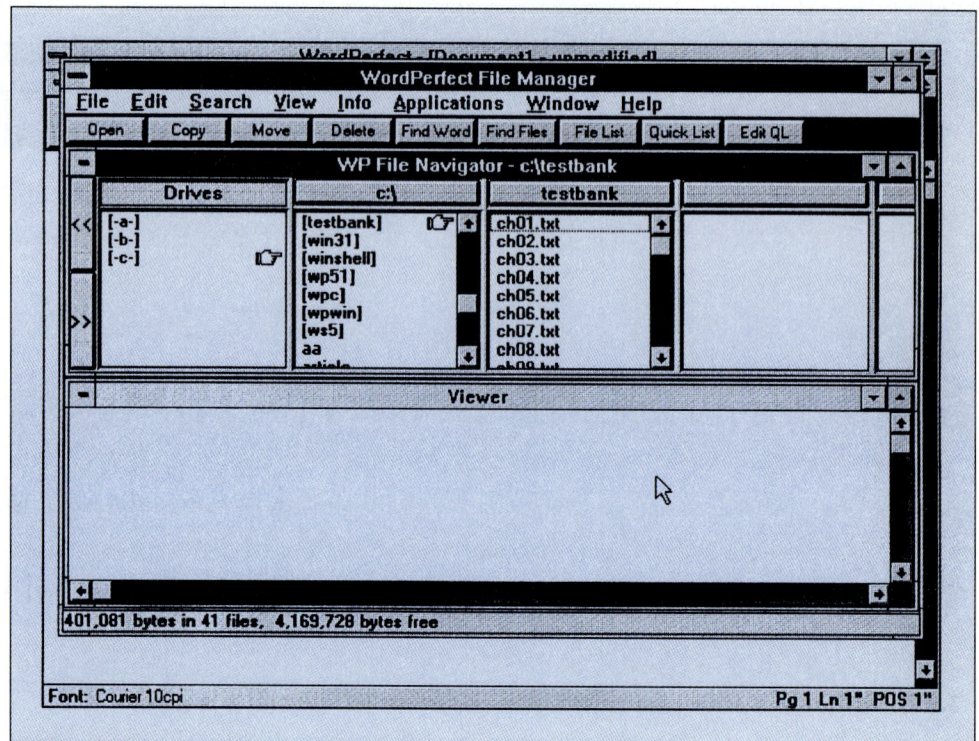

umn. Figure 7–8 does not have a directory in the third column—just documents. Notice that all directories are identified by a pair of brackets: [ ].

To change drives, double-click on the desired drive icon. For example, double-click on the [-a-] to change to drive A. As soon as you do this, the contents of this drive will be displayed in the second column.

Also notice in Figure 7–8 that File Manager includes several buttons in its button bar that perform the *most* common tasks. We will explain these buttons later in this chapter.

7–3–2 Overview of the File Manager Menu

The File Manager includes eight menu options (see Figure 7–8). Let us briefly consider each option.

The File menu includes commands for opening, printing, deleting, and copying files. It also allows you to run an application and perform some of the advanced DOS operations such as creating a directory, changing a directory, and changing file attributes. For example, using the Change Attributes option from the File menu, you can make a file a read-only file, thereby guarding against accidental erasure of the file.

The Edit menu allows you to select files for additional operations. You can also select the selected files through the Edit menu. In addition, you can copy information to the Clipboard and append information from the Clipboard. This information can later be accessed by other Windows applications such as Microsoft Excel.

The Search menu enables you to find words, phrases, and files and search all the active windows. You can also search for the next or previous occurrences of a phrase.

The View menu allows you to view various options such as the Button Bar, Button Bar Setup, Font, and File Navigator.

The Info menu provides you with information regarding your system, Windows setup, printer, and disk in your system.

The Applications menu gives you access to the WordPerfect for Windows screen, speller, thesaurus, and macro facility.

The Window option allows you to arrange the open windows in tile or cascade format, arrange icons, or close all the open windows. When you select the Close All option from this menu, the Navigator window disappears.

Finally, the Help menu provides you with online help about various aspects of the File Manager.

The remaining parts of this chapter concentrate on the major operations performed by the File Manager through the options on the button bar.

7–3–3 Opening a File

To open a file click on the Open button in the File Manager. As soon as you do this the open dialog box is displayed; see Figure 7–9. In the Files box type the file name with its complete path and click on the Open button. An alternative method of opening a file is to first view a listing of all the files in the selected drive and/or directory. Click the file folder icon to the right of the Files box in Figure 7–9. When you do this you will see a screen similar to the one in Figure 7–10. Click on the desired file and click on the Select button in the Select File dialog box. You can also double-click on the desired file. In either case, you will return to the Open dialog box with the selected file. Click on the Open button.

The fastest way to open a file is from the file Navigator. Highlight (click on) the file first; then double-click on the file; then click on the Open button.

Figure 7–9

Open dialog box in the File Manager.

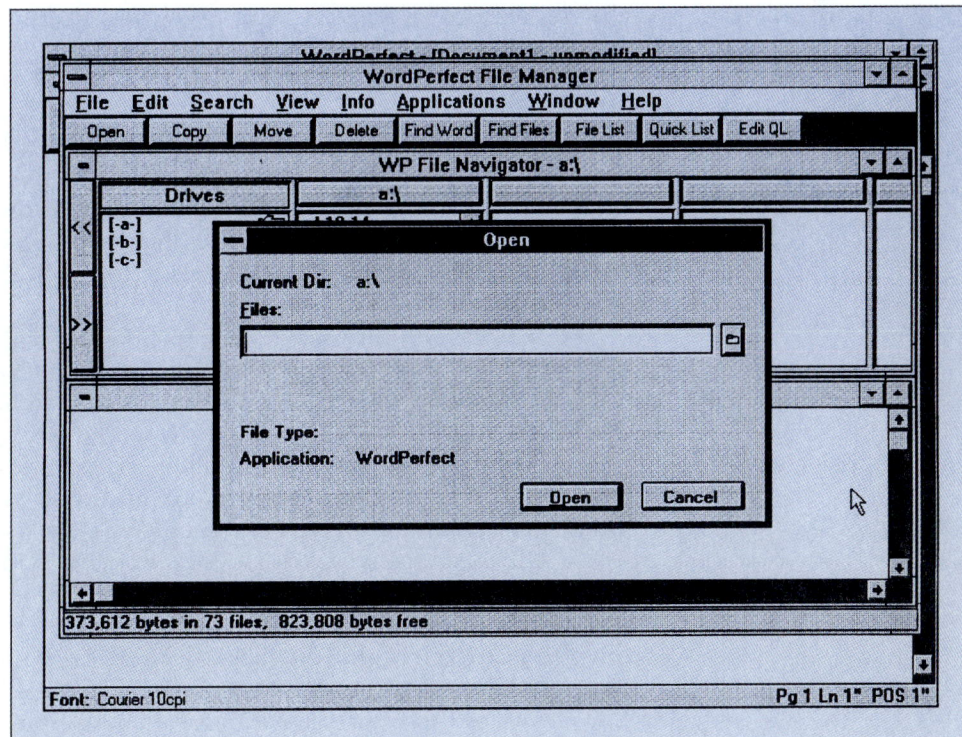

Figure 7–10
Select File dialog box.

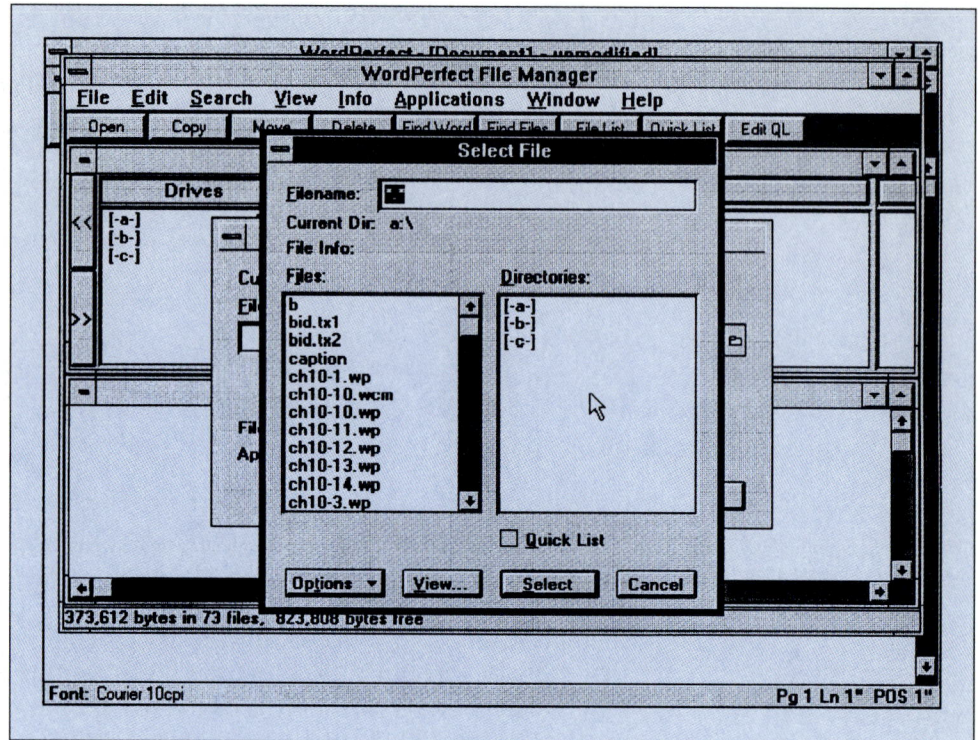

Figure 7–10
Select File dialog box.

7–3–4   Viewing the Contents of a File

To view the contents of a file, highlight the file, which means click on the file. As soon as you do this the contents of the file is displayed in the **Viewer** window. The Viewer only displays as much information as can fit in the window. To see more, click on the scroll icon.

7–3–5   Copying a File

To copy a file or a series of files, first highlight them; then click on the Copy button. This opens the Copy File[s] dialog box. In the To or To Directory box type the destination. If you only type a drive name in the box, the file will be copied under its present name. However, you can type a new name if you want to change the name of the file after being copied. To finalize the process, click either the Copy or Copy All button.

Let us walk through an example. We highlighted five files in our current drive and clicked on the Copy button. As you can see in Figure 7–11, the Copy File[s] dialog box displays the names of the highlighted files and the space needed for copying these files. In this case, the space required is 25,809 bytes. We want to copy all these files into a directory in drive B named TEST. To do this, type *B:\TEST* in the To Directory box and click on Copy All. WordPerfect for Windows proceeds as directed and shows the percentage copied as it progresses.

If you are copying a series of files that are in sequence, click and drag to highlight all the desired files. If the files are not in sequence, press the Ctrl key while you click on the desired files one by one. To unselect the selected files, press the Ctrl key while you click on the desired files one by one, or select the Unselect All option from the Edit menu. By using the Select All option from the Edit menu instead of using the mouse, you can select all the files and directories in a given drive as well.

Figure 7–11
Copy File[s] dialog box.

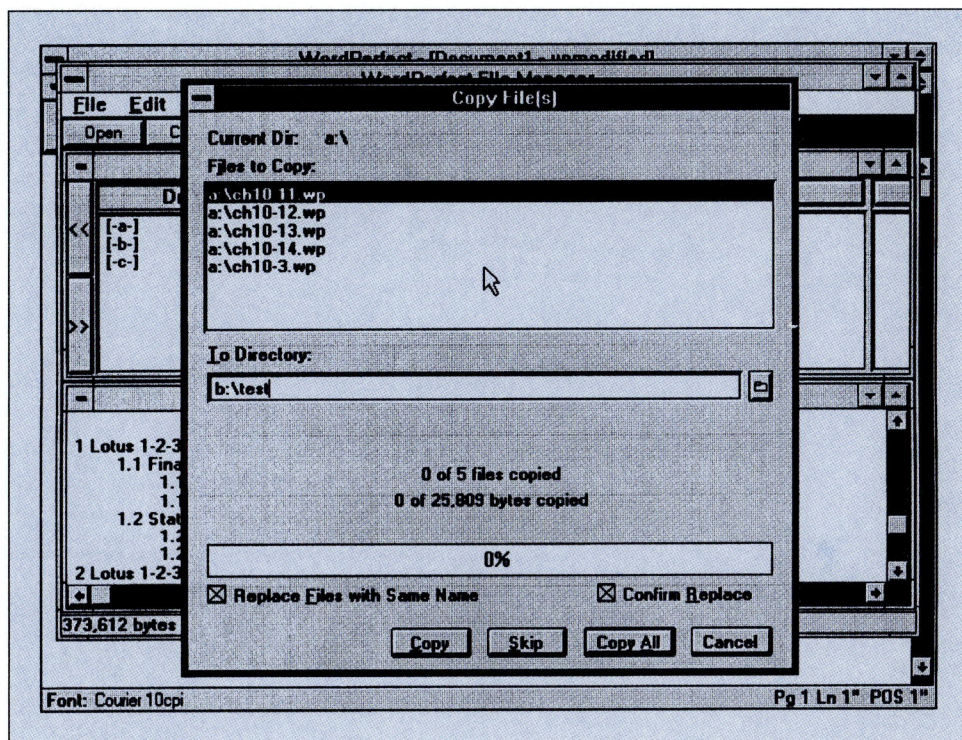

Figure 7–11
Copy File[s] dialog box.

7–3–6   Moving a File

To move a file or a series of files from one location to another, first highlight them; then click on the Move button. The Move dialog box will appear as displayed in Figure 7–12. In the To box type the name of the file or directory with the complete path and click on the Move button.

While you are moving a file, you can rename it at the same time by typing a new name for the file in the To box.

7–3–7   Deleting a File

To delete a file first highlight it; then click on the Delete button. The Delete File[s] dialog box will appear as displayed in Figure 7–13. Click on the Delete button. Be careful! When you delete a file the disk allocation table is updated to reflect the deletion of the specified file(s). At this point, the only way to get the file back is to use the UNDELETE command if you are using DOS 5 or higher or one of the many utility programs on the market that offers undelete capabilities.

If you are deleting more than one file, when you click on the Delete button the File Manager displays the confirmation box. So you have one final chance to change your mind before you delete each file. To continue, click the Delete button again. If you click on the Delete All, the confirmation dialog box is not displayed, and the remaining files are deleted without further confirmation. So selecting Delete All is somewhat risky!

7–3–8   Finding Words

Let us say you have written memos to several people and you want to find out which memo or memos have mentioned Mr. Morris. You can't remember which

Figure 7–12
Move/Rename File[s] dialog box.

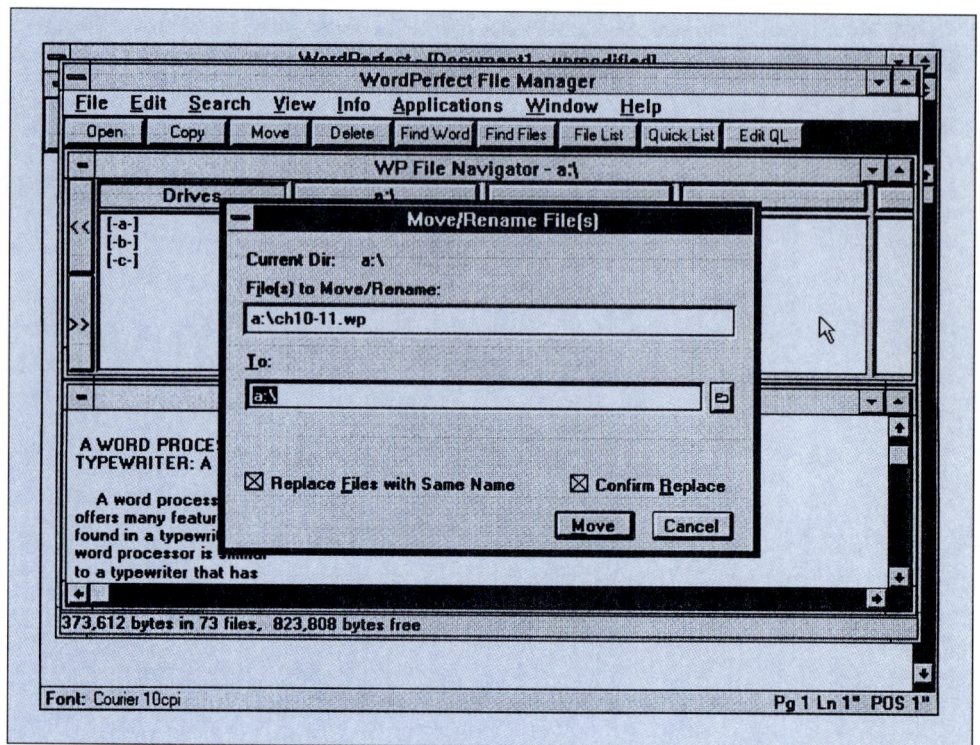

Figure 7–13
Delete File[s] dialog box.

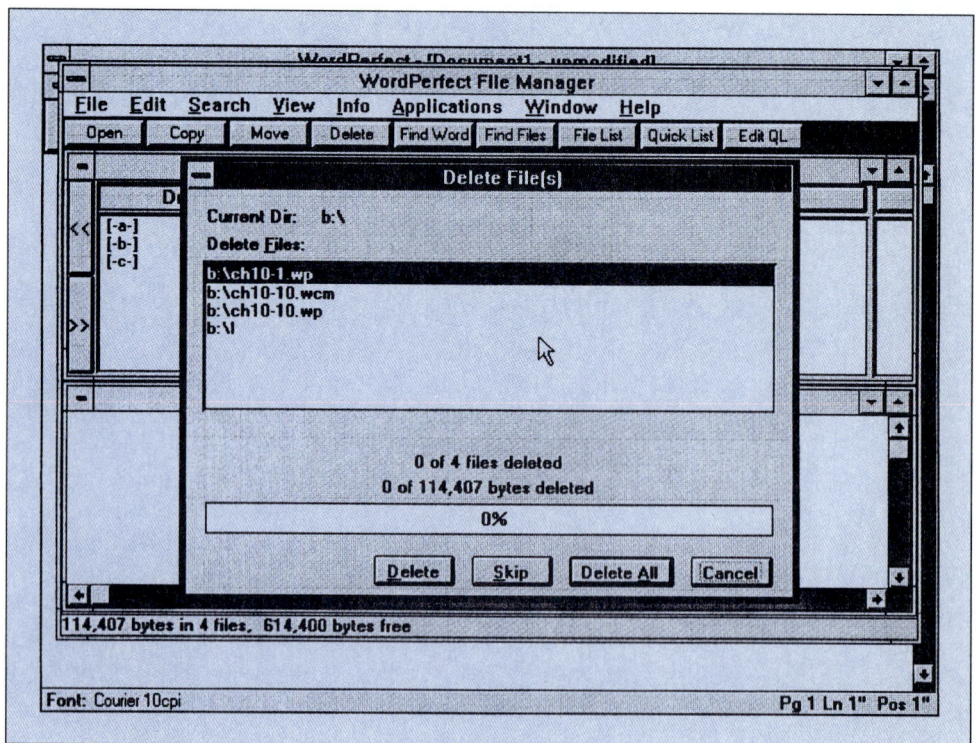

memos include this name. The Find Word button in the File Manager can take care of this problem for you. This is how you do it:

1. Highlight the drive and/or directory or files that you think may include the name Mr. Morris. The more specifically you define this information, the faster you will find the name. For example, highlighting five files will bring results much faster than highlighting the entire drive. We highlighted five files that we think may include Mr. Morris.
2. Click on the Find Word button. The Find Words dialog box will appear; see Figure 7–14.
3. In the Word Pattern box type *Morris* and click on Find.
4. As soon as you click on Find, the File Manager goes to work and provides you with results. In this case it provided the names of four files that include the name Morris; see Figure 7–15.

7–3–9

Finding Files

You may be interested in finding a specific file in a drive or in a particular directory, for example, a file named Sales or all files that start with certain characters. The Find Files button does this for you very effectively.

If you click on the Find Files button you will be presented with a dialog box similar to the one in Figure 7–16. In the File Pattern box type the desired file name or pattern of characters that you remember. For example, if you type *.WK1,* the result would be all your WK1 files in the current drive. If this is not the drive and directory that you want, click on the correct drive in the Drives column.

The * (asterisk) is a wildcard, which acts like a placeholder. The * represents up to eight characters. If you type *CH*.*,* for example, the File Manager will find all the files that start with CH, and the rest of the characters can be anything.

Figure 7–14
Find Words dialog box.

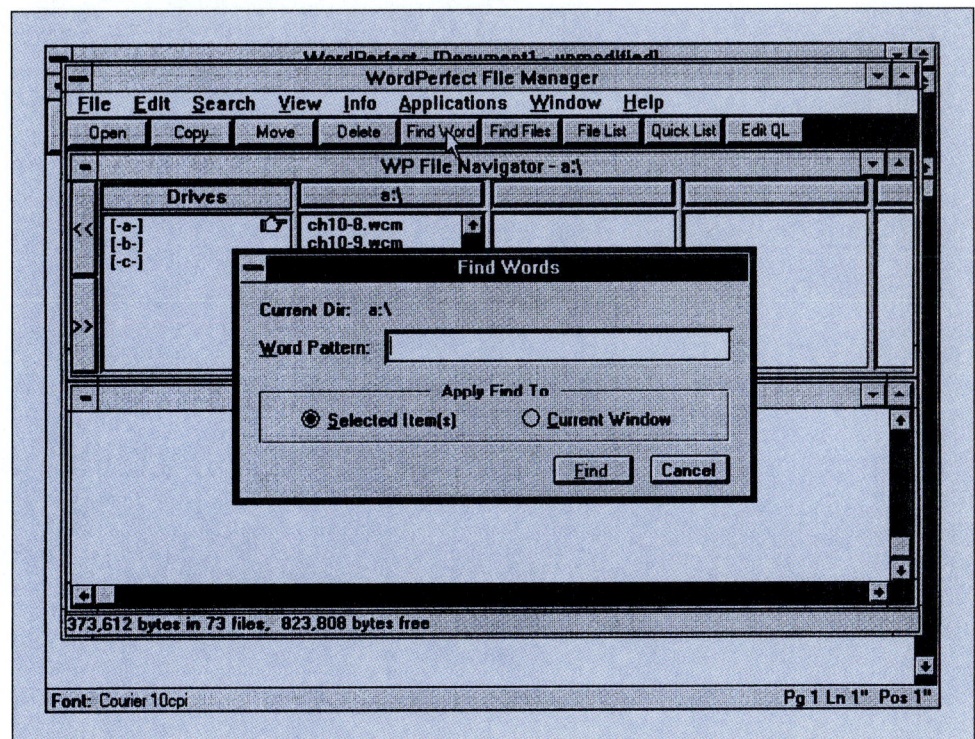

Figure 7–15
Search results for "Morris" text.

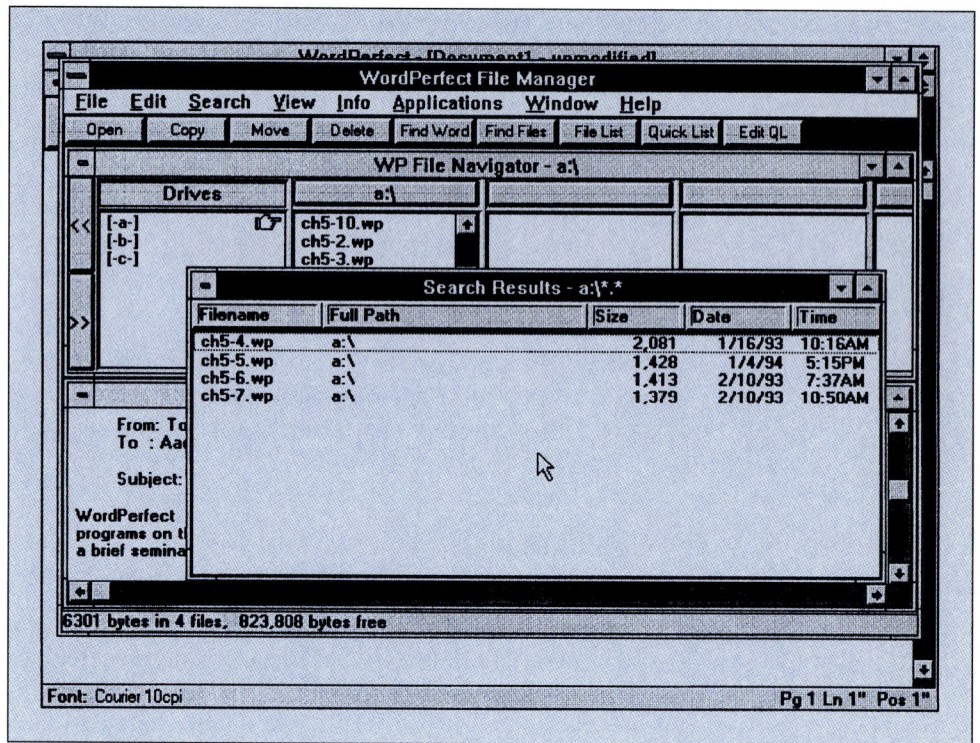

Figure 7–16
Find Files dialog box.

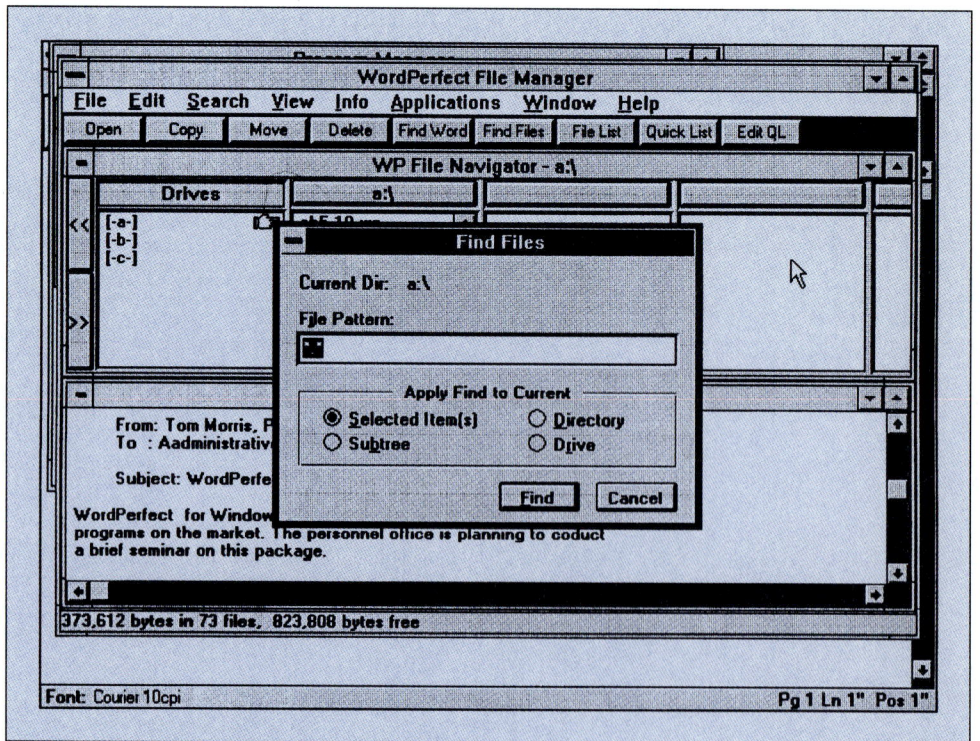

To find all the files with a WP extension in drive A, type *.WP* in the File Pattern box. After typing the name, click on Find. Figure 7–17 is the result of the search for all *.WP files. To see the rest of the files, you must click and drag the down-arrow icon. To see the contents of a specific file, highlight it. You will see the contents of the highlighted file in the Viewer window. To open the Open dialog box, double-click on the desired file.

The other wildcard that you can use is the ? (question mark). For example, if you type *.WK?* you will generate a listing of all WK1, WKS, WKE, and WK3 files. In other words, the question mark represents any character in one location.

7–3–10

Listing Files

The File List button is similar to the DOS DIR command. By means of the File List button you can generate a directory listing of any drive and/or directory in your system. These files can be WordPerfect files or files generated by any other application. This is how you do it:

1. Click on the File List button.
2. In the Dir box type the name or pattern in which you are interested.

After generating the list, you can highlight the file to see its contents in the Viewer window, or you can double-click on it to display the Open dialog box.

7–3–11

Using the File Manager Quick List

If there are certain files that you use more often than others, consider adding them to the Quick List. You can save a considerable amount of time by not going through a long list of files to locate a desired file.

Figure 7–17
Search results.

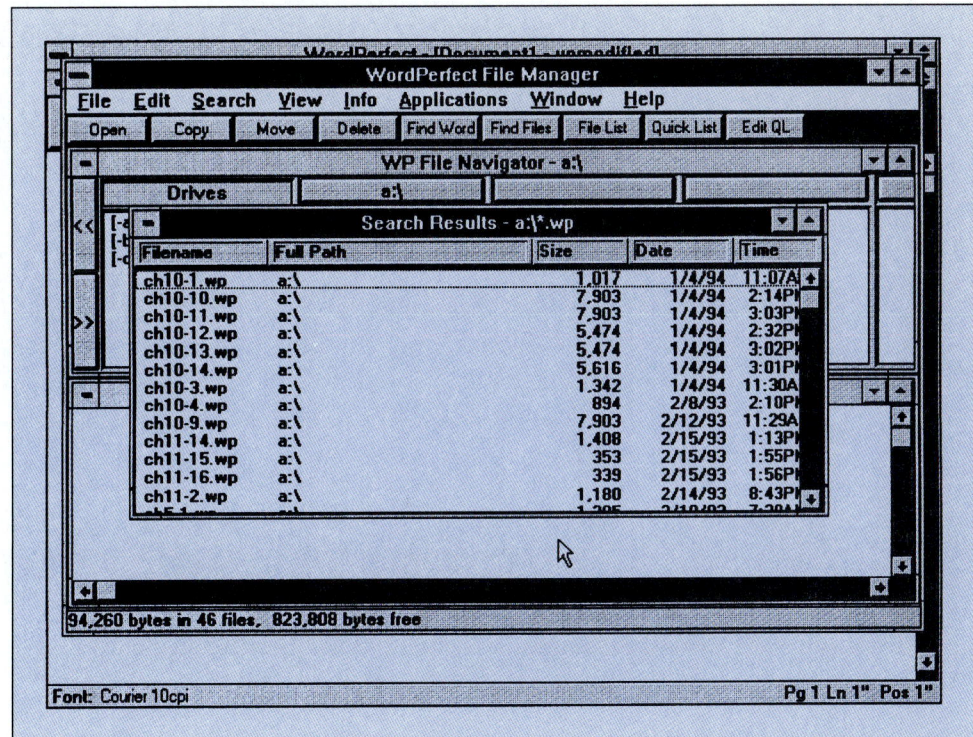

If you click the Quick List button you will see a dialog box similar to the one in Figure 7–18. This is the default listing. You can add any other file(s) to this list (see the next section).

Adding Files to the Quick List.   To add a file to the Quick List, follow these steps:

1. Click on the Edit QL button. You will be with a dialog box similar to the one in Figure 7–19.
2. Click on the Add button. You will be presented with the Add Quick List Item dialog box (see Figure 7–20).
3. In the Directory/Filename box type the name of the desired file with its complete path. We typed *A:CH6-10.WP.*
4. In the Descriptive Name box enter a name that describes this category of files. We typed *WordPerfect Book.*
5. In the Add Quick List Item dialog box click on OK.
6. To finalize the process, click on OK in the Edit Quick List dialog box.

From now on when you click on Quick List, you will see the WordPerfect Book category. Later you can add more files to this category.

Deleting and Editing a Quick List Item.   If you change your mind, you can delete a Quick List item from the list by selecting the Delete button from the Edit Quick List dialog box. You can also change the description of an item by selecting the Edit button from the Edit Quick List dialog box.

Figure 7–18
Quick List default listing.

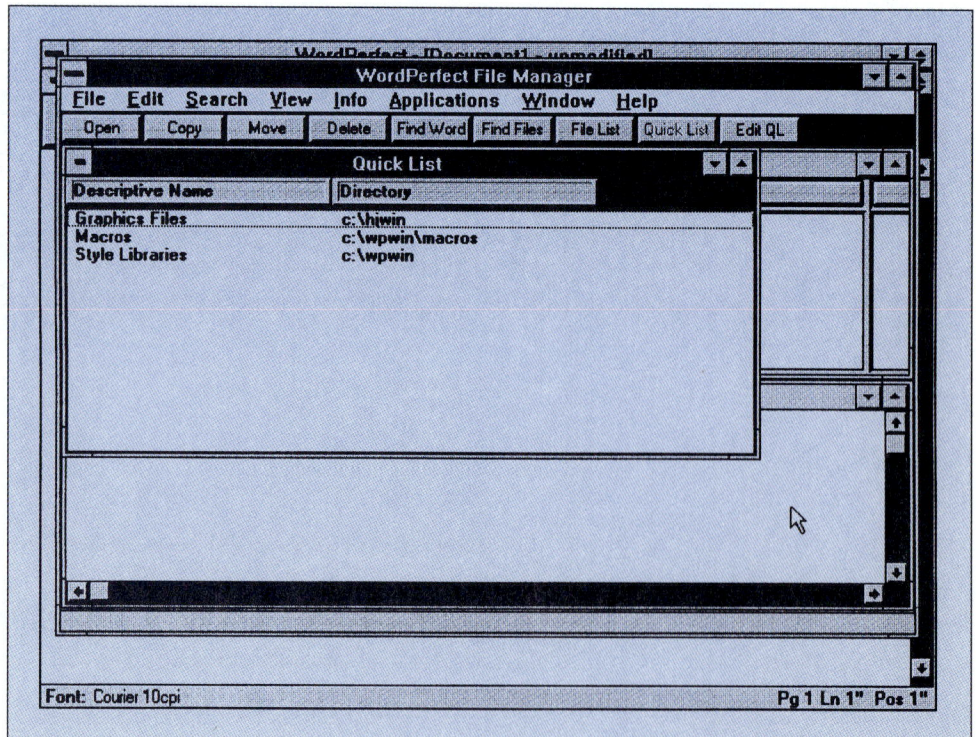

Figure 7–19
Edit Quick List dialog box.

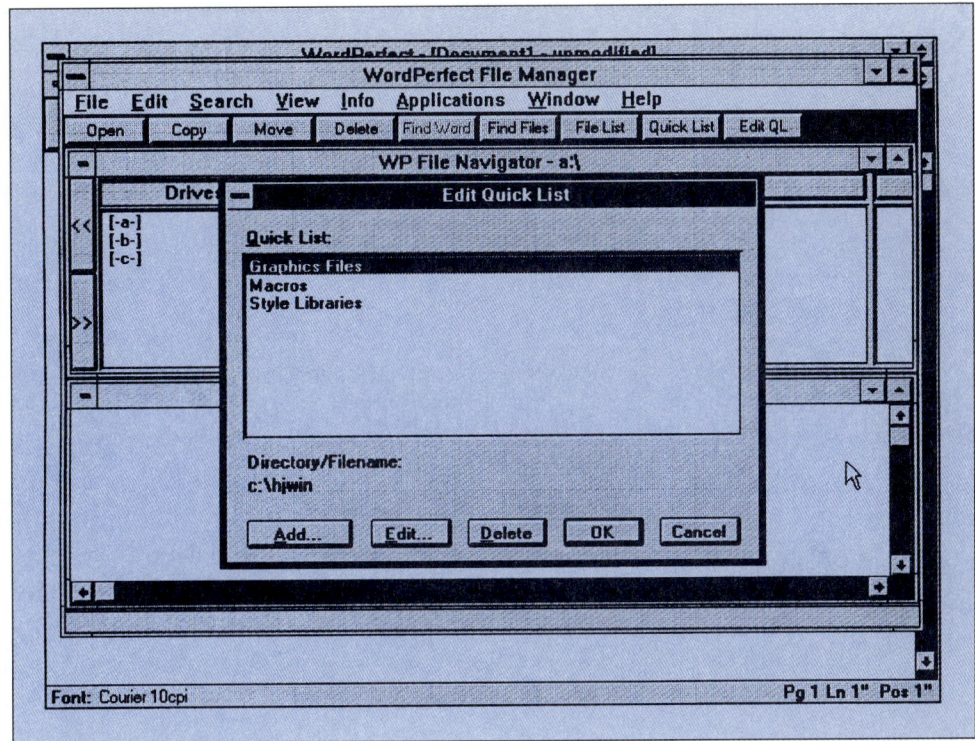

Figure 7–20
Add Quick List Item dialog box.

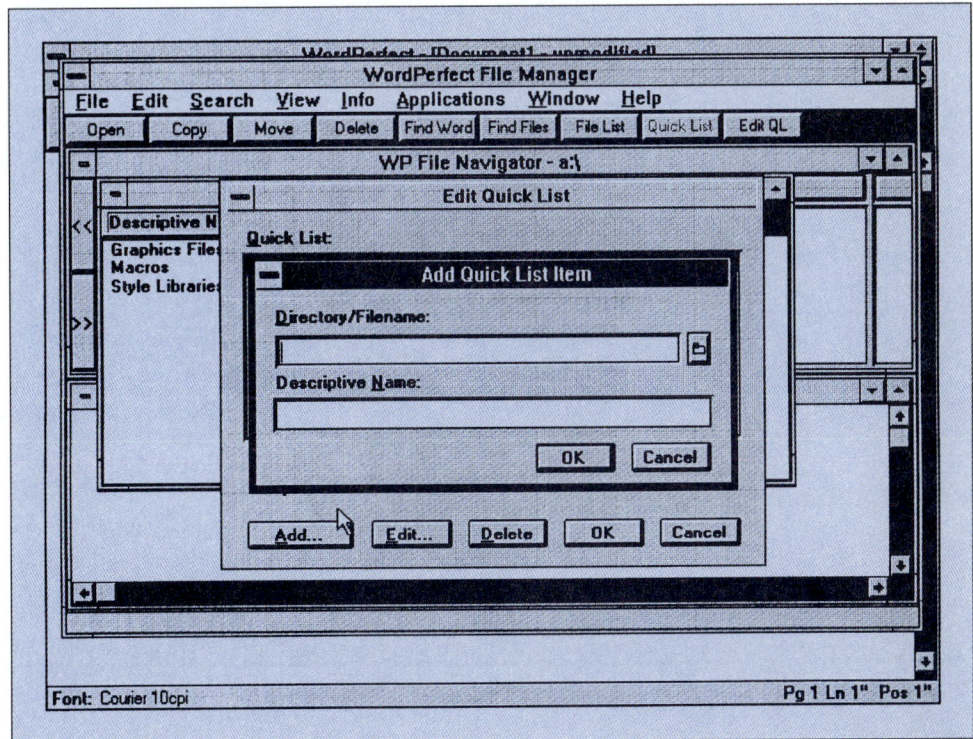

SUMMARY

This chapter explained button bars and the File Manager as two powerful features of WordPerfect for Windows. First, the chapter described the process of using, editing, creating, and selecting button bars. The second part of the chapter discussed the File Manager as a powerful tool for organizing, viewing, copying, and moving WordPerfect for Windows and other files available in your system.

REVIEW QUESTIONS

*These questions are answered in Appendix A.
  1. What is a button bar?
 *2. What are the default buttons on the button bar?
  3. Give some of the advantages of using button bars.
  4. How do you move the button bar from one location to another location?
  5. Describe how to create your own button bar.
 *6. What file extension is attached to a button bar file?
  7. How do you delete a button from the button bar?
  8. How do you rearrange the buttons on the button bar?
 *9. How do you select a different button bar? How do you hide the button bar to save space?
 10. What is the File Manager?
 11. Name some of the typical tasks performed by the File Manager.
 12. What is the Navigator window in the File Manager screen?
*13. What are the menu options in the File Manager?
 14. How do you open a file using the File Manager? How do you view a file?
 15. Explain how to copy a file from drive C to drive A using the File Manager.
*16. How do you move a file from drive A to drive C using the File Manager? How do you delete an unwanted file?
 17. How do you find a word using the File Manager?
 18. How do you find a specific file using the File Manager?
 19. What are wildcards and how do you use them to find a series of files?
 20. Describe how to list files using the File Manager.
*21. How do you view one of the files displayed in the Navigator window?
*22. How do you open one of the files that you found using the Find Files button?
 23. What is the Quick List?
 24. Explain how to add two files of your choice to the Quick List.
*25. How do you edit the description of a file in the Quick List?
 26. How do you remove one of the files in the Quick List?
 27. What are some of the applications of the Quick List?

HANDS-ON EXPERIENCE

  1. Start WordPerfect for Windows and do the following:
     a. Hide the button bar.
     b. Reveal it.
     c. Move the button bar to all four possible locations.
     d. Move the button bar back to its default location.

2. Create a button bar with four buttons that perform the following tasks, respectively: count words in a document, underline selected text, boldface selected text, italicize selected text.

3. By using the Select option from the Button Bar Setup menu, access different button bars provided by WordPerfect for Windows. What does each specific button bar do?

4. Access the File Manager and do the following:
   a. Change from the C drive to the A drive.
   b. By clicking on one of the displayed files in the Navigator window, display its contents.
   c. By double-clicking on one of the displayed files and clicking on the Open button, open it.
   d. By using the Copy button, copy one of the files in drive C to drive A.
   e. By using the Delete button, erase the copied file from drive A.
   f. Exit the File Manager.

5. Start the File Manager again and do the following:
   a. Using the Find Word button, search for a particular word of your choice in drive A.
   b. Using the File List button, generate a listing of drive A.
   c. Add three files of your choice to the Quick List under the description Try.
   d. Erase these files.
   e. Exit the File Manager.

KEY TERMS

Button bars

File Manager

Navigator window

Viewer

KEY COMMANDS

File Manager (to access WordPerfect File Manager)

View Button Bar (to enable or disable the button bar)

View Button Bar Setup (to access the Button Bar Setup menu)

MISCONCEPTIONS AND SOLUTIONS

Misconception Your screen does not show the button bar. This makes your ordinary word processing tasks more difficult.

Solution Select the View menu and click on Button Bar to display the button bar on the screen.

Misconception You start WordPerfect for Windows and notice that the button bar displayed is not the default button bar.

Solution WordPerfect for Windows remembers your last button bar. To display the default button bar, you must select View, Button Bar Setup, and Select; double-click on wp{wp}.wwp, which is the default button bar.

Misconception You are not satisfied with the order of the buttons on the button bar. You think you are stuck with this configuration.

Solution You can rearrange the buttons on the button bar. Select the Edit option from the Button Bar Setup menu; click and drag the buttons, one by one, anywhere that you want on the bar.

Misconception   Using the mouse, you are trying to highlight the entire disk for copying. This is time consuming.

> **Solution**   From the Edit menu (in the File Manager window) choose the Select All option, or just press the Ctrl+S key combination to highlight the entire disk.

ARE YOU READY TO MOVE ON?

Multiple Choice

1. Which one of the following is *not* among the buttons available in WordPerfect for Windows?

   a. Close
   b. Open
   c. Save
   d. Print
   e. They all are available.

2. To hide the button bar, which menu must you activate?

   a. View
   b. File
   c. Layout
   d. Tools
   e. Window

3. To change the position of the button bar, which option should you select?

   a. Button Position
   b. Button Bar Setup
   c. Button Rotation
   d. View Button
   e. none of the above

4. To create your own button bar, select the New option from which menu?
   a. File
   b. Layout
   c. Button Bar Setup
   d. Ruler
   e. Tools

5. When you save a button bar under a name, what extension does WordPerfect for Windows attach to it?

   a. BAK
   b. WS
   c. WP
   d. WWB
   e. COM

6. To select a different button bar, which option must you choose from the Button Bar Setup menu?

   a. Select
   b. Edit
   c. Options
   d. New
   e. Save As

7. The default button bar is saved under the name

   a. wwb
   b. wp{wp}.wwb
   c. wp.wwp
   d. {wp}.wwb
   e. none of the above

8. Under which menu will you find the WordPerfect for Windows File Manager?
   a. Tools
   b. Layout
   c. View
   d. Edit
   e. File

9. Which of the following options is not among the File Manager menu options?
   a. View
   b. Search
   c. File
   d. Save
   e. Edit

10. In the File Manager window, directories are identified by
    a. \
    b. {}
    c. []
    d. /
    e. *

True/False

1. The File option is among the menu selections of the File Manager.
2. A selected file cannot be unselected through the File Manager menu; it must be unselected by using the mouse.
3. Through the Info menu of the File Manager, you can receive information about the disks in your computer.
4. To arrange your open windows in tile or cascade format, you must access the Applications menu in the File Manager.
5. To view the contents of a file in the Viewer window, simply double-click on the file.
6. Using the Copy button in the File Manager, you can copy only one file from one location to another. There is no way to copy several files.
7. To unselect a selected file, press the Ctrl key while you click it.
8. The File Manager allows you to delete an entire directory at once.
9. The Find Word button in the File Manager assists you in locating information in any drive or directory.
10. The File Manager does not provide any facility for generating a complete listing of a drive or directory.

ANSWERS

Multiple Choice		True/False	
1.	e	1.	T
2.	a	2.	F
3.	b	3.	T
4.	c	4.	F
5.	d	5.	F
6.	a	6.	F
7.	b	7.	T
8.	e	8.	T
9.	d	9.	T
10.	c	10.	F

Layout Design and Merge Printing

8

8–1   INTRODUCTION

In this chapter we consider various features of WordPerfect for Windows that enable you to design the layout of a document. Page breaks, page numbers, headers, and footers are discussed. The Print Preview command for viewing a document before it is printed is highlighted. The second part of the chapter focuses on merge printing as one of the strongest features of WordPerfect for Windows. Merge printing enables you to combine fixed and variable documents together—a helpful feature for mass mailings.

8–2   LAYOUT DESIGN

In the next few pages we will discuss the general design, or **layout design**, of a document. Page breaks allow you to exercise full control over the start and stop of a page in your document. The page number feature lets you include page numbers on your document, and headers and footers enable you to include additional information at the top or bottom of document pages. Let us look at each feature in more detail.

8–2–1   Page Breaks

As soon as you type enough text to fill one page, WordPerfect for Windows automatically enters a soft page break and moves to the next page. A soft page break is identified by a single, solid line (———) on the document and by the [SPg] code in the Reveal Codes window. If for some reason you want to end a page before its normal termination, you must enter a hard page break. Let us say you have a table and you want to make sure that the entire table appears on one page. To do this, start a new page and enter the table in this new page. Now to enter a hard page break, move the insertion point to the desired position and select Layout, Page, and Page Break (or press Ctrl+Enter). You will see a double, solid line (═══) on the document and [HPg] code in the Reveal Codes window. If you look at the status line, you will see that the text under the double, solid line is on page 2. Figure 8–1 illustrates a document with a hard page break. To remove a hard page break, move the insertion point to the line above the break and press the Del key.

8–2–2   Page Numbers

You can number the pages of your document in several different ways. The WordPerfect for Windows default setting prints pages *without* page numbers. In any case, **page numbers** of a document do not show up on the screen. To see page numbers, you must either print the document or, by using the Print Preview (Shift+F5) command (discussed in the next section), display the document on the screen. When the page number feature is turned on, it can be suppressed whenever necessary. For example, you can number pages 1 through 6 and suppress the number on page 7 (this page may include diagrams and you do not want to include a page number). You can resume the numbering from page 8.

Let us use the page number feature to number the document presented in Figure 8–1. Do the following:

1. Move the insertion point to the beginning of the document.

Figure 8–1
Document with a hard page break.

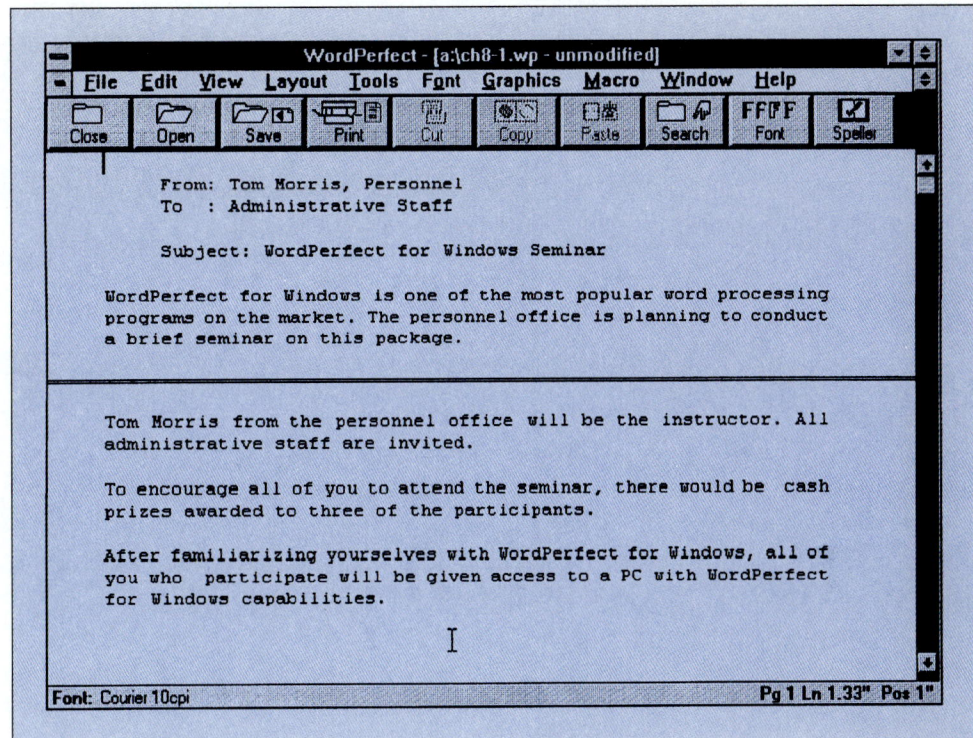

2. Select Layout and Page (Alt+F9). Then select the Numbering option. A screen similar to Figure 8–2 will be displayed.

3. Click and hold on the pop-out icon in the Position box. As you can see in this menu, No Page Numbering is the default option. However, you can select any one of the following options for the position of the page number:

   - Top Left
   - Top Center
   - Top Right
   - Alternating Top
   - Bottom Left
   - Bottom Center
   - Bottom Right
   - Alternating Bottom

   Simply click on the desired option, for example, the Top Center option. As soon as you do this, the sample facing pages in the Define Page Numbering box indicate 2 and 3 as page numbers at the top center position. See Figure 8–3.

4. In the Numbering Options box click and hold on the Numbering Type pop-out icon. The menu gives you the following three options:

   - Arabic, for example, 1, 2, 3, 4. This is the default.
   - Lowercase Roman i, ii, iii, iv, and so on.
   - Uppercase Roman I, II, III, IV, and so forth.

Figure 8–2
Page Numbering dialog box.

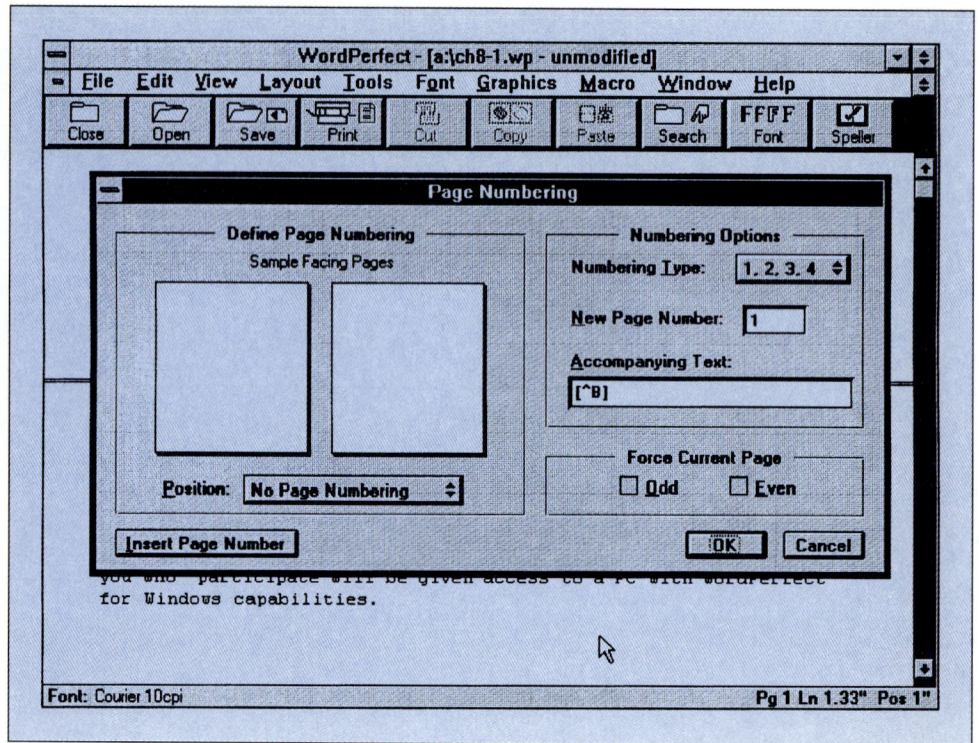

Figure 8–3
Page Number dialog box and sample facing pages.

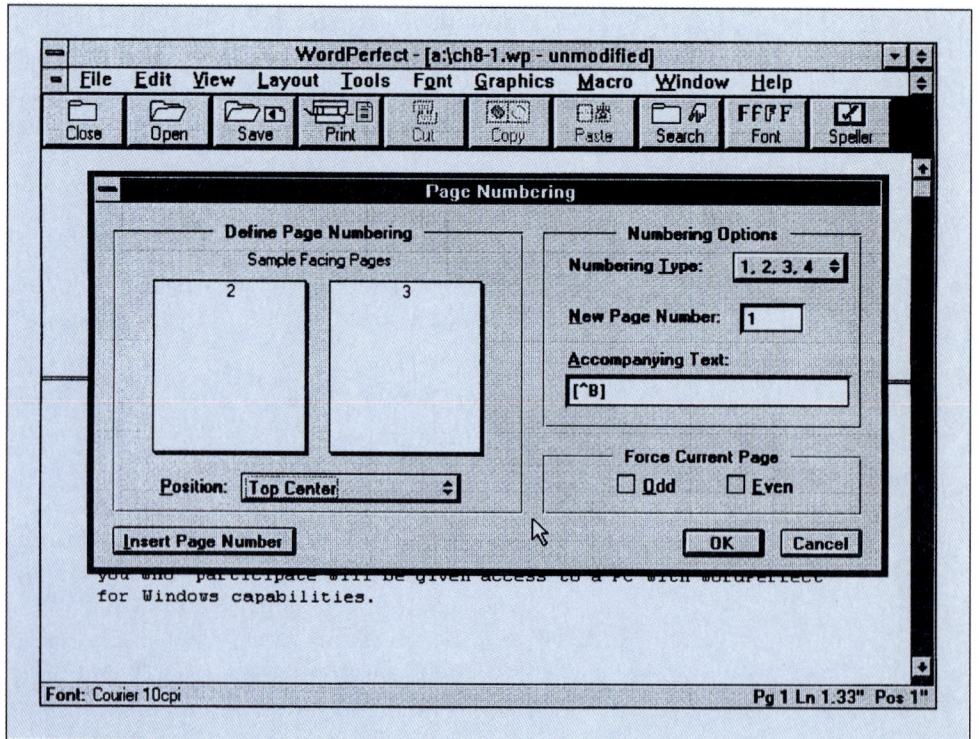

Click on the desired option. We selected the default option, hence the Arabic numbers in Figure 8–3.

5. You can instruct WordPerfect for Windows to start page numbering from certain pages. For example, page 100. In the New Page Number box type the desired page number. When you do this, the sample facing pages will display 100 and 101, respectively.

6. Click on OK to get back to the document.

If you print this document by using the Print command from the File menu and by selecting the Full Document option, you will see that the document is numbered page 1 and 2 and the page numbers appear at the top center of both pages. This document is presented in Figure 8–4.

To suppress a specific page number, follow these steps:

1. Move the insertion point to the top (upper left corner) of the desired page.

2. From the Layout menu select Page; then select the Suppress option. You will be presented with the Suppress dialog box; see Figure 8–5.

3. Click on the Page Numbers box; then click on OK.

8–2–3   Previewing a Document

When you add page numbers and other features such as headers and footers to a document, you do not see these features until you print the document. By using the Print Preview (Shift+F5) command from the File menu, you can review the layout of your document before it is printed. The preview command, by generating a temporary document, displays headers, footers, footnotes, endnotes, margins, and page numbers. You cannot perform any editing in this mode, but you

Figure 8–4
Document with page numbers.

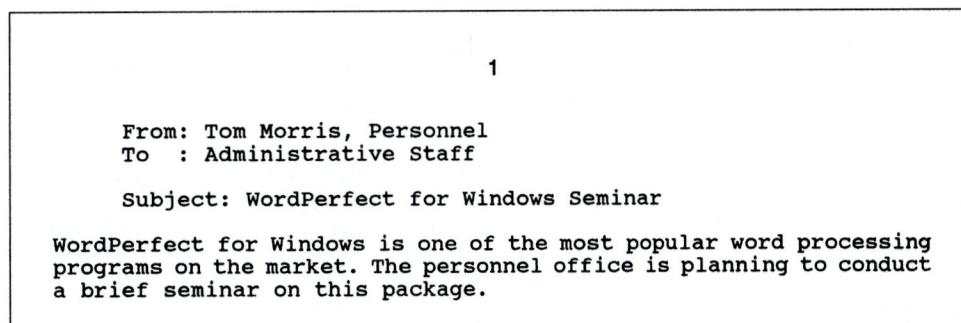

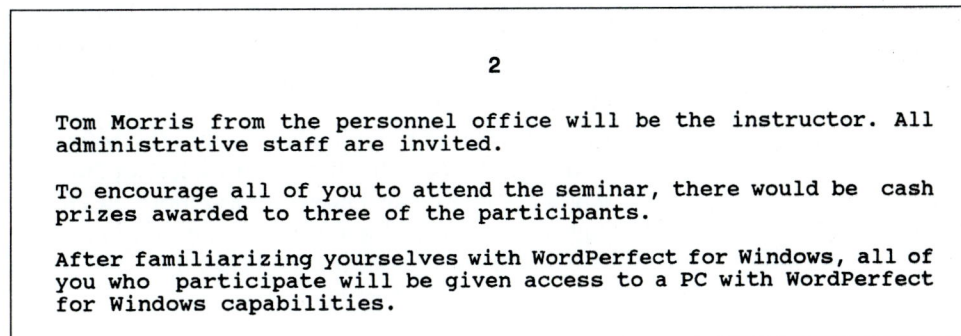

```
                                      1


        From: Tom Morris, Personnel
        To  : Administrative Staff

        Subject: WordPerfect for Windows Seminar

WordPerfect for Windows is one of the most popular word processing
programs on the market. The personnel office is planning to conduct
a brief seminar on this package.
```

```
                                      2


Tom Morris from the personnel office will be the instructor. All
administrative staff are invited.

To encourage all of you to attend the seminar, there would be  cash
prizes awarded to three of the participants.

After familiarizing yourselves with WordPerfect for Windows, all of
you who  participate will be given access to a PC with WordPerfect
for Windows capabilities.
```

Figure 8–5
Suppress dialog box.

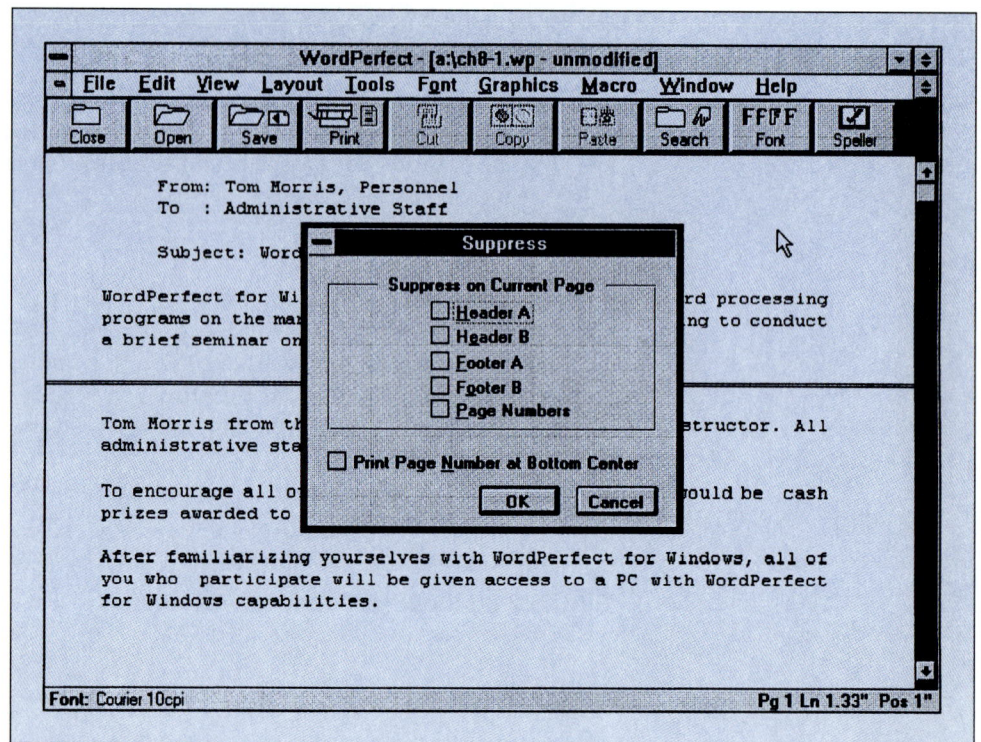

can view your document and then return to the original to make corrections as needed.

Let us say you would like to preview the document presented in Figure 8–4, which, as you recall, includes page numbers. Follow these steps:

1. Retrieve the document by selecting the Open option from the File menu and by typing the file name.
2. Select the Print Preview option from the File menu. You will see a screen similar to the one in Figure 8–6.

Note the series of buttons on the button bar along the left side of the screen. Let us briefly consider each one.

The Close button closes the Print Preview window and returns you to your document.

The Print button prints out a copy of your document; selecting this option is similar to selecting the Print command from the File menu. When you make this selection, the Print dialog box will be displayed. As usual, you have to specify the desired options and click on Print.

The Full Page button shows the preview as a full page.

The FacingPg button reveals the facing page in the document. This option is useful only when the document has more than two pages, and it will show more than one page only when the insertion point is positioned on the second page or higher. At the lower left of the screen a message tells you which pages are being previewed. For example, in Figure 8–7 the message indicates that pages 2 and 3 are being previewed. The message also tells you the actual page size that these images represent (in this case, 58%).

The PrevPage button switches you to a preview of the previous page.

Figure 8–6
Print Preview screen.

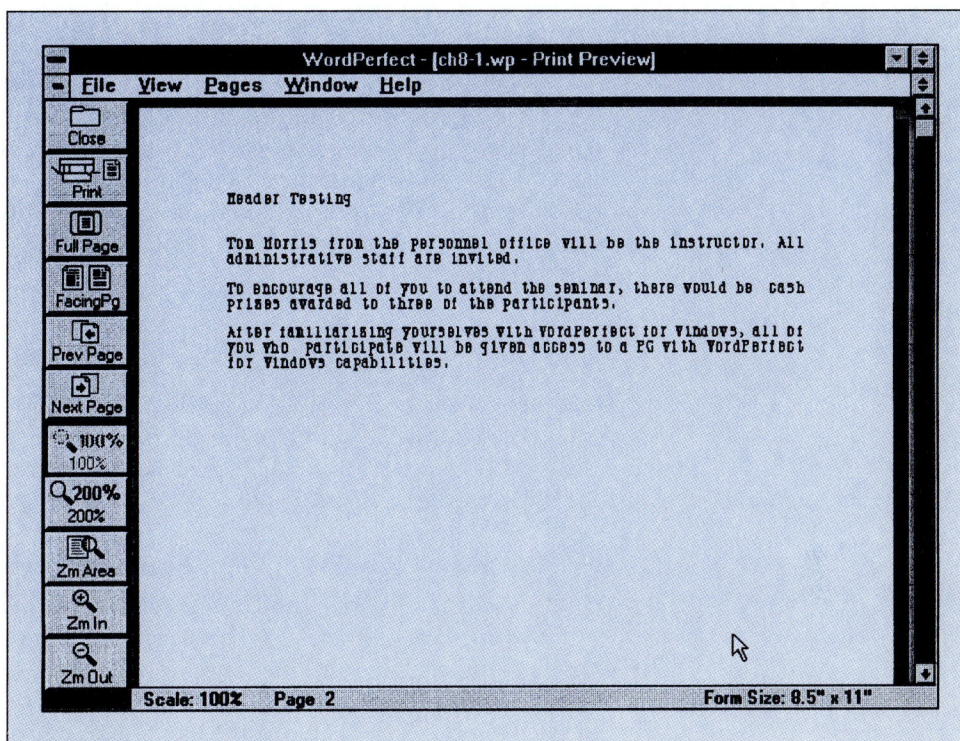

Figure 8–7
Previewing facing pages.

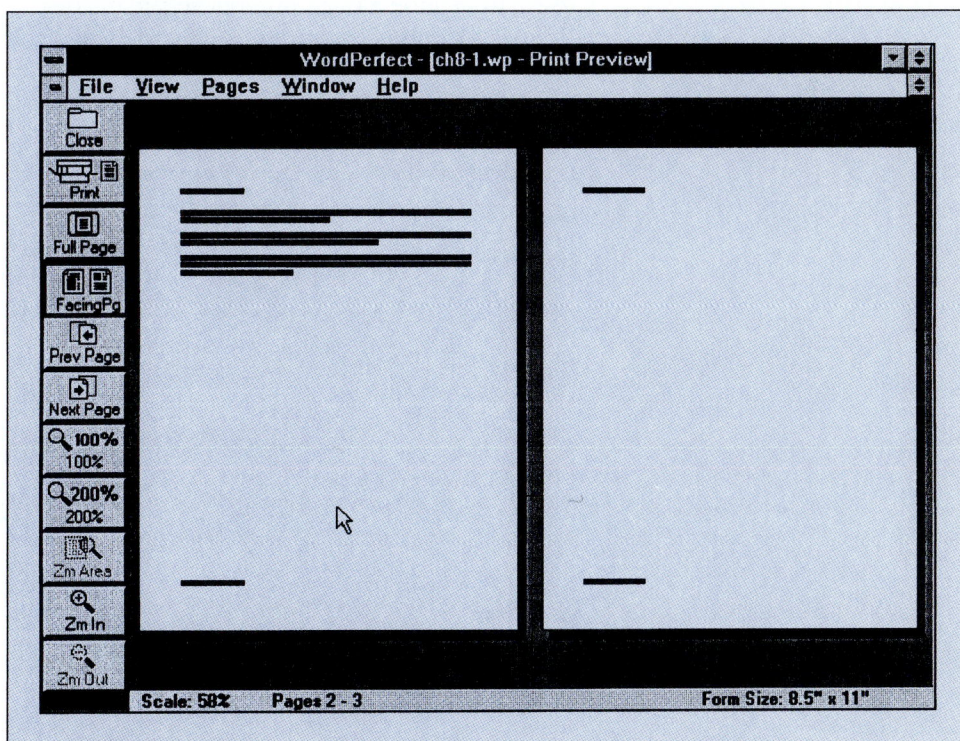

The Next Page button switches you to a preview of the next page, which is the case in Figure 8–6.

The 100% button provides an actual-size view of the page.

The 200% button displays a 200% view of the page, that is, twice the actual size. This option is useful for viewing the fine details of graphics and fonts.

The Zm Area button enables you to select an area of a document. The Zm In button allows you to zoom in on or magnify the view of the selected area. Similarly, the Zm Out button allows you to zoom out or reduce the view of the selected area.

8–2–4

Inserting Headers and Footers into Documents

Headers consist of information printed at the top of the page where the first line of text normally prints. **Footers** are printed at the bottom of a page.

Let us insert a header and a footer into the document presented in Figure 8–4. To enter a header, follow these steps:

1. Move the insertion point to the beginning of the document.

2. After selecting Layout and Page, select the Headers option. You will see the Headers dialog box (Figure 8–8). There is no difference between Header A and Header B as long as you want only one header. If you want two headers, then you must select A and B, and they will appear as two different headers. As an example, think of chapters in a book. On odd pages the header may say "Information Systems Literacy" and on even pages the header may say "WordPerfect for Windows."

3. Click on Create. You will be presented with a screen similar to the one in Figure 8–9. To include a page number in the header click on the Page Number button. If you select this option the ^B code will appear, but it will not be printed. If you click on the Placement button, you will see a placement screen similar to the one in Figure 8–10. Click on the desired option; then click on OK.

Figure 8–8
Headers dialog box.

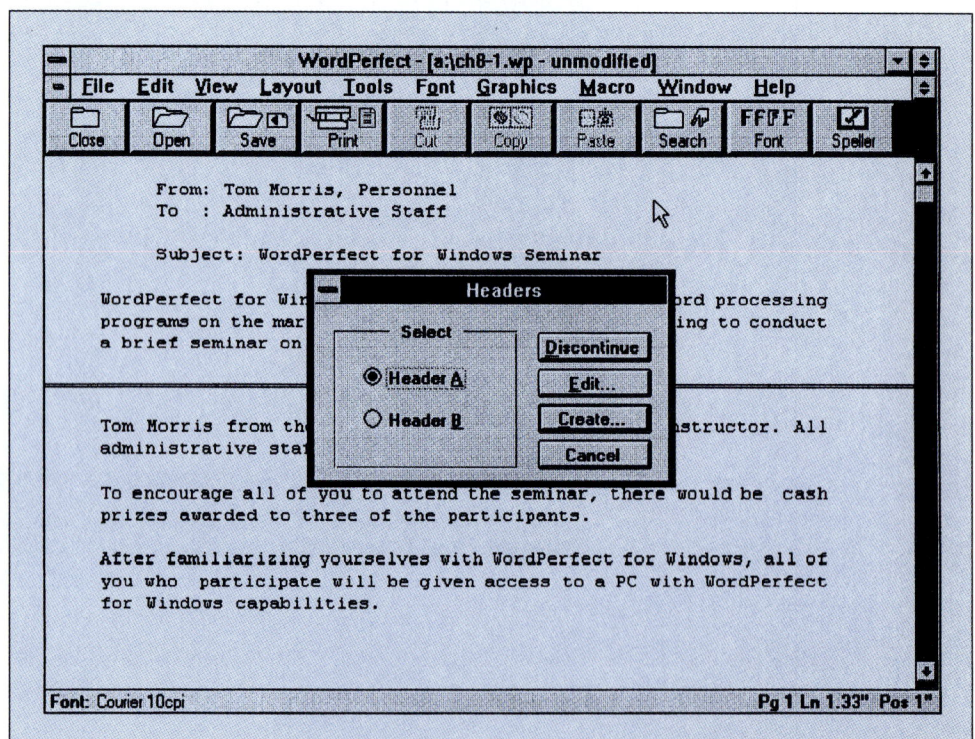

Figure 8–9
Headers screen.

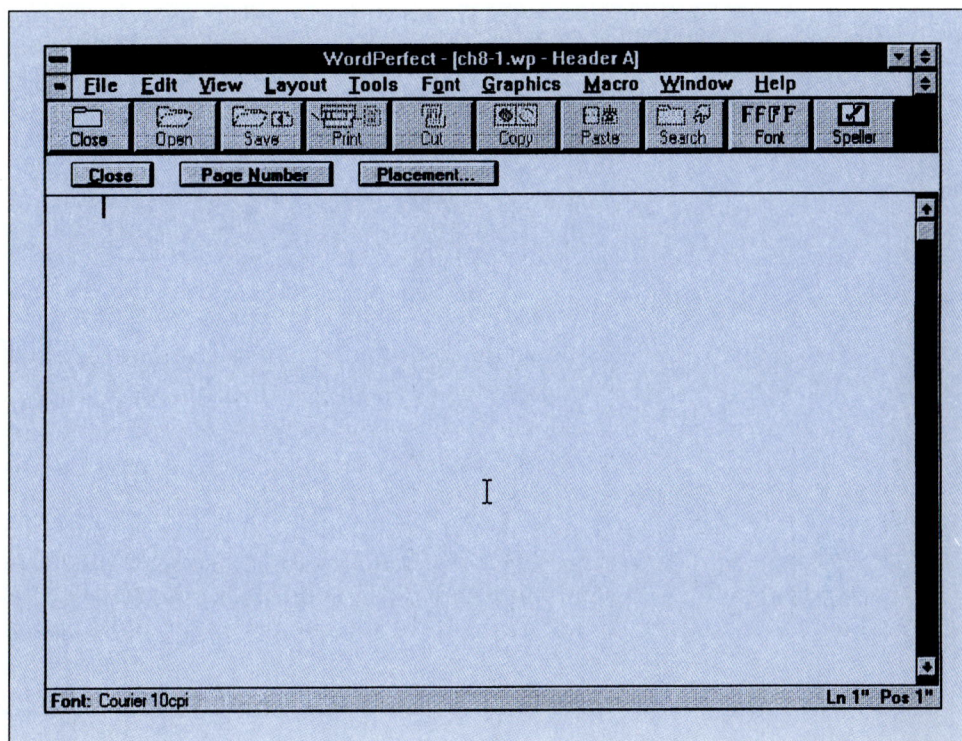

Figure 8–10
Placement dialog box.

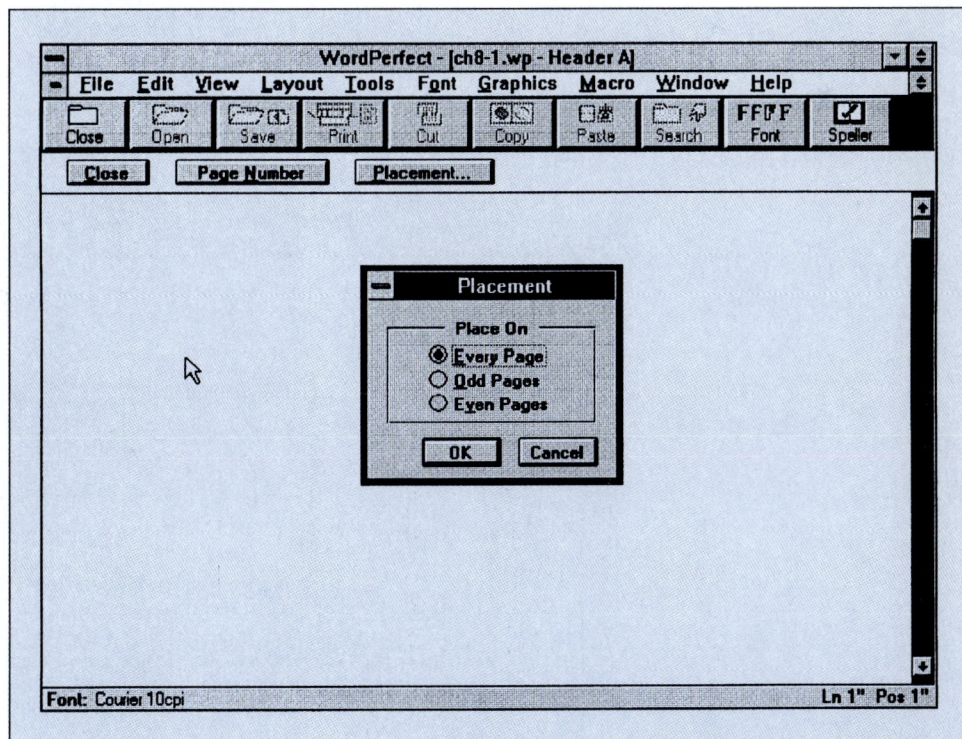

4. We clicked on the Every Page option to let the header appear on every page and then on OK.

5. In the clear screen that is provided, type *Header-Testing* (or anything else that you choose).

6. Click on Close; you will return to the document.

Now you can preview this document and see that, indeed, the header has been inserted at the top of each page.

Now, let us insert a Footer into this document.

1. Move the insertion point to the beginning of the document.

2. Select Layout and Page; then select the Footers option. You will see a screen similar to the one in Figure 8–11. Select the Create option.

3. In the clear screen that is provided, type *Footer-Testing* and click on Close.

Print this document by selecting the Print option from the File menu; then select the Full Document option. Your report should resemble the one shown in Figure 8–12. Remember, you can also preview this document to see that the header is at the top and the footer at the bottom of both pages.

8–2–5

Changing Headers and Footers After They Are Inserted

Headers and footers can be changed or modified after they have been inserted. They can be underlined, boldfaced, and/or printed in a font that is different from the text. Other formatting features can also be applied to headers and footers. To display and change the header in Figure 8–12, follow these steps:

Figure 8–11
Footers dialog box.

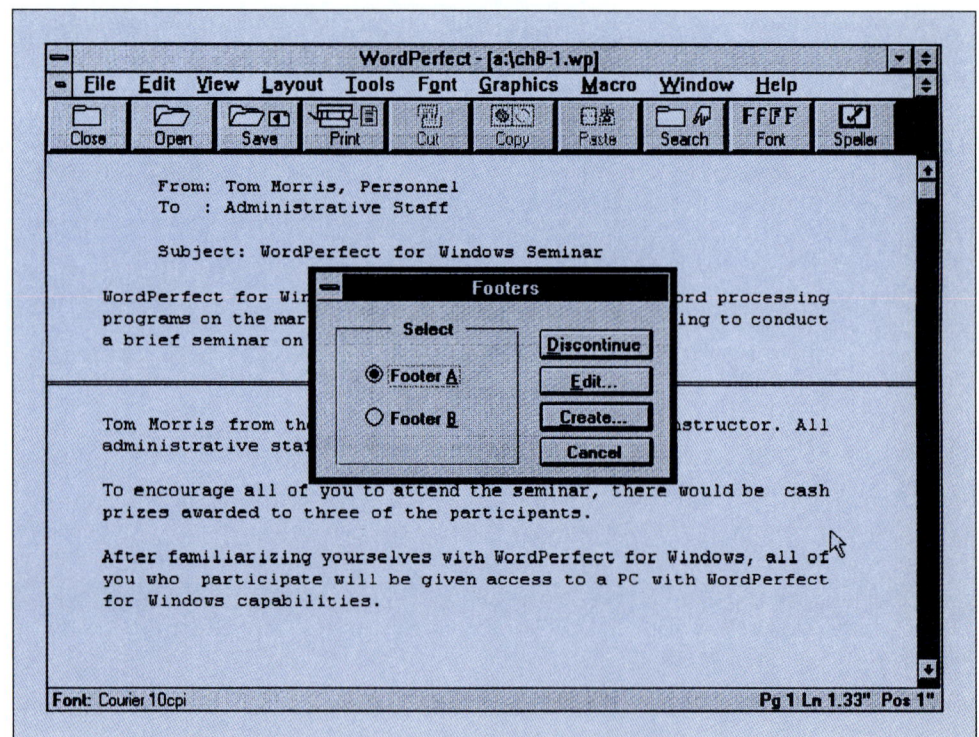

Figure 8–12
Report with page number, header, and footer.

```
Header-Testing                    1


        From: Tom Morris, Personnel
        To  : Administrative Staff

        Subject: WordPerfect for Windows Seminar

WordPerfect for Windows is one of the most popular word processing
programs on the market. The personnel office is planning to conduct
a brief seminar on this package.




Footer-Testing
```

```
Header-Testing                    2


Tom Morris from the personnel office will be the instructor. All
administrative staff are invited.

To encourage all of you to attend the seminar, there would be  cash
prizes awarded to three of the participants.

After familiarizing yourselves with WordPerfect for Windows, all of
you who  participate will be given access to a PC with WordPerfect
for Windows capabilities.




Footer-Testing
```

1. Select the Page option from the Layout menu; then select the Headers option. You will see a screen similar to Figure 8–8.
2. Select the Edit option. At this point the text "Header-Testing" will be displayed. You can make any changes to the header using the editing features of WordPerfect for Windows.
3. Click on Close to get back to the document.

8–3   MERGE PRINTING

In many situations an organization sends the same letter to several hundred or several thousand of its customers. You may even send an invitation letter for a wedding or a big party to several hundred people. Typing individual letters to all the customers or guests would be a time-consuming task. WordPerfect for Windows provides a **merge printing** facility that can expedite this process. Merge printing can be particularly helpful for form letters, for standard billing documents, for promotional letters, for brochures describing new products, and for organizational notices.

In merge printing, the primary file contains the **constant document** and the secondary file contains the **variable document** such as names, addresses, and so on. For example, the primary file might be an organizational notice and the secondary file a mailing list.

The primary file is entered from the keyboard or from a computer file stored on a floppy or hard disk. You enter codes in the primary file that indicate the insertion of relevant information from the secondary file. If data is being merged from the secondary file, the codes in the primary file refer to the field(s) in the secondary file. Each code represents one field of data. For example, first name or last name or both. It is up to you to define the amount of information to be considered as a field. It depends on how you set up your secondary file.

Let us say you would like to mail the following letter to 2,000 customers of the Northwest Craft Company.

Dear:
I am pleased to inform you that the credit department has approved your credit request.

Sincerely yours,

Diana Thomas
Credit Manager

The following names and addresses are two of the 2,000 customers.

Mr. John Jones
3100 Ashe Road, #200
Portland, OR 97201

Ms. Dona Brown
1627 Broadway Avenue, #11
San Diego, CA 92112

8–3–1   Merge Codes

As mentioned, WordPerfect for Windows uses a series of codes for merge printing. Table 8–1 lists some of these codes. They are applicable to numerous tasks, and we will use some of them here. Figure 8–13 illustrates the Insert Merge Codes dialog box. To display this dialog box select Merge from the Tools menu; then select the Merge Codes option from this menu. The codes are listed in alphabetical order. Scroll down to locate the desired code.

8–3–2   Creating the Primary File

To create the primary file start with a clear screen. To create the document (a form letter) presented in Figure 8–14, complete the following steps:

1. From the Tools menu select the Merge option (Ctrl+F12).
2. From this menu select Merge Codes. You will see a screen similar to the one in Figure 8–13. The codes are arranged alphabetically. Move the insertion point to the desired code then either click on the Insert button or double-

Table 8–1
Selected Merge Codes

{DATE}	Inserts the system date into the document at the position of the insertion point (system date should be entered as the current date when the system is booted)
{END RECORD}	Marks the end of a record in a secondary file
{FIELD NAMES}name1˜. . . nameN˜˜	Merges the text from the specified field into the document being created
{INPUT}	Temporarily stops the merge process allowing for text to be entered from the keyboard. Select Tools, Merge, and End Field or just press (Alt+Enter) to continue
{NEXT RECORD}	Looks for the next record in the secondary file. If it does not find the next record, it ends the merge process
{QUIT}	Stops the merge process
{END FIELD}	Marks the end of a field in a secondary file

Figure 8–13
Insert Merge Codes dialog box.

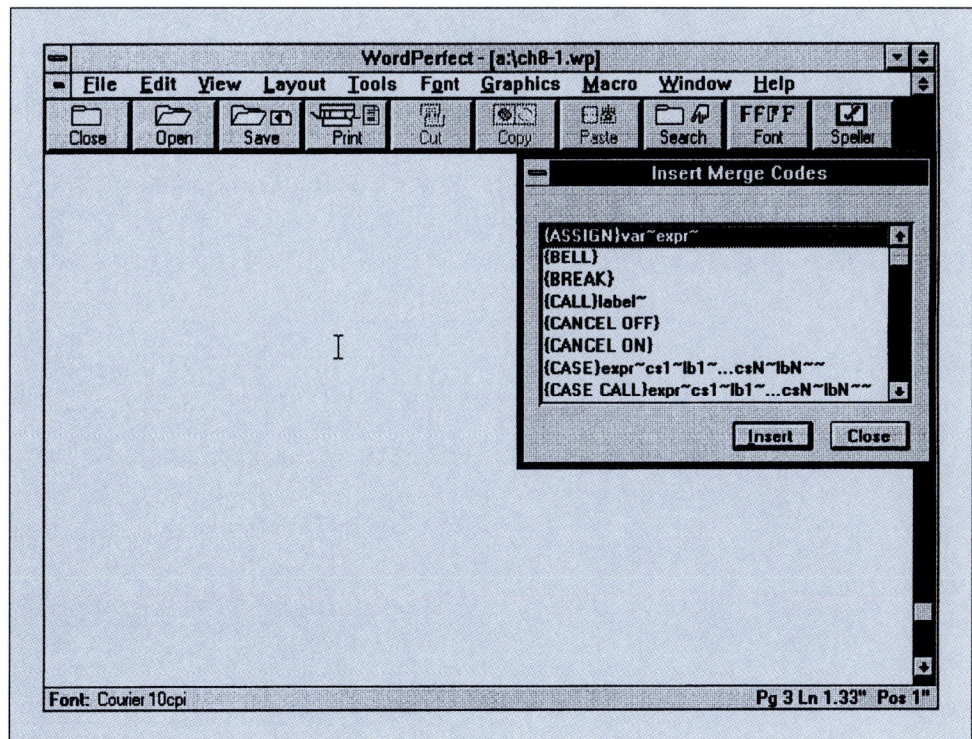

click on the desired code to enter it to the document. We selected the {DATE} code to enter the system date into our letter. Click on Close to close the Insert Merge Codes dialog box.

3. Press the Enter key twice to move the insertion point down two lines.

4. From the Tools menu select the Merge option; then click on Field. You will be presented with a screen similar to the one in Figure 8–15. Type *NAME*;

Figure 8–14
Sample form letter.

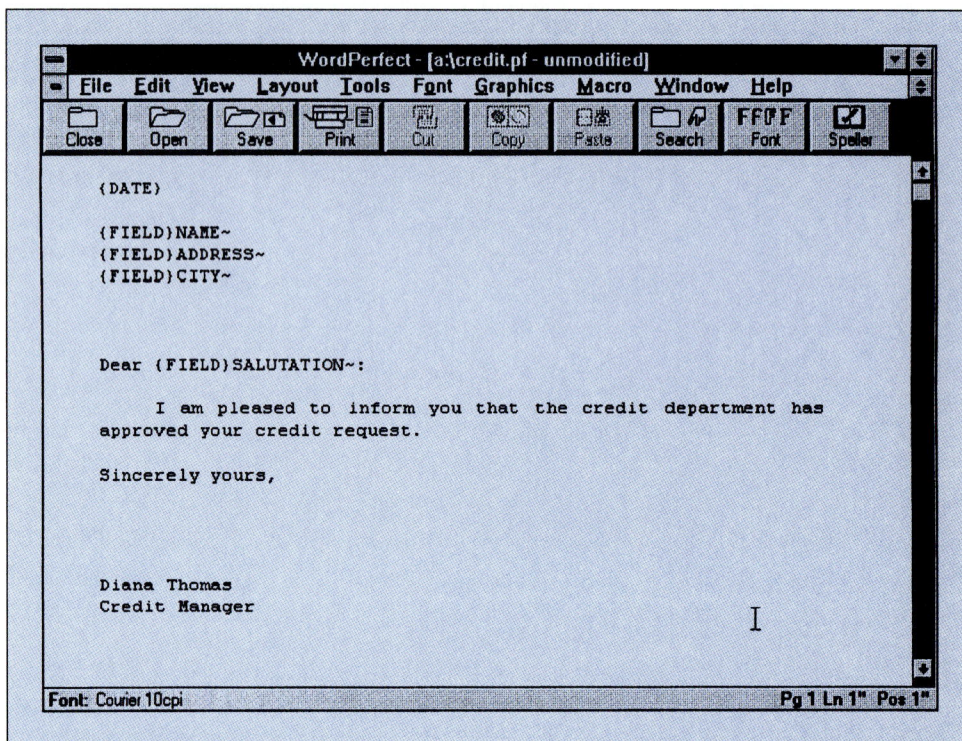

then click on OK. As soon as you do this, {FIELD}NAME~ appears on the screen.

5. Press the Enter key. Follow the same steps to enter a field called ADDRESS and a field called CITY.

6. After entering the CITY field, press Enter four times to skip four blank lines.

Figure 8–15
Insert Merge Code dialog box.

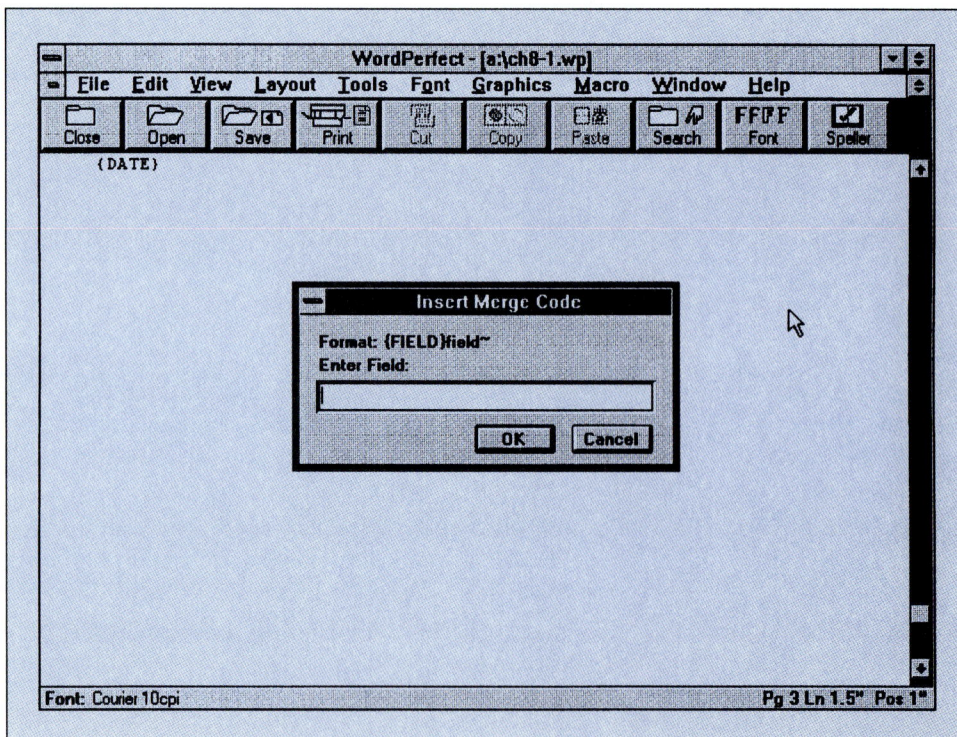

7. Type *Dear* and then press the space bar.

8. Select the Merge option from the Tools menu and click on Field. In the Enter Field box type *SALUTATION* and click on OK.

9. Type : and press Enter twice.

10. Press the Tab key; then type: *I am pleased to inform you that the credit department has approved your credit request.*

11. Press Enter twice.

12. Type *Sincerely yours*; then press the Enter key four times.

13. Type *Diana Thomas* and press Enter

14. Type *Credit Manager* and press Enter.

15. Save the document by selecting the Save As option from the File menu and by naming it CREDIT.PF. In this case, the file name tells you the contents of the file and the extension tells you that it is a primary file.

8–3–3

Creating the Secondary File

To create the secondary file (in this case, the file that contains the names and addresses), follow these steps:

1. Start with a clear screen. Select Tools, Merge, then Merge Codes.

2. Click on {FIELD NAMES}Name1~ . . . nameN~~.

3. Click on the Insert button. You will be presented with Merge Field Name[s] dialog box; see Figure 8–16. Notice that you are prompted to enter the name for Field Number 1 in the dialog box.

4. Type *NAME* and click on the Add button.

5. To enter the name for Field Number 2, move the insertion point to the Field Name box, click, and type *ADDRESS*.

Figure 8–16
Merge Field Name[s] dialog box.

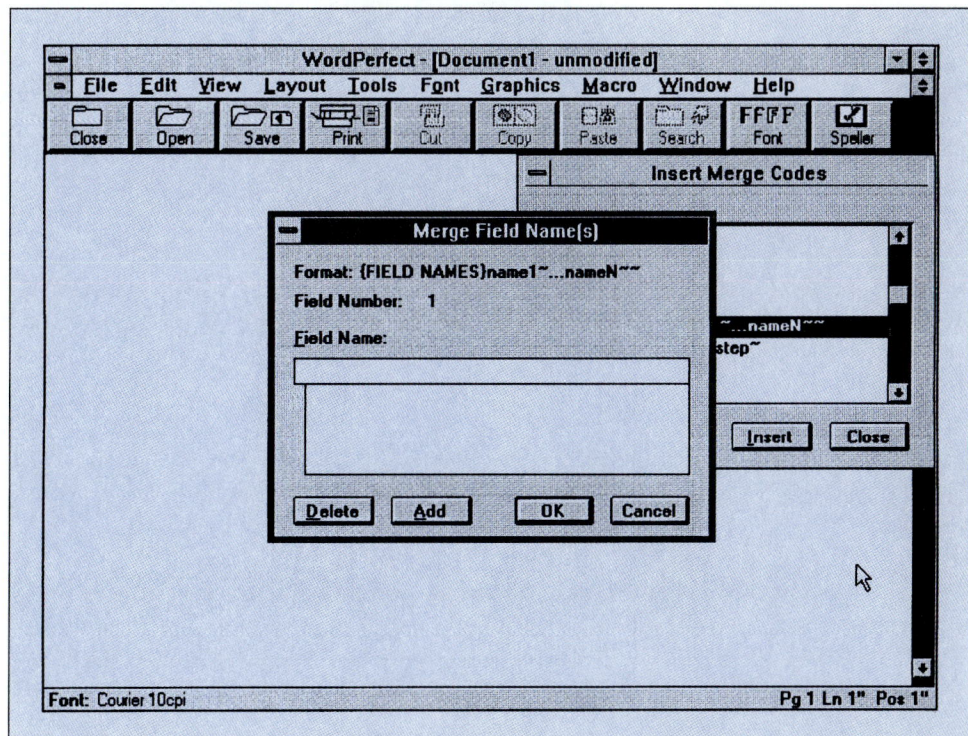

6. Click on Add.

7. Do the same two steps for the CITY and SALUTATION fields.

8. To end naming the fields, click on OK.

9. To close the Insert Merge Codes dialog box, click on Close.

At this point your screen should be similar to the one in Figure 8–17. Now you have to enter the information for the two records in this secondary file.

10. Type *Mr. John Jones* and from the Merge menu select {End Field}, or press Alt+Enter. This marks the end of the field.

11. Type *3100 Ashe Road, #200* and from the Merge menu select {End Field}.

12. Type *Portland, OR 97201* and from the Merge menu select {End Field}.

13. Type *Mr. Jones* and from the Merge menu select {End Field}.

14. Now you are done with the first record. To mark the end of this record from the Merge menu, select {End Record} or press Alt+Shift+Enter. This marks the end of the first record. It also places a hard page break (i.e., ══════) after the record.

Next you have to enter the second record:

15. Type *Ms. Dona Brown* and from the Merge menu select {End Field}. This marks the end of the first field.

16. Type *1627 Broadway Avenue, #11* and from the Merge menu select {End Field}.

17. Type *San Diego, CA 92112* and from the Merge menu select {End Field}.

18. Type *Ms. Brown* and from the Merge menu select {End Field}.

Figure 8–17

Merge codes for four fields are entered.

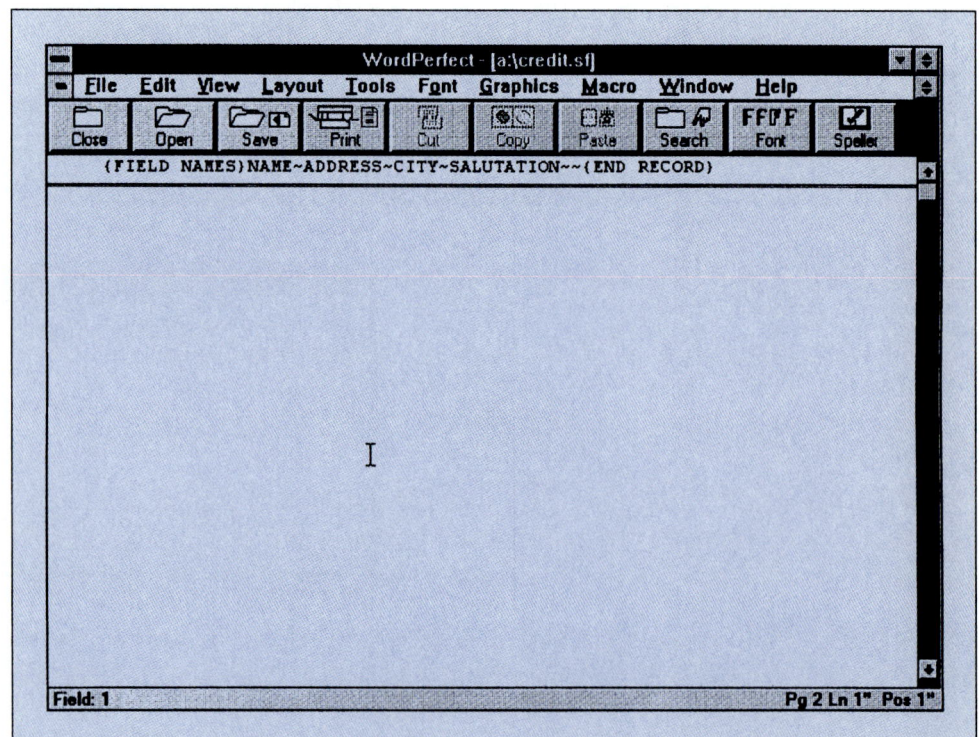

Figure 8–18
Secondary file (mailing list).

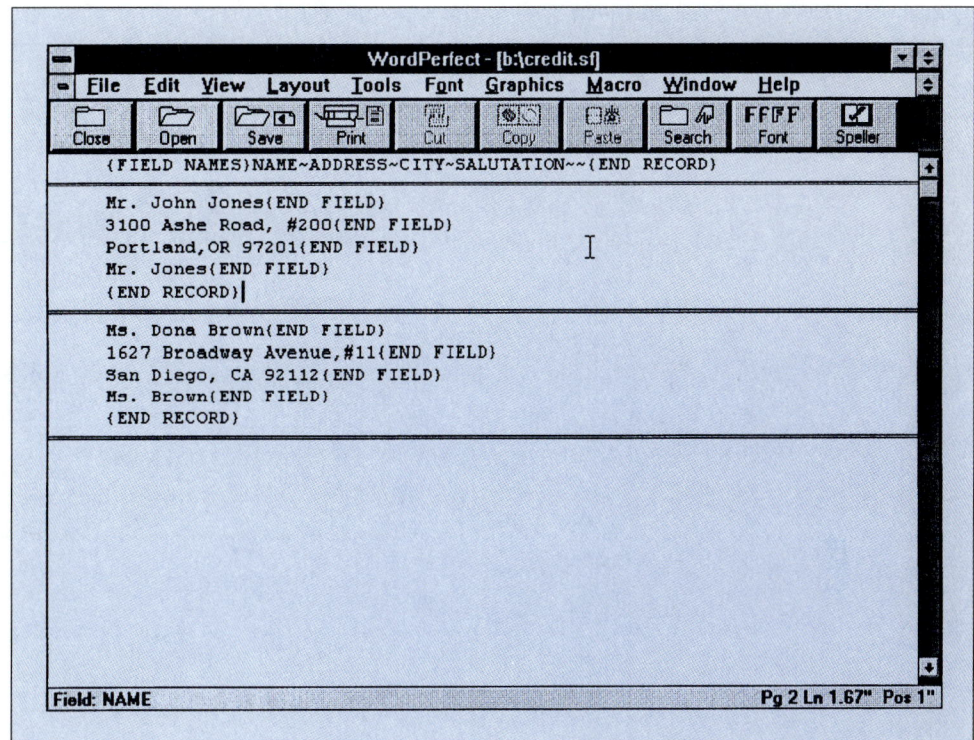

Figure 8–18
Secondary file (mailing list).

19. From the Merge menu select {End Record}. This marks the end of the second record; it also places a hard page break. This file is displayed in Figure 8–18.

20. Save this file with the Save As option and name it CREDIT.SF. The file name identifies the contents of the file, and the extension identifies it as a secondary file.

8–3–4 Starting the Merge Print Operation

To merge the primary file (Figure 8–14) and the secondary file (Figure 8–18), complete these steps:

1. At a clear screen, select the Merge option from the Tools menu. Click on the Merge option. You will be presented with the Merge dialog box as presented in Figure 8–19.

2. In the Primary File box type *A:CREDIT.PF* (your primary file). Alternatively, you can click on the file folder icon to the right of the box to see a listing of all the files in your default drive; double-click on the desired one.

3. In the Secondary File box type the name of the secondary file. We typed *A:CREDIT.SF* (our secondary file). Again, as an alternative, you can click on the file folder icon to see a listing of all your files in the default drive; select the appropriate file. Click on OK. After a few seconds both letters are available on the screen. However, you will only see the second letter, because the first one has been scrolled up. Press the Page Up key or the up-arrow icon to see the first letter. The current date is inserted on the top of each letter.

Figures 8–20 and 8–21 display the two sample letters. You can also save the merged file under a new name and access it whenever needed.

Figure 8–19
Merge dialog box.

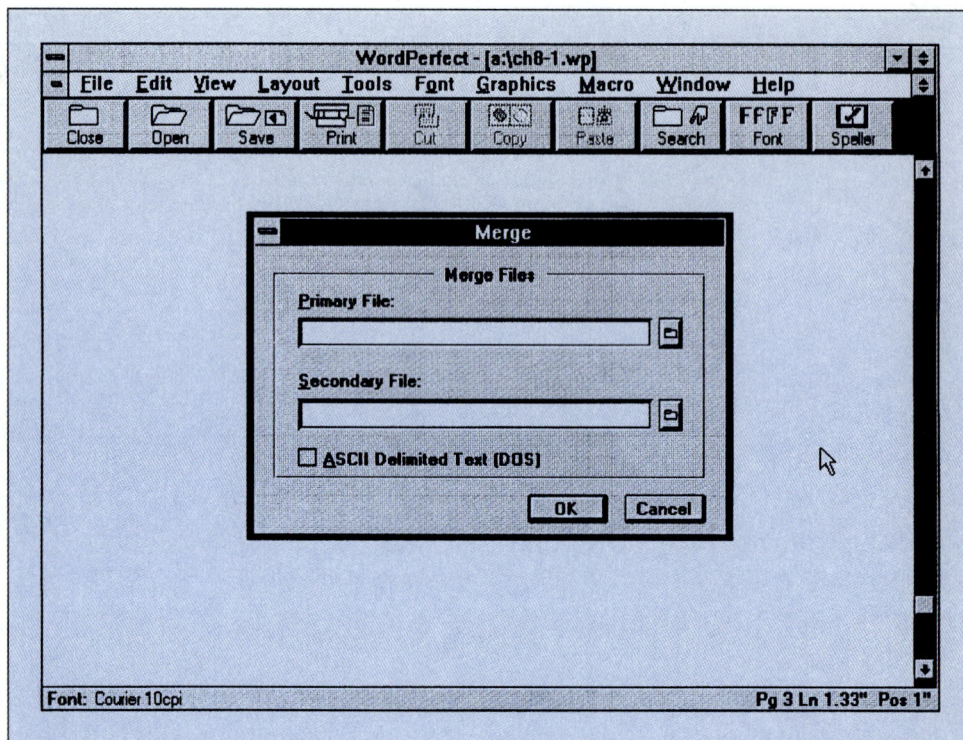

Figure 8–20
First sample letter.

```
January 1, 1994


Mr. John Jones
3100 Ashe Rd #200
Portland, OR 97201


Dear Mr. Jones:

     I am pleased to inform you that the credit department has
approved your credit request.

Sincerely yours,



Diana Thomas
Credit Manager
```

```
January 1, 1994

Ms. Dona Brown
1627 Broadway Ave #11
San Diego, CA 92112


Dear Ms. Brown:

     I am pleased to inform you that the credit department has
approved your credit request.

Sincerely yours,



Diana Thomas
Credit Manager
```

When you establish your secondary file, remember that all the records must be consistent. For example, if one of the fields is missing, you must still enter it as {End Field}. Let us say in a mailing list you include four fields for each customer. The fields are name, title, street address, and city/state. If one of your customers does not have a title, in the title field for that customer, you must enter the merge code {End Field}. This indicates that this field exists but it is empty for this particular customer. In the top part of the letter if you want to address the customer by his or her first name, just type the first name. In our example the fourth field would be *John*{End Field} or *Dona*{End Field}. If you would like to have both first and last names appear, just enter them as *Mr. John Jones*{End Field} or *Ms. Dona Brown*{End Field}.

8–3–5   Making Merge Printing an Interactive Process

You can insert codes in the primary file to accomplish **interactive merge printing**. For example, say in your primary document you have a word or phrase that will vary depending on the customer to whom you are referring. The interactive process allows you to insert the desired information while merge printing is taking place.

Let's walk through this process using our sample primary and secondary documents. In this example, we wish to inform each customer of the line of credit for which they have been approved. Follow these steps:

1. Retrieve the primary document file, A:CREDIT.PF, and move the insertion point to the information you wish to alter. In this case, we would like our notice to read: I am pleased to inform you that the credit department has approved your credit request of ____.

2. After typing *of,* open the Merge Codes menu (see Figure 8–13); in the Insert Merge Codes dialog box, double-click on {INPUT}message˜. WordPerfect for Windows responds with the Insert Merge Code dialog box; in the Enter Message box type *Enter Amount*; click on OK and click on Close. When you are finished, the line on your document should read:

```
your credit request of {INPUT}Enter Amount˜
```

Figure 8–22
Primary file with keyboard input.

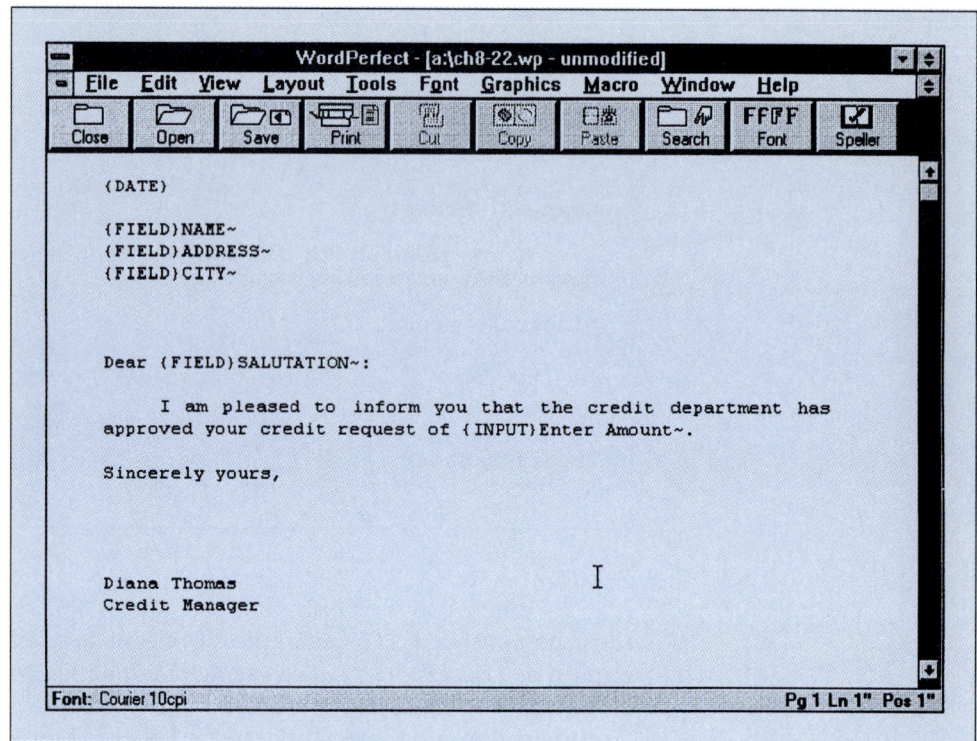

```
                    WordPerfect - [a:\ch8-22.wp - unmodified]
  File   Edit   View   Layout   Tools   Font   Graphics   Macro   Window   Help

  Close   Open   Save   Print   Cut   Copy   Paste   Search   Font   Speller


     {DATE}

     {FIELD}NAME~
     {FIELD}ADDRESS~
     {FIELD}CITY~



     Dear {FIELD}SALUTATION~:

          I am pleased to inform you that the credit department has
     approved your credit request of {INPUT}Enter Amount~.

     Sincerely yours,




     Diana Thomas
     Credit Manager


  Font: Courier 10cpi                                          Pg 1 Ln 1" Pos 1"
```

See Figure 8–22. This input code will stop the execution of the merge printing process and wait for your input. The prompt appears only on the screen, not on printed output. Often, you enter the variable data from the keyboard. To continue to the next customer, select Tools, Merge, and End Field.

SUMMARY

This chapter described various features of WordPerfect for Windows for designing the layout of a document: page breaks, page numbers, headers, and footers. The Print Preview command allows you to review a document before printing it. The second part of the chapter explained merge printing for combining a constant (primary) and a variable (secondary) document.

REVIEW QUESTIONS

*These questions are answered in Appendix A.

1. What is a soft page break?
2. What is a hard page break?
3. How is a soft page break entered? Is this the user's responsibility or WordPerfect's responsibility?
*4. How do you enter a hard page break? How do you remove a hard page break?
5. Explain how to open the Page Numbering dialog box.
*6. Can page numbers appear any place in the document or must they always be in a fixed position?
7. How do you preview a document? What is displayed when you preview a document?
*8. Can you edit a document in the preview mode?

9. How do you enter a header in a document?
10. How do you enter a footer in a document?
11. Can you change a header or a footer after it has been inserted? If yes, how do you do this?
12. What is merge printing?
13. Name some of the applications of merge printing.
*14. What are merge codes? What do they do?
15. What code is used to mark the end of a field? What code marks the end of a record?
16. How do you create primary and secondary documents?
*17. How do you start the merge process?
18. How do you know if the merge process has been a success?
19. Can you make the merge printing an interactive process? If so, how?
20. Describe how to print the result of merge printing.
21. How do you continue the merge process after entering variable data from the keyboard?

HANDS-ON EXPERIENCE

1. Load Figure 8–1 to your computer from the disk provided and do the following:
    a. Insert a hard page break after every paragraph.
    b. Number the four pages of the document from page 1 to page 4. Place the page number at the bottom center of every page.
    c. Preview this document to see if the page numbers are entered properly.
    d. Suppress the page number on page 2 of the document. Use the Print Preview command to verify your work.
    e. Insert "Header A" as a header on every page.
    f. Delete this header and enter a header on all the odd pages.
    g. Insert "Footer A" as a footer on all the even pages. Using the Print Preview command verify your work.
    h. Change the header to "New Header."
    i. Change the Footer to "New Footer."

2. Use the merge printing feature of WordPerfect for Windows to merge the following two documents. Primary document:

    Dear Valued Customer:

    I am extremely pleased to announce that we are opening a new branch of our department store in your neighborhood. There is a grand opening party on the first Tuesday of next month. You and your family are invited to attend. We are looking forward to seeing you there.

    Sincerely,

    John Thomson
    Marketing Manager

The sample secondary document is as follows:

    Ms. Susan Smith
    Chief Executive Officer
    16201 South Jefferson
    Portland, OR 97201

Mr. Tony Adam
151 North Cliff
Portland, OR 97112

Ms. Mary Thomas
Product Manager
1691 East Hampton
Portland, OR 97112

3. Retrieve the EXERCISE.WP document from your disk and do the following:
   a. Number this document using lowercase Roman format, for example, i, ii, and so on on every page at bottom center.
   b. Enter a header as "Header-Test" and a footer as "Footer-Test" and print the document.
   c. By using the Print Preview command, preview this document.
   d. Try all options of the Print Preview command. What are the applications of the zoom feature?
   e. Insert the following header and footer as the second header and footer to this document:

   Second Header - This is a practice document
   Second Footer - This document will be saved under NEW

   f. Save this document under NEW.WP.

KEY TERMS

Constant document (primary file)	Interactive merge printing	Page number
Footer	Layout design	Previewing
Header	Merge codes	Variable document (secondary file)
	Merge printing	

KEY COMMANDS

Alt+Enter (to end a field)	Ctrl+Enter (to enter a hard page break)	Shift+F5 (to preview a document)
Alt+Shift+Enter (to end a record)	Ctrl+F12 (to display the Merge menu)	
Alt+F9 (to display the Page menu)		

MISCONCEPTIONS AND SOLUTIONS

Misconception   The merge printing facility does not generate information in the order you want.

   Solution   Sort the secondary (variable document) file based on any desired key; then start the merge operations. The sort operation is discussed in the next chapter.

Misconception   Sometimes you would like to generate a partial merge print document from the secondary document. To generate the whole list and use half of it would be a waste of resources.

   Solution   Enter a {QUIT} code in your secondary document in the position at which you want to terminate the merge printing.

ARE YOU READY TO MOVE ON?

Multiple Choice

1. A soft page break is identified by
   a. a single, solid line (———)
   b. a double, solid line (═══)
   c. a line of asterisks (****)
   d. a line of plus signs (+++)
   e. none of the above

2. To enter a hard page break, place the insertion point in the desired position and press
   a. Enter
   b. the Backspace key
   c. Ctrl+Enter
   d. Ctrl+Backspace
   e. Ctrl+Home

3. Page numbering is available from the
   a. Layout, Paragraph menus
   b. Layout, Page menus
   c. Layout, Line menus
   d. Layout, Column menus
   e. none of the above

4. To preview a document, use the Print Preview option available by pressing
   a. Ctrl+F5
   b. Shift+F8
   c. Alt+F9
   d. Shift+F5
   e. none of the above

5. The preview feature can
   a. display a single page of the document at a time
   b. zoom in 100 percent
   c. zoom in 200 percent
   d. display facing pages
   e. do all of the above

6. The Headers or Footers menu is selected from the
   a. Layout, Line menus
   b. Layout, Page menus
   c. Layout, Paragraph menus
   d. Layout, Column menus
   e. none of the above

7. In merge printing, WordPerfect for Windows makes use of two documents—a primary document and a secondary document—which are sometimes referred to as
   a. constant and variable documents
   b. bold and underlined documents
   c. letter and address documents
   d. variable and secondary documents
   e. none of the above

8. To create a constant document (e.g., a form letter), the merge code to insert at the end of each variable field is
   a. {END}
   b. {FIELD}
   c. {REGRD}

    d. {END FIELD}

    e. none of the above

9. To create a variable document (e.g., a mailing list), the merge code to insert to indicate the system date is

    a. DATE

    b. {D}

    c. {TEX}

    d. {CODE}

    e. {DATE}

10. When {END RECORD} is placed in the variable document, it signifies

    a. the end of a field

    b. the end of a line

    c. the end of a record

    d. the end of a page

    e. none of the above

True/False

1. As soon as you enter enough text to fill a page, WordPerfect for Windows automatically enters a soft page break and moves to the next page.

2. No method is available to remove a hard page break, so you must be positive that you want to place one in your document.

3. If you decide to include page numbers in your document, they will not be displayed on the standard edit screen; you must either print the document or use the Print Preview feature.

4. Once the page numbering feature is turned on, a page number must be placed on every page.

5. While previewing a document using the Print Preview command, you can edit and make any changes desired.

6. You can define as many as two headers and two footers in a document.

7. Once they are created, headers and footers cannot be changed.

8. WordPerfect for Windows has no provision for merge printing.

9. A variable data item in the constant document (primary file) is denoted by a special merge code that links that item to a specific field in the variable document (secondary file).

10. The {INPUT} code is used to momentarily pause the merge operation and ask for input from the keyboard.

ANSWERS

Multiple Choice		True/False	
1.	a	**1.**	T
2.	c	**2.**	F
3.	b	**3.**	T
4.	d	**4.**	F
5.	e	**5.**	F
6.	b	**6.**	T
7.	a	**7.**	F
8.	d	**8.**	F
9.	e	**9.**	T
10.	c	**10.**	T

Footnotes, Sort Operations, Line Drawing, and Graphics

9

9–1   INTRODUCTION

This chapter introduces four advanced features of WordPerfect for Windows: footnotes and endnotes, sort operations, line drawing, and graphics. Footnotes and endnotes are important elements of scientific and research-oriented documents. Sort operations help you to perform data management operations on documents. Line drawing features allow you to draw boxes and lines in and around your documents. The graphics feature enables you to integrate various graphs into documents.

9–2   FOOTNOTES

When you write a term paper or conduct a research project, you must provide citations for the published materials that you referenced. **Footnotes** are citations printed at the bottom of the page on which the references are made. If all the citations appear at the end of a chapter or section, they are called **endnotes**. Besides the location of printing, there are no other differences between footnotes and endnotes.

9–2–1   Entering Footnotes into Documents

To cite a published work, enter a footnote or endnote number right after the author's name or in a specific place within your document where the work is referenced. WordPerfect for Windows automatically numbers the citations for you. If later you delete one or several of the citations, WordPerfect for Windows automatically renumbers the remaining footnotes and references. It is also easy to insert footnotes between existing notes. In this case, WordPerfect for Windows renumbers the remaining footnotes and references.

Although several formats are acceptable for footnotes, for illustration purposes, the examples in this chapter follow the style of the Modern Language Association (MLA).

Let us say you would like to enter the following paragraph and make two citations:

> Windows-based systems are designed to assist decision makers in all levels of the organization. Quattro Pro, which has gained popularity in recent years, is used as a decision-making tool.

The first citation should be entered immediately after the word "organization." The second citation should be entered after the word "tool." Here are the two citations:

1. Bidgoli, Hossein. *Information Systems Literacy: Windows 3.1.* New York: Macmillan Publishing Company, 1993.
2. Bidgoli, Hossein. *Information Systems Literacy: Quattro Pro.* New York: Macmillan Publishing Company, 1993.

To enter these citations, follow these steps:

1. Move the insertion point to the space immediately after the period that follows "organization."

2. Select Footnote from the Layout menu. From this menu select Create.

3. You will be presented with a blank screen with the number 1 at the top left. See Figure 9–1.

4. Type the first citation.

5. Remember to underline the title of the book by using the Ctrl+U command.

6. Click on Close to exit the footnote screen.

Now a superscript 1 (^{1}) appears after the word "organization."
To enter the second citation, follow these six steps:

1. Move the insertion point to the space after the word "tool."

2. Select Footnote from the Layout menu. Select Create from this menu.

3. Number 2 will be displayed at the top left of a blank screen.

4. Type the second citation.

5. Remember to underline the title of the book by using the Ctrl+U command.

6. Click on Close to exit.

If you preview or print this document, you will see both footnotes at the bottom of the page. The document is illustrated in Figure 9–2.

9–2–2

Editing an Existing Footnote

If you make mistakes when entering citations, don't worry. The editing feature of WordPerfect for Windows enables you to easily correct your mistakes. To edit a footnote, complete these steps:

Figure 9–1
Footnote blank screen.

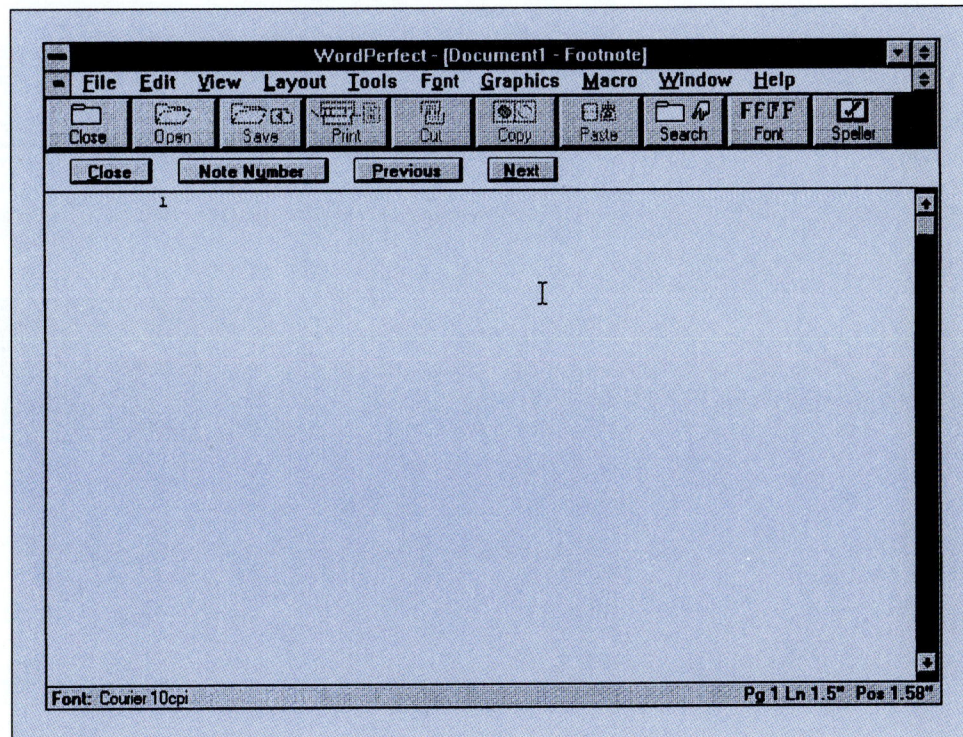

Figure 9–2
Document with two footnotes.

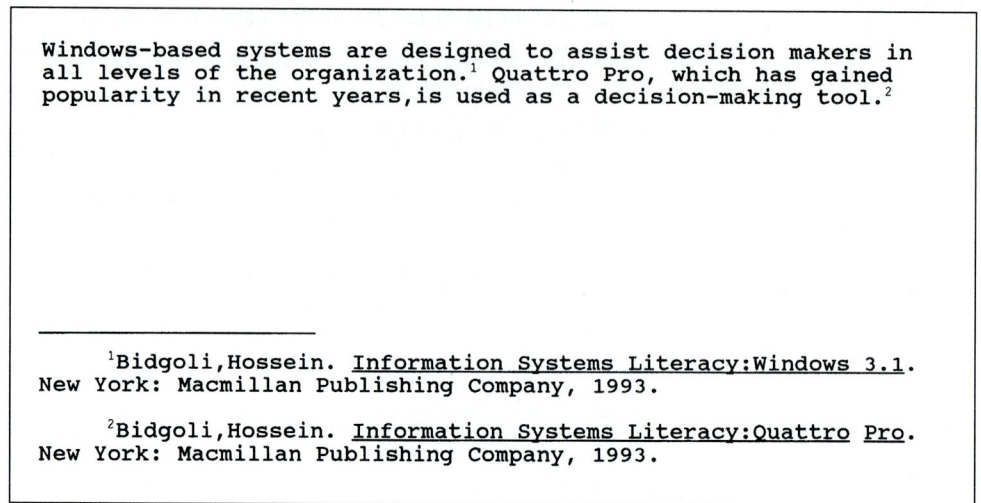

```
Windows-based systems are designed to assist decision makers in
all levels of the organization.¹ Quattro Pro, which has gained
popularity in recent years,is used as a decision-making tool.²

                    _____

        ¹Bidgoli,Hossein. Information Systems Literacy:Windows 3.1.
New York: Macmillan Publishing Company, 1993.

        ²Bidgoli,Hossein. Information Systems Literacy:Quattro Pro.
New York: Macmillan Publishing Company, 1993.
```

1. Move the insertion point to the beginning of the document.
2. Select Footnote from the Layout menu.
3. From this menu select Edit. The Edit Footnote dialog box appears; see Figure 9–3. The Footnote Number box indicates 1. This means you can edit footnote 1. If you want to edit any other footnote, just type in the number. Click on OK and footnote 1 is displayed for editing. You can now perform any editing tasks.
4. Click on Close to return to the document.

Figure 9–3
Footnote Editing dialog box.

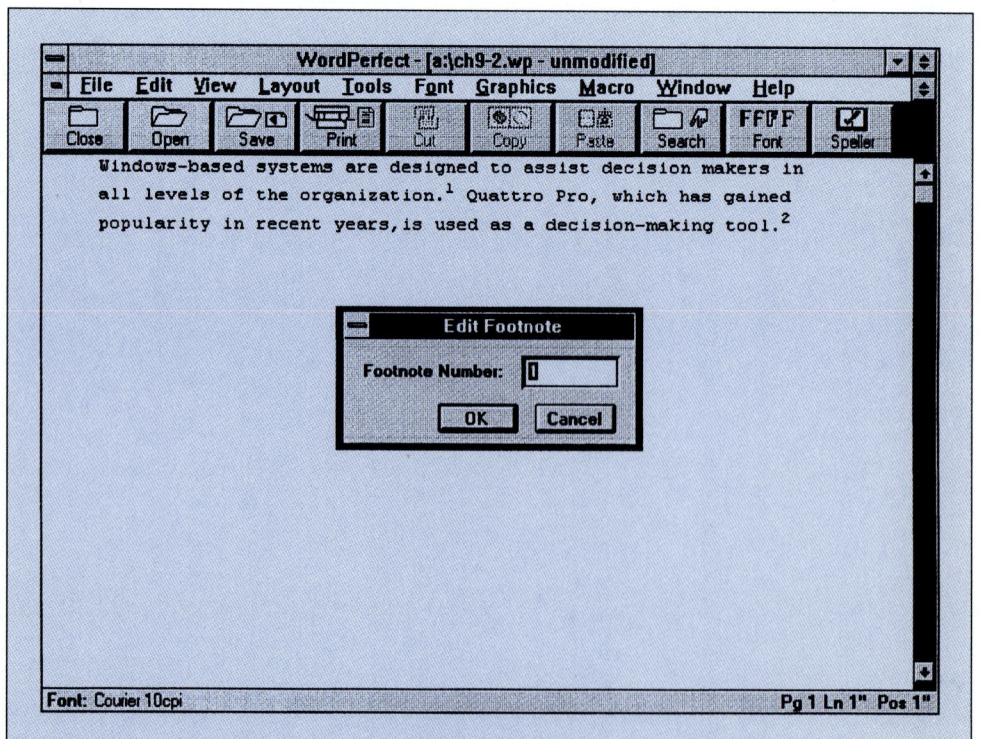

9–2–3   ## Changing Footnote Options

We just created footnotes using the WordPerfect for Windows default setting. However, WordPerfect for Windows provides a variety of options from which you can choose. To choose from these options, follow these instructions:

1. Select Footnote from the Layout menu.
2. From this menu select Options. Figure 9–4 will be displayed. You can choose any of these options by clicking on the desired one. Some of these options include a pop-out menu. For example, if you click on the Numbers pop-out icon in the Numbering Method option, you will see numbers, characters, and letters. You can choose any of the options by clicking on it. For most applications the default settings will be adequate.
3. After making your changes, click on OK to return to the document.

9–3   SORT OPERATIONS

WordPerfect for Windows offers some data management operations, including **sort operations**. To perform sort operations you must make three decisions. First, decide how much of the document is going to be sorted. It can be the entire document, several paragraphs, one paragraph, a block, a column, and so forth. Second, decide which **key** you want to use for the sort. The key is the information used by WordPerfect for Windows to sort your document. For example, account number, last name, and credit limit can be keys. To create a comprehensive sorted file, your key should be unique. Social Security and account numbers are examples of unique keys. However, if your **primary key** is not unique, you must

Figure 9–4
Footnote options.

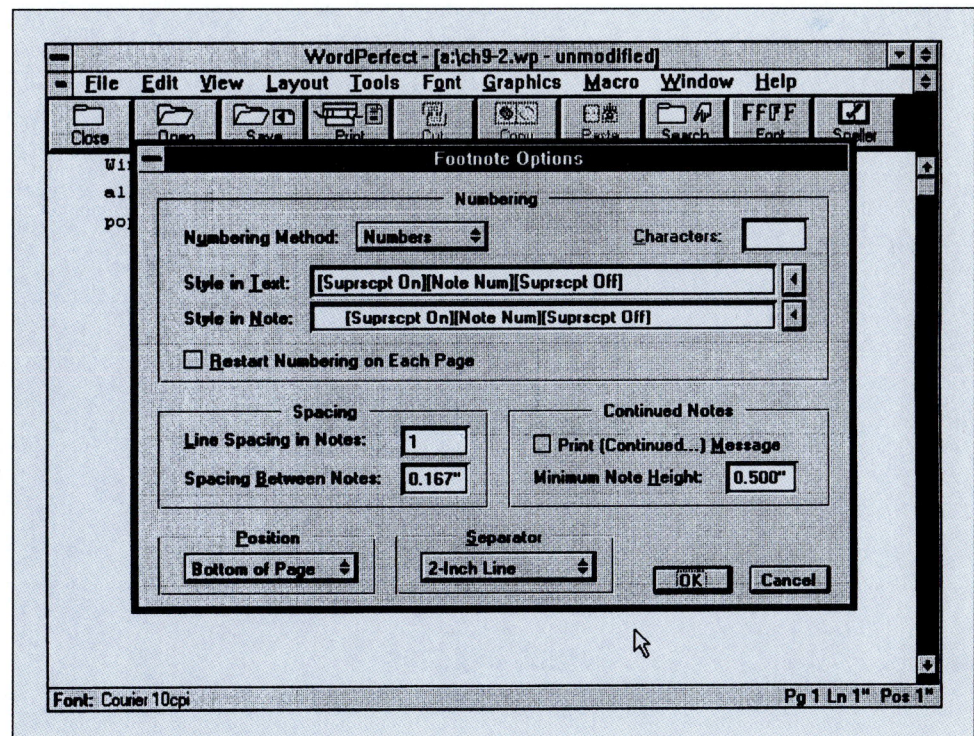

select a **secondary key** in order to sort. (For example, if your document includes 10 customers with the last name Brown, you must use a secondary key to distinguish among the Browns. WordPerfect for Windows allows you to set up to nine keys for sorting. Third, decide how you wish your data sorted, that is, in **ascending** order or **descending** order. Ascending order means A to Z, for example, and descending order means Z to A.

WordPerfect for Windows followings this sorting sequence:

- Special characters (@, #, . . .) come first.
- Numbers (0 through 9 come second.
- Uppercase letters (A, B, . . .) come third.
- Lowercase letters (a, b, . . .) come fourth.

To see how sort operations work, let us walk through some examples. Create the following table, which is a part of the customer database of Alpha-Talk, a manufacturer of wood products.

FNAME	LNAME	GENDER	AGE	CREDIT
Bob	Brown	M	33	1000
Jan	Brown	F	80	2000
Tom	Brown	M	21	9000
Mary	Smith	F	31	1200
Marty	Thomson	M	52	2500
Sandy	Jones	F	26	1100
Brian	Vigen	M	51	5000

To create this document using WordPerfect for Windows we have to set up tabs. Follow these steps:

1. From the View menu select the Ruler (Alt+Shift+F3) option.
2. Clear the predefined tabs either by using the mouse or by selecting the Clear Tabs option from the Tab Set dialog box in the Layout and Line menus.
3. Create a tab in positions 1, 2.2, 3.4, 4.6, and 5.8. To do this, click the mouse pointer on the left tab icon and drag it to these positions one by one and release it.
4. Click on View, then on Ruler, to return to a clear screen.
5. Type *FNAME* (this is in position 1").
6. Press Tab and type *LNAME*.
7. Press Tab and type *GENDER*.
8. Press Tab and type *AGE*.
9. Press Tab and type *CREDIT*.
10. Press Enter
11. Enter the table data until the entire table is constructed. It is displayed in Figure 9–5.

9–3–1

Sorting by Lines

Let us say you decide to sort Figure 9–5 by the rows of the table. This means the table will be sorted based on the first character of each record. Remember that the block of data begins with Bob Brown and ends through Brian Vigen. Do not

Figure 9–5
Sample table for sort operations.

```
FNAME        LNAME        GENDER        AGE        CREDIT
Bob          Brown        M             33         1000
Jan          Brown        F             80         2000
Tom          Brown        M             21         9000
Mary         Smith        F             31         1200
Marty        Thomson      M             52         2500
Sandy        Jones        F             26         1100
Brian        Vigen        M             51         5000
```

include the headings in the block. If you do, they will be sorted within your data—something that you do not want! Also remember that in this table your first tab is in the margin position, which is position 1".

To sort this table by lines, follow these steps:

1. Move the insertion point to "B" of Bob (Brown).
2. Highlight the entire block by clicking the mouse button and moving the insertion point to the right (to 1000) then down through the 5000 for Brian Vigen; then release the mouse button.
3. From the Tools menu select the Sort option (Ctrl+Shift+F12). Figure 9–6 will be displayed.

The menu in Figure 9–6 shows the default settings. By default the primary key is the first field (1) and the sort order is ascending (Ascending). Also, the type of the first field is alphanumeric (Alpha). These default settings fit our table description and the sort we wish to perform. Click on the OK button to perform the sort operation. The table sorted by the first field in ascending order is presented in Figure 9–7.

Figure 9–6
Sort menu.

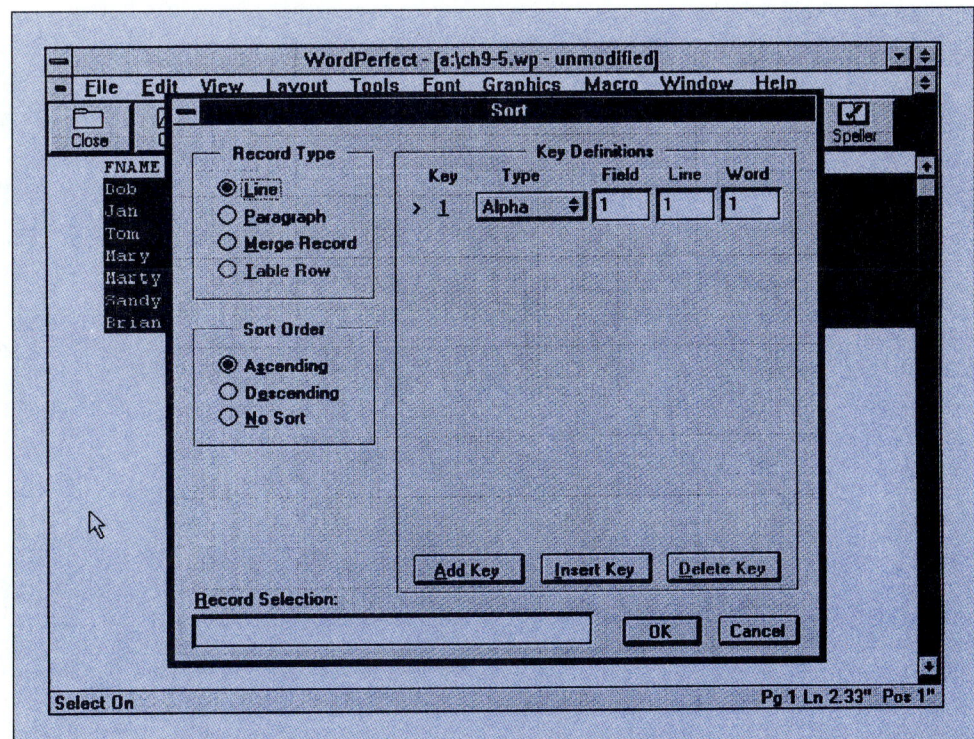

Figure 9–7
Sort by one key.

```
FNAME        LNAME       GENDER      AGE       CREDIT
Bob          Brown       M           33        1000
Brian        Vigen       M           51        5000
Jan          Brown       F           80        2000
Marty        Thomson     M           52        2500
Mary         Smith       F           31        1200
Sandy        Jones       F           26        1100
Tom          Brown       M           21        9000
```

9–3–2

Sorting by Two Keys

Now you decide to sort Figure 9–5 by gender and age. Gender will be the primary key and age will be the secondary key. When the sort is finished, all the female customers will be followed by all the male customers. Each group will be in ascending order by age. To do this, complete these steps:

1. Move the insertion point to "B" of Bob and highlight all the data except the headings.

2. From the Tools menu select the Sort option. Figure 9–6 will be displayed. In this example field 3 will be your key number 1 and field 4 will be your key number 2.

3. Click on the Field box and replace 1 with *3*. This instructs WordPerfect for Windows that your first key is field 3.

4. Click on the Add Key button. The default setting for key 2 will be displayed. In the Field box for this key type *4*. This instructs WordPerfect for Windows that your second key is field 4.

5. Click on the pop-out icon in the Type box and select the Numeric option since your second key (i.e., age) is numeric.

6. Now your sort screen should be similar to the screen in Figure 9–8.

Figure 9–8
Sort screen for a two-key sort.

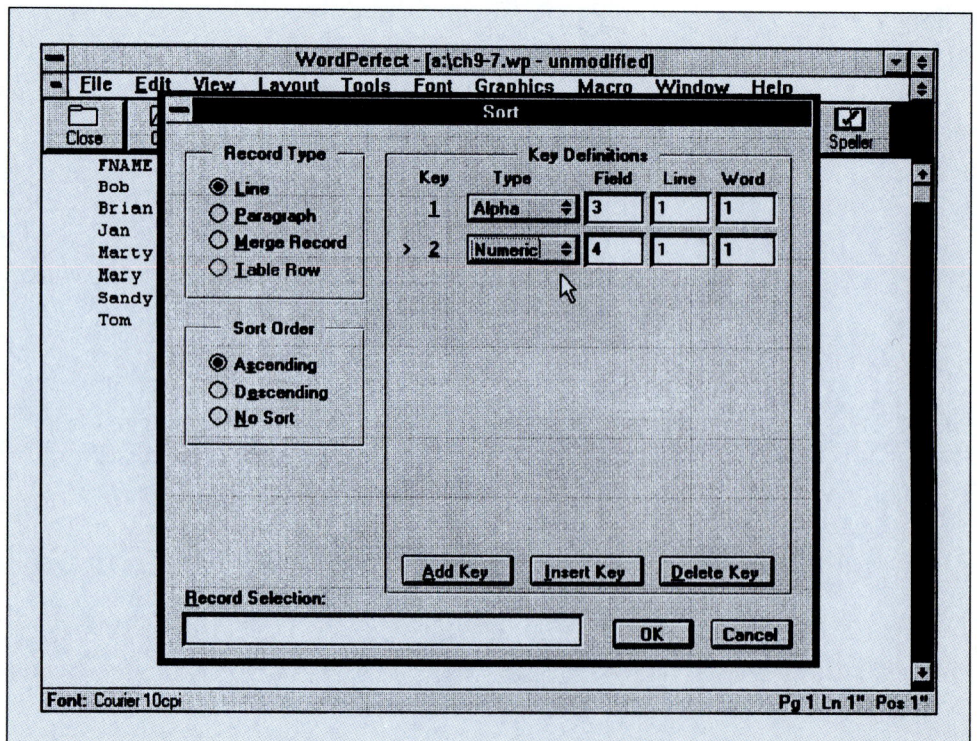

Figure 9–9
Table sorted by gender and age.

```
FNAME          LNAME          GENDER        AGE          CREDIT
Sandy          Jones          F             26           1100
Mary           Smith          F             31           1200
Jan            Brown          F             80           2000
Tom            Brown          M             21           9000
Bob            Brown          M             33           1000
Brian          Vigen          M             51           5000
Marty          Thomson        M             52           2500
```

7. Click on the OK button. Your sorted table should look like Figure 9–9.

9–4   LINE DRAWING CAPABILITIES

Sometimes you may want to highlight a portion of text by putting it in a box, or you may want to draw a simple chart such as an organization chart, structure chart, or command map. The WordPerfect for Windows **line drawing** feature allows you to perform all these tasks.

To display the Line Draw dialog box select the Line Draw (Ctrl+D) option from the Tools menu. You will be presented with a screen similar to the one in Figure 9–10.

As soon as you select Line Draw, your computer switches to Draft mode. Click on the Close button to return to the normal mode.

By default, WordPerfect for Windows displays 10 characters that you can choose for drawing (see bottom left of Figure 9–10). To select one of these characters, move the insertion point to the desired character and click. If none of the default characters satisfies your requirements, you can choose other characters from the WordPerfect's 1,500 character set. To do this, click on Character (bottom

Figure 9–10
Line Draw dialog box.

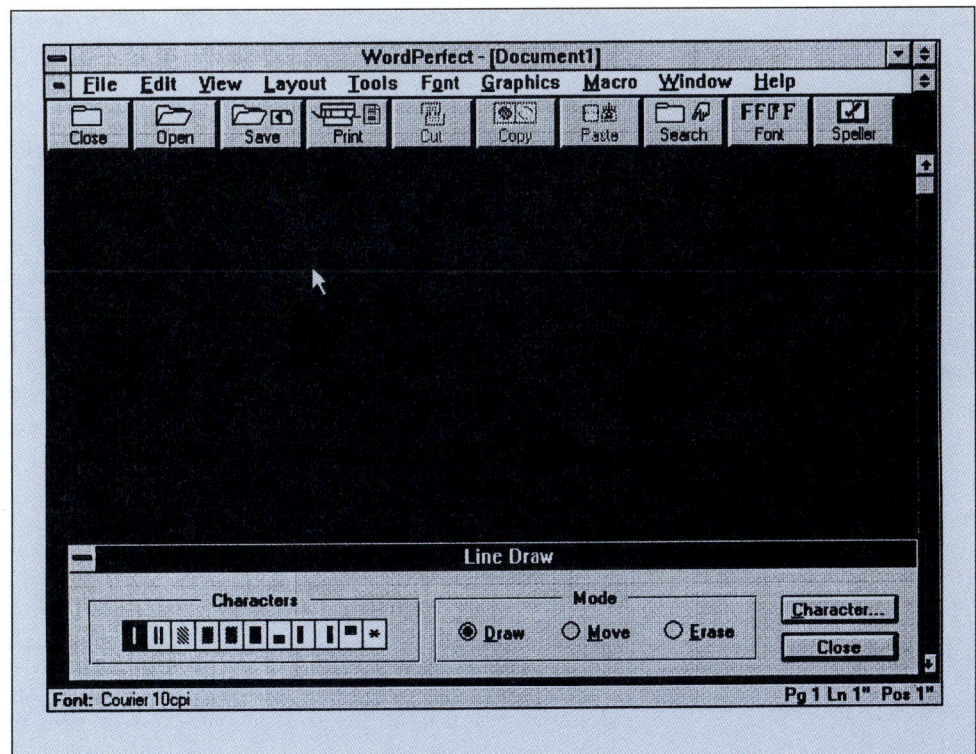

Table 9–1
Keystrokes for Quick Drawing

Keystroke	Task
Home or Ctrl+ ←	Extends to left margin
End or Ctrl+ →	Extends to right margin
Ctrl+ ↑	Extends to top margin
Ctrl+ ↓	Extends to bottom margin

Figure 9–11
Box drawn with the line draw feature.

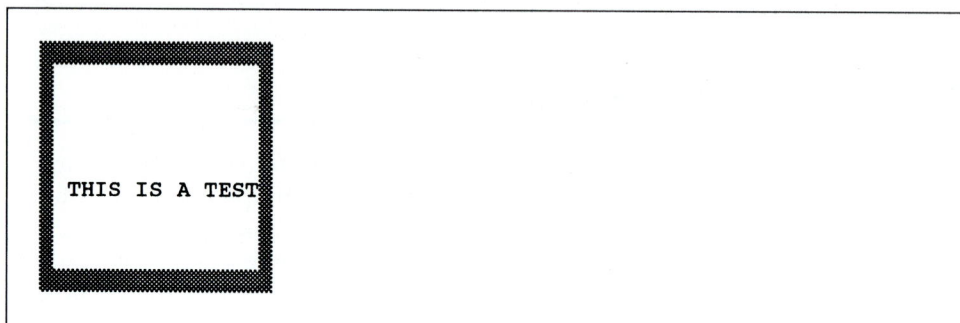

THIS IS A TEST

right) and type in the desired character from the keyboard. You can also press Ctrl+W while the Line Draw character dialog box is displayed to see the WordPerfect Characters dialog box. Select the desired set by clicking on the pop-out menu in the Set box, select the desired character by clicking it, and click on Insert and Close in this dialog box. To finalize the process click on the OK button.

All drawing is done by means of the arrow keys. You cannot use the mouse pointer for drawing. To move the cursor from one point to another point *without* drawing or erasing, click on the Move option and then move the cursor. To move and erase, click on the Erase option and then move the cursor. When you are finished drawing, click on the Close button.

For quick drawing, use the keystrokes shown in Table 9–1.

Now let's try drawing a box around text. Start with a clear screen. By using the Enter key and space bar, move the insertion point to position Ln 2.5" Pos 2.5". In this position type *THIS IS A TEST*. To draw a box around this text follow these instructions:

1. From the Tools menu select the Line Draw option.
2. In the Characters box, click on the fourth character from the left.
3. Press the up arrow 6 times.
4. Press the left arrow 16 times. Press the down arrow 10 times. Press the right arrow 16 times. Press the up arrow until the box is connected.
5. Click on Close.

Your final work should be similar to Figure 9–11.

9–5   WORDPERFECT FOR WINDOWS GRAPHICS

WordPerfect for Windows handles graphics and text similarly. When you print a document that includes graphics, to your printer it's the same as printing a document with only text.

Graphics make your documents more pleasant looking and in some cases make a document more meaningful. For example, if you are generating a report regarding various costs in your department, a pie chart may make the cost breakdown more readily understood.

In WordPerfect for Windows you can include two types of graphics in your reports. The first group is among the several readily available in the C:\WPWIN\GRAPHICS directory. These graphics are saved under the .WPG file extension. You can incorporate any of these graphics into your document at any time. The second group consists of graphics created in other software such as PC Paintbrush, Freelance, or Harvard Graphics. You should be able to bring these graphics into your WordPerfect for Windows documents with no difficulty.

9–5–1

Examples of Graphics

Figure 9–12 illustrates four of the graphics available in the WordPerfect for Windows graphics directory. To incorporate these graphics into your document, follow these steps:

1. Click on Graphics.
2. Click on Figure.
3. Click on Retrieve (F11).

At this point you will be presented with a listing of all the graphics available in the C:\WPWIN\GRAPHICS directory. If for some reason your directory has been changed, you must change to C:\WPWIN\GRAPHICS to see the listing of WordPerfect for Windows graphics files. Double-click on the desired graphic. The names of the four sample graphics in Figure 9–12 are DUCKLING.WPG, COMPUTER.WPG, DEGREE.WPG, and BIRTHDAY.WPG. Remember that you must carry out the three steps for each graphic. As a shortcut, press the F11 function key to see the listing of the graphics files; then double-click on the desired one.

Practice retrieving all of these graphics one by one and examine them. You may be able to use them on specific occasions. For example, you may design a birthday letter for a friend with a happy birthday graphic (BIRTHDAY.WPG) on it, or you may want to insert a computer picture on the cover page of a term paper in a computer class.

When you invoke the Graphics option from the main menu, WordPerfect for Windows gives you Figure, Text Box, Equation, Table Box, and User Box options. The process of creating and working with graphics is the same in all of these. For this reason, we will only discuss figure graphics.

Figure 9–12
Four sample graphics selected from C:\WPWIN\GRAPHICS subdirectory.

9–5–2

Changing the Size of a Graphic

Follow these steps to create the graphic presented in Figure 9–13.

1. Click on Graphics.
2. Click on Figure.
3. Click on Retrieve.
4. Double-click on JET-2.WPG.

As you can see, this graphic, similar to the others that you have seen previously, has a border. Later you will learn how to eliminate the border.

Click anywhere inside the border. As soon as you do this your graphic is surrounded by a dashed border. This means that your graphic has been selected; see Figure 9–14. To deselect a graphic, click anywhere outside of the graphic boarder.

One way to change a graphic's size is to drag one of its **handles** (the squares that appear on the graphic's border when it is selected—see Figure 9–14). To change the graphic width click and drag one of the handles at the left or right of the border. To change the height of the graphic, click and drag one of the handles from the top or bottom. Keep in mind that by doing this you may skew the proportions of the graphic. To change the width and height of the graph at the same time, click and drag one of the handles from the graphic corners.

9–5–3

Moving a Graphic Around

To move a graphic around on your document, complete these two steps:

1. Click inside of the desired graphic and drag the graphic to any location.
2. Release the mouse button.

Figure 9–13
Sample graphic (JET-2.WPG).

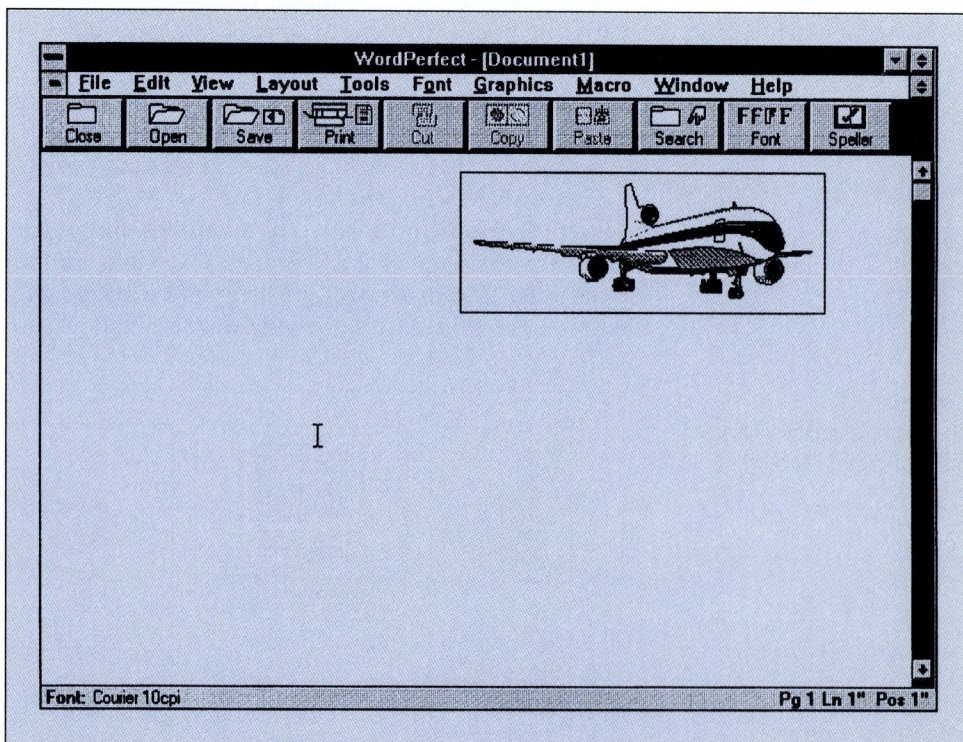

Figure 9-14
Sample graphic is selected.

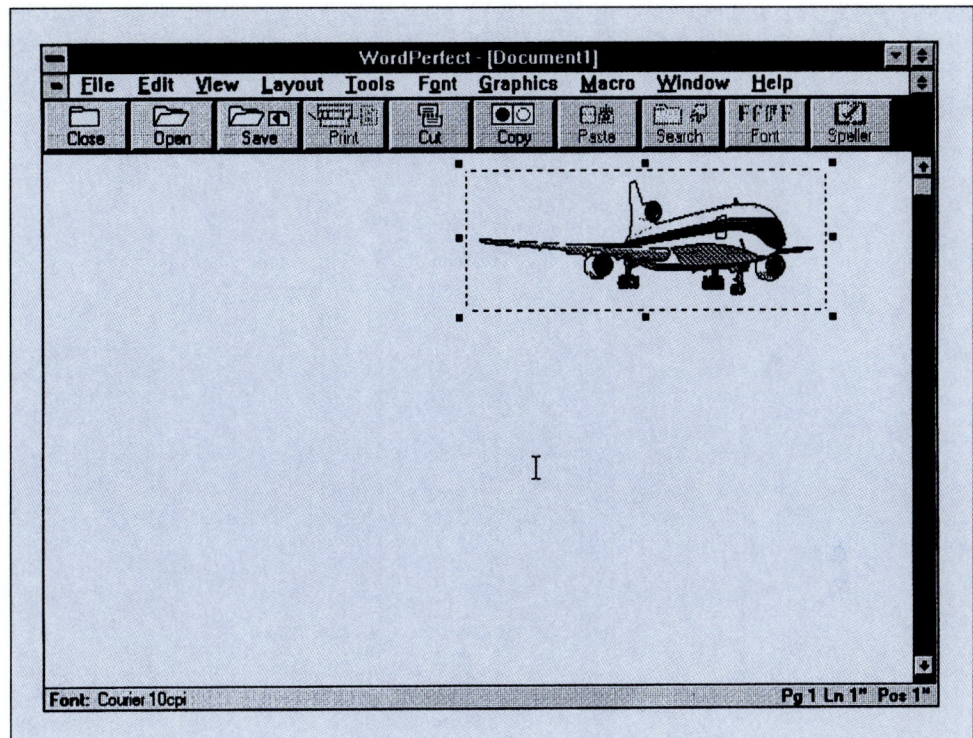

If you drag the graphic through text, the text will move to make room for the graphic.

9-5-4

The Figure Editor Button Bar

If you choose the Create option after selecting the Graphics and Figure menus, you will see a screen similar to the one in Figure 9-15. You can also press Shift+F11. This is the **Figure Editor** screen which includes several buttons that can be used to effectively manipulate your graphics. Let us briefly explain these buttons.

The Close button closes the Figure Editor window. When you are done manipulating your graphic, click on the Close button to return to your document.

The Retrieve button allows you to bring any of the .WPG files to your document.

The Fig Pos button generates the Box Position and Size dialog box (see Figure 9-16). This box allows you to adjust the position of the graphic on the page as well as its size. By means of this box you can be a lot more precise than you can be by using the mouse to drag a graphic around.

The Move button is used for moving a graphic within its border. If you use the Move command, you must use the arrow keys to move a graphic inside of the graphic box. Remember, the box will not move, only the graphic will move.

The Rotate button allows you to rotate a graphic, thereby changing its orientation.

The Enlarge button enables you to enlarge the size of a graphic. The ResetSize button is used to reset the size of the image to what it was before any changes were made to it.

The Mirror button creates a mirror image of the graphic. The Outline button creates an outline of the image.

Figure 9–15
Figure Editor screen.

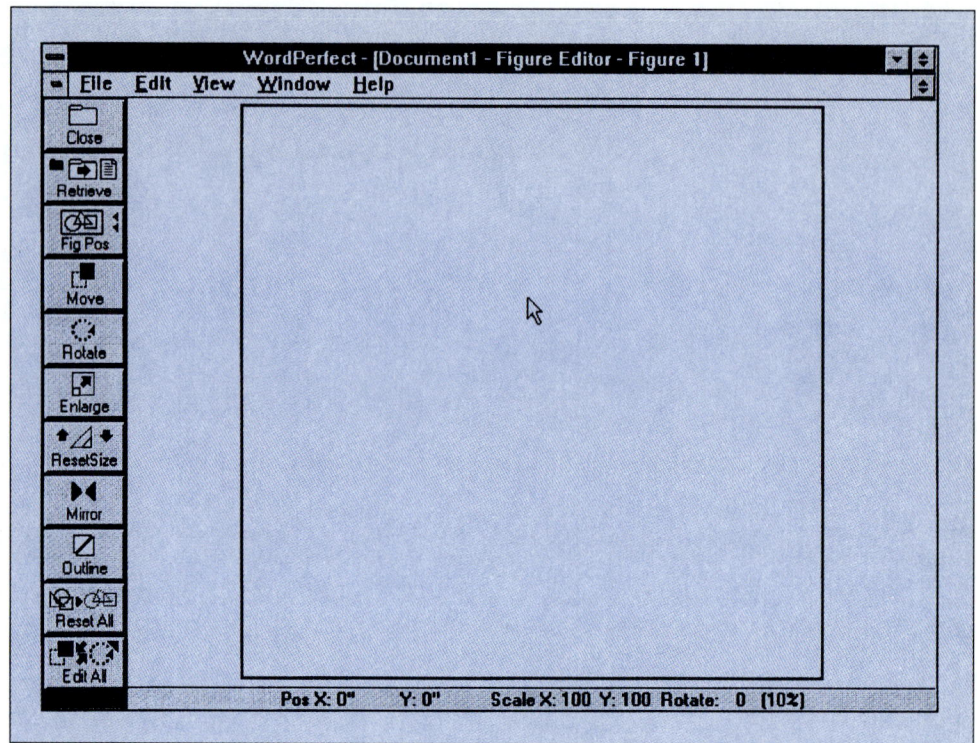

Figure 9–16
Box Position and Size dialog box.

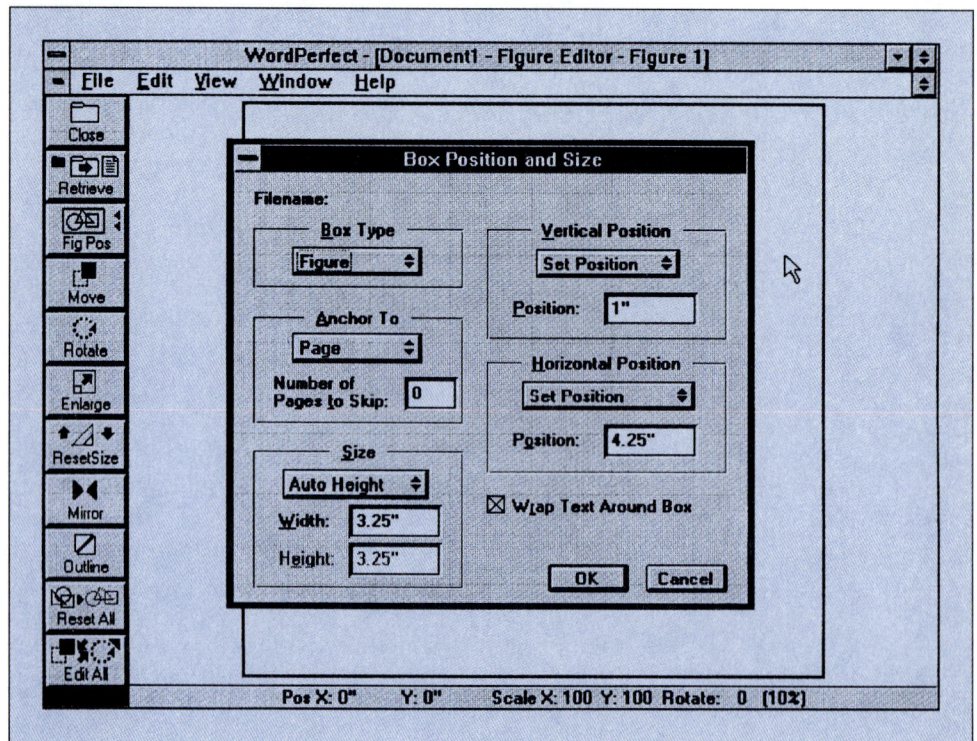

The Reset All button displays the figure as it appeared when you retrieved it (with the default settings).

Finally, the Edit All button serves various editing purposes, such as changing the size, position, rotation, and so forth.

9–5–5   Using the Position and Size Dialog Box

As you have already seen, you can modify the size of a graphic by dragging one of the handles. You can also move around a graphic by means of the click and drag technique. These actions may not, however, generate a precise position and size for you. The Box Position and Size dialog box enables you to define a position as finely as possible.

To display the Box Position and Size dialog box, either click on the Fig Pos button in the Figure Editor button bar or select Figure from the Graphics menu and click on Position. In either case, you will see a screen similar to the one in Figure 9–16. If you have several active graphics, remember to specify the figure number in the Box Position and Size dialog box, which will be displayed if you have more than one graphic active.

As you see in Figure 9–16, width and height can be defined by using the pop-out menu in the Size region. The horizontal position can be adjusted by clicking on the pop-out menu and selecting the desired position. The vertical position can be adjusted in the same manner.

9–5–6   Adding a Caption

Your graphics become more meaningful if you add **captions** to them. WordPerfect for Windows automatically keeps track of graphics and captions. They always appear in sequence. To add a caption to a graphic, follow these steps:

1. Select the figure to which you want to add a caption.
2. From the Graphics menu select the Figure option.
3. From this menu select the Caption option. At this point the Edit Figure Caption dialog box appears. In the Figure Number box type in the figure number. For example, type *1* and click on OK.
4. You will be presented with a blank screen with Figure 1 displayed at the upper left.
5. Type your desired caption, for example, *This is a sample WordPerfect for Windows graphic.*
6. Click on the Close button.

As you can see in Figure 9–17, the typed caption is displayed below the graphic.

9–5–7   Rotating a Graphic

To turn a graphic around or change its orientation, use the Rotate button from the Figure Editor screen. This is how to do it:

1. Select the desired graphic and double-click on it to open the Figure Editor screen.
2. Click on the Rotate button in the Figure Editor screen. As soon as you do this, two perpendicular lines that cross to form a right angle appear.

Figure 9–17
Graphic with caption.

Figure 1 This is a sample
WordPerfect for Windows graphic

Figure 9–18
Graphic turned upside down.

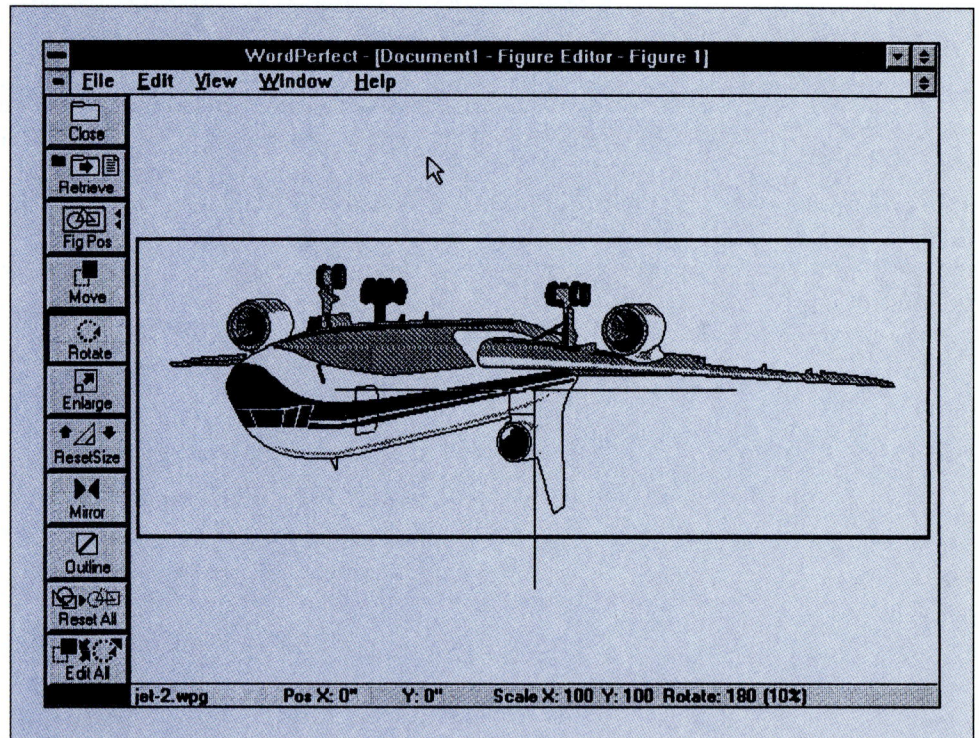

To rotate the graphic 90 degrees counterclockwise, click on the vertical axis. To turn the graphic upside down, click on the left horizontal axis. Figure 9–18 shows our sample graphic upside down.

9–5–8   Modifying a Graphic Border

By default, WordPerfect for Windows generates a border that is a solid line on the left, right, top, and bottom of a graphic. However, this border can be modified as follows:

1. Select the Graphics option from the main menu.
2. Click on Figure. Select the Options menu.

This will display the Figure Options dialog box; see Figure 9–19.

Figure 9–19
Figure Options dialog box.

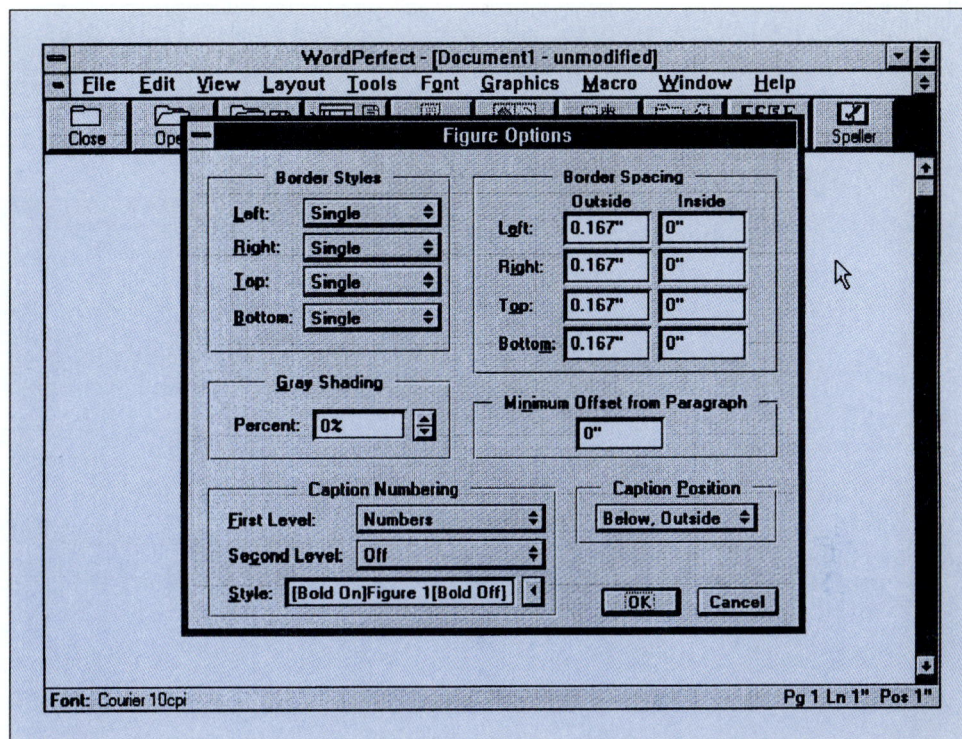

Notice the Border Styles region at the upper left of this screen. Click and hold on the pop-out menu for the left border. You will see the following options: None, Single, Double, Dashed, Dotted, Thick, and Extra Thick. Click on the desired one. Follow the same procedure for the right, top, and bottom borders. For example, to eliminate the border completely, select None for all four borders. When you are done, click on OK. Your next graphic will conform to your new specification—it will not have a border.

9–5–9

Creating Lines

In some cases, you may want to draw a vertical and/or a horizontal line in your document. For example, you can create a letterhead by using a horizontal line or you can draw attention to a portion of text by drawing a vertical line. You may even use a horizontal line to separate one graphic from another. The Line option from the Graphics menu will do all of these for you. Follow these steps:

1. For a horizontal line, select Line from the Graphics menu.
2. Select Horizontal. You will be presented with the Create Horizontal Line dialog box as presented in Figure 9–20. The steps for vertical line are the same except you select Vertical (Ctrl+Shift+F11) instead.

The Line Size region allows you to select the length and thickness of the line. The Gray Shading region allows you to select the percentage of gray in which the line prints. As you can see in Figure 9–20, the default value is 100%; this is completely black. If your line is thin, a lower percentage of gray shading won't show up very well. But a thicker line with medium shading will add special effects. The Vertical Position is the distance from the top margin down to the line. The Horizontal Position is the location of the line in reference to the left and right margins. Figure 9–21 shows a couple of examples of horizontal and vertical lines.

Figure 9–20
Create Horizontal Line dialog box.

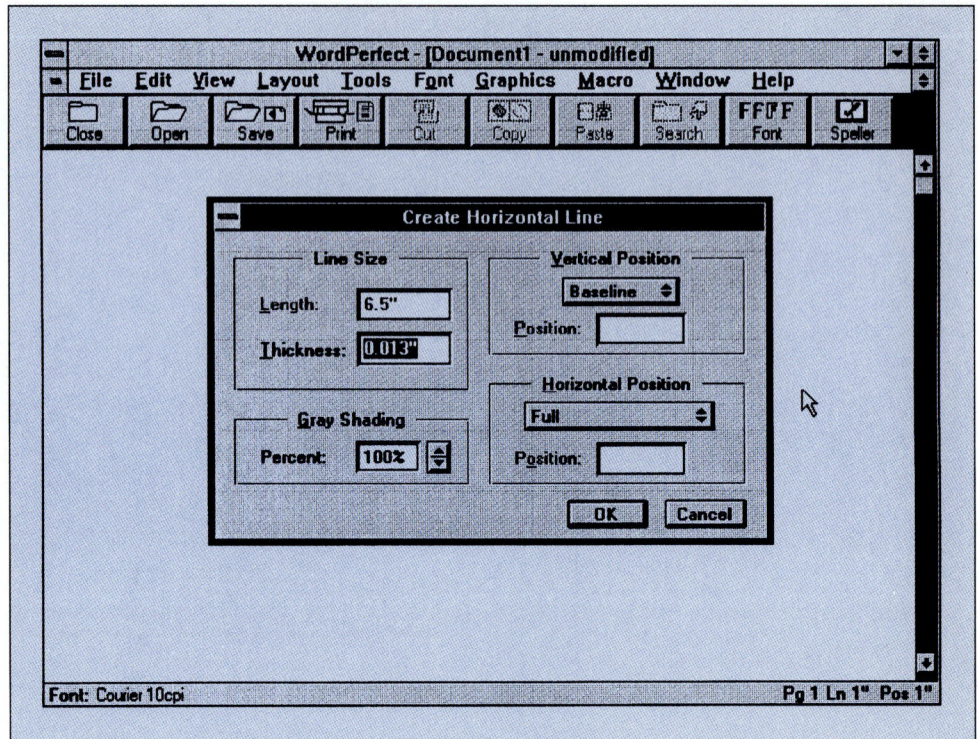

Figure 9–21
Examples of vertical and horizontal lines.

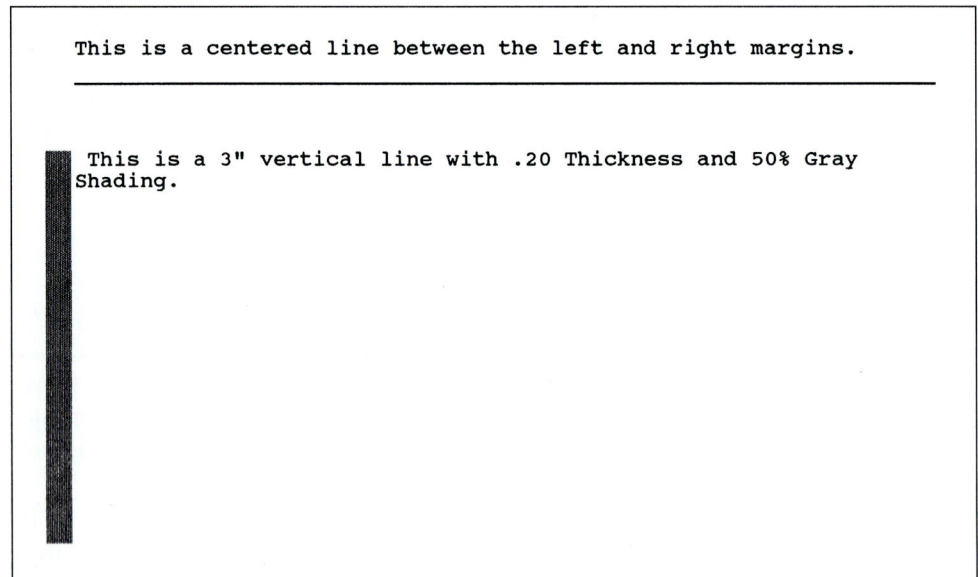

SUMMARY

In this chapter we discussed four advanced features of WordPerfect for Windows: footnotes and endnotes, sort operations, line drawing, and graphics. The footnotes and endnotes feature assists you in designing scientific and research-oriented documents. Sort operations accomplish data management tasks. The line drawing feature enables you to draw lines and boxes in and around your document. The graphics feature allows you to generate pleasant looking documents by integrating graphics in them.

REVIEW QUESTIONS

*These questions are answered in Appendix A.

1. What are footnotes? How are they created?
*2. What is the difference between footnotes and endnotes?
3. Is there a shortcut key for accessing the Footnote option?
4. Under what menu is the Footnote option?
*5. How do you exit the footnote screen?
6. Explain how to edit an existing footnote.
7. What are the Footnote options? What is the default option?
8. How do you exit the footnote screen after typing your first footnote?
9. Describe sort operations.
10. What is a primary key? What is a secondary key?
*11. How many sorting keys are allowed in WordPerfect for Windows?
12. What is the sort order?
13. What is an alphanumeric key?
*14. How do you start the sort operation?
15. Explain how to exit the Sort menu.
16. How do you change the sort key?
17. Can the sort key type be changed from numeric to alphanumeric?
18. Name some of the applications of the line drawing features of WordPerfect for Windows.
*19. How do you display the Line Draw dialog box?
20. How many symbols are available for drawing lines?
21. How do you erase a portion of a line?
22. What command is used for moving the cursor without erasing in Line Draw mode?
23. Describe the process of drawing a box.
24. What is the default value of the symbol for drawing?
25. Name the two types of graphics that can be included in WordPerfect for Windows documents.
*26. What is the file extension of a graphic in WordPerfect for Windows?
27. How do you retrieve one of the .WPG files?
28. In which directory are the .WPG files stored?
29. How do you change a graphic size?
*30. How do you move a graphic?
31. What are some of the buttons in the Figure Editor screen?
32. Explain how to add a caption to a graphic.
*33. How do you rotate a graphic 180 degrees?
34. How do you create a thick horizontal line and a thick vertical line?

HANDS-ON EXPERIENCE

1. In the following document enter the three footnotes in the specified places.

   Since silicon technology is not able to emit light and has speed limitations, computer designers have concentrated on gallium arsenide technology. In gallium arsenide, electrons move almost five times faster than in silicon. Devices made with this synthetic compound can emit light, withstand higher temperatures, and survive much higher doses of radiation than silicon devices.[1]

The fifth-generation project in Japan has specified these goals:[2] (1) Listen when spoken to; then do what it is told; (2) Help the program itself; (3) Sort through volumes of facts to find and use only what is pertinent.

Teleshopping may also become a reality by incorporating other senses, such as touch, smell, and taste, into the telecommunications system.[3] For example, a consumer may be able to purchase an item by using his or her computer. The consumer may not only see the product but he or she may also be able to touch and taste it as well.

The three footnotes are as follows:

[1]Posa, John J. 1987. "Using Silicon and Gallium Arsenide." *High Technology* (March):38-41.

[2]Miller, Richard K. 1987. *Fifth Generation Computers*. Lilburn, GA: The Fairmount Press, Inc., p. 3.

[3]Cornish, Edward. 1986. "Did You Hear the One About the Human Who . . .?" *ComputerWorld* (November):28-29.

  a. By using the Print Preview command, check to see if the footnotes are properly inserted.
  b. Edit the second footnote by changing the last name of the author to all capital letters.
  c. By using the Footnote Options dialog box, change the style of footnote 1 to a style of your choice.
  d. Change all footnotes to endnotes.

2. Set up the following table:

Name	Credit	Age
John	1000	39
Bob	500	50
Sue	700	61

  a. Sort this table by lines.
  b. Sort by age (in descending order).
  c. Sort first by age and then by credit limit (in ascending order).
  d. Sort the table by credit in ascending order.

3. Using the line drawing features of WordPerfect for Windows, draw boxes around the following text:

Input

Process

Output

The boxes should be connected vertically to one another.

4. Repeat exercise 3 using a different symbol.

5. Display all the .WPG files in your system one by one. Select two of the desired ones and print them.

6. Retrieve one of the .WPG files and do the following:
   a. Reduce it to half.
   b. Rotate it by 90 degrees.
   c. Rotate it by 180 degrees.
   d. Add a caption to it.
   e. Print it.

KEY TERMS

Ascending order   Footnote   Line drawing

Caption   Graphic   Primary key

Descending order   Handle bar   Secondary key

Endnote   Key   Sort operations

Figure Editor

KEY COMMANDS

Alt+Shift+F3 (to display   Ctrl+Shift+F11 (to   Ctrl+W (to display the
the Ruler)   display the Create Vertical   WordPerfect Characters
                               Line dialog box)   dialog box)
Ctrl+D (to display the
Line Draw dialog box)   Ctrl+Shift+F12 (to   F11 (to retrieve a graphics
                               display the Sort dialog   file)
Ctrl+F11 (to display the   box)
Create Horizontal Line   Shift+F11 (to display the
dialog box)   Ctrl+U (to underline)   Figure Editor screen)

MISCONCEPTIONS AND SOLUTIONS

Misconception   You just finished drawing a box or boxes for one document. To do the
same steps over again for another document would be time consuming.

    Solution   Using the Edit command you can copy or move sections of your draw-
ings to another document.

Misconception   Although you can display the Figure Editor screen by invoking Graphics,
Figure Create, or Edit, this seems time consuming.

    Solution   The fastest way to get to the Figure Editor is by double-clicking any-
where inside a graphic.

ARE YOU READY TO MOVE ON?

Multiple Choice

1. The footnote feature allows the following choices except for:
   a. create
   b. edit
   c. selecting the footnote format
   d. choosing a new starting number
   e. selecting a numbering style

2. Under which menu does the Footnote option appear?
   a. Edit
   b. File

    c. Tools

    d. Layout

    e. Font

3. After you select the Footnote option, you can select all of the following options except

    a. Create

    b. Save

    c. Edit

    d. New Number

    e. Options

4. To perform sort operations, you must first decide

    a. how much of the document is to be sorted

    b. which key you want to use for the sort

    c. the manner in which to sort (ascending or descending)

    d. which sequence to use for the sort

    e. none of the above

5. If you sort a file first on the key LNAME, and then on the key FNAME, the key FNAME is known as the

    a. primary key

    b. secondary key

    c. major key

    d. minor key

    e. none of the above

6. If you want to create a box or draw simple charts, you should use WordPerfect's line drawing feature. Under which menu is it found?

    a. Layout

    b. View

    c. Edit

    d. Tools

    e. Font

7. How many characters that you can choose from (without going to WordPerfect character set) does the line draw feature allow by default?

    a. 25

    b. 2

    c. 3

    d. 1

    e. 10

8. By default, the first key used in WordPerfect's sort operation is

    a. the first field

    b. the last field

    c. any numeric field

    d. the field that contains the person's last name

    e. none of the above

9. What extension identifies WordPerfect graphic files?

    a. .PRN

    b. .WPG

    c. .BAK

    d. .PIC

    e. .DBF

10. The boarder of a graphic can be all of the following except

    a. single line

    b. double line

    c. dashed line

    d. dotted line

    e. all of the above

True/False

1. To invoke the screen for drawing lines you can press the Ctrl+D key combination.
2. If you are using WordPerfect's footnote feature, footnotes are renumbered automatically if you make changes to them.
3. Once you create a footnote, you cannot edit it.
4. WordPerfect for Windows does not support any data management operations.
5. You must not include column headings within the block of data to be sorted.
6. WordPerfect for Windows cannot sort on more than one key.
7. WordPerfect's line drawing feature can draw only single lines; it cannot draw double lines or use other characters.
8. A graphic can be rotated to any angle.
9. The border of a graph cannot be eliminated.
10. WordPerfect for Windows supports several numbering options for footnotes including numbers, letters, and characters.

ANSWERS

Multiple Choice		True/False	
1.	c	1.	T
2.	d	2.	T
3.	b	3.	F
4.	a	4.	F
5.	b	5.	T
6.	d	6.	F
7.	e	7.	F
8.	a	8.	T
9.	b	9.	F
10.	e	10.	T

Outlines, Macros, and Columns

10

10–1   INTRODUCTION

In this chapter three additional advanced features of WordPerfect for Windows are described. These powerful features are creating outlines for term papers and other writing projects, developing macros for simplifying repetitive tasks, and designing newspaper and parallel columns for reports.

10–2   Creating Outlines: An Overview

The **outlining** feature of WordPerfect for Windows enables you to create outlines that are easy to use and modify. Outlines help you organize your thoughts. You start by setting up a rough outline. As you generate new ideas, enter them and WordPerfect for Windows will organize and renumber your outline for you. If you add or delete a number in the sequence of the outline, the remaining numbers are updated automatically.

The outline feature allows numbered and indented outlines. Here is an example:

1. Level 1 item
    1–1   Level 2 item
    1–2   Another level 2 item
    1–3   Another level 2 item
        1–3–1 Level 3 item
        1–3–2 Another level 3 item
2. Another level 1 item
    2–1   Level 2 item
    2–2   Another level 2 item

WordPerfect for Windows also generates numbered paragraphs. (We will discuss this in section 10–3.)

10–2–1   Creating Your First Outline

The following text is a portion of a table of contents from a Lotus 1-2-3 textbook.

1. Lotus 1-2-3 Functions
    1–1   Financial Functions
        1–1–1   Present Value
        1–1–2   Future Value
    1–2   Statistical Functions
        1–2–1   Average
        1–2–2   Sum
2. Lotus 1-2-3 Graphics
    2–1   Pie Charts
    2–2   Line Graphs

You can use WordPerfect for Windows to create this outline and modify it. Start with a clear screen and follow these steps:

1. From the Tools menu click on Outline.
2. From this menu click on the Outline On option. As soon as you do this, the status line at the lower left reads Outline.
3. Press Enter to enter the first outline number, that is, I.
4. Press F7 to indent.
5. Type *Lotus 1-2-3 Functions* and press Enter. The number II. will be displayed.
6. Press Tab. At this point the II. is changed to A. and is indented.
7. Press F7 to indent.
8. Type *Financial Functions.*
9. Press Enter and B. is displayed.
10. Press Tab once. The B. is changed to a 1. and is indented.
11. Press F7 to indent. Type *Present Value.*
12. Press the Enter key and 2. is displayed.
13. Press F7 to indent. Type *Future Value.*
14. Press the Enter key and 3. is displayed.
15. Press Shift+Tab. The 3. is changed to B.
16. Press F7 once. Type *Statistical Functions.* Press Enter and C. is displayed. Press Tab and 1. is displayed.
17. Press F7. Type *Average.* Press Enter and 2. is displayed. Press F7.
18. Type *Sum.* Press Enter and 3. is displayed.
19. Press Shift+Tab twice. This will change the 3. to II.
20. Press F7. Type *Lotus 1-2-3 Graphics.* Press Enter and III. will be displayed. Press Tab. The III. is changed to A. and will be indented. Press F7.
21. Type *Pie Charts.* Press Enter and B. will be displayed. Press F7.
22. Type *Line Graphs.*

Your work should be similar to Figure 10–1. From the Tools menu select the Outline option, and from this menu select the Outline Off option to turn the outline mode off. This process may seem time consuming, but once the outline is established, modifications can be done easily.

If you want to add to your outline, move the cursor to the end of the line below which you want to make the insertion. Press Enter. If the insertion is not a first-level entry, tab to the correct position with the Tab key. Press F7 and type your new entry.

Figure 10–1
Example of an outline.

```
I.   Lotus 1-2-3 Functions
     A.    Financial Functions
           1.    Present Value
           2.    Future Value
     B.    Statistical Functions
           1.    Average
           2.    Sum
II.  Lotus 1-2-3 Graphics
     A.    Pie Charts
     B.    Line Graphs
```

To delete an outline item, place the insertion point on the item you want to delete and use the Del key to erase it. WordPerfect for Windows automatically renumbers the remaining entries in the outline. You also can change the level number manually using the methods described above.

10–2–2

Changing the Outline Numbering Format

WordPerfect for Windows allows different numbering formats for outlines. To change the format of the outline presented in Figure 10–1 to legal format, do the following:

1. Retrieve the document (if it is not already on the screen).
2. If necessary, move the insertion point to the beginning of the document.
3. From the Tools menu select the Outline option; then click on the Define (Alt+Shift+F5) option. Figure 10–2 will be displayed.
4. Click on the Outline pop-out menu; then click on the Legal option. Click on OK. The numbering format is changed immediately; Figure 10–3 displays this new outline.

10–3 NUMBERING PARAGRAPHS

If you have several paragraphs that you wish to number, first enter the text and then complete these steps:

1. Move the insertion point to the left of the paragraph that you wish to number.
2. From the Outline menu select the Paragraph Number (Alt+F5) option. The Paragraph Numbering dialog box will appear.

Figure 10–2
Define Paragraph Numbering dialog box.

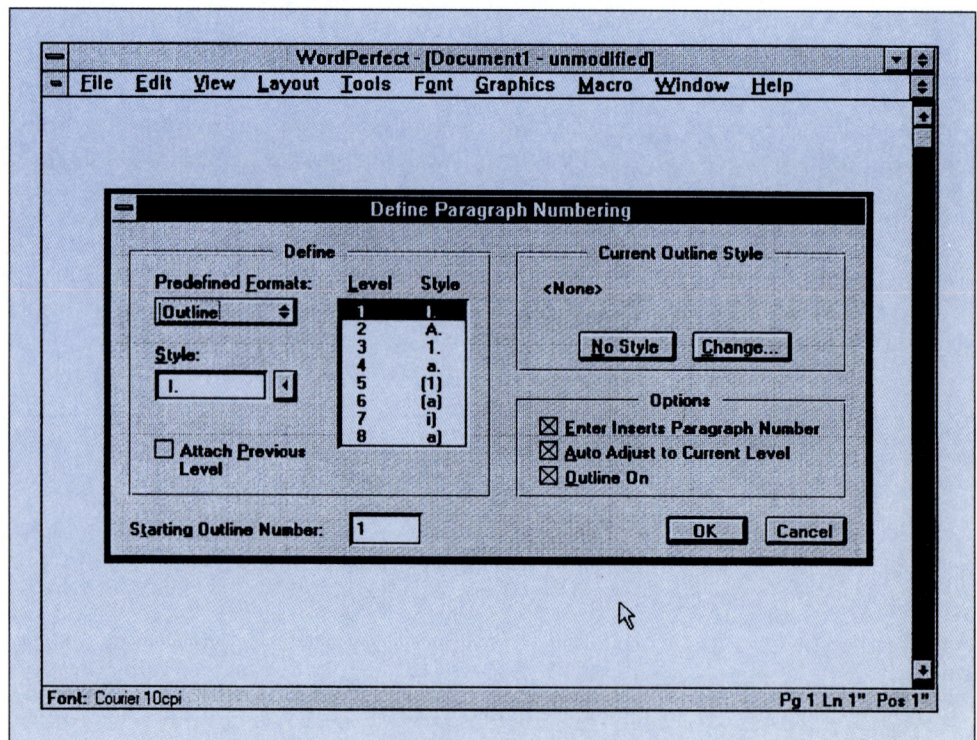

Figure 10–3
Outline renumbered in legal style.

```
1    Lotus 1-2-3 Functions
     1.1 Financial Functions
          1.1.1    Present Value
          1.1.2    Future Value
     1.2 Statistical Functions
          1.   Average
          2.   Sum
2    Lotus 1-2-3 Graphics
     2.1 Pie Charts
     2.2 Line Graphs
```

Figure 10–4
Example of numbered paragraphs.

```
I.   WordPerfect for Windows is one of the most popular word
processing programs on the market. The personnel office is planning
to conduct a brief seminar on this package.

II.  Tom Morris from the personnel office will be the instructor.
All the administrative staff are invited.

III. To encourage all of you to attend the seminar, there will be
cash prizes awarded to three participants.

IV.  After familiarizing yourselves with WordPerfect for Windows,
all of you who participate will be given access to a PC with
WordPerfect for Windows capabilities.
```

3. Click on Insert. The paragraph will be numbered.

4. Continue this process until all the paragraphs are numbered. Figure 10–4 shows an example of **numbered paragraphs**. If you delete one of these paragraphs, the rest will be renumbered automatically.

10–4   MACRO OPERATIONS

The majority of WordPerfect for Windows operations are performed by a series of keystrokes. These keystrokes can be recorded and played back later. A WordPerfect for Windows **macro** is a collection of keystrokes designed to perform a specific task. Whenever you are doing repetitive tasks, think of macros. They can help you simplify the task as well as improve accuracy.

A macro can be run in a batch mode or in an interactive mode. In batch mode, the macro is executed from beginning to end without any user intervention. In interactive mode, the user is able to enter certain keystrokes during the macro execution. WordPerfect for Windows comes with a number of macros stored in the C:\WPWIN\MACROS subdirectory. All these macros are saved with the .WCM file extension. You can retrieve any of these macros and use them. Consult the WordPerfect for Windows manual for detailed specifications of these predefined macros.

10–4–1   Developing a Macro

Macro design involves several steps. The terminology in these steps is explained in the sections that follow.

1. Start the recording process.
2. Give the macro a name. The name can be similar to a file name, with up to eight characters.
3. Describe the macro.
4. Enter the desired keystrokes (the function of the macro).
5. Stop recording.
6. Execute the macro. The macro can be executed anywhere on the screen. However, be sure to execute the macro in an area that does not include text; otherwise, the macro will overwrite the existing text in Typeover mode or shift text to the right in Insert mode.

10–4–2

Your First Macro

Tom always closes his business letters as follows:

> Sincerely yours,
>
> Tom Johnson, Ph.D.
> Director
> Management Information Systems Dept.

Since this closing is repeated in every letter, it is a good application for a macro. To design this macro, follow these steps:

1. Start with a blank screen.
2. Click on Macro; then click on Record (Ctrl+F10) to turn on the recording feature. The Record Macro dialog box will be displayed; see Figure 10–5.

Figure 10–5
Record Macro dialog box.

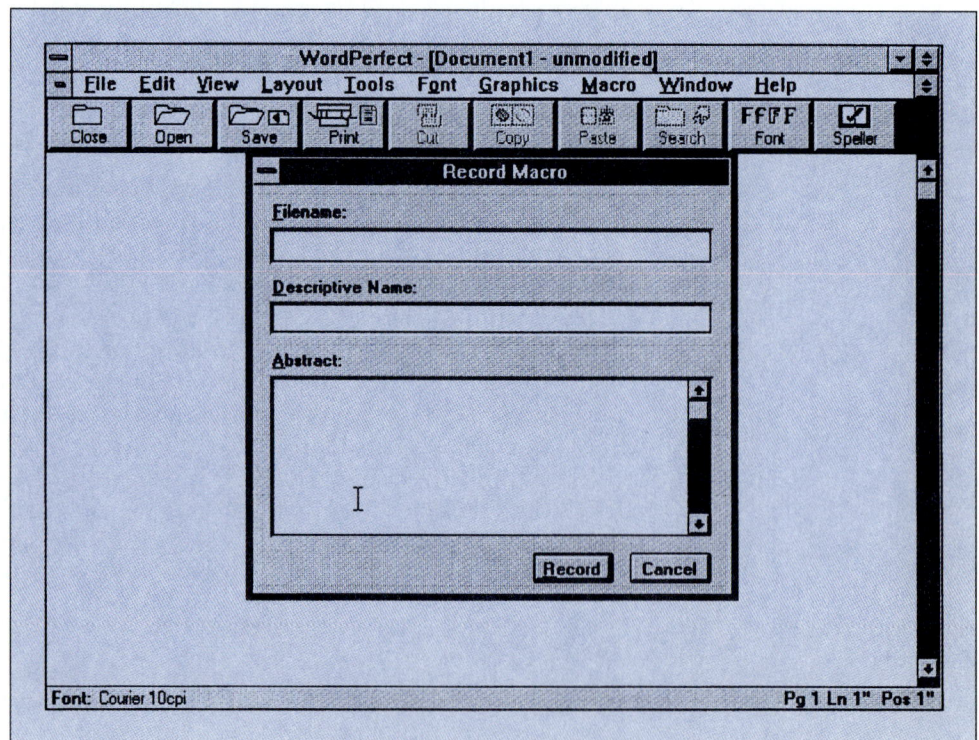

3. In the Filename box type *A:Finish* for your macro name. In the Descriptive Name box type a brief description for your macro. Type *Closing* as your description and click on the Record button. You can also click on the Cancel button to get out of the recording process. At this point the status line displays

```
Recording Macro
```

and the mouse pointer takes the shape of a circle.

4. Type *Sincerely yours,* and press the Enter key four times (this will insert three blank lines).

5. Type *Tom Johnson, Ph.D.* and press Enter.

6. Type *Director* and then press Enter.

7. Type *Management Information Systems Dept.* and press Enter. To temporarily stop the recording process, click on the Pause option from the Macro menu. For example, you may want to look for a command. When you are ready again to continue the recording process, click on the Pause option again.

8. Select Stop (Ctrl+Shift+F10) from the Macro menu to turn off the recording mode. The Recording Macro message disappears from the status line.

This macro has been saved in drive A. You can specify any drive and directory in your system. If you do not specify a drive, it will be saved on your default drive. The Finish macro, which is saved on the disk in drive A with WCM as its extension, is presented in Figure 10–6.

10–4–3   Executing a Macro

To accomplish **macro execution**, the insertion point to a blank area of the screen and follow these directions:

1. Select Macro; then click on Play (Alt+F10). The Play Macro dialog box will appear.

2. Type *A:Finish* and click on the Play button. The macro is executed immediately and you will see the result.

10–4–4   Editing a Macro

To edit the macro that you just created, you must retrieve it by using the File and Open commands. When you retrieve the Finish.WCM macro you will see a screen similar to the one in Figure 10–7. Macro files are made up of a series of commands called **functions**. Every WordPerfect for Windows command has a corresponding function. Suppose you want to add the title "and Chief Financial Officer" after the word "Director."

Figure 10–6
Your first macro.

```
Sincerely yours,


Tom Johnson, Ph.D.
Director
Management Information Systems Dept.
```

Figure 10–7
Editing screen for the Finish.WCM macro.

```
Application (WP;WPWP;Default;"WPWPUS.WCD")
Type
(
    Text:"Sincerely yours,"
)
HardReturn()
HardReturn()
HardReturn()
HardReturn()
Type
(
    Text:"Tom Johnson, Ph.D."
)
HardReturn()
Type
(
    Text:"Director"
)
HardReturn()
Type
(
    Text:"Management Information Systems Dept."
)
HardReturn()
```

Notice that there are three functions in this macro:

1. The Application function on the top tells the macro to perform each command in WordPerfect rather than some other application software. Each macro begins with an application function.

2. The Type function allows you to enter text as a part of a macro. As you can see in Figure 10–7, there are four of these functions in this macro. Each appears immediately before you enter text. The argument for the Type function begins with the word "Text:" followed by a series of characters that you enter. The text that you entered appears within quotation marks.

3. The HardReturn function places a hard return in a macro. During macro construction, each time you press the Enter key, WordPerfect for Windows enters a HardReturn function in the macro.

To insert "and Chief Financial Officer" after "Director" move the insertion point after the "r" of "Director"; press the space bar and type *and Chief Financial Officer*.

The new macro is displayed in Figure 10–8. Save the macro again under a new name using the File and Save As commands. Be sure to include the .WCM extension. When you play the new macro, you will see the new title for Tom Johnson.

10–4–5   An Interactive Macro

There are many cases in which most keystrokes in a macro are fixed but a few must be changed every time the macro is executed. In our previous example, let us say you want to keep all the information about Tom Johnson except his title, which you want to change every time you execute the macro; or perhaps you want to use a name other than Tom Johnson every time you execute the macro. Still another appropriate use of a macro is for the commands to retrieve a file: the File and Open commands are fixed but the file name changes.

WordPerfect for Windows offers a feature that handles these situations. It allows keyboard input during macro execution. To establish an **interactive macro**

```
Application (WP;WPWP;Default;"WPWPUS.WCD")
Type
(
    Text:"Sincerely yours,"
)
HardReturn()
HardReturn()
HardReturn()
HardReturn()
Type
(
    Text:"Tom Johnson,Ph.D."
)
HardReturn()
Type
(
    Text:"Director and Chief Financial Officer"
)
HardReturn()
Type
(
    Text:"Management Information Systems Dept."
)
HardReturn()
```

you must enter PAUSEKEY(key:character) in the macro at the location at which want to enter data from the keyboard. The character is the key that you will press to end the pausing of the macro. You can use the Enter key, the Esc key, or any other single-character key. For example, if you designate the key to end the pausing as Enter!, then you must press the Enter key to resume the macro operation. (The exclamation point is part of the command; it is a convention of WordPerfect.)

Let us walk through this interesting feature by changing the macro in Figure 10–6 to an interactive macro so you can enter other names beside Tom Johnson. Follow these steps:

1. Open the FINISH.WCM macro (presented in Figure 10–6).
2. Move the insertion point to the left of the second Type function and click on it.
3. Highlight the Type function and the next three lines. Press the Del key.
4. Type *PAUSEKEY(Key: Enter!)*
5. Press Enter. At this point your screen should be similar to the one in Figure 10–9.
6. Save this macro as INTERACT.WCM.

Now play the macro by selecting the Play option from the Macro menu. After Sincerely yours, is displayed, the cursor pauses. Type *Mary Brown, MS.* and press Enter. Now the rest of the macro will appear, that is, Director and then Management Information Systems Dept.

10–4–6 Deleting a Macro

If a macro is no longer needed, delete it from your disk to provide space for other applications. Recall that your macro files have a .WCM extension. By default, macros are stored in the C:\WPWIN\MACROS subdirectory. However, you could save your macros to any desired drive and/or directory. To delete a macro, follow these steps:

Figure 10–9
Interactive macro.

```
Application (WP;WPWP;Default;"WPWPUS.WCD")
Type
(
    Text:"Sincerely yours,"
)
HardReturn()
HardReturn()
HardReturn()
HardReturn()
PAUSEKEY(Key:Enter!)

HardReturn()
Type
(
    Text:"Director"
)
HardReturn()
Type
(
    Text:"Management Information Systems Dept."
)
HardReturn()
```

1. Select File and File Manager.
2. Select the desired macro.
3. Select File; then click on Delete.
4. Click on the Delete button.

To close the File Manager, select File and Exit.

10–4–7   Your Second Macro

The first macro that you created in this chapter recorded a series of text that can be used repeatedly. You can also record a series of menu options to simplify a time-consuming task. In this example we would like to design a macro that removes the frame from a graphic. As you recall, all WPG graphics are surrounded by a frame on all four sides (i.e., top, bottom, left and right). This is how to do it:

1. Click on Macro; then click on Record.
2. In the Filename box type *A:FRAME.*
3. In the Description Name box type *Removing the Frame from a Graphic.*
4. Click on the Record button.
5. Click on Graphics, Figure, and Options.
6. In the Border Styles region, click on the Left pop-out icon; then click on None.
7. Click on Right pop-out icon; then click on None.
8. Click on the Top pop-out icon; then click on None.
9. Click on Bottom pop-out icon; then click on None.
10. Click on OK to finalize the process.
11. Click on Macro, then click on Stop.

This macro is presented in Figure 10–10. Now if you play this macro and then retrieve any graphic file, the graphic will not have any borders. Try it!

Figure 10–10
Macro for removing graphic borders.

```
Application (WP;WPWP;Default;"WPWPUS.WCD")
BoxOptions
(
    Type:Figure!;
    LeftBorder:None!;
    RightBorder:None!;
    TopBorder:None!;
    BottomBorder:None!
)
```

10–5   CREATING COLUMNS

So far all the documents presented as figures in this book have appeared in a solid-page format. On some occasions, however, this format may not be appropriate. For example, the text in newspapers, newsletters, scripts, and brochures may look better in column format.

WordPerfect for Windows handles two types of columns: newspaper columns and parallel columns. In **newspaper columns** text starts at the beginning of the page, fills an entire column, and continues in the next column on the same page. In **parallel columns** text is presented in a side-by-side manner; that is, the left column corresponds to the right column. For example, the left column lists 10 items and the right column provides a description of each item.

10–5–1   Creating Newspaper Columns Using the Ruler

The fastest method for creating newspaper columns is to use the Ruler. The Ruler, however, is not capable of creating parallel columns. To create newspaper columns, follow these steps:

1. Move the insertion point to the beginning of the text.
2. Click on View; then click on Ruler (Alt+Shift+F3).
3. Click and hold on the third icon (columns) from the right.

The Ruler allows you to select 2, 3, 4, or 5 columns.

The nicest feature about the Ruler is that you can easily adjust the left or right margin. In Figure 10–11, we set the margins to 1 and 3.5 inches and 5 and 7.5 inches by dragging the margin marker to these positions. The default is in positions 1, 4, 4.5, and 7.5 inches.

When you create columns, they remain in effect until you select the Column Off option, either from the columns icon on the Ruler or from the Columns menu available on the Layout menu.

10–5–2   Creating Newspaper Columns Using Menus

Fancier and more precise columns can be created using the Columns (Alt+Shift+F9) option on the Layout menu. When you work with columns, newspaper or parallel, you have two options: you can enter text first and then set up columns, or you can set up columns first then enter text. The options are a matter of preference; choose whichever you like.

This is how to create newspaper columns using the Columns option:

1. From the Layout menu select the Columns (Alt+Shift+F9) option. If Columns On is not enabled, click on it to enable it.

Figure 10–11
Sample newspaper column.

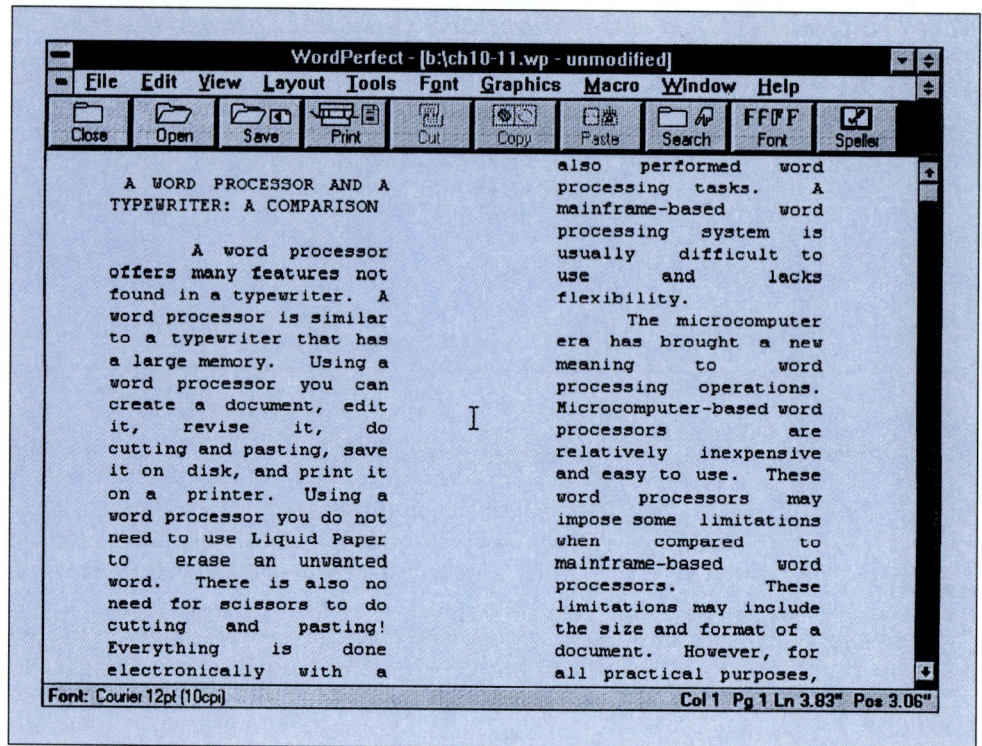

2. Click on the Define option. You will be presented with the Define Columns dialog box as shown in Figure 10–12. As you can see, by default the number of columns is two per page. The default for type of column is Newspaper. The left margin is set to 1 and 4.5 inches, and the right margin is set to 4 and 7.5 inches. You can change any of these settings by moving the insertion point to

Figure 10–12
Define Columns dialog box.

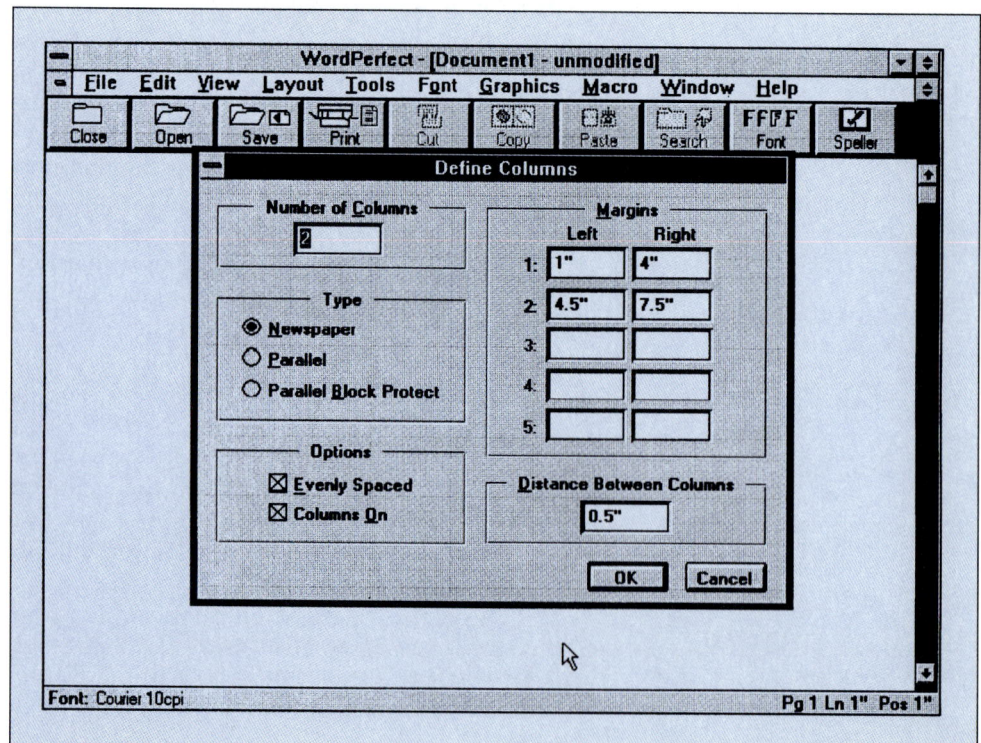

the position and changing the number. The default distance between columns is set to 0.5 inch. If you are satisfied with these settings, click on OK. You can also change any of these settings and then click on OK.

Any of the formatting features that you have learned so far can be applied to dress up your document. We boldfaced the headings and italicized the subheadings, and by using the line feature (discussed in the previous chapter) drew a thick line under the heading. See Figure 10–13.

10–5–3

Creating Parallel Columns

Parallel columns can only be created through menus; the Ruler cannot perform this task. Follow these instructions:

Figure 10–13
Newspaper column created by using the Layout and Columns menus.

A WORD PROCESSOR AND A TYPEWRITER: A COMPARISON
BY Hossein Bidgoli

A word processor offers many features not found in a typewriter A word processor is similar to a typewriter that has a large memory. Using a word processor you can create a document, edit it, revise it, do cutting and pasting, save it on disk, and print it on a printer. Using a word processor you do not need to use Liquid Paper to erase an unwanted word. There is also no need for scissors to do cutting and pasting! Everything is done electronically with a high degree of efficiency and effectiveness. Throughout this book you will learn many powerful features of WordPerfect for Windows as one of the most popular word processing programs on the market.

WORD PROCESSING REVOLUTION

Word processing machines have gone through a major revolution. The earliest word processors were dedicated machines, meaning they were only capable of performing word processing tasks. These machines were relatively expensive. Only medium-size and large organizations could afford them.
In the past decade mainframe computers have also performed word processing tasks. A mainframe-based word processing system is usually difficult to use and lacks flexibility.
The microcomputer era has brought a new meaning to word processing operations.

Microcomputer-based word processors are relatively inexpensive and easy to use. These word processors may impose some limitations when compared to mainframe-based word processors. These limitations may include the size and format of a document. However, for all practical purposes, microcomputer-based word processors perform major word processing tasks in an efficient and effective manner.

WORDPERFECT FOR WINDOWS: THE ENTIRE PACKAGE

WordPerfect for Windows is considered by many experts to be one of the best word processing programs on the market. The tasks performed by WordPerfect for Windows can be classified into five major components: word processor, speller, thesaurus, merge, and advanced features.
The word processor component is a full-featured word processing program. A document can be created, indented, boldfaced, underlined, saved, and printed. Electronic cut and paste, and variable spacing, are easily done using this component of the WordPerfect program.

1. Enter the title of your document and apply any desired formatting features.
2. Position the insertion point where you want columns to begin. This is the beginning of your text.
3. Select Columns from the Layout menu.
4. In the Define Columns dialog box, click on the Parallel button.
5. Click on OK.
6. Enter the text for the first column; for example, type *Component Number 1*.
7. To move to the next column while you are in Parallel mode, press the Ctrl+Enter key combination. This will move the insertion point over one column to the right.

Figure 10–14
Example of parallel columns.

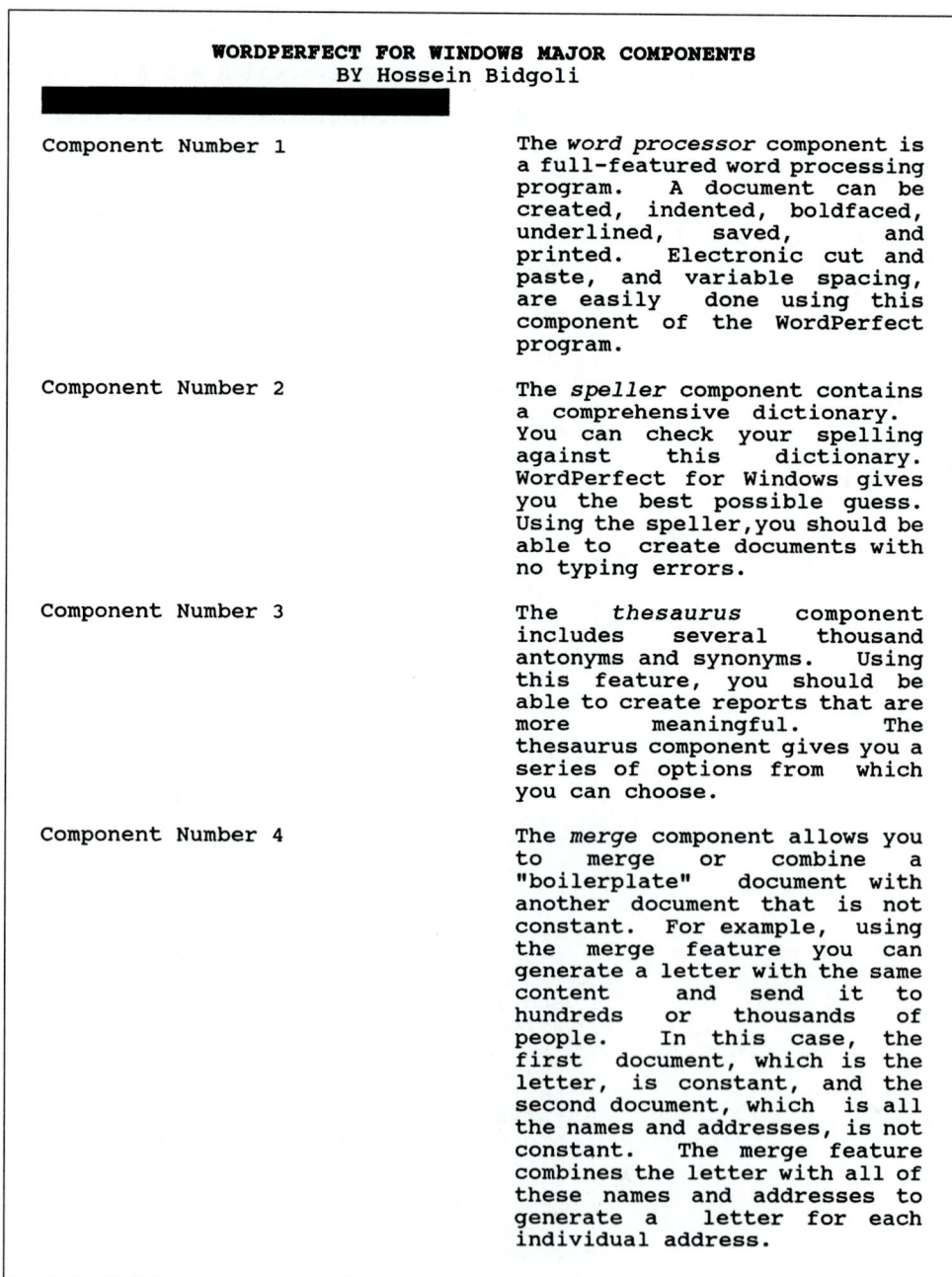

WORDPERFECT FOR WINDOWS MAJOR COMPONENTS
BY Hossein Bidgoli

Component Number 1	The *word processor* component is a full-featured word processing program. A document can be created, indented, boldfaced, underlined, saved, and printed. Electronic cut and paste, and variable spacing, are easily done using this component of the WordPerfect program.
Component Number 2	The *speller* component contains a comprehensive dictionary. You can check your spelling against this dictionary. WordPerfect for Windows gives you the best possible guess. Using the speller,you should be able to create documents with no typing errors.
Component Number 3	The *thesaurus* component includes several thousand antonyms and synonyms. Using this feature, you should be able to create reports that are more meaningful. The thesaurus component gives you a series of options from which you can choose.
Component Number 4	The *merge* component allows you to merge or combine a "boilerplate" document with another document that is not constant. For example, using the merge feature you can generate a letter with the same content and send it to hundreds or thousands of people. In this case, the first document, which is the letter, is constant, and the second document, which is all the names and addresses, is not constant. The merge feature combines the letter with all of these names and addresses to generate a letter for each individual address.

8. Enter the text that constitutes component 1, for example, *The word processor component . . .*
9. Continue this process by moving back and forth using the Ctrl+Enter keys. Your final work should be similar to Figure 10–14.

As you did in newspaper columns, you can use any formatting commands to further dress up your text.

SUMMARY

This chapter began by explaining the outline feature of WordPerfect for Windows. This feature enables you to create outlines for projects and papers and easily revise them as necessary. Next, macro operations were described. Using macros, you can simplify repetitive tasks, thereby improving the efficiency and the accuracy of your work. The last feature discussed in the chapter was the process of creating columns. This feature allows you to create two types of columns: newspaper and parallel. The columns feature is useful for designing newspapers, brochures, scripts, and so forth.

REVIEW QUESTIONS

*These questions are answered in Appendix A.
1. What is an outline?
2. What capabilities are provided by the outline feature of WordPerfect for Windows?
3. When an outline is finished, can you modify it?
*4. How do you start the outline feature?
5. How can you change the outline numbering?
6. How many different numbering formats are available in the outline feature?
7. Explain how to number paragraphs.
*8. What is a macro?
9. What are some of the applications of macros?
10. List the steps in developing a macro.
11. How do you start macro recording?
*12. How do you stop the recording operation?
13. Describe how to execute a macro.
14. What is the convention in naming a macro?
15. How do you edit a macro?
16. Give some examples of type functions in macros.
17. What key(s) can be used to pause a macro?
18. Name some of the applications of interactive macros.
19. What file extension is attached to a macro file name?
20. How do you delete an unwanted macro?
21. What are some applications of columns?
22. What are two types of columns handled by WordPerfect for Windows?
23. Explain the difference between newspaper and parallel columns.
*24. What type of columns can be created by the Ruler?
25. What is the maximum number of columns that can be created by the Ruler?
26. Under which menu option is the Columns command?

27. By default, what is the number of columns in the Define Columns dialog box?

*28. What key combination is used to switch the insertion point between columns in Parallel mode?

HANDS-ON EXPERIENCE

1. Using the outline feature of WordPerfect for Windows, set up the following outline:

1. Word Processing Major Functions
   1-1   Document Creation
   1-2   Cut and Paste
   1-3   Merge Printing
   1-4   Macro Design
2. Spreadsheet Major Functions
   2-1   What-If Analysis
   2-2   Graphics Analysis
   2-3   Financial and Statistical Analyses
3. Database Management Functions
   3-1   Search Operations
          3-1-1 Single Criterion Search
          3-1-2 Multiple Criteria Search
   3-2   Sort Operations
          3-2-1 Numeric Sort
          3-2-2 Nonnumeric Sort

2. Change the outline in exercise 1 to the legal format.

3. Design a macro to print:

> Dear Classmates:
> We all have learned so much about WordPerfect for Windows.

4. Design an interactive macro to input the name for the following closing:

> Sincerely yours,
>
> Any Name, Ph.D.
> Marketing Director

Remember, the name will be entered during the macro execution.

5. Using the columns features of WordPerfect for Windows, design the following parallel columns. Steps for solving a problem:

Step 1	Problem Definition
Step 2	Feasibility Study
Step 3	Systems Analysis
Step 4	Systems Design
Step 5	Systems Implementation

6. Type section 10–2 of this chapter in a blank screen. Using the Ruler, design a newspaper column with three columns in your desired location. By dragging the margin markers around, change the margins. Now, change the number of columns to two.

KEY TERMS

Column format	Macro design	Newspaper columns
Function	Macro execution	Outlining
Interactive macro	Numbering paragraphs	Parallel columns
Macro		

KEY COMMANDS

Alt+F5 (to invoke the paragraph numbering feature)

Alt+Shift+F3 (to display the Ruler)

Alt+Shift+F5 (to invoke the Define Paragraph Numbering dialog box)

Alt+Shift+F9 (to invoke the Columns menu)

Alt+F10 (to play a macro)

Ctrl+Enter (to switch between columns in Parallel mode)

Ctrl+F10 (to start the macro recording process)

Ctrl+Shift+F10 (to stop the macro recording process)

ARE YOU READY TO MOVE ON?

Multiple Choice

1. To turn on the outline feature, which menu should you select first?
   a. View
   b. File
   c. Edit
   d. Tools
   e. Window

2. WordPerfect for Windows macros are good candidates for all of the following except
   a. typing a fixed heading
   b. typing a fixed closing
   c. typing a term paper
   d. automating a series of repetitive commands
   e. all of the above

3. A macro name is
   a. similar to a file name (it can have up to eight characters)
   b. only digits 1 through 9
   c. only capital letters
   d. only letters A through H
   e. only names that start with A or B

4. To turn off the macro recording feature, press
   a. Alt+F5
   b. Ctrl+Shift+F10
   c. Enter
   d. Esc
   e. none of the above

5. To play a macro,
   a. type the macro name when the cursor is flashing
   b. press Alt+F9

      c. press Alt+F5
      d. do any of the above
      e. press Alt+F10 first; then type the macro name

6. How many types of columns does WordPerfect for Windows handle?
      a. 5
      b. 4
      c. 3
      d. 2
      e. 6

7. How many columns at most does the Ruler allow for creating newspaper columns?
      a. 5
      b. 4
      c. 3
      d. 2
      e. 1

8. WordPerfect for Windows handles
      a. newspaper columns
      b. parallel columns
      c. both A and B
      d. columns with only odd numbers
      e. only columns with no headings

9. To number paragraphs, press
      a. Shift+F8
      b. Alt+F5
      c. Shift+F5
      d. Alt+F7
      e. Ctrl+F5

10. You know that the outline feature is on if
      a. the screen is blinking
      b. you see OU at the lower right
      c. you see OU at the lower left
      d. all of the above
      e. the word "Outline" is displayed at the lower left of the screen

True/False

1. WordPerfect for Windows does not include a feature for outlining a table of contents of a book.
2. To turn on the outline feature in WordPerfect for Windows, you must first select the Tools menu.
3. To turn off the outline feature, you must click on the Outline Off option in the Outline menu.
4. Legal numbering is not one of the options in numbering paragraphs or outlines.
5. To turn on the macro recording feature, you must press Ctrl+F10.
6. WordPerfect for Windows offers editing features for macros.
7. You cannot pause an interactive macro for keyboard entry.
8. When you open a saved macro, you see the macro function and all the codes.
9. The file extension for a macro is WXM.
10. To stop the macro recording, press Ctrl+Enter.

ANSWERS

Multiple Choice		True/False	
1.	d	1.	F
2.	c	2.	T
3.	a	3.	T
4.	b	4.	F
5.	e	5.	T
6.	d	6.	T
7.	a	7.	F
8.	c	8.	T
9.	b	9.	F
10.	e	10.	F

Table Handling, Working with Multiple Documents, and Changing Fonts

11

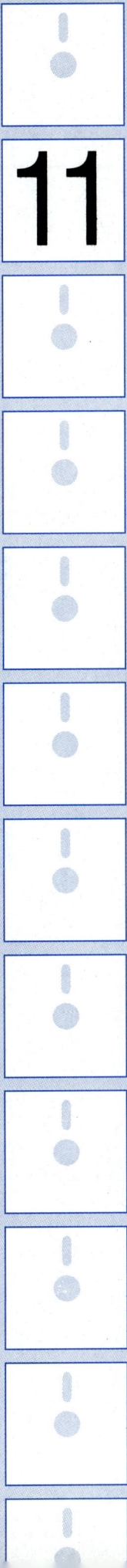

11–1   INTRODUCTION

This chapter introduces three more advanced features of WordPerfect for Windows: table handling, working with multiple documents, and changing fonts. By using the tables feature, you can design complex tables such as electronic spreadsheets. After you enter data in the tables, WordPerfect for Windows provides accurate results in a timely manner. The second part of the chapter concentrates on multiple document handling. This feature allows you to access text from any of nine open documents. You can display the documents in tile or cascade format, and you can save and retrieve each document individually. The chapter concludes by describing font capabilities of WordPerfect for Windows. By means of this feature, you can further enhance the appearance of your documents.

11–2   WHAT IS A TABLE?

WordPerfect for Windows offers an elegant and sophisticated capability for creating and handling **tables**. Tables serve a variety of purposes, including organizing data in a spreadsheet format, creating calendars, and designing forms. Any situation that can fit into a row and column format can benefit from this powerful feature of WordPerfect for Windows.

A table can be described as a set of rows and columns of information. The rows run horizontally across the table and the columns run vertically. Up to 32 columns and 32,765 rows can be specified in a WordPerfect for Windows table. The intersection of any row with any column is called a **cell**. Rows are numbered from 1 through 32,765 and columns are labeled from A to AF. When the insertion point is positioned in any of the cells in a table, you will see the **cell address** in the status line. For example, A1 means column A and row 1, AF5 means column 32 and row 5, and so forth.

11–2–1   Creating a Table

To create a table select Layout; then click on Tables (Ctrl+F9). From this menu click on the Create option. You will be presented with the Create Table dialog box as shown in Figure 11–1. Notice in the dialog box that the number of columns by default is 3 and the number of rows is 1. Click on OK to accept this dimension, or change these numbers to desired ones and then click on OK.

To create a table of five rows and four columns, type *4* in the Columns box and *5* in the Rows box and click on OK. Your table should be similar to the one in Figure 11–2.

11–2–2   Moving the Insertion Point Around in a Table

You can move the mouse pointer to any cell in the table by clicking the left button of the mouse. If there is no data in a cell, arrow keys (↑, ↓, →, ←) move the insertion point one cell up, down, right, or left. If there is data in a cell, you must use the Alt key *and* an arrow key to move in the four directions. For example, Alt+← moves the insertion point one cell to the left.

You can also use the Go To option from the Edit menu to move the insertion point around. To do this, select Go To (Ctrl+G) from the Edit menu. Then from the Go To Page Number pop-out menu select the cell reference. The insertion point must be positioned in one of the cells of the table before you can invoke the Go To command. Table 11–1 lists other important keys for moving the insertion point in a table.

Figure 11–1
Create Table dialog box.

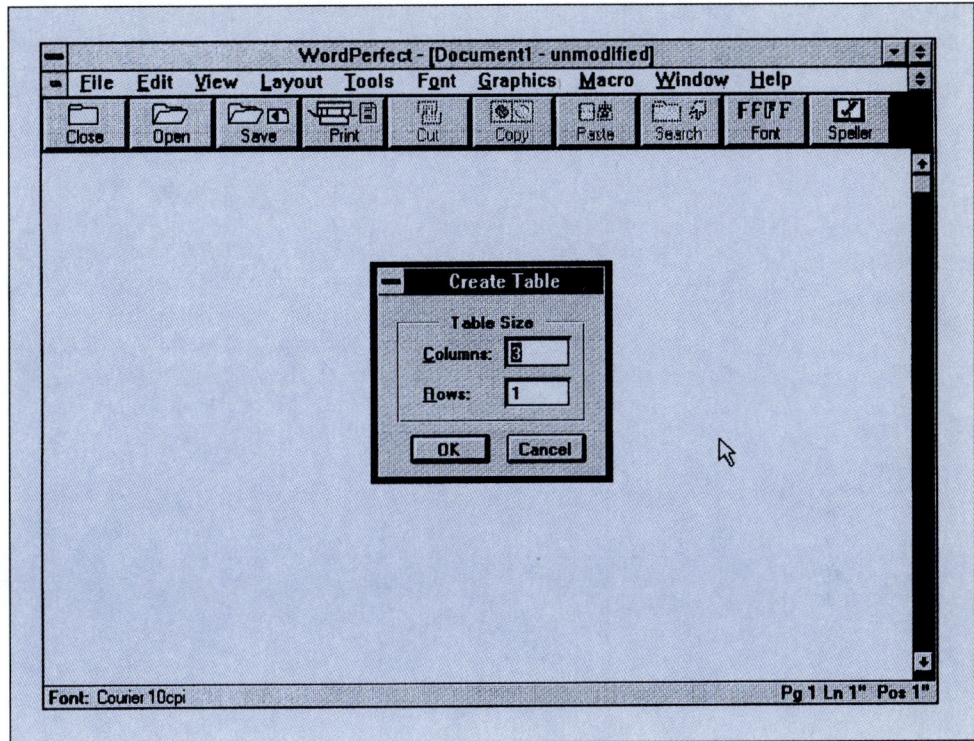

Figure 11–2
Table with five rows and four columns.

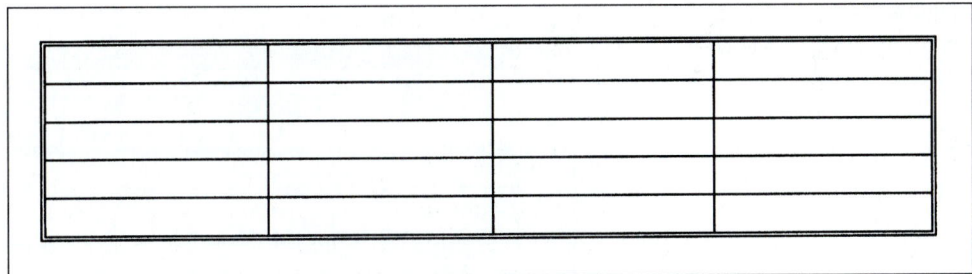

Table 11–1
Important Keys for Moving the Insertion Point in a Table

Keystroke	Moves
Alt+↑	One cell up
Alt+↓	One cell down
Alt+→	One cell right
Alt+←	One cell left
Tab	One cell right
Shift+Tab	One cell left
Ctrl+Tab	Five spaces to the right within a cell
End,End	To the last cell in row
Home,Home	To the first cell in row

Figure 11–3
Example of vertical selection bar.

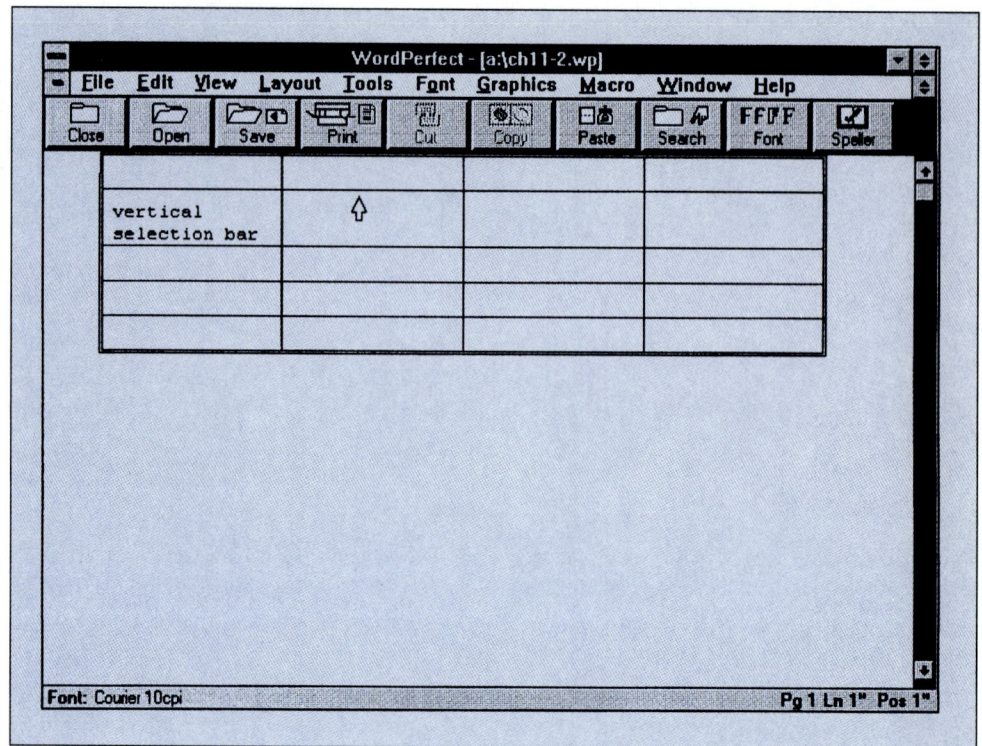

Figure 11–4
Example of horizontal selection bar.

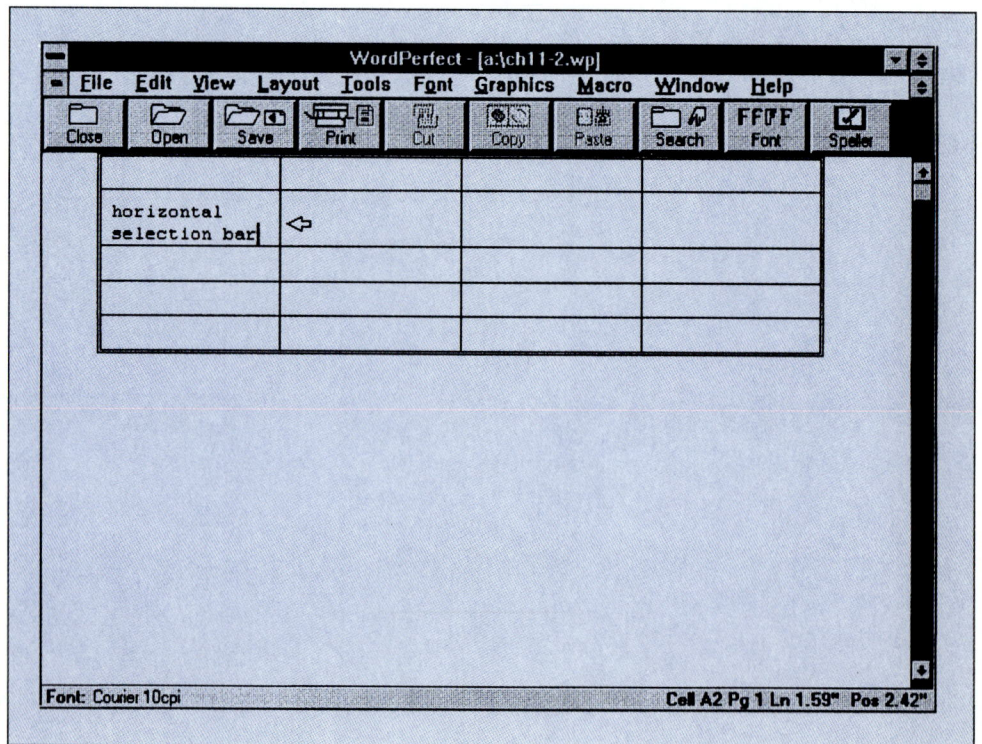

Table 11–2
Techniques for Selecting a Table

Selecting	Mouse Action
A cell	Click while the mouse pointer is a selection arrow
Several cells	Select the first cell and click and drag the mouse pointer across the other cells
A row	Double-click while the mouse pointer is a horizontal selection arrow
A column	Double-click while the mouse pointer is a vertical selection arrow
A table	Triple-click while the mouse pointer is a selection arrow (horizontal or vertical)

Text can be entered and edited in tables as you have been doing all along.

11–2–3   Techniques for Selecting Cells in a Table

To manipulate a section of a table, you must first select it. When you move the mouse pointer vertically from cell to cell, you will see a vertical selection arrow. When you move the mouse pointer horizontally from cell to cell, you will see a horizontal selection arrow. Figure 11–3 illustrates a vertical selection bar and Figure 11–4 illustrates a horizontal selection bar. Table 11–2 summarizes the mouse actions for selecting different sections of a table.

As soon as you select a portion of a table, you can perform any of the editing commands such as Copy and Cut.

11–2–4   Editing a Table

After a table is constructed, you can perform various editing tasks on it. Select Layout and Tables; you will be presented with a menu similar to the one in Figure 11–5. Let us briefly explain these menu options:

The Create option, as you have already seen, allows you to create a table with up to 32 columns and 32,765 rows.

Options allows you to change the size of the table, modify a cell margin, change gray shading, change the appearance of negative numbers, and change the table position. When you select Options, you will see a dialog box similar to the one in Figure 11–6. You can change any of these options and click on OK.

The Join option joins several columns or rows together. To do this, select the desired row or column by using techniques specified in Table 11–2; then select the Join option.

The Split option splits a column or a row. To do this, move the insertion point to the desired row or column. Then select the Split option. You will be presented with the Split Column/Row dialog box as shown in Figure 11–7. Enter the desired number in the Column or Row box and click on OK.

The Insert option enables you to insert rows or columns in your table. When you select this option, you will be presented with the Insert Columns/Rows dialog box as shown in Figure 11–8. Identify the number of rows or columns to be inserted and click on OK. The rows or columns specified will be entered before the present row or column. For example, if you are in row 5, the new rows will be entered before row 5.

Figure 11–5
Tables menu options.

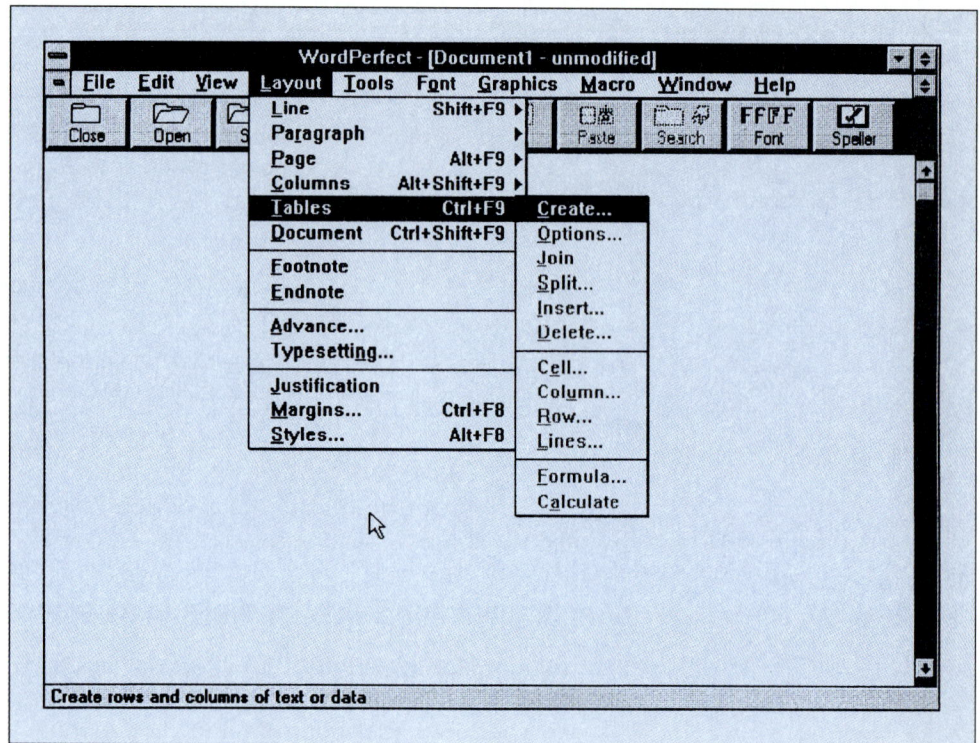

Figure 11–6
Table Options dialog box.

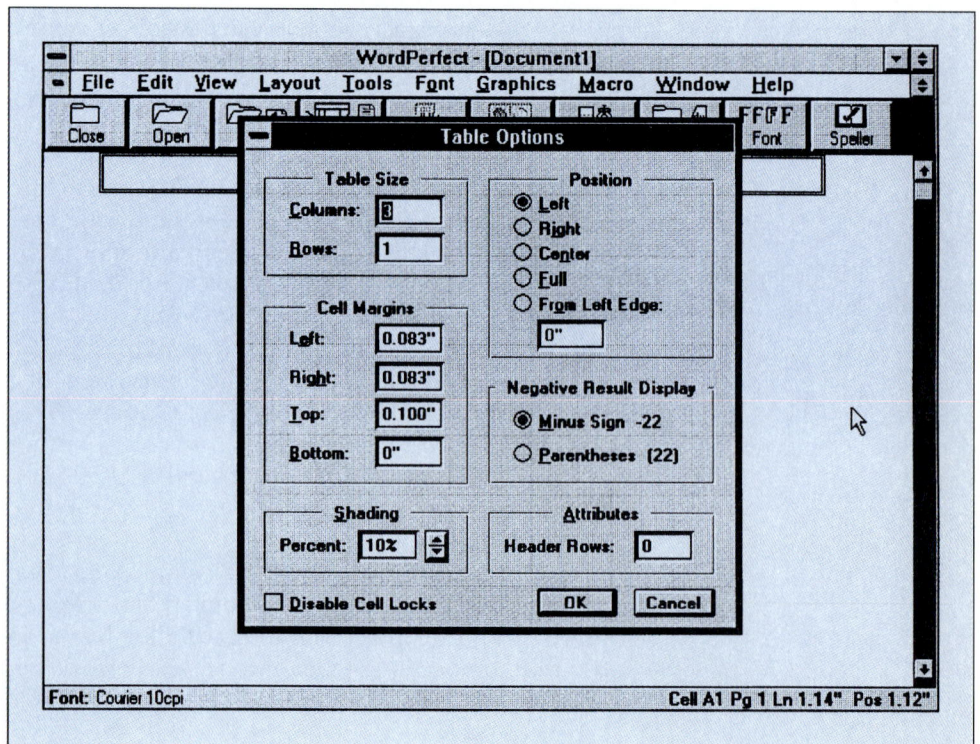

Figure 11–7
Split Column/Row dialog box.

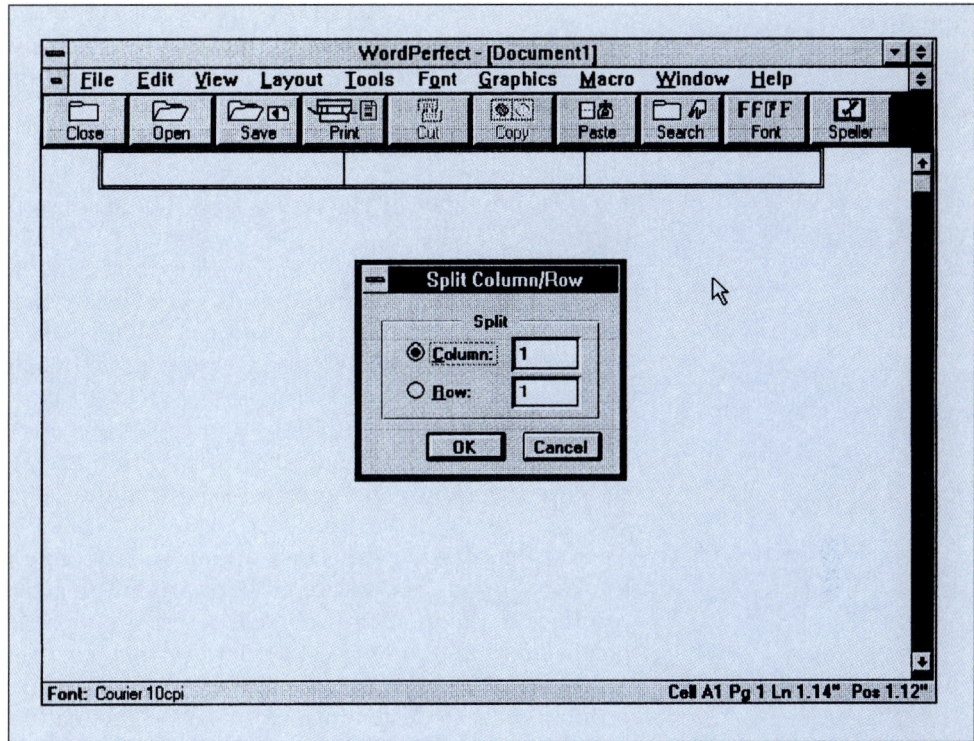

Figure 11–8
Insert Columns/Rows dialog box.

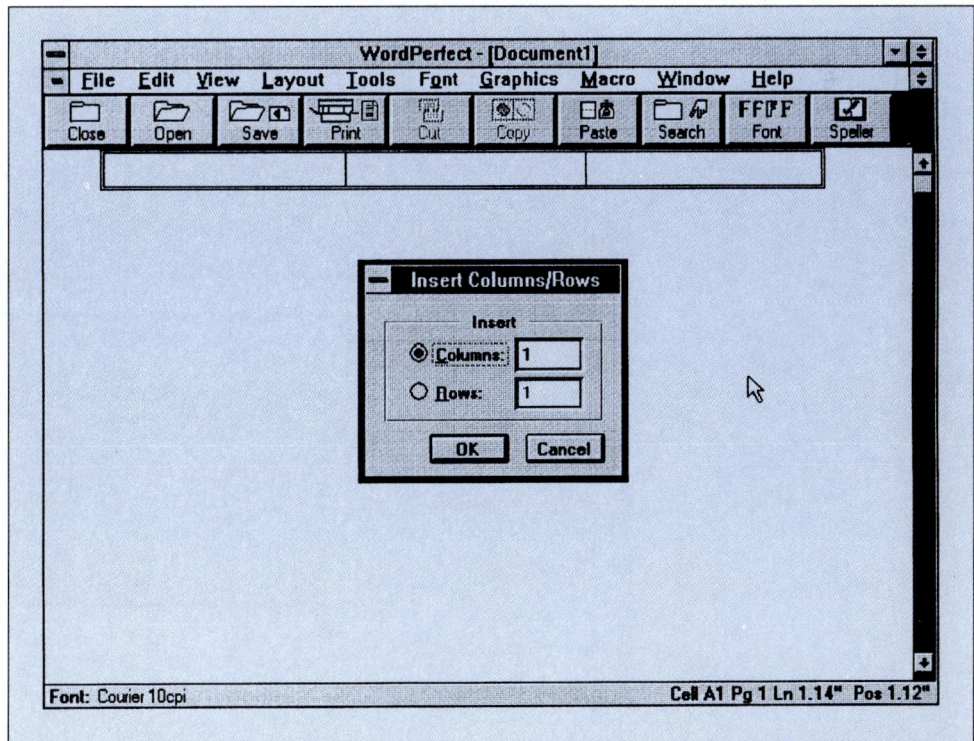

By selecting the Delete option you can delete a series of rows or columns. When you choose this option, the Delete Columns/Rows dialog box will be displayed as presented in Figure 11–9. Specify the number of columns or rows, then click on OK.

The Cell option allows you to change the appearance, size, justification, and alignment of text or numbers in a cell. When you select this option the dialog box presented in Figure 11–10 will be displayed. Change the desired option; then click on OK.

The Column option allows you to change the appearance, size, or justification of text in a column. You can also adjust the column width or specify the number of decimal places in a column. When you select this option, you will see a dialog box similar to the one in Figure 11–11. Change any of these options and click on OK.

The Row option allows you to set the number of lines per row and the height of a row. When you select this option the Format Row dialog box will be displayed as shown in Figure 11–12. Change any of these settings and click on OK.

By selecting the Lines option you are able to change the lines and their thickness around the entire table or around selected cells. If you want to change the lines for more than one cell, select the area, invoke the Table Lines dialog box as presented in Figure 11–13, perform your changes, and click on OK.

The Formula option allows you to create formulas and place them in one or more cells. To design formulas, you use the math operators such as + (addition), – (subtraction), * (multiplication), and / (division). When you invoke the Formula option, you will see a dialog box similar to the one in Figure 11–14. Select the desired cell, construct your formula in the Formula box, and click on OK.

The formula that you created can be copied as many times as you wish—down or right. WordPerfect for Windows keeps track of the relative addresses of

Figure 11–9
Delete Columns/Rows dialog box.

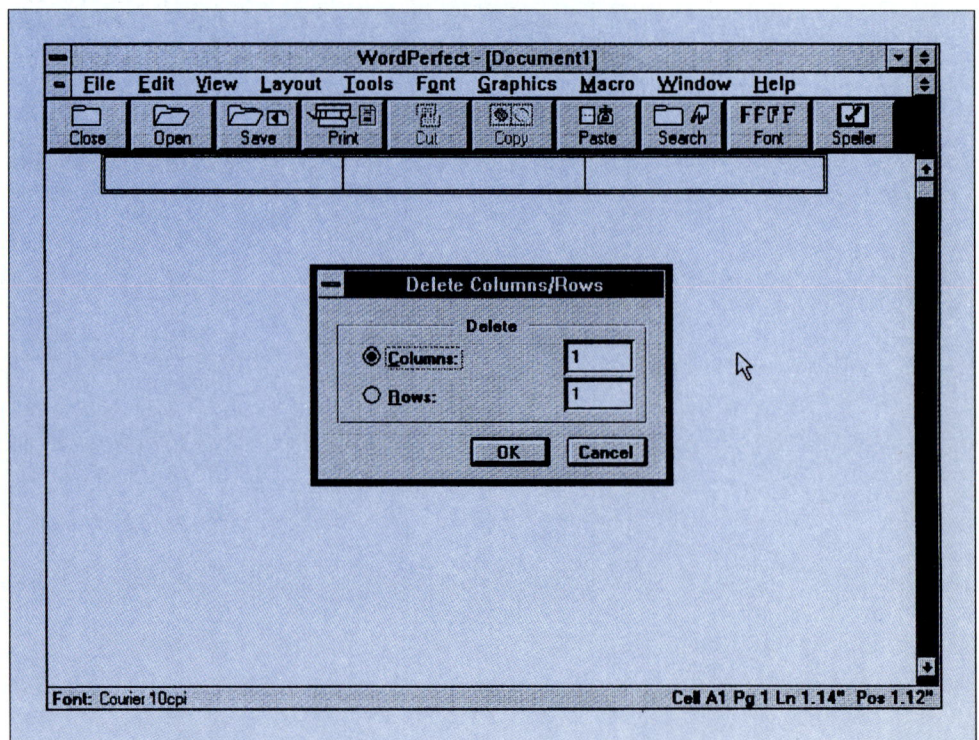

Figure 11–10
Format Cell dialog box.

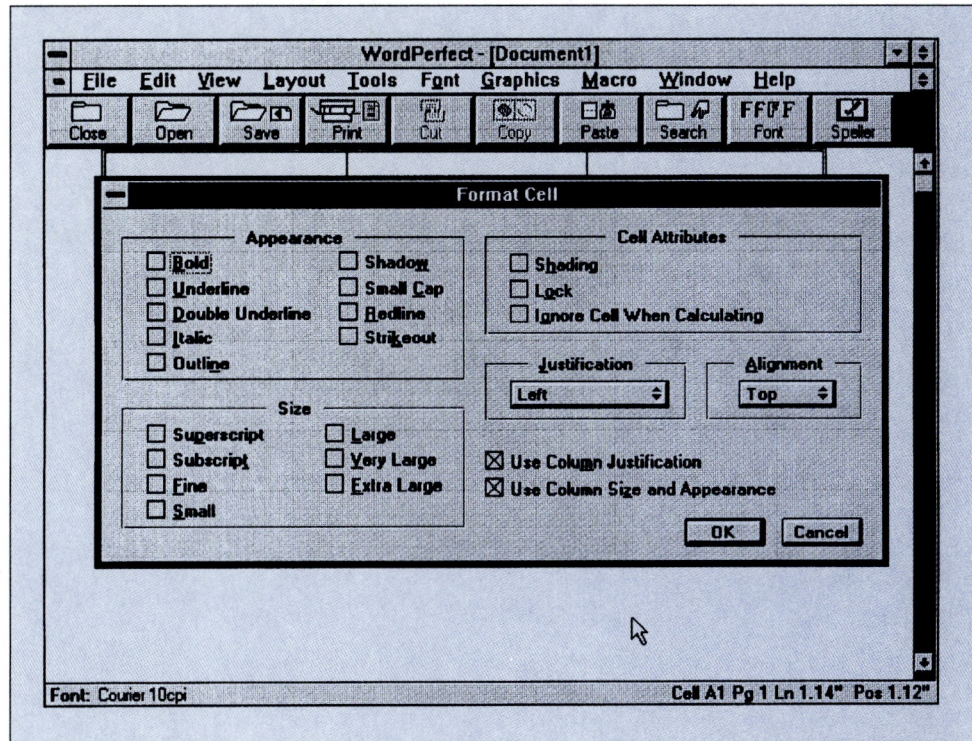

Figure 11–11
Format Column dialog box.

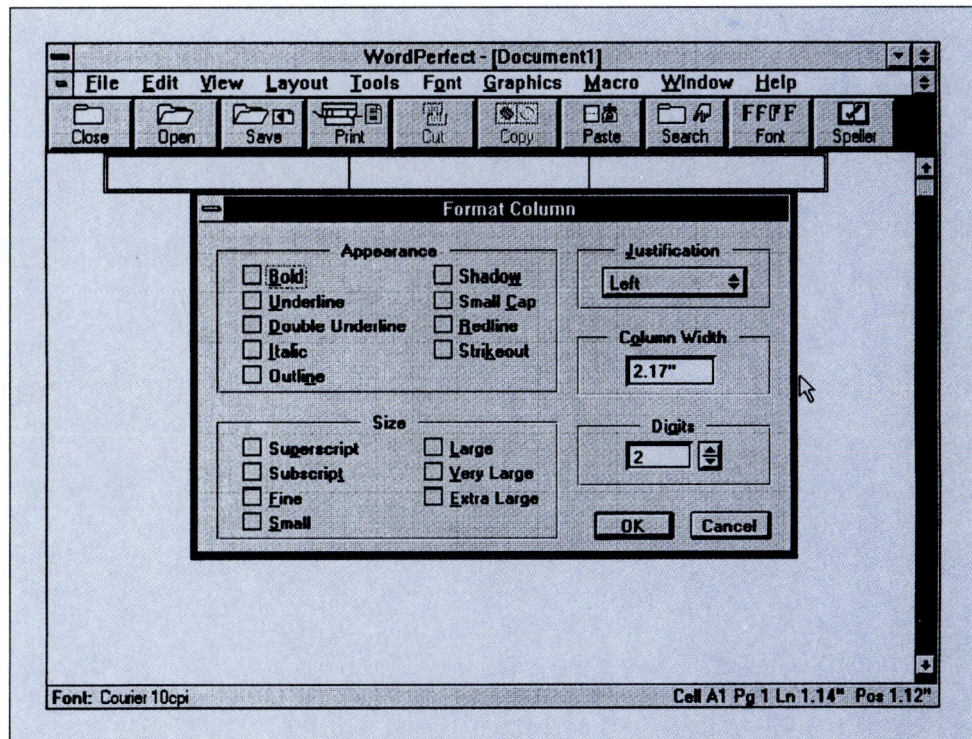

Figure 11–12
Format Row dialog box.

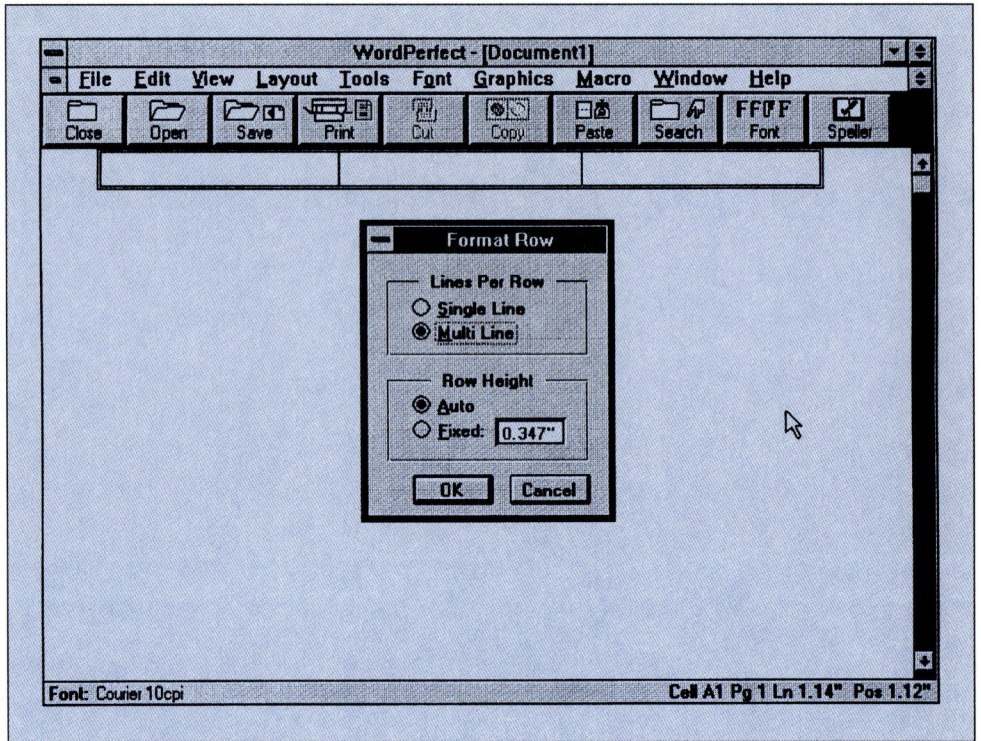

Figure 11–13
Tables Lines dialog box.

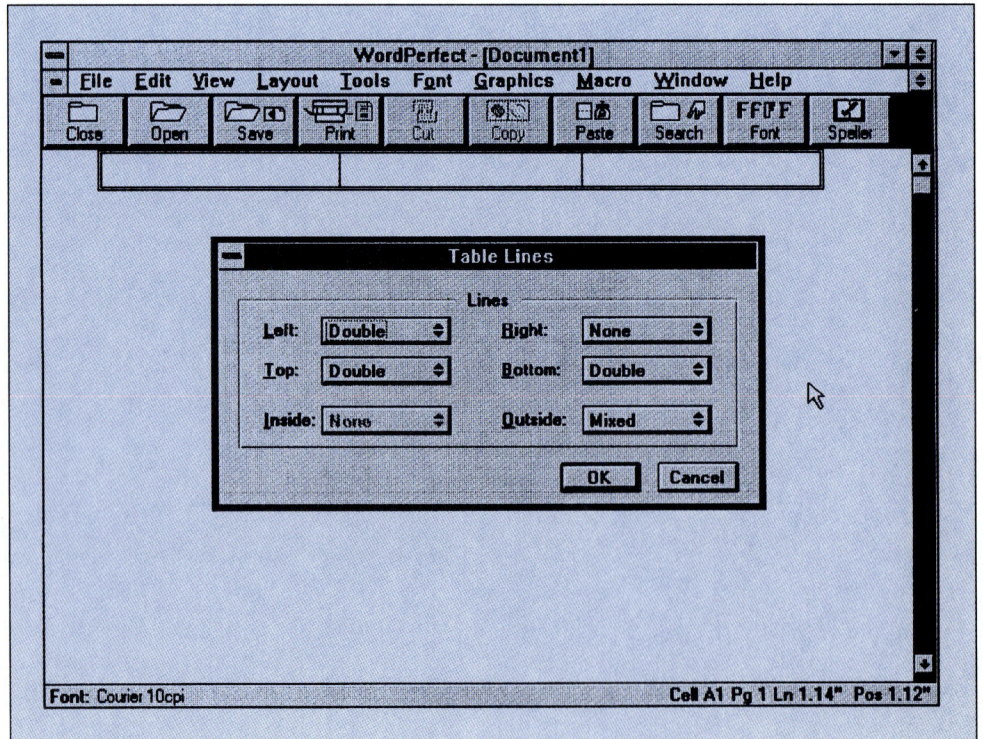

Figure 11–14
Tables Formula dialog box.

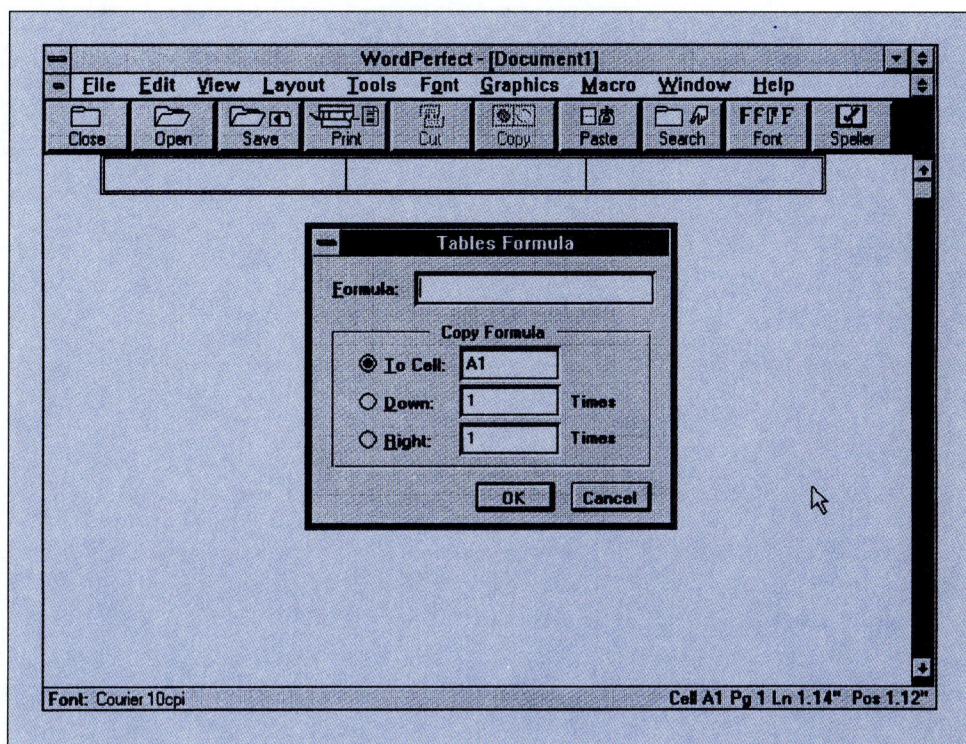

formulas. This means that when you copy, for example, A1+A2+A3 from cell A4 to cell B4, the formula in cell B4 automatically becomes B1+B2+B3, and if you copy the formula in cell C4, it becomes C1+C2+C3.

Finally, the Calculate option calculates the most recent values of the formulas in a table. For example, if you change some of the values in a table and click on the Calculate option, the table is recalculated.

11–2–5   Using the Button Bar with Tables

WordPerfect for Windows has made the table processing job even easier by creating the TABLES.WWB button bar. All table commands have a representative button. To activate the button bar, follow these steps:

1. From the View menu select the Button Bar Setup option; then click on the Select option.
2. From the Select Button Bar dialog box select TABLES.WWB by double-clicking on it. You will be presented with a screen similar to the one in Figure 11–15. Remember that to make the buttons on the button bar active, the insertion point must be in a cell of a table.

At the upper left of the button bar note the left- and right-arrow icons; move these to the left or right to see the buttons that are not currently visible. As usual, you can click on any of these buttons to activate the desired option.

11–2–6   An Example of a Table

Start with a clear screen. Click on Layout, then on Tables (Ctrl+F9), then on Create. The Create Table dialog box will appear. In the Columns box type *4*, in the

Figure 11–15
TABLES.WWB button bar.

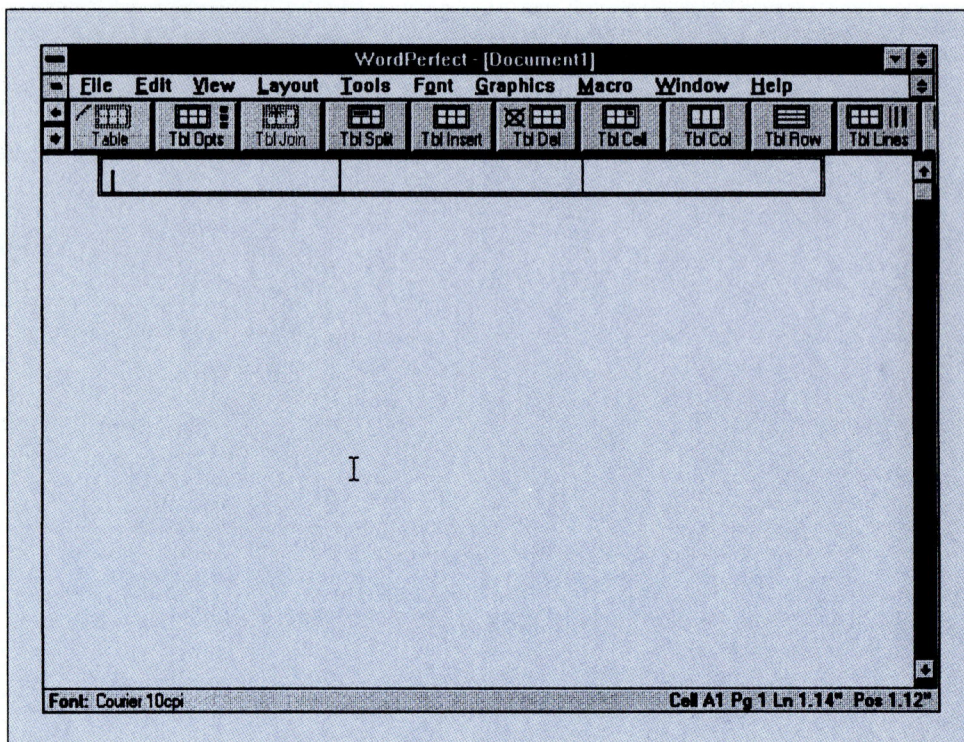

Rows box type *4*, and click on OK. You will be presented with a 4-by-4 table. The status line indicates that you are in cell A1 of the table, and the insertion point is blinking in cell A1. Activate the TABLES.WWB button bar if it is not already active. Now follow these instructions:

1. Place the mouse pointer in the table and move the pointer for a small distance to the right until you see the horizontal selection bar. By triple-clicking the mouse button select the entire table.

2. Click on the Tbl Cell button. The Format Cell dialog box will be displayed.

3. Click on the pop-out menu of the Justification box; then click on Center and on OK. This instructs WordPerfect for Windows to center all the entries in the table.

4. Move the mouse pointer outside of the table and click the left button of the mouse to unselect the table.

5. Move the insertion point to cell A1. Please notice that the insertion point is blinking in the center of cell A1.

6. Type the following information and press the keys indicated:

Type	Press
REGION	Right arrow
QUARTER 1	Right arrow
QUARTER 2	Right arrow
TOTALS	Down arrow once and left arrow three times
WEST	Right arrow
51,200	Right arrow
57,550	Down arrow once and left arrow twice

EAST	Right arrow
49,250	Right arrow
54,600	Down arrow once and left arrow twice
GRAND TOTAL	Right arrow three times and up arrow twice

7. Click on Tbl Form (for formula). The Tables Formula dialog box appears. Type *B2+C2* and click on OK. As soon as you do this, the number 108,750.00 will be displayed in cell D2.

8. Click on the Tbl Form button again. Note that the B2+C2 formula is still displayed in the formula box. Click on the down button in this box. This means that you want to copy the formula B2+C2 to the next cell down.

9. Click on OK. As soon as you do this, the number 103,850.00 will be displayed in cell D3.

10. Move the insertion point to cell A4.

11. Select cells A4, B4, and C4 by using the click and drag technique.

12. Click on the Tbl Join button. As soon as you do, the cells A4, B4, and C4 become one cell and the GRAND TOTAL label is centered in this new cell.

13. Move the insertion point to cell D4 and click on Tbl Form. The Tables Formula dialog box will be displayed.

14. In the Formula box type + (a plus sign) and click on OK. As soon as you do, the number 212,600.00 will be displayed in cell D4. Your final work should be similar to Figure 11–16. Using the + (plus sign) is a shortcut for calculating the total.

Figure 11–17 is another example of a table. What formula was entered into cells C6, C12, C13, and C15?

Figure 11–16
Example of a table.

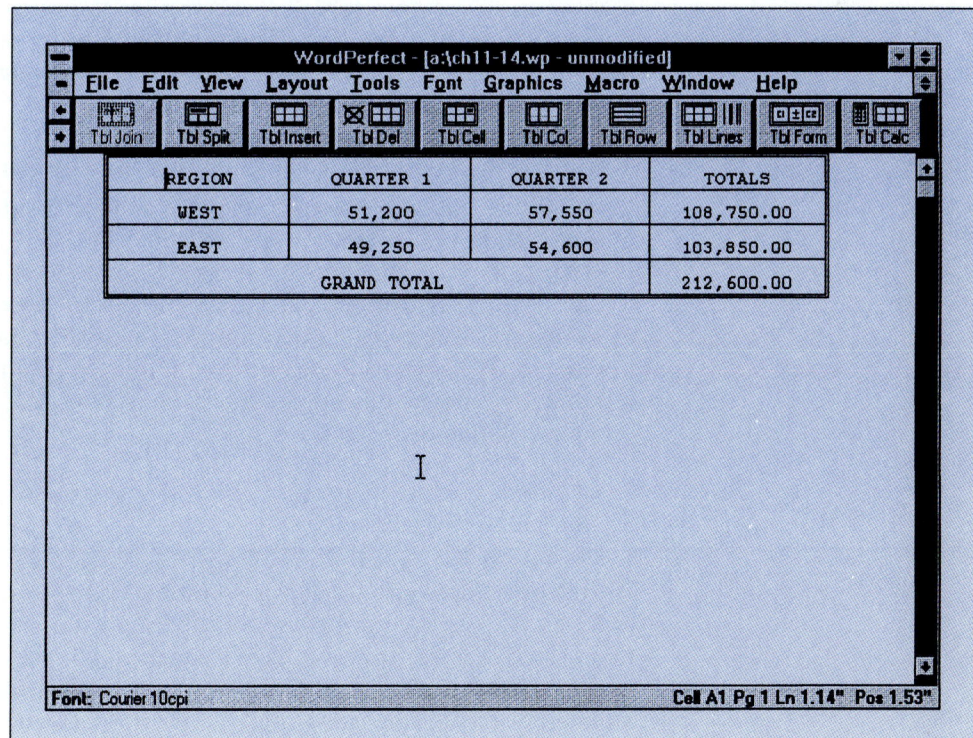

Figure 11–17
Another example of a table.

```
                    WordPerfect - [Document1]
  File  Edit  View  Layout  Tools  Font  Graphics  Macro  Window  Help

  Close  Open  Save  Print  Cut  Copy  Paste  Search  Font  Speller

  SALES
                        NORTH        100
                        SOUTH        200
                        EAST         300
                        WEST         400
          TOTAL SALES                1,000.00
  COSTS
                        NORTH        -50
                        SOUTH        -120
                        EAST         -200
                        WEST         -250
          TOTAL COSTS                -620.00
          NET INCOME                 380.00
          ROYALTY                    500
          GRAND TOTAL                880.00

  =C13+C14                            Cell C15 Pg 1 Ln 5.06" POS 6.03"
```

11–2–7   Creating a Table Using the Ruler

Tables can also be easily created by using the Ruler. Click on View and on Ruler (Alt+Shift+F3). The Table button on the Ruler (the fourth button from the right) allows you to create a table by clicking on the button and dragging the mouse pointer across the table grid. The number of cells you highlight in the table grid determines the size of the table. Let us say you want to create a table with four rows and three columns. Follow these steps:

1. Click on View and on Ruler. Click and hold on the Table button on the Ruler.
2. Drag the mouse pointer across three columns and four rows. Then release the mouse button.

Notice that when using the Table button on the Ruler, by default the size of the grid is 10 rows by 10 columns. To create a larger table, drag the mouse pointer to the right to increase the number of columns or down to increase the number of rows displayed on the grid. When you are satisfied with the table dimensions, release the mouse button.

11–3   PROCESSING MULTIPLE DOCUMENTS

WordPerfect for Windows allows you to open up to nine documents at any given time. Each document appears in a separate window on your screen. All the commands and features that you have learned so far work with **multiple documents**.

Multiple documents can be opened by using the Open (F4) command and can be created by using the New (Shift+F4) command. WordPerfect for Windows numbers your opened documents from Document1 through Document9.

11–3–1   ## Creating Two Documents

Follow these steps to create two documents:

1. Make sure that on the top of the screen you see Document1. This means your default document is document number 1. If there are other documents opened, close them one by one by using the Close (Ctrl+F4) command. Type *Test1*.

2. Select the New option from the File menu. You will be presented with a clear screen, and on the top of the screen you will see Document2.

3. Type *Test2*.

Now you have created two documents. The content of the first document is Test1 and the content of the second document is Test2. The last document that you opened is your active document.

To see a listing of your open documents click on the Window option in the main menu.

11–3–2   ## Viewing Multiple Documents

Multiple documents can be viewed either in Cascade or Tile mode. In **Tile mode** you see multiple windows side by side, so they do not overlap each other. In **Cascade mode** you see the title bar of each window. Figure 11–18 illustrates the Tile mode, and Figure 11–19 illustrates the Cascade mode.

To arrange your open documents in Tile mode select the Window and Tile options. To arrange your open documents in Cascade mode, select Window and Cascade.

Figure 11–18
Example of Tile mode.

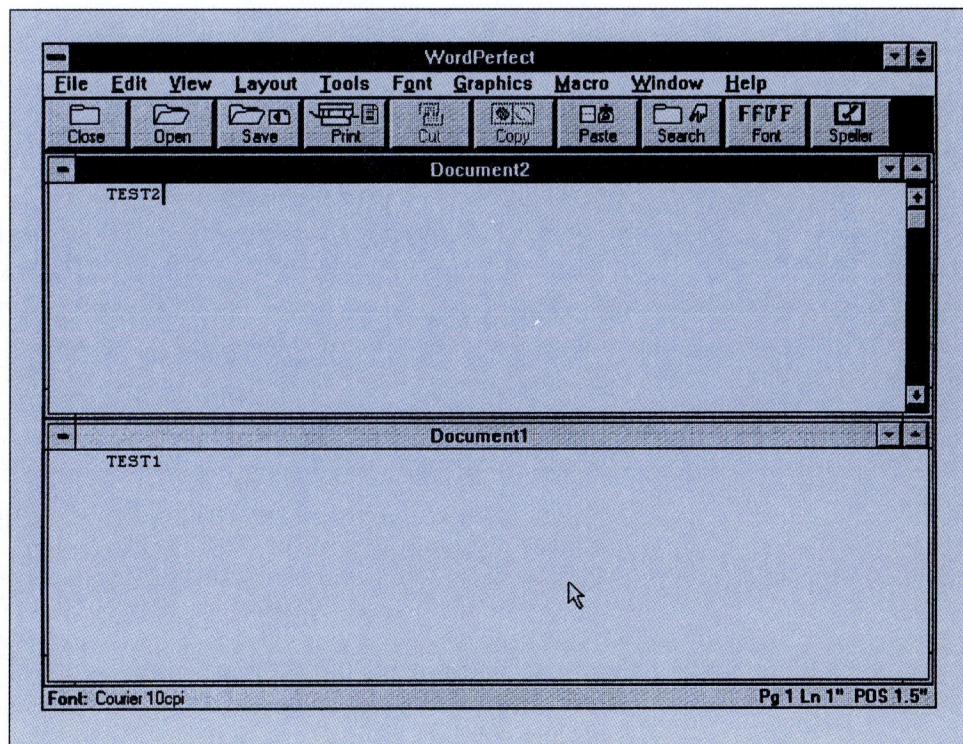

Figure 11–19
Example of Cascade mode.

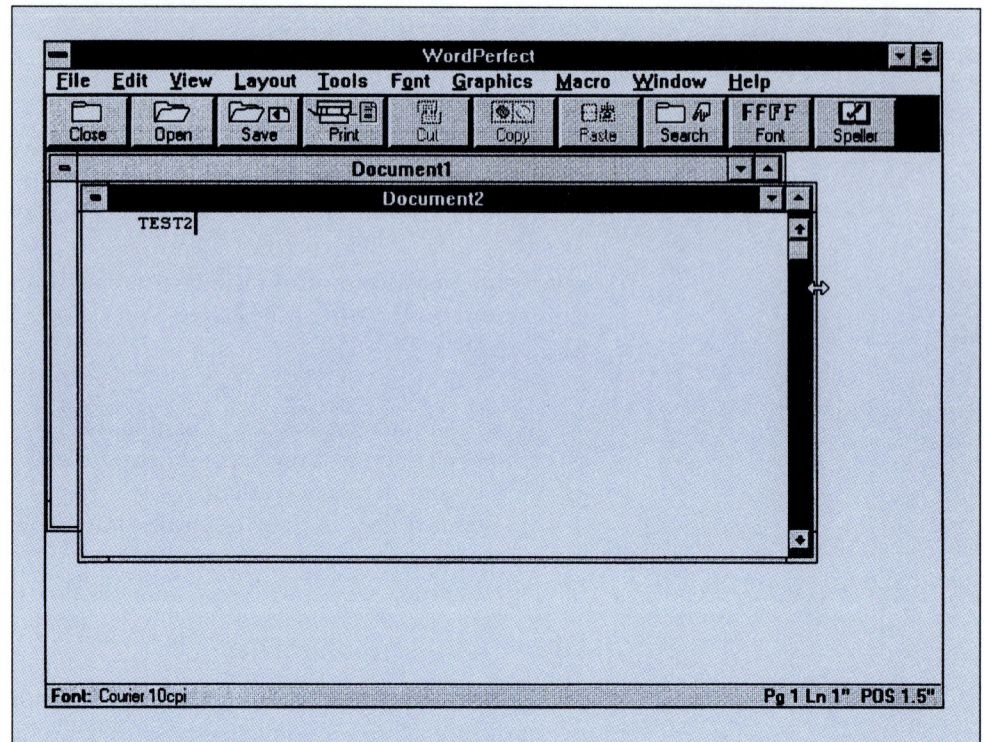

11–3–3   An Application of Multiple Documents

One of the most common applications of multiple documents is cutting, or copying, text from one document and pasting it to another document. This is how you do it:

1. Open two documents, one by one, by using the Open command.
2. Select Window and Tile. Both of your documents will be displayed in Tile mode. Let us say you want to copy one paragraph from document 1 and paste it to the end of document 2.
3. Highlight the desired text in document 1.
4. From the Edit menu select the Copy (Ctrl+Ins) command.
5. Move the insertion point to the desired location in document 2.
6. From the Edit menu select Paste (Shift+Ins). The selected text from document 1 is pasted into document 2.

11–4   FONT CAPABILITIES

The font feature of WordPerfect enables you to change the size and style of displayed and printed text. A **font** is a particular style (typeface) of characters at a particular size. What types of fonts are available to you varies depending on whether you are using a WordPerfect or Windows printer driver. For example, a Windows printer driver gives you access to a set of scalable Truetype fonts (Truetype fonts and scalable fonts will be explained shortly), but a WordPerfect printer driver does not. Truetype fonts enable even a dot matrix printer to have scalable fonts measured in "points."

The following terms are introduced to help clarify our discussion of fonts:

Typeface	A typeface is a particular style, or shape, of text. Examples of common typefaces are Courier, Times Roman, and Helvetica.
Serif	A serif is the tiny line that appears at the top and bottom of letters. A serif font is any font that includes these tiny lines.
Sans serif	A sans serif font is any font that does not have the tiny lines that appear at the top and bottom of letters.
Size	For laser printers, the most commonly used increment of text size is in terms of "points." Since 1 point is 1/72 of an inch tall, a font set to 18 points would be 1/4 inch tall, a 36-point font would be 1/2 inch tall, and so on. A popular size for laser printer output is 12 points. Dot matrix printers, on the other hand, typically use characters per inch (cpi) as the increment of measurement—5 cpi, 10 cpi, 17 cpi, and so on.
Spacing	Spacing refers to whether individual letters are monospaced or proportionally spaced. Monospacing allocates the same amount of space to each character. Proportional spacing allocates only as much space as necessary to each letter.
Scalable fonts	A **scalable font** is a font for which you can specify any size, such as 14 points or 18 points. If your printer has scalable fonts and you use any of the fonts in the font dialog box to change the font in a document, you must select a size in the Point Size list box or type a size in the Point Size box. The largest point size possible is 1199.9.
Truetype fonts	**Truetype fonts** are fonts that are scalable and sometimes generated as bitmaps (images stored as a pattern of dots) or soft fonts, depending on the capabilities of your printer. Truetype fonts can be sized to any height, and they print exactly as they appear on the screen.

Let's experiment with font capabilities. Begin with a clear screen and type the text in Figure 11–20. Do not be concerned if your paragraph varies somewhat from the paragraph in the figure. After you have finished typing the paragraph, print the document.

Now move the insertion point to the top of the document. Click on Font; then click on Font (F9) again. This will display the Font dialog box as presented in Figure 11–21. WordPerfect for Windows displays the list of fonts that your printer is capable of producing. This list varies by type of printer and whether a WordPerfect or a Windows printer driver is being used. As mentioned earlier, a Windows printer driver gives you access to a full set of scalable typefaces. In this example we are using the Windows printer driver. Click on one of the selections

Figure 11–20
Sample document.

```
WordPerfect  for Windows can be used to generate a variety of
fonts. With a little practice, you will be able to use fonts in
your reports,memos,documents,and letters that make your printed
output much more visually interesting. You should be very careful
when deciding how to use and combine fonts in a document;do not
overuse this feature.
```

Figure 11–21
Font dialog box.

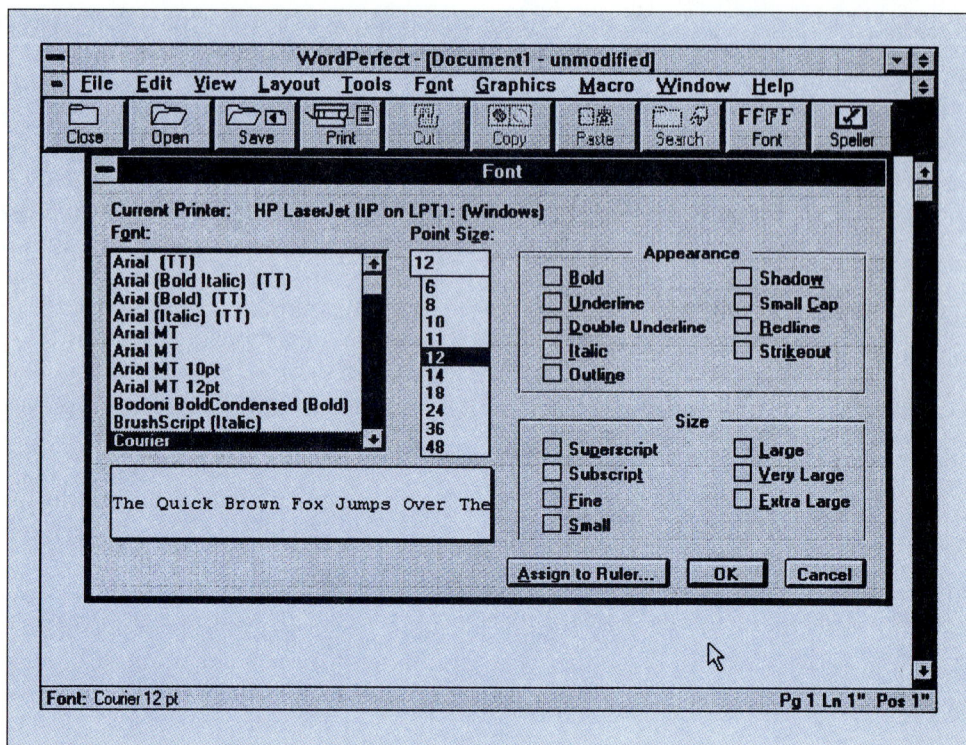

Figure 11–22
Example of size and font features.

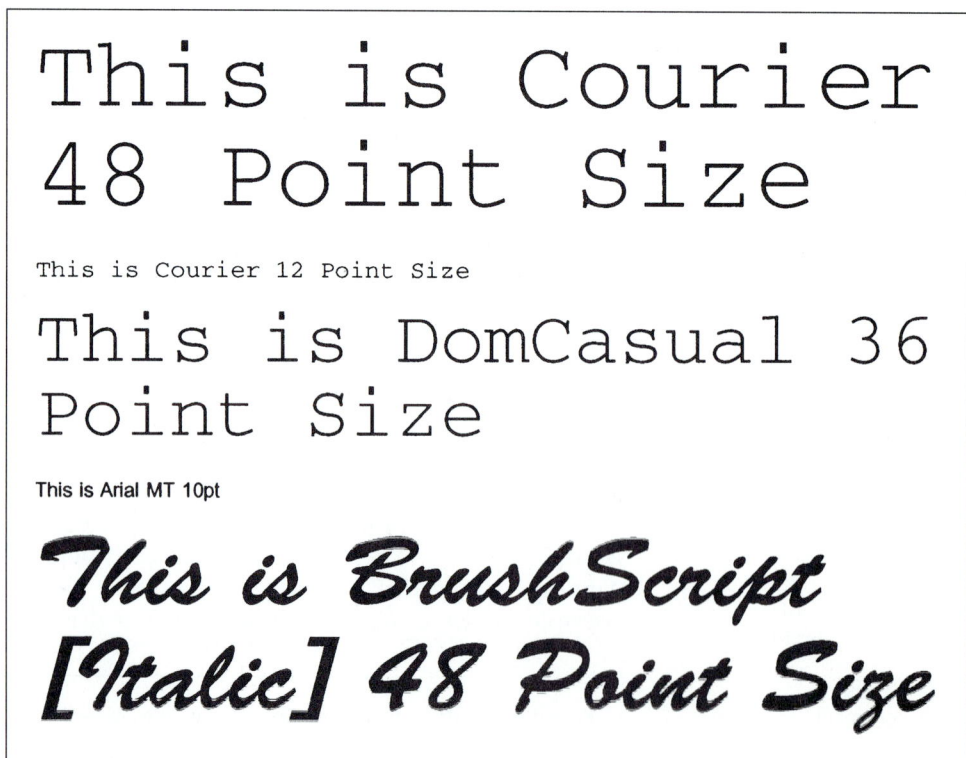

available in the font list. As soon as you do this, sample text will be displayed in the last box in the font region in Figure 11–21 (lower left). From the appearance region (at right of screen) you can select a desired format by clicking on it. From the size region you can select the desired size. To finalize the process click on OK.

From this point on your text will be printed or displayed with the selected options. The options stay in effect until you select others. Figure 11–22 is a sample document created with various fonts and size attributes.

SUMMARY

This chapter explained three powerful features of WordPerfect for Windows: tables, multiple document processing, and font capabilities. By using the tables feature you can create spreadsheets and other documents that benefit from a grid format. Multiple document processing allows you to open several documents, view them in Tile or Cascade mode, and move or copy text between documents. The font capabilities help you to significantly improve the appearance of your documents.

REVIEW QUESTIONS

*These questions are answered in Appendix A.

1. What are some of the applications of tables?
*2. How many rows and columns can be supported by a WordPerfect for Windows table?
3. What key combination is used to invoke the Tables menu?
4. By default, what is the size of a table?
5. What will the arrow keys do if there is no data in the table? What will they do if there is data in the table?
*6. Can you use the Go To command to move around in a table?
7. What does the Home,Home key combination do? What does End,End do?
8. Explain how to select a row, a column, an entire table, and a specific cell using the mouse.
9. Describe the function of the Options option in the Tables menu.
10. What are the applications of the Join command?
11. What does the Split option do? Can you split only rows or columns or both?
12. How do you delete two columns from a table?
*13. How do you change the appearance of a cell in a table?
14. Which option from the Tables menu allows you to change lines around an entire table or around specified cells?
15. Explain how to enter a formula in a cell.
16. Can you copy a formula from one cell to another? If yes, how?
*17. Can a formula be constructed based on cell addresses?
18. Name the four major mathematical operators used for constructing a formula.
19. What is the application of the Calculate command?
20. How do you activate the button bar for simplifying table operations?
*21. Under what name is the tables button bar saved?
22. How do you update a table?
23. How do you create a table using the Ruler?
24. What is the size of the table grid in the Ruler?

*25. How many documents can be opened at once?

26. How can you see the names of all your documents?

27. Describe how to copy one page of one document to another document.

28. How many ways are there to display documents?

*29. In which mode can you see your documents side by side?

30. List some of the applications of multiple document processing.

31. What is a font?

32. How do you access WordPerfect for Windows font capabilities?

33. What are the applications of fonts?

*34. What are Truetype fonts and scalable fonts?

HANDS-ON EXPERIENCE

1. Create a table that includes five columns and five rows. In row 1, type *Division1, Division2, Division3, Division4,* and *Division5.* Do the following:
   a. Type three numbers of your choice for each division.
   b. Using a formula, calculate the total of division 1.
   c. Using the Copy option, copy this formula for the other divisions.
   d. Now change one number for each division. Use the Calculate option to recalculate the table.
   e. Save this table under TABLE1.WP.

2. Insert two rows on the top of the table in exercise 1 and do the following:
   a. Use the Join option to join the cells in rows 1 and 2 (the new rows) into one.
   b. Type the following title and center it: *THIS IS A SAMPLE TABLE.*
   c. Center all the entries in this table.
   d. Save this table under TABLE2.WP.

3. Using the tables feature of WordPerfect for Windows create a calendar as follows:
   a. Make seven rows for seven days of the week.
   b. Make nine columns for the hours 8 a.m. through 4 p.m.
   c. Enter a title for this calendar as *MY CUSTOMIZED CALENDAR.*
   d. Enter the first appointment for 10 a.m. on Monday as *Breakfast with VP.*
   e. Save this calendar under TABLE3.WP.

4. Start with a clear screen and do the following:
   a. Type five lines of your desired text.
   b. Save this document under DOC1.WP.
   c. Using the New command, type another five lines of text.
   d. Save this under DOC2.WP.
   e. Using the New command, type the following title: *The Merge of DOC1 and DOC2.*
   f. Press the Enter key three times.
   g. Now using the multiple document feature of WordPerfect for Windows, merge DOC1.WP and DOC2.WP under the heading that you just typed.

5. Using the Tile option, tile DOC1 and DOC2. Using the Cascade option, display DOC1 and DOC2. In Cascade mode, how do you switch to a document that is not active?

6. Retrieve the memo presented in Figure 5–1 and print it using five different fonts. What are the differences among these fonts?

7. In a clear screen type *This is a test.* Print this message in a desired font using five different point sizes.

KEY TERMS

Cascade mode	Font	Table
Cell	Multiple documents	Tile mode
Cell address	Scalable font	Truetype font

KEY COMMANDS

Alt+Shift+F3 (to display the Ruler)

Ctrl+F4 (to close an open document)

Ctrl+F9 (to display the Tables menu)

Ctrl+G (to invoke the Go To dialog box)

Ctrl+Ins (to copy a block)

F4 (to open a saved document)

F9 (to Invoke the Font dialog box)

Moving the insertion point around from the keyboard (see Table 11–1)

Shift+F4 (New)(To open a new document)

Shift+Ins (to paste a block)

Techniques for selecting a table (see Table 11–2)

ARE YOU READY TO MOVE ON?

Multiple Choice

1. In WordPerfect for Windows, how many columns can a table have?
   a. 32
   b. 18
   c. 24
   d. 100
   e. 500

2. Using WordPerfect for Windows, you can create a table with up to how many rows?
   a. 10,000
   b. 52,000
   c. 18,000
   d. 17,672
   e. 32,765

3. Which of the following is not a good application of tables in WordPerfect for Windows?
   a. a small inventory system
   b. a calendar
   c. a small spreadsheet
   d. a term paper
   e. they all are

4. Which of the following keys cannot be used for moving the insertion point around?
   a. Alt+↑
   b. Alt+→
   c. Ctrl
   d. Tab
   e. End-End

5. The Go To command from the Edit menu allows you to move the insertion point to all of the following except
   a. top of cell
   b. middle of a cell with text

    c. bottom of cell
    d. first cell
    e. last cell

6. The mouse lets you select all of the following except
    a. a cell
    b. several cells
    c. a row
    d. a column
    e. they all can be selected

7. To change the appearance of negative numbers, which option should you select from the Tables menu?
    a. Create
    b. Options
    c. Join
    d. Split
    e. Insert

8. To insert a series of rows or columns to a table, which option must you select?
    a. Insert
    b. Split
    c. Join
    d. Delete
    e. Cell

9. To change the appearance, size, and justification of text in a column which option must you select?
    a. Options
    b. Row
    c. Cell
    d. Column
    e. Lines

10. To change the lines around a table which option must you select?
    a. Column
    b. Row
    c. Lines
    d. Options
    e. Join

True/False

1. You can change several of the values in a table and then click on the Calculate option to recalculate the table.

2. The button bar for table manipulation is saved under TAB.WWP.

3. There are buttons for only six of the tables functions.

4. A point size can be 12, 48, and so forth.

5. By default, the size of a table created using the Ruler is 10 rows by 10 columns.

6. To see the names of all your open documents, you must select the Edit option.

7. Open documents can be displayed in Tile mode.

8. In the Tile mode you can see only the title bar of each window.

9. WordPerfect for Windows allows up to nine documents to be opened.

10. Open documents can be merged.

ANSWERS

Multiple Choice		True/False	
1.	a	1.	T
2.	e	2.	F
3.	d	3.	F
4.	c	4.	T
5.	b	5.	T
6.	e	6.	F
7.	b	7.	F
8.	a	8.	F
9.	d	9.	T
10.	c	10.	T

Appendix A:
Answers to Selected
Review Questions

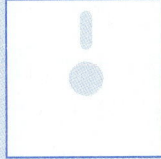

Chapter 1

2. Keyboard and mouse.
6. Floppy disks and hard disks.
13. It varies from 1 to 4 megabytes and higher.
17. Keep it in a dust-free environment. Protect it against excessive heat and humidity.
22. Every application program provides an editing feature so you can edit your mistakes. Or, in the worst case, you can type over your mistakes.
27. The priority of arithmetic operations is as follows:

   - Expressions inside parentheses have the highest priority.
   - Exponentiation (raising to power) has the next highest priority.
   - Multiplication and division have the third highest priority.
   - Addition and subtraction have the fourth highest priority.
   - When there are two or more operations with the same priority, operations proceed from left to right.

Chapter 2

3. Because all your programs and data files will be saved with that information. Later, you can determine when a document was created, which version of a document is the most recent one, and so on.
7. Type *A:* and press Enter. Type *C:* and press Enter.
15. A batch file is a disk file that includes a series of commands and statements. To execute this file, you must type the file name. An autoexec file starts execution as soon as you get your computer started.
16. Internal commands: COPY, DATE, TIME; external commands: FORMAT, DISKCOPY, DISKCOMP

Chapter 3

2. Type *CD WIN31* and press Enter. Then type *WIN* and press Enter.
8. Restore, Move, Size, Close, and Minimize.
12. Press the Ctrl+Esc key combination to activate the Task List; then double-click on the desired application in the Task List dialog box.

Chapter 4

3. Word processing, speller, thesaurus, merge, and advanced component.
8. The WordPerfect for Windows button bar includes a series of buttons that perform common word processing tasks.
16. Insert mode is the default option. When you press the Insert key, you are changing to the Typeover mode. In Typeover mode you write over the existing text.
19. Select the Save or Save As command from the File menu.
21. Click on the Print command in the File menu or click on the Print button in the button bar.
27. No. Saving is your own responsibility.

Chapter 5

1. Click on Layout, Line, and Center or press Shift+F7; then type your text.
5. Click on Font; then click on Subscript or Superscript.
11. Click on Edit; then click on the Convert Case option; choose Uppercase. Yes.
18. Click on Tools then on Speller, or press the Ctrl+F1 key combination. Also, you can press the Speller button in the button bar.
22. Click on Tools then on Thesaurus, or press the Alt+F1 key combination.

Chapter 6

3. No.
6. Click on Replace in the Edit menu (Ctrl+F2); then in the Search and Replace dialog box, click on Codes. Double-click on the desired code for Search For and double-click on the desired code for Replace With. Click on the Replace button to finalize it.
11. Click on the margin icon and drag the mouse pointer back to the original position and release it; or select the Undo option from the Edit menu.
15. Click on the Clear Tabs option to erase all the tabs, or click on the Clear Tab option to erase one tab at a time.
20. A block of data can be a character, a word, a paragraph, and so forth.
26. Yes. Click on Edit and Undo.

Chapter 7

2. Close, Open, Save, Print, Cut, Copy, Paste, Search, Font, and Speller.
6. WWB (WordPerfect for Windows Button).
9. Click on Edit, Button Bar Setup, and Select. From the list presented double-click on the desired button bar. To hide the button bar, click on View and Button Bar.
13. File, Edit, Search, View, Info, Applications, Window, and Help.
16. Select File and Move/Rename; then identify the name of the file in the File To Move/Rename box and identify the destination in the To box. To delete a file, select the Delete command from the File menu.
21. Just click on the file.
22. In the Search Results dialog box, click on the file; then click on Open (in the Open dialog box).
25. Click on EDIT QL; then click on the Edit button.

Chapter 8

4. Press Ctrl+Enter. To remove it, press the Del key.
6. You have a flexibility regarding the position of the page numbers. Click on the Position box as shown in Figure 8–2.
8. No.
14. Merge codes instruct WordPerfect for Windows to perform certain tasks. For example, the {DATE} code inserts the system date into a document.

17. From the Tools menu select the Merge option; then click on Merge again. Enter the name of the primary and secondary files in the Merge dialog box and click on OK.

Chapter 9

2. Endnotes are listed at the end of a document; footnotes are listed at the bottom of the page where the reference is made.
5. Click on Close.
11. Nine.
14. Select Tools; then select Sort.
19. Select Line Draw (Ctrl+D) from the Tools menu.
26. .WPG.
30. Click on it to select it; then click and drag the graph.
33. Click on the Rotate button in the Figure Editor screen. To rotate the graphic by 180 degrees, click on the left horizontal axis.

Chapter 10

4. Click on Tools; then click on Outline.
8. A macro is a series of keystrokes that can be recorded and then played back later.
12. Select Stop from the Macro menu or press the Ctrl+Shift+F10 key combination.
24. Newspaper columns.
28. Ctrl+Enter.

Chapter 11

2. 32,765 rows and 32 columns.
6. Yes.
13. Select the Cell option from the Tables menu.
17. Yes.
21. TABLES.WWB.
25. Nine.
29. In Tile mode.
34. Truetype fonts in Windows and all Windows applications display the fonts on the screen exactly as they appear when printed. A scalable font is a font for which you can specify any size, such as 14 or 18 points.

Appendix B:
Sharing Information Among Windows Applications

B

B–1   INTRODUCTION

This appendix provides general guidelines for sharing information among Windows applications. The appendix first briefly reviews the commands and capabilities available within various Windows applications for sharing information. Then it describes the Windows Clipboard as a tool for exchanging information among Windows applications. Object linking and embedding are introduced as two prominent techniques for sharing information among Windows applications. This presentation should assist you in making your data more portable, and it should increase your efficiency and effectiveness in using Windows applications.

B–2   BUILT-IN CAPABILITIES OF SELECTED SOFTWARE

Several Windows software packages include Export/Import commands that enable you to share information over a wide array of Windows applications. Quattro Pro and Paradox for Windows are two examples of such applications. All you have to do is to select the Export/Import command and follow the prompts.

Other Windows application packages such as Excel, Word, WordPerfect, and Lotus 1-2-3 for Windows allow you to save a file in a variety of formats. This is done when you are using the Save or Save As commands. As soon as you save a file under a given format, that file can be readily available to the target application.

More powerful information exchange is available through the Clipboard and object linking and embedding, which are the main topics of the rest of this appendix.

B–3   THE WINDOWS CLIPBOARD

Windows Clipboard serves as a temporary location for storing information. You can copy or move information from one application to the Clipboard; then you can copy (paste) the contents of the Clipboard to another application. The information that you copy to the Clipboard stays there until you clear the contents of the Clipboard or copy other information to it.

The Clipboard can also serve as a buffer for exchanging information among several applications. When you exit Windows or turn your computer off, the contents of the Clipboard is erased.

B–3–1   Moving or Copying Information to the Clipboard

When you are using a Windows application, you can easily move or copy text to the Clipboard. You can also move or copy an image to the Clipboard. To copy or move information to the Clipboard, follow these steps:

1. Highlight or select the text or the information that you want to move or copy. Remember, you can copy or move text, graphics, or both. In most applications, clicking left anywhere on a graph will select it for moving or copying.

2. From the application's Edit menu (e.g., the Edit menu of Lotus 1-2-3 for Windows), select Cut or Copy. Cut removes the selected text or image from its current position. Copy only takes a snapshot—the existing information remains intact.

To copy the contents of an entire screen to the Clipboard, display the desired screen and press the Print Screen key (or Shift+Prtsc or Alt+Prtsc). This process puts a snapshot (also called a bitmap) of the screen onto the Clipboard.

B–3–2

Transferring Information from the Clipboard

To transfer the contents of the Clipboard to another Windows application, follow these steps:

1. Start the desired application.
2. Position the insertion point at the place that you want the information from the Clipboard to appear.
3. From the application's Edit menu, select Paste.

B–3–3

Working with the Clipboard Viewer

By means of the Clipboard Viewer, you can view, save, retrieve, and delete the contents of the Clipboard. To view the contents of the Clipboard, follow these steps:

1. Switch to the Program Manager (if you are not already there). You can do this by pressing the Ctrl+Esc key combination to display the Task List; then double-click on the Program Manager option.
2. Open the Main group window (if it is not already an open window).
3. Double-click on the Clipboard Viewer icon. Click left on the maximize button to let Clipboard fill the entire screen. You will see a screen similar to the one shown in Figure B–1. The sample text was copied to the Clipboard from the Write application. Write, one of the accessories available in Windows 3.1, is a word processing program.

Figure B–1
Clipboard Viewer menu.

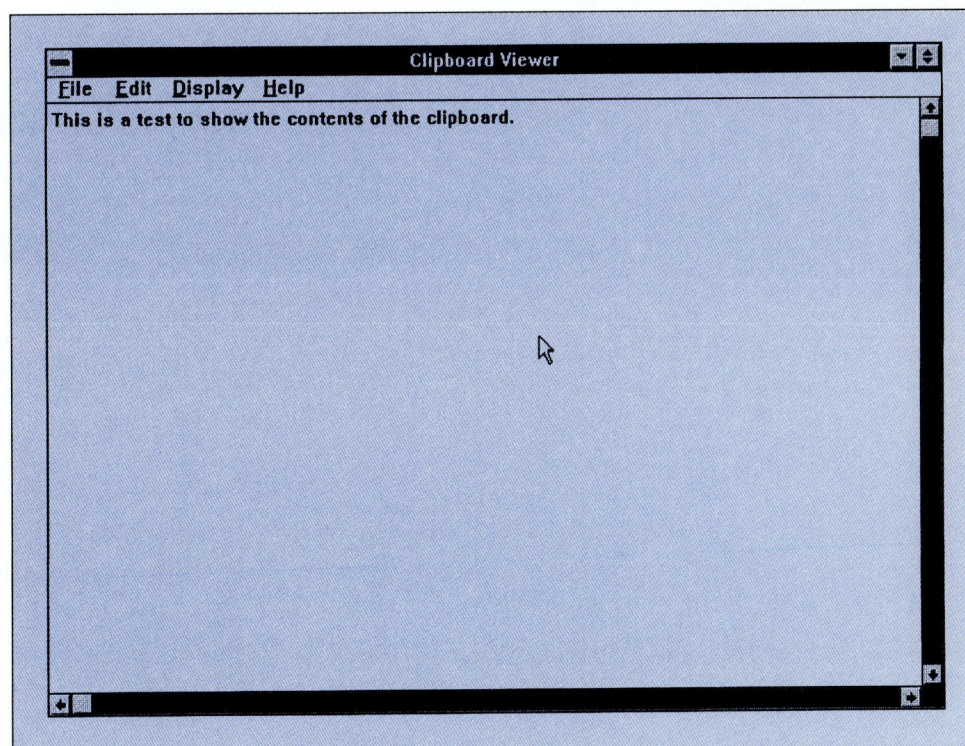

You can view the information in the Clipboard in any of the formats that were supplied by the original application. To view the text in a different format from the Display menu, select the desired format; for example, choose Text. The Auto option displays the Clipboard contents in the format that it had when it was placed on the Clipboard. The other options are different formats supported by Windows and a specific Windows application. To return to the previous format that was displayed, from the Display menu, select Auto.

B–3–4

Saving the Contents of the Clipboard to a File

The contents of the Clipboard can be saved in a file for future use. To do so, follow these steps:

1. From the File menu in the Clipboard Viewer, select the Save As option. The Save As dialog box appears; see Figure B–2.
2. Type in a name of up to eight characters. You must specify the complete path if you are saving to a directory and drive different from the default one. The Clipboard automatically attaches a CLP extension to the file name.
3. Select OK to finalize the save procedure.

B–3–5

Retrieving a Clipboard File

To retrieve a clipboard file, follow these steps:

1. Select Open from the File menu in the Clipboard Viewer. The Open dialog box appears; see Figure B–3.
2. Select the .CLP file that you want to retrieve.
3. Select OK.

Figure B–2

Save as dialog box of the Clipboard Viewer.

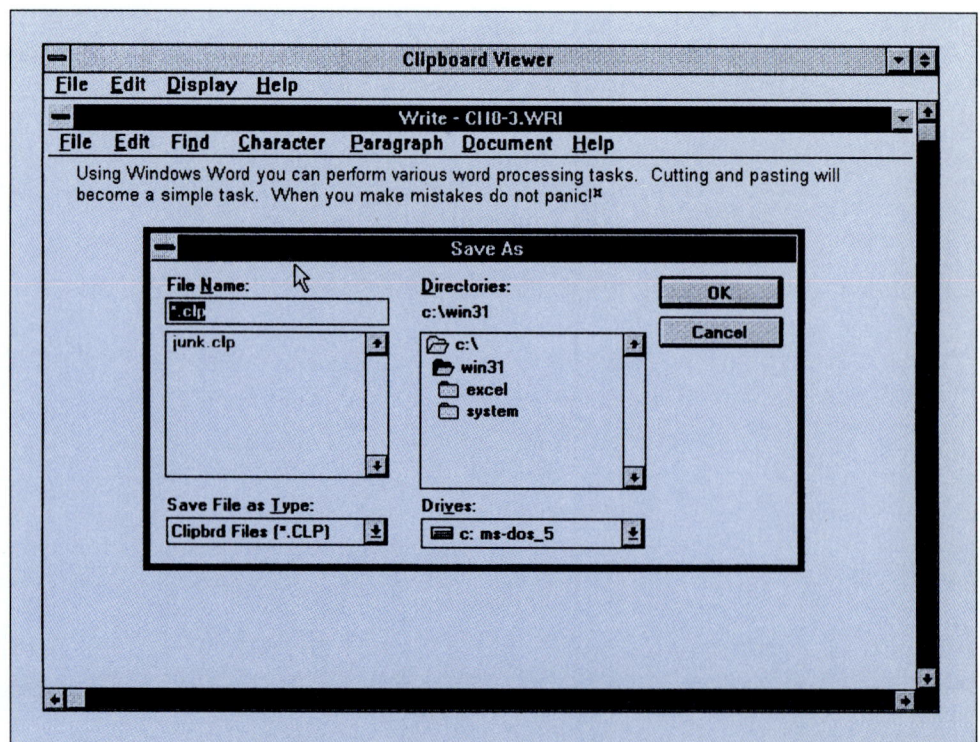

Figure B–3
Open dialog box of the Clipboard Viewer.

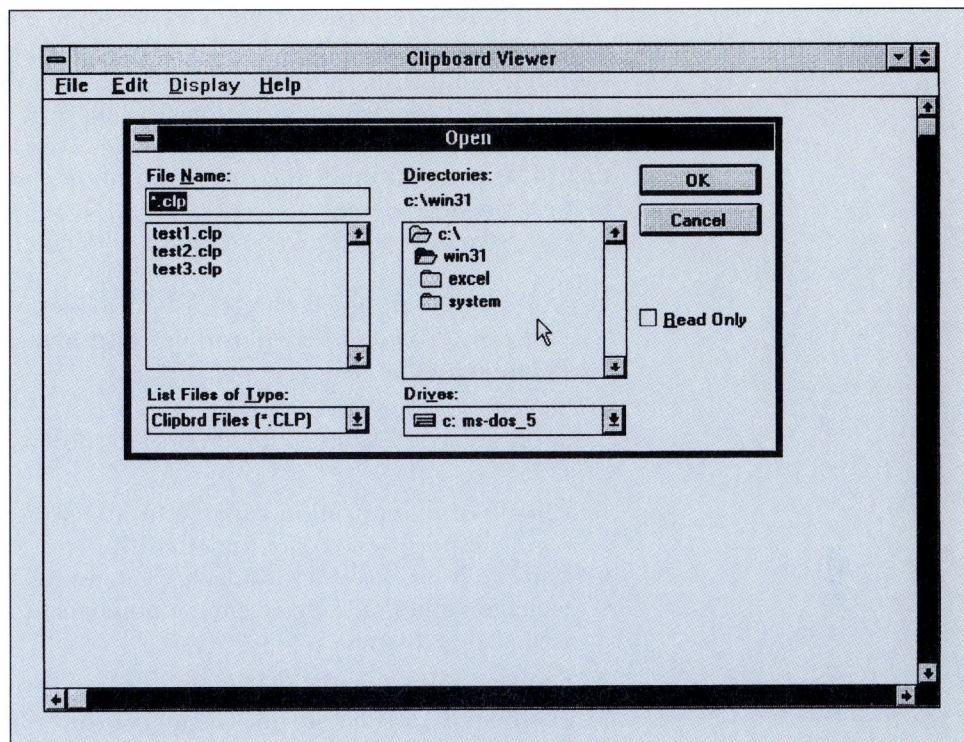

B–3–6

Clearing the Contents of the Clipboard

To clear the contents of Clipboard, follow these steps:

1. Select Edit from the Clipboard Viewer menu.
2. Select Delete. You will be prompted with the Clear Clipboard dialog box displaying Yes and No options. Selecting Yes will erase the contents; selecting No will not erase the contents of the Clipboard.

When you are in Clipboard Viewer, simply pressing the Del (Delete) key will also allow you to clear the contents of the Clipboard. Clearing the contents of the Clipboard frees up some of your computer resources. Remember, however, that placing new contents into the Clipboard automatically erases the old contents regardless of any differences in size.

B–4   OBJECT LINKING AND EMBEDDING

Windows 3.1 offers a powerful tool in the form of object linking and embedding (OLE—pronounced "oh-lay"). Windows has always allowed users to copy graphics or other objects between applications. With earlier versions of Windows, however, if you decided that you wanted to change a Paintbrush graphic, for example, that had been copied into a Write document, you had to delete it from your Write document, reload Paintbrush, load and edit the graphic to make the desired changes, save the graphic, and then copy it back into the Write document. Now, by means of OLE, you can create the graphic using Paintbrush, embed the graphic into your Write document, and edit the graphic from within the Write document—you don't have to delete it!

To be more specific, you can open the Paintbrush application automatically from within the Write document by double-clicking on the graphic. In this scenario, Paintbrush appears on the screen with the graphic already loaded and ready for editing. Any changes that you make to the graphic in Paintbrush are automatically made to the graphic in the Write document, because a dynamic link exists between the Paintbrush application and the graphic that is embedded in the Write document.

Several terms are important for understanding OLE:

1. Object—any graphic or item of information. For example, a spreadsheet, a range or a single cell from within a spreadsheet, a table, and a graph are all examples of objects.
2. Server—any application whose objects can be linked or embedded into other applications. Paintbrush and Sound Recorder are examples of server applications.
3. Client—any application capable of accepting objects that are created by a server application. Write and Cardfile are examples of client applications. Cardfile is an accessory available in Windows 3.1. The Cardfile can help you manage names, addresses, phone numbers, and other information critical to your daily activities.
4. Source document—the document in which the object was created
5. Destination document—the document into which the object is embedded or linked

B–4–1   Embedding an Object Versus Linking an Object

There is an important distinction between embedding an object and linking an object. When you embed an object, you are actually making a copy of the object from the server application and placing the copy into the client application. You may then make editing changes to the object from within the client application simply by double-clicking on the object. The server application that was used to create the object is automatically loaded, with the object ready for editing.

Now here is the distinction. Any changes that you make to an embedded object do not change the original object that was copied from the source document in the server application. Any editing changes appear only in the destination document of the client application; the source document object is left in its original form. On the other hand, linking an object involves creating a link, or reference, to the original object in the source document. Once an object is linked into the destination document, simply double-clicking on the object automatically loads the server application that was used to create the object, with the object ready for editing. At this point, changes made to the linked (client) object do change the source object in the source document.

B–4–2   Example of Object Linking

Let's say that you are the business office manager for a school district and you maintain budget data using a spreadsheet application. At some point during the year, you must send a budget report containing a copy of the spreadsheet to your school district board, the county office of education, and the state department of education. The three reports contain the same spreadsheet data, but each report also contains other pieces of information relevant only to the respective entity.

You create the three reports using Write, and in each of the reports (destination documents) you create a link to the spreadsheet (source document). You finish the reports and suddenly remember that you forgot to add a budget item into the spreadsheet (source document). No problem! Retrieve any one of the three reports (destination documents) into Write (the client application) and double-click on the spreadsheet (object). Automatically, the spreadsheet application (server) appears with the spreadsheet (source document) loaded on the screen. Make your editing changes, save the spreadsheet (source document), and exit the spreadsheet application (server). The links automatically update each of the three spreadsheets contained within the reports with the missing piece of information, and you can print reports and send them on their way.

B–4–3

Hands-On Example of Object Embedding

We will now walk through an example of how to embed a graphic created in Paintbrush into a Write document. Follow these steps:

1. Open Paintbrush. To do this, double-click on the Accessories group icon then double-click on the Paintbrush icon.
2. Click on the maximize button at the upper right of the screen to allow Paintbrush to fill the entire screen.
3. Select the hollow circle tool from the toolbox and create a circle in the upper-left corner of the drawing area.
4. To save the drawing, select Save from the File menu and specify TEST as the name; then click left on OK.
5. Using the pick tool (the second tool from the top) from the toolbox, select the drawing by clicking left above and to the left of the drawing; then drag the mouse down and to the right so that a dashed box surrounds the circle.
6. From the Edit menu, select Copy. This places a copy of the drawing in the Clipboard.
7. Exit Paintbrush by selecting the Exit option from the File menu.
8. Open Write. To open Write double-click on its icon in the Accessories group.
9. Click on the maximize button at the upper right of the screen to allow Write to fill the entire screen.
10. Move the insertion point to the location where you would like to position the embedded object.
11. From the Edit menu, select Paste. A copy of the drawing is placed (or embedded) into your Write document.

Now let's say that you want to jazz up the drawing a little. To do this, double-click left anywhere on the object (the circle). Paintbrush will open with a copy of the drawing already displayed and ready for editing. Follow the steps outlined next to modify the object:

1. Click left on the paint roller (the fourth tool from the top left) tool in the toolbox.
2. Click left on a different color in the color palette at the bottom of the screen.
3. Click left anywhere inside of the circle. Your circle should fill with the selected color.

4. Select Update from the Paintbrush File menu. The circle in the Write document should instantly fill with the selected color. As mentioned earlier, editing an embedded object does not change the appearance of the object in the source application. Editing changes made to an embedded object change only the appearance of the object in the destination application. You can verify this by opening the Test.bmp file. You will see that all the improvements are not reflected here.

5. Select Exit & Return to [Untitled] from the Paintbrush File menu. Paintbrush will close, and you will be returned to your Write document so that you can continue working. Click left anywhere outside of the circle to deselect it; then you may continue editing your Write document. When you are finished editing, save your document under TEST and exit the Write application.

B–4–4
Hands-On Example of Object Linking

Follow the steps outlined next to link an object from Paintbrush to a card in Cardfile and a document in Write.

1. Open Paintbrush.
2. Click on the maximize button at the upper right of the screen to allow Paintbrush to fill the entire screen.
3. Select the hollow square (the seventh tool from the top left) tool from the toolbox and create a square in the upper-left corner of the drawing area.
4. Save the drawing by selecting the Save option from the File menu; then specify TRY as the name and click left on OK.
5. Using the pick tool (the first tool from the top right) from the toolbox, select the drawing by clicking left above and to the left of the drawing; then drag the mouse down and to the right so that a dashed box surrounds the square.
6. From the Edit menu, select Copy. This places a copy of the drawing in the Clipboard.
7. Switch back to the Program Manager by means of the Ctrl+Esc key combination.
8. Open Cardfile.
9. Click on the maximize button at the upper right of the screen to allow Cardfile to fill the entire screen.
10. Select Picture from the Edit menu.
11. Select Paste Link from the Edit menu. A copy of the drawing will be placed in the upper-left corner of the card.
12. Exit Cardfile by selecting the Exit option from the File menu; then click left on Yes to save your changes. Cardfile will respond by displaying the Save As dialog box.
13. Type *LINKTEST* and click left on OK to give the file a name. After saving the file, you will be returned to the Program Manager.
14. Open Write.
15. Click on the maximize button at the upper right of the screen to allow Write to fill the entire screen.
16. Select Paste Link from the Edit menu. A linked copy of the drawing will be placed in the upper-left corner of the document.

17. Exit Write by selecting the Exit option from the File menu; then click left on Yes to save the changes. Write will respond by displaying the Save As dialog box.

18. Type *LINKTEST* and click left on OK to give the document a name. Don't worry about the document having the same name as in the Cardfile—the extensions are different. After saving the file, you will be returned to the Program Manager.

You have now created and saved an object in the source application (Paintbrush) and placed a linked copy of the object into a Cardfile card and a Write document. In addition to placing a copy of the drawing into the Cardfile card and Write document, Windows also created a direct link between these two drawings and the application that created the drawing (Paintbrush). We will now test the links by making a change to the original object in Paintbrush, and opening the LINKTEST.CRD card file and LINKTEST.WRI document to see if the objects in these two files are updated with the changes.

19. Switch to Paintbrush by using the Ctrl+Esc key combination or by clicking anywhere on its Window (if it is already on the screen).

20. Select the Paint roller tool from the toolbox (the fourth tool from the top left).

21. Click left on a different color in the color palette at the bottom of the screen.

22. Click left anywhere inside the box that you created. The box should be filled with the specified color.

23. Select Exit from the File menu; then click left on Yes to save your changes. You will be returned to the Program Manager.

24. Open Cardfile.

25. Click on the maximize button at the upper right of the screen to allow Cardfile to fill the entire screen.

26. Select Open from the File menu. Cardfile will display the Open dialog box.

27. Double click left on LINKTEST.CRD to open this file. Cardfile will display a screen similar to Figure B–4 to alert you that this card file contains links to other documents and that the links may need updating.

28. Click left on OK. Your Cardfile with the object inside the card will be displayed. Notice that the change we made to the original object in Paintbrush has not appeared.

29. Select Picture from the Edit menu.

30. Select Link from the Edit menu. Cardfile will display the Link dialog box (Figure B–5). This screen allows you to update your links, change or cancel your links, and view link information.

31. Click left on Update Now; then click left on OK. The link will be updated, and you should now see the changes that you made to the original object in Paintbrush.

32. Select the Exit option from the File menu; then click left on Yes to save your changes. You will be returned to the Program Manager.

33. Open Write.

34. Click on the maximize button at the upper right of the screen to allow Write to fill the entire screen.

35. Select Open from the File menu. Write will display the Open dialog box.

Figure B–4
Cardfile link warning dialog box.

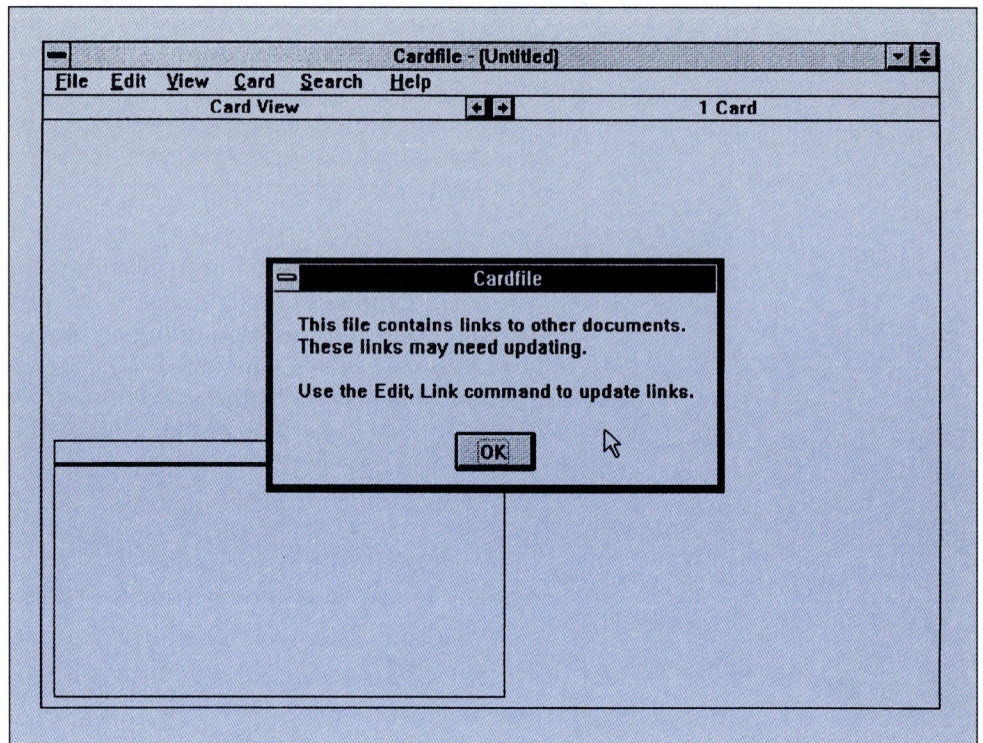

Figure B–5
Cardfile Link dialog box.

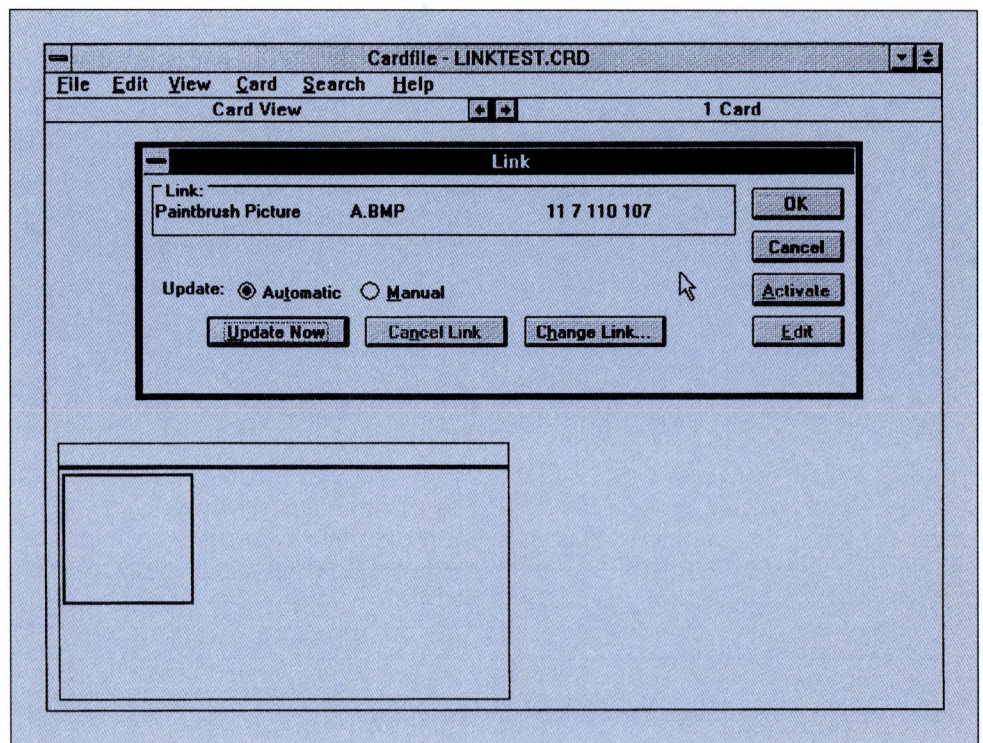

36. Double-click left on LINKTEST.WRI to open this file. Write will display a screen similar to Figure B–6 to alert you that this file contains links to other documents and to prompt you about whether to update the links now.

37. Click left on Yes. Your document will be displayed on the screen with your changes already displayed.

38. Select the Exit option from the File menu; then click left on Yes to save your changes. You will be returned to the Program Manager.

At this point, you may not be sure about the difference between linking an object (as we just did) and embedding an object as we did in the first example. When would you use one method and not the other? As you already know, double-clicking on the drawing automatically loads the application that created the drawing (Paintbrush) with the drawing ready for editing. If the drawing is linked in the destination application, any changes that you make to the drawing using the server application alter both the original object and all linked copies of the graphic in any client application (Cardfile, in this case). Alternatively, if the drawing were embedded, any changes that you made to the embedded drawing in the Cardfile would not alter the original file in the server application. In any case, you may edit the linked object using the same sequence of steps used to edit an embedded object.

B–4–5

Dynamic Data Exchange Versus OLE: What's the Difference?

The OLE feature of Windows 3.1 represents a significant improvement over the way that previous versions of Windows allowed the exchange of data between applications. In versions of Windows prior to 3.1, the capability to move objects among applications as we have been discussing was called dynamic data exchange (DDE).

Figure B–6
Write Link dialog box.

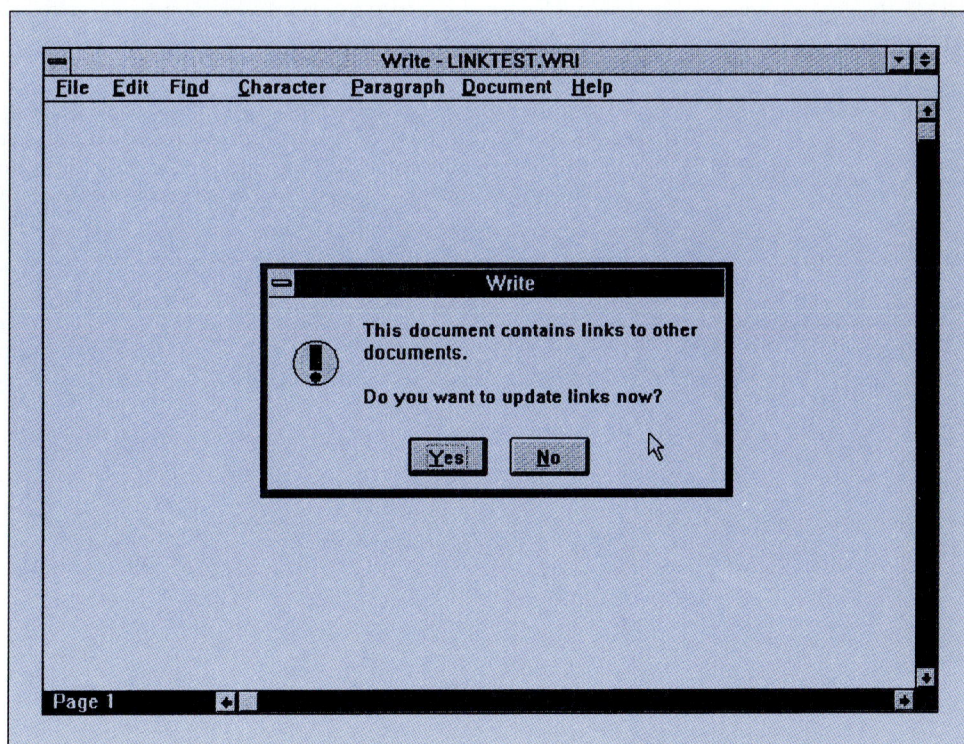

To share information among different applications using DDE, all the applications must be running on the Windows desktop and the related files must be opened. And more important, the updating process occurs only one way: from the server to the client. The data can only be edited in the server application. So, OLE is the next logical step in technological progress beyond the DDE capabilities. By means of OLE, sharing information among different applications becomes document driven rather than application driven. Updating can take place in either direction.

The OLE feature also represents an improvement over DDE in its use of dynamic link libraries to maintain the link information used between applications. In previous versions of Windows, DDE link information was stored within the linking (server) application itself. This created overhead for each server application and opened the door to problems because such a wide variety of linking protocols existed between the various server application programs. With OLE, linking information is stored within dynamic link libraries, thereby freeing the various server application programs from having to store the information. Instead of many applications each storing link information, all link information is now stored under the single umbrella of dynamic link libraries. The application programs are free of the overhead and simply refer to the libraries as necessary to gain access to the link information they require. Thus, OLE is more application independent and flexible and forms a more reliable platform for using its powerful capabilities.

In our discussion of object linking and embedding we used Paintbrush, Cardfile, and Write. They were selected because any Windows application has access to them. You can apply the same principle to the application of your choice. Also, you should consult the documentation of your desired software to see if it supports OLE. The older versions of Windows applications support DDE, whereas the newer versions mostly support OLE in addition to DDE.

SUMMARY

This appendix provided general guidelines for sharing information among Windows applications. It discussed export/import capabilities and saving with different file formats, the Clipboard, and object linking and embedding. This information should improve your efficiency and effectiveness as you use various Windows applications.

Index

ISBN 0-02-309591-1